CRIME ANALYSIS WITH CRIME MAPPING

CRIME ANALYSIS WITH CRIME MAPPING

Dr. Anne Wade

SOCIETY
Publishing

www.societypublishing.com

Crime Analysis with Crime Mapping

Dr. Anne Wade

Society Publishing
4164 Lakeshore Road
Burlington, ON L7L 1A4
Canada
www.societypublishing.com
Email: orders@arclereducation.com

ISBN: 978-1-77956-394-1 (Hardcover)

ABOUT THE AUTHOR

Dr. Anne Wad has been a researcher and a professor in the Criminal Justice field for over 30 years. She currently holds a position as a Provost/CAO in a University, and Director of Research at another university. She holds an Ed.D. in Educational Leadership and a Ph.D. in Public Safety Leadership/Criminal Justice. Her research interests are in Criminology, Victimology, and the Human Services. She is married to Wesley Wade. She is an artist, writer, researcher, professor, and university administrator.

TABLE OF CONTENTS

List of Figures .... *xi*

List of Tables .... *xv*

Preface .... *xvii*

Chapter 1 Crime Analysis and the Profession 1

Introduction 2

1.1. Definition of Crime Analysis 2

1.2. Definitions of GIS and Crime Mapping 6

1.3. History of Crime Analysis 7

1.4. History of Crime Mapping 12

1.5. Crime Analysis as a Career Track 16

1.6. Theoretical Foundations of Crime Analysis 24

1.7. Displacement and Diffusion of Benefits 39

References 42

Chapter 2 Crime Analysis and Evidence-Based Policing 55

Introduction 56

2.1. Research on Crime Analysis and Crime Reduction 56

2.2. Stratified Policing: Framework for Crime Analysis 70

2.3. Evidence-Based Policing 79

2.4. Crime Analysis and Evidence-Based Policing Strategies 87

2.5. The Role of Crime Analysts in Evidence-Based Policing 98

References 104

Chapter 3 Analyzing Reading Cases and Statutes 111

Introduction 112

3.1. Analyzing by Reading 112

3.2. The Science of Observation 126

3.3. Analyzing by Asking and Listening 136
3.4. Sources of Statutes 153
References 158

Chapter 4 Crime Analysis Process, Application, and Data 161
Introduction 162
4.1. The Crime Analysis Process 162
4.2. Types of Crime Analysis 168
4.3. Crime Mapping by Type of Analysis 177
4.4. Crime Analysis Data and Technology 179
4.5. Databases Used in Crime Analysis 185
4.6. Using Calls-for-Service Data to Study Crime Problems 199
References 205

Chapter 5 Geographic Data and Crime Mapping 207
Introduction 208
5.1. Geographic Data 209
5.2. Crime Mapping Techniques 216
References 236

Chapter 6 Crime Mapping and Analysis Using GIS 239
Introduction 240
6.1. Crime Mapping 241
6.2. GIS for Crime Mapping 242
6.3. Role of Geospatial Technology in Crime Mapping 246
6.4. Crime-Place Relationship and Role of Place in Assessing Crime 257
References 273

Chapter 7 Crime Analysis Purpose and Audience 279
Introduction 280
7.1. Crime Analysis Purpose 280
7.2. Crime Analysis Audiences 283
7.3. Crime Analysis Typology 285
7.4. Situational Awareness Examples 285
7.5. Crime Reduction Examples 291
References 301

Chapter 8 Analyzing Repeat Victimization 303
Introduction 304
8.1. Patterns of Repeat Victimization 304
8.2. Understanding Your Local Repeat Victimization Pattern 318
8.3. Data Sources and Limitations of Revictimization 329
References 335

Chapter 9 Pattern Identification Process 339
Introduction 340
9.1. Crime Pattern Identification Process 340
9.2. Persons Crime and Property Crime 352
9.3. Potential Responses to Patterns by Police 355
9.4. Identifying Meaningful Patterns 360
9.5. Property Crime Pattern Key Characteristics and Examples 367
9.6. Describing and Disseminating Known Patterns 377
References 388

Chapter 10 Administrative Crime Analysis 391
Introduction 392
10.1. Overview of Administrative Crime Analysis 392
10.2. Crime Reduction Accountability 394
10.3. Crime Reduction Goal Development 396
10.4. Crime Analysis for Weekly Action-Oriented Accountability Meetings 399
10.5. Crime Analysis for Monthly Evaluation-Orientedetings 402
References 417

Index 419

LIST OF FIGURES

Figure 1.1. The definition of crime analysis
Figure 1.2. Sample crime analysis unit organizational chart
Figure 1.3. The problem analysis triangle
Figure 1.4. Offender and victim activity space example
Figure 2.1. Process for diagnosing and curing a patient
Figure 2.2. Crime analysis process in crime reduction
Figure 2.3. Stratified policing structure
Figure 4.1. The crime analysis process
Figure 4.2. Map of student pathways to school and hangouts
Figure 5.1. Point and line feature map
Figure 5.2. Polygon feature map
Figure 5.3. Satellite photo example
Figure 5.4. Geocoding: street segment matching
Figure 5.5. Single-symbol mapping example
Figure 5.6. Buffer map example
Figure 5.7. Graduated-size map example
Figure 5.8. Graduated-colour map example
Figure 5.9. Pie chart map example
Figure 5.10. Graduated-colour map indicating presence of a freeway
Figure 5.11. Unique-symbol map indicating banks or stand-alone ATMs
Figure 5.12. Graduated-size point map: natural breaks classification
Figure 5.13. Graduated-size line map: natural-breaks classification
Figure 5.14. Graduated-colour polygon map: natural-breaks classification
Figure 5.15. Graduated-color polygon map: equal-interval classification
Figure 5.16. Graduated-color polygon map: quantile classification
Figure 5.17. Graduated-colour polygon map: standard-deviation classification

Figure 5.18. Graduated-color polygon map: custom classification (January)
Figure 5.19. Graduated-colour polygon map: custom classification (February)
Figure 5.20. Density map: search radius 0.5 miles
Figure 5.21. Density map: search Radius 2 miles
Figure 6.1. Data clock of crime provide temporal hotspot analysis
Figure 6.2. Crime (Murder, Dacoity and Robbery) in India in lakh from 2001–2015
Figure 6.3. Crime (burglary, theft, riots) in India in lakh from 2001–2015
Figure 6.4. Crime map of India (a: crime density 2015, b: crime map percent change 2015, c: crime density 2014, d: crime map percent change 2014, e: crime density 2013, f: crime map percent change 2013, g: crime density 2012, h: crime map percent change 2012, i: crime density 2011)
Figure 6.5. City crime 2015 (murder, dacoity, robbery, burglary, theft, riots and other IPC crime)
Figure 7.1. Relationship between responsibility and problem complexity
Figure 7.2. Typology of crime analysis results
Figure 7.3. Four weeks of car prowls in Seattle, Washington—2015: Southwest Precinct
Figure 7.4. Two months of calls-for-service comparison: District 4
Figure 7.5. Part I crime in Gainesville, Florida—2010
Figure 7.6. Western region: residential burglary by month
Figure 7.7. California unsolved homicides, 1987–2006
Figure 7.8. Theft from vehicle incidents and patterns: April–May
Figure 7.9. Problem analysis results: ABC apartment
Figure 7.10. Residential burglary response evaluation
Figure 8.1. Time course between repeat commercial burglaries Montgomery County, MD
Figure 8.2. Time course between repeat commercial burglaries: Indianapolis, IN
Figure 8.3. Repeat commercial robberies
Figure 8.4. Distribution of burglaries by address and frequency
Figure 8.5. Distribution of burglaries by address and frequency
Figure 8.6. Sample table for recording number of victimizations: residential burglary
Figure 9.1. Pattern identification: deduction
Figure 9.2. Pattern identification: induction
Figure 10.1. Monthly trend chart
Figure 10.2. Average trend analysis for 6 months, 1 year, and 5 years
Figure 10.3. Problem areas: 6-month comparison

Figure 10.4. Selected crime incidents and patterns: June–November 2017
Figure 10.5. Performance indicators (output): January–December 2017
Figure 10.6. Long-term residential burglary trend chart for 3 years
Figure 10.7. Seasonal residential burglary trend chart for 3 years
Figure 10.8. Crime type comparison chart
Figure 10.9. Jurisdiction comparison chart
Figure 10.10. Density map of crime reduction goal: 2016
Figure 10.11. Density map of crime reduction goal: 2017

LIST OF TABLE

Table 1.1. Techniques to situational prevention

Table 2.1. Summary of crime analysis assessment

Table 3.1. Data collection

Table 4.1. Data matrix example

Table 4.2. Sample crime incidents data table

Table 4.3. Sample arrest data table

Table 4.4. Sample call for service data table

Table 4.5. Sample traffic crash data table

Table 4.6. Sample database: primary data collection

Table 5.1. Point feature attribute data

Table 5.2. Line feature attribute data

Table 5.3. Polygon feature attribute data

Table 5.4. Number of robberies by address

Table 5.5. Number of robberies by area (polygon)

Table 5.6. Number of robberies by area, Sorted in ascending frequency to determine quantiles

Table 5.7. Summary of mapping classification

Table 7.1. Calls for service at 345 at S apple ST

Table 7.2. Arrests by district per shift

Table 7.3. Commercial robberies, previous 24 hours

Table 7.4. Counts and percentage of change: Part I Crime Types

Table 7.5. Release burglary offenders living in pattern area

Table 7.6. Daily roll call sheet

Table 7.7. Command briefing report

Table 7.8. Top addresses for disorder: precinct 33

Table 7.9. Crime pattern summary information

Table 7.10. Top violent offenders residing in district 5: January–June 2017
Table 8.1. Estimates of repeat victimization international victimization survey
Table 8.2. Estimates of repeat victimization for assault
Table 8.3. Estimates of repeat victimization for property crime: British crime survey
Table 8.4. Estimates of repeat victimization: crime reports
Table 8.5. Concentration of repeats among victims
Table 8.6. Contribution of repeat victims to burglaries
Table 8.7. Time course of repeat victimization by offense type: crime reports
Table 10.1. Example of crime reduction goal components
Table 10.2. Response statistics by pattern

PREFACE

In today's world, crime analysis and crime mapping have become integral tools in the fight against crime, leveraging technology and data to enhance public safety and law enforcement effectiveness. Crime analysis involves the systematic examination of crime data to identify patterns, trends, and correlations. This analysis helps law enforcement agencies understand the nature and dynamics of criminal activities, predict potential hotspots, and deploy resources more strategically. Crime mapping complements this analysis by visualizing crime data geographically, often using Geographic Information Systems (GIS). This spatial representation allows for the identification of crime hotspots, trends over time, and spatial relationships between different types of crime. Maps can reveal areas with high crime rates, enabling law enforcement to focus their efforts on these regions and implement targeted interventions. Additionally, crime mapping can help communities and policymakers understand the distribution of crime, leading to better-informed decisions about urban planning, resource allocation, and community safety initiatives.

The integration of advanced technologies has significantly enhanced both crime analysis and mapping. For example, predictive policing tools use algorithms to analyze historical crime data and predict where future crimes are likely to occur. These tools can help prevent crime by anticipating where and when it might happen and deploying officers accordingly. Moreover, real-time data collection through technologies such as surveillance cameras, social media monitoring, and automated license plate readers contributes to more immediate and actionable insights.

However, the use of crime analysis and mapping also raises concerns about privacy and civil liberties. The collection and use of data must be balanced with the need to protect individuals' rights, ensuring that technology is used ethically and responsibly. Transparency and oversight are essential to maintain public trust and prevent misuse.

The book *Crime Analysis and Crime Mapping* provides a detailed exploration of the methodologies and applications involved in crime analysis and mapping. It is written to offer a comprehensive understanding of how crime data is analyzed and used to inform policing strategies and public safety measures.

Chapter 1 lays the foundation by introducing the field of crime analysis, detailing the role and responsibilities of crime analysts, and explaining how the profession fits into the broader context of law enforcement and public safety.

Chapter 2 explores the integration of crime analysis with evidence-based policing practices. It highlights how crime analysis can support and enhance evidence-based approaches to law enforcement, improving decision-making and resource allocation.

Chapter 3 focuses on the techniques for analyzing reading cases and statutes, providing insights into how legal documents and case studies can inform crime analysis and help shape effective crime prevention strategies.

Chapter 4 covers the crime analysis process, including the collection, application, and interpretation of data. It covers various data sources and methodologies used in crime analysis, emphasizing the importance of accurate and comprehensive data in understanding crime patterns.

Chapter 5 examines geographic data and its role in crime mapping. This chapter discusses how spatial data is used to visualize crime patterns and trends, facilitating better understanding and management of crime through geographic information.

Chapter 6 builds on the previous chapter by detailing the use of Geographic Information Systems (GIS) in crime mapping and analysis. It illustrates how GIS technology can enhance the analysis and visualization of crime data, providing tools for more effective crime prevention and intervention.

Chapter 7 addresses the purpose of crime analysis and its intended audience. It explores how crime analysis serves various stakeholders, including law enforcement agencies, policymakers, and the community, and discusses the objectives of crime analysis in different contexts.

Chapter 8 investigates repeat victimization, analyzing patterns where victims experience multiple incidents of crime. This chapter highlights methods for identifying and addressing repeat victimization to reduce the likelihood of further crimes against these individuals.

Chapter 9 covers the process of pattern identification in crime analysis. It explains how analysts detect and interpret patterns in crime data to identify trends and inform strategic responses to criminal activity.

Chapter 10 focuses on administrative crime analysis, which involves the use of crime data and analysis for administrative purposes, such as policy development, resource allocation, and performance evaluation within law enforcement agencies.

This book is aimed at law enforcement professionals, crime analysts, researchers, and students in criminal justice or criminology. It provides valuable insights for those involved in crime analysis and mapping, including police departments, public safety organizations, and academic institutions. Additionally, it serves as a resource for policymakers and practitioners interested in evidence-based approaches to crime prevention and law enforcement.

–Author

Chapter **1**

Crime Analysis and the Profession

Contents

Introduction 2
1.1. Definition of Crime Analysis 2
1.2. Definitions of GIS and Crime Mapping 6
1.3. History of Crime Analysis 7
1.4. History of Crime Mapping 12
1.5. Crime Analysis as a Career Track 16
1.6. Theoretical Foundations of Crime Analysis 24
1.7. Displacement and Diffusion of Benefits 39
References 42

INTRODUCTION

Crime analysis is a critical function within law enforcement and the broader criminal justice system, focusing on the systematic examination of data related to criminal activities. This profession plays a pivotal role in enhancing public safety, informing policing strategies, and supporting criminal investigations. By analyzing crime patterns, trends, and correlations, crime analysts help law enforcement agencies allocate resources more effectively, predict potential criminal activity, and develop strategies to prevent crime.

The profession of crime analysis encompasses several key responsibilities. Analysts collect and evaluate data from various sources, including police reports, arrest records, and geographic information systems (GIS). They use statistical and analytical tools to identify patterns, such as hotspots of criminal activity, emerging crime trends, and correlations between different types of crimes. This information is crucial for law enforcement agencies to make informed decisions about resource deployment, patrol strategies, and community policing efforts.

Crime analysis is not limited to reactive measures; it also plays a proactive role in crime prevention. By identifying trends and potential threats, analysts can help police departments anticipate and disrupt criminal activities before they escalate. For example, if an analysis reveals a spike in burglaries in a particular neighborhood, law enforcement can increase patrols in that area or engage in community outreach to raise awareness and deter crime.

The profession requires a blend of skills, including data analysis, critical thinking, and a deep understanding of criminology and law enforcement practices. Analysts often work closely with police officers, detectives, and other stakeholders to ensure that their findings are actionable and relevant to ongoing investigations and strategic planning.

Crime analysis is a vital profession that supports the effective functioning of law enforcement agencies. By providing insights into criminal behavior and trends, crime analysts help to enhance public safety, prevent crime, and ensure that law enforcement resources are used efficiently. Their work is integral to modern policing and the broader effort to maintain law and order in society.

1.1. DEFINITION OF CRIME ANALYSIS

Definitions of crime analysis have been developed over the last thirty years by numerous scholars (Bruce, 2008a; Emig, Heck, and Kravitz, 1980; Gottlieb, Arenberg, and Singh, 1994; Vellani and Nahoun, 2001). While definitions of crime analysis vary slightly, they all agree on a few key points: crime analysis serves the police agency's mission, makes use of systematic information and methods, and disseminates information to a variety of audiences. To help the police with criminal apprehension, crime and disorder reduction, crime prevention, and evaluation, crime analysis is the methodical study of problems related to crime and disorder as well as other issues pertaining to the police, such as sociodemographic, spatial, and temporal factors.

Elucidating every facet of this definition facilitates the illustration of the diverse constituents of crime analysis. Studying generally refers to looking into, looking closely at, and/or scrutinizing information. Therefore, crime analysis is the concentrated and methodical study of issues pertaining to crime and disorder as well as other matters pertaining to law enforcement. Rather than being haphazard or anecdotal, crime analysis is theoretically grounded and applies statistical techniques, analytical methods, and social science data collection procedures.

To be more precise, qualitative and quantitative information and techniques are used in crime analysis. When analyzing nonnumerical data to identify the root causes of crime, crime analysts employ qualitative data and methodologies. The qualitative techniques unique to crime analysis include content analysis (looking at police report narratives) and field research (observing features of places and speaking with people who have specific knowledge about a given type of crime). While performing statistical analyses of numerical or categorical data, crime analysts make use of quantitative data and methodologies. The main statistical tools used by crime analysts are frequencies, percentages, means, and rates a large portion of their work is quantitative.

The study of crime is the primary focus of crime analysis (e.g., sexual assault, theft, and break-ins) and chaos (e.g., complaints about noise, burglary alarms, and suspicious activity) issues and details about the types of incidents, criminals, victims, and targets (i.e., inanimate items, like structures or real estate) of these issues. In addition, crime analysts research operational issues pertaining to the police, such as areas of service and staffing requirements. Therefore, despite the name "crime analysis," this field of study actually encompasses much more than just the study of crime.

Crime analysts use three primary types of information: sociodemographic, spatial, and temporal. While many different characteristics of crime and disorder are relevant, these three types of information are crucial to their work. The personal traits of people and groups, such as sex, race, income, age, and education, make up sociodemographic information. To find and identify crime suspects and victims on a personal level, crime analysts use sociodemographic data. More broadly, they use this data to ascertain the traits of groups and the ways in which these traits are connected to criminal activity. To answer questions like "Is there a white male suspect, 30 to 35 years old, with brown hair and brown eyes, to link to a particular robbery?" or "Can demographic characteristics explain why people in one group are victimized more often than people in another group in a particular area?" analysts might utilize sociodemographic data.

Understanding the nature of a problem is largely dependent on the spatial aspect of disorder, crime, and other police-related issues. The availability of electronic data and the development of computer technology have made spatial analysis a major tool in crime analysis. Understanding the nature of crime and disorder requires visual displays of crime and disorder locations (maps), along with their relationships to other events and geographic features. (For a thorough explanation of this kind of analysis, see "crime mapping"). Furthermore, findings from criminological studies in the field of "crime and place" (Weisburd, Bernasco, and Bruinsma, 2009; Weisburd and McEwen, 1997) motivate crime analysts to concentrate on spatial patterns of crime by analyzing circumstances in which victims and offenders coexist in space and time. (For a conversation regarding the significance of "place" in the study of crime. The significance of these patterns is highlighted by the book's title, Crime Analysis with Crime Mapping.

Lastly, a key element of crime analysis is the temporal aspect of disorder, crime, and other police-related concerns. Various levels of temporal analysis are conducted by crime analysts, such as analyzing long-term patterns of crime and disorder over a number of years, by season, by day of the week, and by hour of the day. This book will closely examine methods of analysis that are applied to investigate the temporal aspects of crime at each of these levels.

The purpose and goals of crime analysis are summarized in the last section of the definition, which reads, "to assist the police in criminal apprehension, crime and disorder reduction, crime prevention, and evaluation." Crime analysis's main goal is to assist (i.e., "assist") a police department's operations. Crime analysis as it is defined here would not exist without police.

Since aiding in criminal apprehension is a primary objective of law enforcement, the primary aim of crime analysis is to support this endeavor. For example, a detective might be looking into a robbery where the offender employed a specific method of operation (i.e., manner of the offense). A crime analyst could help the investigator by looking for cases similar to the one in a database of past robberies.

Preventing crime through strategies other than apprehending suspects is another essential police objective. Intervention in the causes of criminal and disorderly events to lessen the likelihood that they will occur and/or the potential severity of their consequences is known as crime prevention (Ekblom, 2005).

The identification, analysis, and guidance of crime and disorder problems, along with the implementation of crime prevention measures by law enforcement, constitute the second objective of crime analysis. For instance, police officers may want to concentrate their resources in areas where residential burglary is most prevalent in order to launch a campaign to prevent residential burglaries. A residential burglary analysis by a crime analyst can help by looking at the how, when, and where of the burglaries as well as the items that were taken. The analyst can then utilize this data to formulate recommendations for actions, like warning local residents to close and lock their garage doors.

According to Ekblom (2005), crime reduction is the process of lowering the quantity and intensity of crime and disturbance. Numerous issues that police handle or are asked to resolve have more to do with issues of disorder and quality of life than they do with criminal activity. Traffic control, neighbor disputes, loud noise complaints, and false burglary alarms are a few instances. The police's goal of lessening disorder and crime is the source of the third goal of crime analysis. Crime analysts can support law enforcement in these endeavors by investigating and evaluating issues like trespass warnings, noise complaints, suspicious activity, and code violations. By doing this, they can give police intelligence that will enable them to resolve these problems before they escalate into more serious criminal offenses.

The ultimate objective of crime analysis is to measure the effectiveness of police organizations and to assess the degree of success of initiatives and programs aimed at controlling, reducing, and preventing crime and disorder. The success of their initiatives and programs for crime prevention and control has drawn more attention from local police departments. For instance, an assessment could be carried out to ascertain the efficacy of a program aimed at preventing crimes through the implementation of Crime Prevention Through Environmental Design (CPTED) principles in multiple apartment communities, or a two-month burglary surveillance system (Crowe, 2000). Additionally, crime analysts support police departments in assessing internal organizational processes, like resource distribution (i.e., the assignment of police officers to patrol zones), the redrawing of geographical borders, the prediction of workforce requirements, and the creation of performance metrics. Such protocols are constantly monitored by police agencies to make sure the agencies are operating efficiently.

The different elements of the definition of crime analysis that are used throughout this book are made clear by the flowchart shown in Figure 1.1. Crime analysis helps police with criminal apprehension, crime prevention, crime and disorder reduction, and evaluation by looking at crime and disorder issues as they arise as well as ongoing police-related issues.

In conclusion, this definition serves as the basis for the remainder of the book and, despite being broad, it covers a variety of tasks that crime analysts perform in support of law enforcement. According to Bruce (2008a), these include resolving crimes, locating, and apprehending offenders, creating strategies and tactics that effectively reduce crime, identifying and resolving issues in the community, enhancing safety and quality of life, streamlining internal operations, informing the public, and making plans for future resource requirements.

1.2. DEFINITIONS OF GIS AND CRIME MAPPING

Police departments have used maps that show the physical characteristics of communities, like streets and city borders, to identify patrol zones and emergency routes as well as to help patrol officers locate specific addresses, ever since these maps became available. Police and crime analysts utilize maps as a crucial tool for crime analysis, as stated in the definition of the term. Traditionally, this process involved manually placing pins on hand-drawn wall maps.

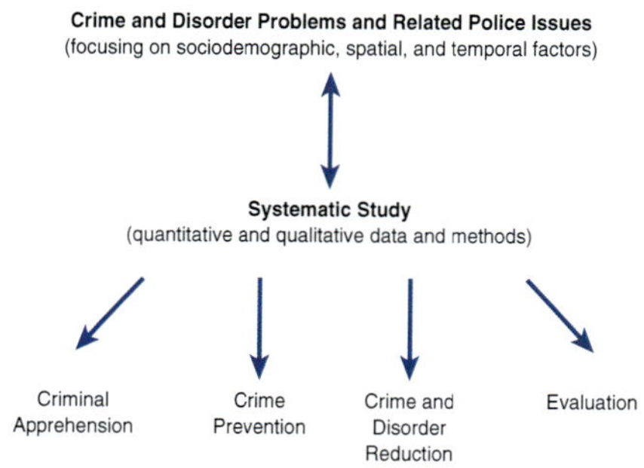

Figure 1.1. *The definition of crime analysis.*

Source: https://www.sagepub.com/sites/default/files/upm-binaries/46973_CH_1.pdf.

Since the 1990s, police innovation and notable advancements in software, hardware, electronic databases, and the Internet have made crime mapping by police departments a common practice (Weisburd and Lum, 2005). As a result, crime mapping is a crucial tool in crime analysis and is discussed extensively in this book; therefore, it is necessary to define key terms before continuing.

An analyst of crime can map crime in a variety of ways using a geographic information system (GIS), ranging from a straightforward point map to a three-dimensional visualization of spatial or temporal data.

A geographic information system (GIS) is a collection of computer-based tools that let usersdit, view, query, and analyze tabular and geographic data.

A GIS's software offers a structure and templates for gathering, organizing, and analyzing data, much like a spreadsheet or word processing application. The user is in charge of selecting which system components to use and how to use them. Beyond just creating paper maps, a GIS lets users view the data hidden behind geographic features, combine different features, work with both the data and the maps, and run statistical operations.

In law enforcement, the practice of performing spatial analysis as part of crime analysis is known as "crime mapping.." The following is the definition of crime mapping used.

Crime mapping is the process of conducting spatial analysis of problems related to crime and disorder as well as other matters pertaining to law enforcement using a geographic information system.

One of the many crucial purposes of crime analysis is to providee locations of various crimes and incidents. Despite the fact thatEven though crime mapping is a subdiscipline of crime analysis, many people discuss this type of analysis as though it is separate from crime analysis because of the special nature of the software used and the importance of geographic data in crime mapping. Within the field of crime analysis, crime mapping fulfills three primary purposes.

1. It facilitates visual and statistical analyses of the spatial nature of crime and other types of events.
2. It allows analysts to link unlike data sources together based on common geographic variables (e.g., linking census information, school information, and crime data for a common area).
3. It provides maps that help to communicate analysis results.

1.3. HISTORY OF CRIME ANALYSIS

Throughout history, people have studied crime and criminal behavior. In other words, people have always observed crime and other unfavorable occurrences (i.e., gathered) and have found connections between those findings (i.e., carried outconducted an analysis). For instance, a rancher in the ancient American West might have observed that he losing one or two head of cattle each week from his grazing land. It'sIt is also possible that he observed that the cattle vanished exclusively at night and from a specific field. After making an analysis of these observations, he might have decided to either relocate the cattle to a different field or spend the night watching them in that one. Ths ideas and deeds amount to a basic kind of crime analysis. Similar toLike this, police have traditionally carried out crime analysis by utilizing recollections to connect important suspects and items to particular connectietween crime incidents.

The types of crime analysis this example showsshow have evolved into the discipline of crime analysis as it exists today. Data about crime and other relevant factors are systematically gathered and kept for extended periods of time. Modern crime analysts use sophisticated computer systems to apply a variety of analytical techniques, ranging from basic pattern analysis to complex statistical analysis. Earlier "crime analysts" relied primarily on their own observations and memories of crime incidents.

1.3.1. Beginnings of Crime Analysis

Although the study of crime has a long history, the discipline of crime analysis got its start with the establishment of the first modern police force in London in the early 1800s. This makes sense considering that aiding the police is the primary goal of crime analysis. England organized roughly a thousand men to form a London police force through the 1820s Metropolitan Police Act. This force established a ive bureau in 1842, whose job it was to find patterns in crimes to aid inaid their investigation. Police information was being gathered, compiled, and analyzed by detective bureau offby 1844, according to London's Metropolitan Police Service (2011). Here'sHere is an illustration:

- **1844:** The Select Committee on Dogs called Commissioner Richard Mayne to testify. He claimed that the number of stolen or lost dogs in the Metropolis was on the rise. Over 600 dogs were lost and 60 were stolen in the year before. As people paid money for the restorati he said that the law was in a very unsatisfactory condition. In order toTo receive the reward, people give money to people the reason to believe have either stolen from them or lured them away.dot . Mayne thought it was organized crime.

Furthermore, according to the Metropolitan Police Service (2011), total crime data for the city of London was obtainable as early as 1847: "Data for the year included 14,091 robberies; 62,181 persons taken into custody, 24,689 of whom were summarily dealt with; 5,920 people went on trial, and 4,551 of them were fouty and sentenced; 31,572 people were released by the magistrates.".".

1.3.2. United States: 1900–1970

Even though police departments were established in many American large cities by the mid-1850s, they were unable to conduct systematic crime analysis due to internal corruption, a lack of organization, and outdated technology. The early 1900s provided the earliest evidence of formal crime analysis in the United

States. August Vollmer, the most well-known police reformer, promoted the use of pin mapping, the routine review of police reports, and the creation of patrol districts based on crime volume in addition to introducing the innovations of vehicle patrol, radio ication, and fingerprinting (Reiner, Greenlee, and Gibbens, 1976).

O. W. The phrase "crime analysis" was first used and defined by Wilson, who collaborated with Vollmer to develop an advanced police training program, in the second edition of his book Police Administration published in 1963. Wilson and McLaren (1977) make a distinction between "operations" and "crime" analysis in that book's fourth edition. They state that crime analysis is the "process of the identification of crime trends and patterns through statistical treatmen of information and through examination of actual investigativpo."

Wilson's writings suggest that crime analysis was conducted being done in police departments in the 1950s and 1960s, or at least that it was advised to do so; however, there is no proof that crime analysis products were produced during that time. Wilson talks about crime mapping and crime analysis in his lesser-known book Police Planning, which was first published in 1952, even though he does not use those terms. He describes the organization of police planning in the second edition of that volume, adding a togrphy unit," which, among other things, "provides tcal advicedot.." Wwhen illustraing patterns or incidents of crime, dot. in designated places of arrests" and a "statistics unit," which encompasses many of the modern-day crime analysis tasks like "interpreting and disseminating crime statistics and other related material to be used as aids for more effective and efficient operation of the department; preparing statistical charts, graphs, and artwork as needed by other department units; maintaining and operating the modus operandi files" (Wilson, 1957).

1.3.3. United States: 1970 to Present

In the 1970s, there was a greater understanding of the application of analysis and evaluation in policing due to the 1968 Omnibus Crime Control and Satreets Act. The act made it possible for federal grants to be awarded given to state and local police departments for any reason related to crime reduction. The U.S. The Omnibus Crime Control and Safe Streets Act of 1968 and Pomrenke, 1969 both describe how the Bureau of Justice Administration, which was created by the act with the primary goal of assisting police agencies, offered copious amounts of support, including training, technical assisthe work funded by tgrants.

Therefore, it appears that police departmentspolice departments had started to heed Vollmer's and Wilson's advice to formalize crime analysis by the 1970s, based on publications about crime analysis techniques and assessments of crime analysis functions. Emig et a. provided an annotated bibliography for the

National Institute of Justice. (1980) offered details on products and publications related to crime analysis from the 1970s. The bibliography contains entries for numerous handbooks written by different nonprofit organizations and supported by the U.S. that cover tactical and strategic crime analysis techniques. S. authority (e.g., Handbook for Police Crime Analysis Units (Austin et al., 1973); Booth, 1979's "Management Function of a Crime Analysis Unit"; Chang, Simms, Makres, and Bodnar, 1979's "Crime Analysis System Support: Descriptive Report of Manual and Automated Crime Analysis Functions").

The 1970s saw the U.S. government organized multiple symposia on crime analysis and convened practitioners and scholars to collaborate on targeted technical assistance projects designed to improve police agencies' capacity for crime analysis (Emig et al., e is proof that official crime analysis units existed during this time periodtime from popular media sources as well. A 1972 article in the New York Times, for instance, discusses crime analysis and states, "On July 21, crime analysts at NYC Police HQ say that record 57 homicides in 7-day period that ended at midnight July 20 is attributed partly to hot weather in met area" (Pace, 1972).

A small number of scholars started highlighting the significance of the attributes of criminal events, their locations, and the geographic analysis of crime in the mid-to late-1970s (Brantingham and Brantingham, 1981). Herman Goldstein (1979) proposed a different focus, problem-oriented policing, also in the late 1970s. As a result, the police began to concentrate more on handling issues related to crime and disturbance than on political and administrative issues. In an ideal world, formal analysis would be used to provide a thorough understanding of crime problems and to develop baseline measurements and methodology that would allow the evaluation of police responses to problems. Problem solving is a systematic process within problem-oriented policing (Scott, 2000). The analysis of crime and disorder problems was first demonstrated by Goldstein and other academics who were collaborating with law enforcement agencies.

The creation of the Commision on Accreditation for Law Enforcement Agencies (CALEA) in 1979.1 indicateds ecognition of crime analysis in the police practitioner c this time. Police agencies had to have crime analysis capabilities in order toto receive CALEA accreditation. Actually, agencies started allocating staff to crime analysis and creating new positions to meet CALEA standards, so having a formal crime analysis unit became more likely as a result of CALEA accreditation (Giblin, 2006).

In the 1980s and early 1990s, practitioners of crime analysis started to organize. In 1982, the Colorado Crime Analysis Association was established, making it the first state association ever. The association's first president,

Dale Harris (personal communication, November 2, 2003), described it as an engaged group of professionals who gained from the sharing of tools and techniques. With more than 350 members, the California Crime Analysis Association was established in 1989 and is currently the biggest state crime analysis organization in the country. A small group of seasoned analysts from Colorado, Texas, Oklahoma, Georgia, Missouri, and Ontario founded the International Association of Crime Analysts (IACA) in 1990 (Dale Harris, personal communication, 2003).

The field of crime analysis in the US expanded slowly in the early to mid-1990s. Herman Goldstein expanded on the function of crime analysis in his 1979 article and book Problem-Oriented Policing (1990), stressing the significance of police departments utilizing data and research to pinpoint issues, comprehend their root causes, and assess crime prevention initiatives.

The mid-1990s saw a number of additional events that encouraged the growth of crime analysis. Police departments all over the nation were adopting the philosophy of community policing, which placed a strong emphasis on problem solving (the method Herman Goldstein outlined) and partnerships with the communities they serve. A common component of these partnerships was the exchange of data and information related to crime analysis. The 1968 Omnibus Crime Control and Safe Streets Act was amended in 1994 by the Violent Crime Control and Safe Streets Act, which also established the Office of Community Oriented Policing Services, or COPS Office, to oversee the hiring of police officers and provided substantial funding for the addition of 100,000 new police officers to the force.

The COPS Office broadened its focus to include crime mapping and analysis in 1997. Grants were intended to support community policing and crime analysis both technically and substantively. Ultimately, the development and application of Compstat by the New York City Police Department in 1994—a data- and mapping-driven police management strategy that was later adopted by other departments—raised awareness of crime analysis and integrated it into the department's routine operations (Weisburd, Mastrofski, McNally, Greenspan, and Willis, 2003).

Significant advancements in computer technology occurred at the same time as and helped to facilitate the previously described events. The speed and memory of computers increased dramatically in the 1990s, and the development of the Windows operating system had a big influence on crime analysis techniques. Police were now able to store official information electronically and analyze vast amounts of data with much greater ease thanks to these changes. Analysts could also use desktop statistical programs and crime mapping software to clean up data and create reports.

Practitioners concentrated in the 1980s and early 1990s on giving police agencies statistical data regarding long-term trends and suggestions for organizational procedures derived from the work of policing planning units (i.e., tactical criminal investigation). While recognizing transient patterns and trends in crime (i.e., tactical crime analysis) was carried out during this period and gained traction in medium- to small-sized agencies in the middle of the 1990s. This came about partly as a result of crime analysis units becoming more decentralized (i.e., specific techniques in crime analysis training at the time, the move away from group operations at headquarters and toward individual crime analysts working in police precincts out in the field, and a renewed focus on the police mission of apprehending criminals.

1.4. HISTORY OF CRIME MAPPING

Even though crime mapping is still important to crime analysis today, technological advancements over the past 15 years have made spatial analysis and the creation of crime maps for distribution commonplace in both policing and crime analysis. Since the history of crime mapping and crime analysis differ slightly, they are discussed separately in this chapter. Not with the founding of the first police force, but rather with the efforts of researchers well before computers were invented, is where the history of crime mapping begins.

1.4.1. Beginnings of Crime Mapping

Researchers in Europe who followed the cartographic school of criminology in the 1800s looked at the rates of crime in various areas (regions) and how these rates related to sociological elements like socioeconomic status (Groff and La Vigne, 2002). For instance, in 1829, utilizing census data on demographics and criminal statistics for the years 1825 to 1827, ethnographer and geographer Adriano Balbi and lawyer AndréMichel Guerry produced the first crime maps. They looked at levels of education, crimes against people, and crimes against property in France and discovered that higher educated people lived in areas with higher rates of property crime and that high levels of property crime had a lower incidence of crimes against people (Weisburd and McEwen, 1997). Moreover, at this time, Quételet, a Belgian statistician and astronomer, employed maps to investigate relationships between crime and racial and cultural differences, educational attainment, and transit routes (Weisburd and McEwen, 1997).

1.4.2. United States: 1900–1970

Compared to Europe, the United States was a little slow to adopt crime mapping. In the 1800s, the United States was still a young nation, so trustworthy maps were hard to come by and census data was not routinely gathered as it was in France and England. Urban sociologists in Chicago carried out the first significant spatial analysis of crime in the United States during the 1920s and 1930s (Shaw and McKay, 1969). Their studies on crime and delinquency connected elements like poverty and social disarray with criminal activity and delinquency. Indeed, one of the best examples of crime mapping in the first half of the 20th century is this group of researchers' spatial analysis of juvenile delinquency and social conditions in Chicago (Groff and La Vigne, 2002).

The concentric zone model, which maintains that various zones (areas with distinct purposes) form around a central business district in an urban setting and that some of these zones are more prone to crime and disorder than are others, was developed theoretically with the help of crime mapping. Gangs were concentrated in areas of the city where social control was weak and social disorganization was high, according to research that used the concentric zone concept to analyze the locations and distribution of gangs in Chicago (Weisburd and McEwen, 1997). The majority of the initial crime mapping projects carried out in the US and Europe looked at overall crime rates by region. Nonetheless, there is proof of a manually drawn map from 1929 by researchers at Chicago schools, which showed the residence addresses of over 9,000 offenders grouped together in specific Chicago neighborhoods (Weisburd and McEwen, 1997).

Sociologists and other individuals with an interest in crime and its causes carried out further research into the sociological elements connected to crime during the 1950s, 60s, and 70s. Due in part to the researchers' emphasis on sociological factors and the lack of appropriate technology, the explanations and geographic methods of analysis employed during this time remained relatively simple (Groff and La Vigne, 2002). Using massive computer systems and crude visualization techniques, academics started analyzing crime in space in the late 1960s (Weisburd and McEwen, 1997).

1.4.3. United States: 1970 to Present

A group of researchers in England, Canada, and the United States changed the focus of their study of crime from the criminal offender—what traditional criminology examined—to the criminal event and its context, which includes the social and physical environments that provide opportunities for crime, between the late 1960s and the early 1980s (Brantingham and Brantingham, 1981; Clarke, 1980, 1983; Cornish and Clarke, 1986). This shift in focus from the aggregate analysis of crime and social factornalysis of individual criminal events and their locations had an impact on crime mapping. In order toTo better understand crime problems and related issues like rape (LeBeau, 1987) and various other crimes (Harries, 1980), as well as the distribution of police personnel (Rengert and Wasilchick, 1985), researchers started incorporating information about geography and environment.

When client-servechnology became more widely available in the early 1980s, several police departments were able to testevaluate crime mapping as a routine part of their operations (Groff and La Vigne, 2002). The "DMAP" (Drug Market Analysis Program) project, which was funded by the National Institute of Justice, brought together academics and professionals from five U.S. cities (Harris, Connecticut; Pittsburgh, Pennsylvania; San Diego, California; Kansas City, Missouri); to employ cutting-edge analytical methods to examine drug markets and monitor their movements over time (Groff and La Vigne, 2002). These projects showed how communities could use GIS tools as a key component of crime control initiatives, and they paved the way for partnerships between practitioners and researchers in the field of crime mapping. The program's main focus was on using geographic police data, but participants discovered that looking at other geographically based data improved their ability to identify problem-solving techniques, brought important partners with various viewpoints together, and made it easier to evaluate their collaborative efforts (Taxman and McEwen, 1997).

When police data systems and computer technology advanced significantly in the early to mid-1990s, electronic crime mapping became a far more useful tool for investigators and law enforcement. With desktop computers becoming faster and more capable of handling large amounts of data, GIS software became available for these devices. Furthermore, computer-aided dispatch systems and electronic records management systems made police data on crimes, arrests, accidents, and service requests electronically accessible. Geographic data, including street and census information, was made widely available in electronic format by numerous government agencies and private businesses for free or at a very low cost. The field of crime mapping has ad beyond the use of labor-intensive, large-scale mainframe mapping systems and manual methods thanks to all ofall these developments.

Together, the Sociology Department at Loyola University of Chicago and the Illinois Criminal Justice Information Authority hosted a computer crime mapping workshop in Chicago in 1993. Many of the workshop participants, who are now among the best researchers and analysts in the field, described spatial analytic techniques and provided helpful guidance for both police professionals interested in implementing computer mapping in their agencies and students of spatial analysis in a publication titled Crime Analysis Through Computer Mapping (Block, Dabdoub, and Fregly, 1995). One of the first attempts to bring researchers and practitioners together to talk about crime mapping was this workshop.

Vice President Al Gore led a federal government campaign in the mid-1990s to support crime mapping techniques and technologies more heavily. Federal funding was provided to police agencies so they could purchase crime mapping technology, and a number of initiatives were created expressly to help them put crime mapping into practice. The U.S. Through a program called MORE (Making Officer Redeployment Effective), the Department of Justice's Office of Community Oriented Policing Services, or COPS Office, provided a sizable amount of funding for crime mapping software and equipment. "Expand the amount of time current law enforcement officers can spend on community policing by funding technology, equipment, and support staff" was the main goal of this funding, according to the Office of Community Oriented Policing Services (2011b). Just over $53 million (90 separate grants) in MORE funding was allotted to crime mapping technology and staff (M.) between 1995 and 2002. Scheider, correspondence with the author, November 10, 2003.

In 1997, the National Institute of Justice of the Department of Justice established the Crime Mapping Research Center, which is currently known as the Mapping and Analysis for Public Safety (MAPS) program. By looking at how "to use maps to analyze crime," "to analyze spatial data," "maps can help researchers evaluate programs and policies," and "to develop mapping, data sharing, and spatial analysis tools," it hopes to support research that assists criminal justice agencies in using mapping to improve public safety (National Institute of Justice, 2009). The MAPS program was founded and has since hosted yearly conferences where researchers and practitioners convene to exchange ideas about research and spatial analytic methods. Developing training curricula, publishing books on crime mapping, funding spatial analysis research and fellowships, conducting a national survey of crime mapping, and assembling researchers and police professionals in a technical working group to discuss spatial analysis of crime issues are some of the other initiatives that have been carried out. The program has greatly increased interest in and development of crime mapping and crime analysis techniques among police departments and researchers in the United States. The Crime Mapping and Analysis Program (CMAP), whose goal was "to provide technical assistance and introductory and advanced training to local and state agencies in the areas of crime and intelligence analysis and geographic information systems (GIS)," was also funded by the National Institute of Justice from 1998 to 2007 (Crime Mapping and Analysis Program, 2004). A sizable number of field officers and crime analysts received training from CMAP.

Compstat, a data-and mapping-driven police management strategy developed by the New York City Police Department and embraced by other police agencies across the United States, is another relatively recent influence on the use of crime mapping in policing (Henry, 2002; Weisburd et al, 2003). Utilizing crime mapping software and analysis in weekly meetings to comprehend local patterns of crime and disorder incidents is a fundamental aspect of Compstat for law enforcement officials. The importance of crime mapping in the Compstat program was highlighted in each episode of CBS's The District, a television series based on New York's Compstat experience, which aired in 2001 (Theodore, 2001).

However, David Weisburd, a renowned professor in the field of crime and place, has looked into the rate of adoption of crime mapping in the 1990s through a number of surveys and his own pilot study. He discovered that "crime mapping has become widely diffused among police agencies, that the diffusion process began in the late 1980s to early 1990s and gained momentum in the mid-1990s, and that the adoption of crime mapping appears to follow the standard's' curve of diffusion of innovation" (Weisburd and Lum, 2005). However, no historical research has been done on the adoption of crime mapping by police agencies.

1.5. CRIME ANALYSIS AS A CAREER TRACK

There is some disagreement about what constitutes a "good" crime analyst, but most people's opinions reflect their personal experiences. Accordingly, a crime analyst with an advanced degree is likely to feel that all crime analysts should have such degrees, and a crime analyst who is a police officer is likely to think that all crime analysts should be police officers. This is an oversimplification, but there is still discussion about the level of education and experience required for crime analysts to perform their duties. Because so much of modern crime analysis relies on computers and software technology, some argue that crime analysts should also be computer experts. However, is it necessary for a crime analyst to have been an officer, so that he or she knows the ins and outs of a police department, or is an advanced degree in statistics more valuable?

A crime analyst should ideally be knowledgeable about the police, skilled in conducting research, and technologically savvy. It is unlikely that a person entering the field of crime analysis will possess every one of these credentials at first; instead, he or she may excel in one area and need to develop the others over time. The knowledge and abilities possessed by a crime analyst should be balanced across these three domains. Even though they may have a more academic background, they should be able to relate to the day-to-day activities of law enforcement and effectively explain data from crime analyses. In addition to having a street-level understanding of crime and police activity, an unschooled individual may also possess technological and statistical analysis abilities.

Hiring civilian crime analysts is a current trend in police departments. Officers frequently switch jobs every few years, and agencies don't want to take the chance of losing the financial commitment that comes with extensive training in crime analysis when an officer leaves. Furthermore, hiring civilians costs police departments less than hiring officers (both in terms of pay and benefits). This makes working as a crime analyst an excellent entry-level position, but there are no opportunities for career-track advancement in this role. The crime analyst is one of the few professional support positions in many police agencies, especially small to medium-sized departments. The only ways for an analyst to advance in their career are by moving to a larger department or taking a different position in the city government. Nevertheless, there are significant differences across police departments in the way they appoint officers and civilians to crime analyst roles. Successful analysts typically possess a strong background in theory, research methodology, statistics, data collection, and data manipulation. When it comes to analysis, investigation, and helping other police officers perform their duties more successfully, the analyst is the expert. Proficient crime analysts possess an understanding of police procedures, police culture, and the features of the community they serve. Crime analysts interact with people in different ways, but in order to succeed, they must be able to communicate intricate concepts to a wide range of people (e.g., managers, law enforcement officers, municipal officials, and residents) in a non-condescending manner. Furthermore, even if they have never been a police officer, crime analysts need to be able to relate to them, operate within the police culture, think clearly under pressure, stand by their opinions on crucial issues, and maintain a sense of humor. A number of profiles of contemporary crime analysts are provided at the end of this chapter to highlight the differences in the amount of training, education, experience, and responsibility that exist among analysts.

1.5.1. Crime Analyst Qualifications and Job Descriptions

Crime analysis positions come in a variety of forms for police departments. While some only have one crime analyst on staff, others have multiple analysts working in what is known as a crime analysis unit, or CAU. In order to illustrate the range of levels and activities in the field of crime analysis as well as the qualifications required for employment at different levels, the following text offers general descriptions of a number of positions related to crime analysis and their roles within CAUs.

1.5.1.1. Interns/Volunteers

For many years, police departments have conducted crime analysis with the help of volunteers. Because there were either insufficient resources or a shortage of crime analysis professionals in the 1970s and 1980s, many police departments used volunteers for this purpose. Volunteers and interns are now frequently used by police departments to supplement and/or improve their productivity in crime analysis. Volunteers are individuals who work unpaid for the police department; they are typically retired or students. Undergraduate or graduate students who want to gain real-world experience and college credit can work as interns in a police department. An internship can frequently act as the intern's "foot in the door," opening doors to future career opportunities.

Police departments and their interns can both greatly benefit from internship programs. In addition to assisting departments with crime analysis tasks, interns acquire real-world experience and the competencies required to become crime analysts. Depending on the needs of their crime analysis units and the availability of students, police departments hire interns from a wide range of academic fields, including criminal justice, sociology, political science, geography, English, psychology, and computer science. Students majoring in geography might be recruited by a police department that is implementing a geographic information system, while students majoring in criminal justice might be recruited by a department that wants to conduct tactical analysis.

The internship programs that place student interns are usually managed by specific academic programs. For these programs, students must typically complete the following requirements: they must write a final paper for grading, record their experiences through field notes, and work as interns for a minimum of one semester (the number of hours per week varies depending on the number of course credits awarded). Depending on the police agency's resources, internships may be paid or unpaid. Within CAUs, volunteers and interns perform a wide range of duties, such as data analysis, tactical data entry, creating monthly strategic reports, and drafting requests to take part in complex analysis projects. A word of caution regarding internships: Some police departments subject applicants to a screening process akin to that which is employed for candidates seeking police officer training and other positions within the department, even though student interns do not ultimately become police officers. e.g., due to the fact that interns have the same access to departmental areas and records as officers do (including drug testing, lie detector tests, and thorough background checks). When applying for internships in police departments, students should be aware that any illegal activity they have engaged in could negatively affect their acceptance and, ultimately, their ability to work in any police agency at all.

1.5.1.2. Crime Analysis Assistant/Technician

An administrative support worker who handles phone answering, data entry, copying, file maintenance, simple standardized report generation, and other administrative tasks in the CAU is known as a crime analysis assistant or technician. A high school degree and one to two years of secretarial or data entry experience are typically requirements for this role. Typically, someone with experience working as a secretary or someone just starting out in the field of crime analysis (e.g., a pupil). As they gain more training and expertise, crime analysis assistants may be able to advance within the CAU.

1.5.1.3. Entry-Level Crime Analyst

One of the roles in a police department's multiple tiers of crime analysis is frequently referred to as an entry-level crime analyst. Since these analysts are usually new to the field, have little experience, and receive a lot of training in their first years of employment, they typically perform relatively routine crime analysis tasks. A year of analytical experience—though not necessarily experience with crime analysis—and an undergraduate degree in criminal justice, political science, sociology, or a related field that includes statistics and research methodology in its curriculum are typically required for this position (a master's degree is often seen as the equivalent of a year of experience). Certain law enforcement agencies mandate that candidates seeking entry-level crime analyst positions possess the crime analysis certification, which is available in multiple states, either at the time of hiring or within a designated timeframe after taking the job.

1.5.1.4. Experienced Crime Analyst

Expert crime analysts can work as lone practitioners in a police agency or as integral members of a CAU. This level is there to give analysts in departments with a large workforce the chance to grow in their careers. The experienced crime analyst is expected to perform more complex analyses and bears greater responsibility than the entry-level analyst.

In addition, a person in this role might be responsible for overseeing lower-level employees, including interns, volunteers, and crime analysis technicians. A bachelor's degree in criminal justice, political science, sociology, or a similar discipline that incorporates statistics and research methodology into its curriculum is typically the minimum requirement for the position of experienced crime analyst, as is two years of experience in the field.

1.5.1.5. Specialty Crime Analyst

An analyst hired to carry out a specific kind of crime analysis is known as a specialty crime analyst. A comparatively large CAU agency might favor hiring specialized crime analysts (i.e., who possess unique sets of specialized knowledge and abilities) as opposed to generalists (i.e., who receive cross-training to ensure that every member of the unit has a comparable level of expertise).

Agencies may occasionally receive grant funding that mandates that crime analysts examine specific kinds of crimes or other activities. The benefit of having specialty crime analysts on staff for police departments is that they are highly skilled and knowledgeable in their specific fields of crime analysis; the drawback is that their work is not readily transferable to other analysts, meaning that in the event of a specialty analyst's resignation, no one else can take up the work until another analyst with the same specialty is hired.

Specialty crime analysts come in a variety of forms, and each one has different requirements for training and work history. However, because both roles necessitate exields, the specialty crime analyst position is generally regarded as being equal to the experienced crime analyst level. The following are some examples of typesexamples of specialty crime analysts:

- **Tactical Crime Analyst:** This type of analyst conducts only tactical crime analysis and does not produce long-term reports or statistics.
- **Problem Analyst:** This type of analyst conducts analysis within the context of problem solving only.
- **Sex Crime Analyst:** This type of analyst conducts tactical, strategic, and administrative crime analysis having to do with sex crimes and is likely to work closely with detectives. The position of sex crime analyst might exist in a large agency that has developed a long-term task force to address sex crimes. (Other types of crime analysts also specialize in particular kinds of crime; these include violent crime analysts, property crime analysts, and robbery crime analysts.)
- **School Safety Analyst:** This type of analyst conducts analysis on the safety in and around schools, working directly with school administrators and school resource officers.
- **Geographic Information Systems Analyst:** This type of analyst specializes in the use of geographic information systems and conducts spatial analysis of crime and various types of police activity. Salaries for GIS analysts are typically higher than those for crime analysts because of the specialized technical skills required and because police agencies must compete for qualified analysts with private companies offering high salaries. Compared with crime analyst positions, significantly fewer GIS analyst positions are available, for a number of reasons: (i) Smaller departments that conduct crime analysis typically have only one crime analyst position, and that is

not a specialist position; (ii) many police officials do not feel that filling a position with a person who works only on spatial analysis of crime is warranted; and (iii) the number of potential applicants for GIS analyst positions (i.e., individuals who have both geography and criminal justice backgrounds) is relatively small.

1.5.1.6. Crime Analysis Supervisor

A person who oversees a crime analysis unit and possesses significant knowledge and experience in the field of crime analysis is known as a crime analysis supervisor. Police managers (sworn personnel) who oversee the crime analysis function as part of their other responsibilities are not covered by this job title. Because the job of a crime analysis supervisor entails doing actual crime analysis work, it is regarded as a "working" position. A crime analysis supervisor's main duties include leading the development of CAU goals and objectives, representing the CAU's interests at high-level organizational meetings (like command staff and patrol or investigations operations meetings), and having local, national, and international expertise in the field of crime analysis. A master's degree in criminal justice, political science, sociology, or a similar discipline is typically required for this position. Additionally, two years of experience in crime analysis and at least one year of supervisory experience are prerequisites.

1.5.2. CAU Organizational Chart

An imaginary CAU organizational chart with the positions covered in the previous section and their minimal requirements is shown in Figure 1.2. The figure's arrows suggest possible career advancement paths.

1.5.3. Developing and Improving a Crime Analysis Unit

Any kind of division, unit, or organization needs a strategic plan that establishes goals, lays out expectations, and provides guidance on how to allocate resources and carry out tasks. The creation of a strategic plan is crucial when creating a new crime analysis unit (CAU) or enhancing the capabilities of an already-existing CAU. This is because the plan serves as a formal mechanism outlining the role and objectives of the CAU within the particular agency. As a result, this portion of the book is a succinct explanation of how a strategic plan could be created for a brand-new or established CAU. College students may not find this material immediately applicable, but it does offer a basis for comprehending the creation of crime analysis units and their function in police departments. The section offers practitioners information to help direct the creation of their own strategic plans. Generally speaking, a CAU's strategic plan ought to be created in accordance with the objectives of the agency, contain precise short- and long-term objectives for the CAU itself, and be reasonable in how resources are allocated (e.g., financing, time, and staff capabilities), and it should outline the organization's future requirements in addition to going over its main areas of focus.

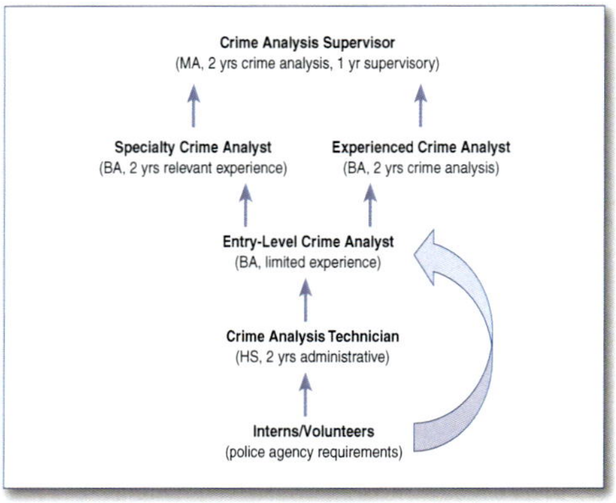

Figure 1.2. *Sample crime analysis unit organizational chart.*

Source: https://www.sagepub.com/sites/default/files/upm-binaries/46973_CH_1.pdf.

Understanding a CAU's current situation and its capacity for crime analysis is the first step in creating a strategic plan for the organization. When evaluating agencies without a crime analysis division, one should take intotrategic objectives, the accessibility of its data sources, and the hardware and software that are available for potential use in crime analysis. The aforementioned concernsconcerns, as well as the quantity, expertise, and work habits of the current crime analysis staff, as well as the kinds of crime analysis products generated and their applications, would all be taken into account for agencies that already have a CAU.

The process of creating a strategic plan for a CAU involves identifying the agency's "needs" in terms of crime analysis. This would be achieved by using three different approaches. An overview of the standards and practices in the field of crime analysis could be obtained by reviewing the literature, which would include this book as well as others. Information would be obtained from staff members informally, depending on each agency, by talking to people there, going onngs," and attending department meetings. Formal methods ation would involve forming a committee to specifically discuss the needs for crime analysis and conductingconduct a departmental survey. Observation conducted on ride alongsrides and in meetings would focthe level of understanding of crime analysis by sworn personnel in the agency and on what type of crime reduction/ prevention strategies are being employed. Possible interviewInterview and survey questions include: How might current products be improved? What additional information is needed? What new products are needed?

The third phase is to draft the strategy plan after the data has been acquired and examined. Essentially, the plan would outline the agency's or the CAU's current status (based on data gathered in the first two steps), rank the needs of the CAU, and include a list of both short-term (one year) and long-term (five years) goals. More specifically, the plan might include the following parts:

- **Structure:** This part would detail the number and type (e.g., civilian, officer, volunteer, student) of personnel conducting crime analysis full or part time and their positions (e.g., crime analysis technician, entry-level crime analyst, specialty analyst, crime analysis supervisor). It would also include job duties and responsibilities for each position and the location of the unit within the organizational chart (i.e., within the chain of command) as well as whether the unit is centralized or decentralized.
- **Functions/Products:** The function (i.e., what type of analyses are conducted) would be determined through collaboration with agency executives who would help prioritize the type of analysis. This part would also describe any standardized products such as reports and bulletins and would lay out the dissemination strategy for each.
- **Data Issues:** This part would describe the quality of current data in terms of timeliness, accuracy, and completeness and would include any limitations imposed by the current data. It would also specify what improvements would be needed to conduct the analysis needed by the agency and identify any new data sources that the agency might pursue.
- **Technology:** This part would describe the hardware and software used for crime analysis, detail replacement and update plans, and list any additional needs.
- **Training and Promotion:** In terms of training, this part would discuss the local and national training opportunities for the analysts and develop a schedule based on the current budget and personnel needs. In terms of promotion, this part would lay out a structure for advancement (e.g., from crime analysis technician to crime analyst to supervisor) and provide suggestions for realizing the structure if it was not already in place.

- **Policies and Procedures:** Because it is important to have formal policies that are not only followed by crime analysts but also are adhered to by customers of crime analysis, this part of the plan would contain each policy and procedure (i.e., methodology). Examples of policies include a citizen request policy, an internal personnel request policy, and a media request policy. Examples of procedures include standardizing product format, methodology for data entry and cleaning, conducting a staffing analysis, and disseminating crime analysis products. Importantly, policies should be developed in collaboration with sworn personnel and approved by the chief or the command staff.
- **Goals:** This section would indicate the achievements the CAU will work toward and would summarize the suggestions for improvements made in each of the previous parts categorized by short-term (e.g., 1 year) and long-term (e.g., 3 to 5 years) goals. It would also include goals focused on the substantive work of the CAU that would include improving the quality and usefulness of crime analysis for crime reduction, prevention, and evaluation.

It goes without saying that the specific details for each of the previously mentioned sections would be specific to the agency for which the plan was created. Furthermore, a written splan can be created in a variety of ways. However, by using this data as a basis, a strategic plan gives a CAU an official set of guidelines for managing and enhancing its crimecrime analysis staff, functions, and capabilities.

1.6. THEORETICAL FOUNDATIONS OF CRIME ANALYSIS

Historically, criminological and criminal justice theory has not been extensively applied in the day-to-day practice of crime analysis. Obtaining and cleaning data, counting incidents, and identifying short-term patterns are tasks that take up a lot of time for crime analysts; applying theory to inform their work takes up far less of their time. However, as the field advances, it is becoming more crucial and typical for analysts to incorporate certain pertincal theories into their work.

- Helping the police deal with regular crime and disorder is the main goal of crime analysis. Theoretical frameworks from sociology and psychology thatpsychology identify personality disorders, social disorganization, and inadequate parenting as the primary causes of criminal behavior areable to crime analysis because police have little control over these causes. Police officers must concentrate on how and why crimes are happening in specific circumstances in order toto find answers for those pressing issues. Police agencies, and crime analysts in particular, deal with people who have already made the decision to commit crimes. Therefore, theories that presume a motivated offender are needed for both crime analysis and law enforcement, rather than theories that attempt to explain why the people became offenders in the first place. The former are regarded as criminology theories, and the latter as theories of criminal justice.

Scholars' attempts to characterize and explain crime events as they occur in daily life have advanced significantl 30 years (Felson and Boba, 2010). These theories collectively refer to as environmental criminology (although the term "criminology" is used here, these theories are actually classifiedclassified as criminal justice theories). They include key ideas that inform crime analysis, crime prevention initiatives, and assessment of those initiatives. This chapter offers a succinct overview of this conceptual model. While the focus of this chapter is on crime, disorder and other issues that affect police and crime analysts can also benefit from the concepts discussed here.

1.6.1. Environmental Criminology

Unlike conventional criminological theories, environmental criminology does not try to explain the underlying causes of crime or the reasons why people commit crimes. Rather, it emphasizes the different facets of the "settings" where crimes are committed. "A location for recurrent use, for a particular activity, at known times" is what Felson (2006) defines as a setting. Every town, city, and even rural area can be classified into environments that are conducive to specific types of behavior. Consider a basketbales at a public park as opposed to a large retail establishment and its parking lot. These various contexts are home to a varietople and behaviors. It is in these particular environmentsenvironments that routine behavior gives rise to the possibility of crimes happening in a methodical manner.

Crucially, a crime doesn'tdoes not happen unless there is a chance for it to happen (e.g., an assault cannot happen if there is only one person in the room; a theft cannot happen if there is nothing to steal. The theories of environmental criminology help us understand how these opportunities are created and subsequently cluster together. Certain settings present more opportunities for crime than others (Felson and Boba, 2010). Understanding the various facets of a criminal event in order to spot behavioral patterns and environmental elements that foster crime and other undesired activity is the aim of environmental criminology, rather than attempting to explain why a particular offender commits a particular crime (Brantingham and Brantingham, 1990). For ane Doe's wallet was taken from her purse, which was in her car in the gym parking lot, while she was working out at the gym. It is not helpful to investigate the offender's background in order toto determine why they stole Jane's wallet in order to stop this crime from happening again. g. poor education, incompetent parenting). Instead, the emphasis should be on how Jane's decision to leave her wallet in her parked car for several hours opens the door to criminal activity (i.e., no wallet, no crime) and on how being aware of people's regular actions in that environment encourages crime (e.g., Every woman knows better than to bring her purse to the gym while working out, and this goes double for potential offenders.

The crime analyst would look at the parking lot itself, the behavior of gym patrons, and the crime data (i.e., the possible crime scene), to recognize the opportunities for criminal activity there and then suggest changes to victim behavior and the surrounding environment to lessen or completely eradicate the likelihood of this kind of crime. In this instance, the crime could be solved by simply taking the personal items out of the car. There are still a few key ideas that need to be clarified before we can continue this conversation.

1.6.2. Problem Analysis Triangle

The idea of the problem analysis triangle (also known as the crime triangle; Center for Problem-Oriented Policing, 2016) forms the basis of the theories that help policing and crime analysis understand crime settings. The little triangle at the center of the figure stands for a specific kind of disorderly or criminal behavior, such as noisy music, unruly children, or similar behaviors. The four essential elements of a crime are located on each of the triangle's three sides and on top of the smaller triangle (for the purpose of simplicity, we will refer to "crime" in this discussion, although the triangle can be applied to any problematic activity). In other words, a crime event happens when a perpetrator and a victim, or target (a target being an inanimate object like real estate, a car, or a building), meet at a specific location at a specific time (the top of the triangle). Even though these are prerequisites for a crime, this does not imply that a crime will always occur when these conditions are met.

As a result, the bigger triangle aids in our comprehension of how opportunities are affected in the context of crime; in other words, opportunities are dynamic and subject to change. The different categories of people or systems that can demonstrate control over targets, and perpetrators are located on either side of the larger triangle. Guardians are individuals with the power to keep an eye on victims or targets and remove them from specific environments in order toto protect them.

Figure 1.3. *The problem analysis triangle.*

Source: Rachel Boba Santos, Crime Analysis With Crime Mapping, ISBN: 9781506331034.

For instance, security guards and neighbors keep an eye on each other's properties and people, respectively, in semipublic spaces like shopping centers and residential neighborhoods. Parents take theircific places—like a park where fights are known to occur—and people hide or remove belongings by putting stuff in a car's trunk or taking a purse out of the vehicle entirely.

Managers are in charge ofoversee establishments like homes, hotels, retail establishments, and apartment complexes. They oversee the locations and impose rules. The physical layout of the location, the rules themselves, and how they are applied, all influence the likelihood of crimes. Organizers of places (e.g., the manager of a shopping center or school) are crucial to consider when analyzing potential crime scenes because they typically have a broad area of influence. For instance, a bar owner who has lax policies regarding underage drinking and overserving is making it more likely that there will be fights, drunk driving, and sexual assaults.

Lastly, those in positions that enable them to keep an eye on and/or exert control over the behavior of potential offenders are known as handlers. A friend is an example of a handler who might encourage potential offenders by pushing them to fight in a bar or get intoxicated and rowdy at a sporting event. Parents and parole officers are examples of handlers who might discourage offenders from committing a crime by establishing a curfew.

The ability of guardians, managers, and handlers to discourage or limit opportunities as well as to encourage or increase opportunities for criminal activity is a significant aspect of their influence. Understanding what is going on in a specific crime setting that gives rise to opportunities for crime is crucial, but so is knowing how those opportunities can be reduced through changing existing conditions. Using Jane Doe's stolen wallet as an example once more, Jane left her purse unattended by leaving it in her car despite being a guardian of herself and her belongings. The parking lot is the location, ar is the place manager, in charge of the area's lighting, security personnel count, and parking spot placement (e.g., beforehand the gym vs. where no one can see them, behind the gym). Ultimately, theThe perpetrator is the person who decides to steal the purse after assessing the circumstances. They may act alone or with a friend, known as a handler. This example highlights a fundamental idea: crime does not always happen when opportunities are available. Instead, opportunities for crime are very specific. The offender might have decided not to take the wallet because it seemed too risky if they had strolled through the parking lot while Jane Doe or another gym patron was present or if there had been a security camera in the parking lot (guardianship).

These concepts have significant ramifications for the study of crime. They recommend that analysts employ particular methods to recognize and comprehend patterns of occurrences, and that comprehension can then guide police actions to deal with or avoid disorder and crime. For example, a location and time-of-day analysis of car thefts may reveal that certain cars are targeted in the evening hours of a shopping mall parking lot. If the affected area of the lot is investigated further, it might be discovered that it is close to a theater and that people frequently leave the goods they have just bought from mall stores in their cars before heading to the movies. Actions intended to help protect the targets (e.g., concealing the belongings in the trunk) or better oversee the parking lot (e.g., to lessen the likelihood of this crime, security guards should monitor that specific area of the parking lot during the times when theft occurs most frequently. Nevertheless, the development of targeted crime prevention measures requires a thorough examination of the criminal incidents and behavior that occur there.

The fundamental idea of how opportunities for crime are influenced is explained by the problem analysis triangle. The three related theories that follow can be used to better understand and predict how criminals decide which crimes to commit as well as how routine behavior by offenders and victims leads them to meet at specific times and places. They shed light on behavioral patterns in three domains: society (routine activities theory), social interaction (crime pattern theory), and individual (rational choice theory).

1.6.3. Rational Choice Theory

Rational choice theory states that criminals decide whether to commit crimes based on expected benefits and risks. According to the theory, everyone will commit a crime if given the chance or the appropriate "opportunity" (Felson and Clarke, 1998). It may be clear why a drug addict without money would want to rob someone, but it can be harder to comprehend why, in some situations, seemingly law-abiding individuals commit crimes; rational choice theory explains why.

When the reward exceeds the chance of being caught, someone who wouldn't normally steal may choose to do so. For instance, at a home improvement store, someone loads ten bags of garden soil onto a cart. The customer leaves the store with 10 bags after paying for only 8, counts only 8 bags, does not object, and leaves. Since the clerk made a mistake in counting, technically this is not theft; however, it is criminal activity when the person chooses not to notify the clerk of the error. The person balances the benefit of receiving two bags at no cost with the possibility of being discovered (i.e., whether the store manager or clerk will notice before the customer loads the soil into the car).

It's also critical tomber that rational choice theory, in contrast to some criminological theories that imply criminal behavior is inevitable, contends that people will choose not to commit crimes when the risks are too greatgreat, or the rewards are insufficient. Teenagers might want to get together and drink, for instance. On a Saturday night, they might spend it searching through their parents' liquor cabinets or locating a phony ID to buy alcohol. However, they might decide not to drink at all that night if these opportunities are closed off (parents locking up their alcohol) or the risk is too high (they hear the police are cracking down on underage alcohol purchases). Creating strategies to stop crimes in the future can be facilitated by understanding why people choose to commit crimes or not in specific situations.

Understanding why certain criminal groups choose to commit specific crimes on a regular basis is crucial for crime analysis and law enforcement, which is why rational choice theory is helpful in these domains. To have a more widespread influence on crime, crime analysis and police must comprehend patterns of behavior rather than just one or two isolated incidents. Understanding offenders' perceptions can assist law enforcement agencies and communities in taking action to alter the opportunities for crime and discourage offending, should offenders choose to commit crimes based on the perceived risks and expected rewards of their actions. Using the gym parking lot example once more, an analysis might reveal, for example, that over time, criminals are primarily targeting vehicles parked in the back row, which is furthest from the gym's front doors. The lack of guardianship in this area, or the comparatively low chance of being caught while committing the crimes, appears to be the reason why repeat offenders choose these cars. Based on this information, police may suggest to the gym's owners that they install security cameras or improve lighting in order to raise the perceived risk of detection for any potential offenders.

1.6.4. Crime Pattern Theory

The goal of crime pattern theory is to comprehend how individuals congregate in crime scenes over time and space. This theory states that criminal activity is most likely to happen in areas where potential victims/targets and potential offenders' activity spaces overlap (Brantingham and Brantingham, 1993; Felson and Clarke, 1998). The area that a person gets to know through daily activities—such as where they live, work, commute, and shop—is their activity space. To put it simply, a place's location constitutes its activity space.

Figure 1.4 provides a basic example of how an offender's activity space intersects with a victim's, showing instances such as work, movie theaters, and retail locations. According to crime pattern theory, an offence involving this perpetrator and this victim can only take place in or originate from where their activity spaces intersect. With people's actual activity spaces being so large, this is a relatively simple example. More generally, crime pattern theory would imply that a downtown area containing eateries, movie theaters, and retail stores would be worthy of investigation since many people, including potential offenders and victims, may frequent the area and contribute to a significant amount of crime. To understand why and how the different types of victims/targets and potential offenders who frequent this area come together, a crime analyst studying the data would break it down into specifics. Due to the heavy traffic of vehicles, thefts from cars and auto theft from parking lots may be an issue in this area. Given how many potential victims there are who carry their purses while shopping, it might also have a problem with purse snatching.

Furthermore, research and the theory of crime patterns both indicate that criminals commit crimes in familiar or frequent locations. In an area where they currently reside or have previously lived, offenders are more than 22 times more likely to commit crimes than in a comparable area where they have never lived, according to a study by Bernasco (2010). This effect is also true for auto theft, robbery, and burglary. According to the research's implications, analysts may start their search for suspects for a specific crime series with local residents or people who frequently visit that location on a regular basis. This also implies that offenders who are unfamiliar with a certain area might need to spend some time "casing" it in order to get a sense of the people or behavior there. A good example of this can be found in the movie Home Alone, where one burglar demonstrates to the other that he has been watching the neighborhood for several days and knows exactly when each home's Christmas lights will go on. In light of this theory, a crime analyst may seek out prior interactions with dubious individuals in a region where burglaries have occurred in order to identify potential suspects. Therefore, crime pattern theory offers a methodical approach for examining and analyzing behavioral patterns for crime analysts.

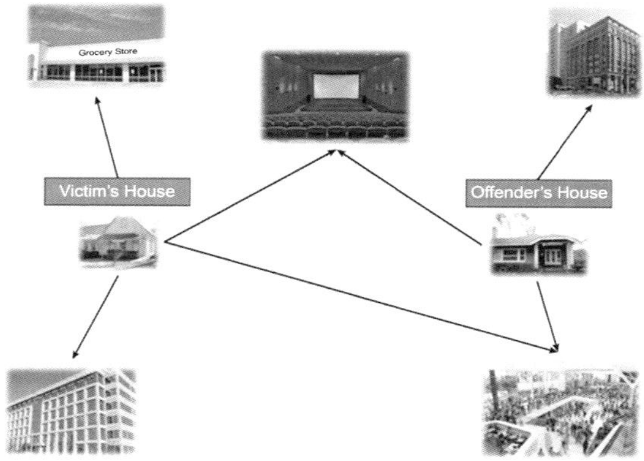

Figure 1.4. *Offender and victim activity space example.*

Source: Rachel Boba Santos, Crime Analysis With Crime Mapping, ISBN: 9781506331034.

1.6.5. Routine Activities Theory

The theory of routine activities focuses on how societal behavioral shifts can alter the opportunities for criminal activity. For instance, Felson and Boba (2010) address how notable modifications to Americans' daily routines contributed to a rise in crime during the middle to late 19th century in the United States. They point out that during that time, there was a notable increase in the number of Americans who regularly left their homes to go to work. Because there was less guardianship over homes, there were more opportunities for crimes like residential burglary, which changed the behavior in the home (setting). Furthermore, as more people entered the workforce, there were more potential targets—cars and other personal property—and victims—individuals. This led to an increase in the likelihood of crimes like rape, robbery, and vehicle theft.

Recalling the example of Jane Doe's stolen wallet, routine activities theory would contend that the rise in popularity of working out at a gym and the practice by many gym patrons of leaving their wallets and/or purses in their cars while they worked out for several hours created new opportunities for crime. Because going to the gym is a part of their own regular routine, it is also important for offenders to learn about the behaviors of their victims in the gym setting.

The use of smartphones is the most notable example of how routine activity has changed on a societal level in recent years. Due to the widespread use of smartphones, there are now many more opportunities for certain types of crimes in the United States and many other countries. Smartphones and mini computers share many functionalities. There are more opportter-related crimes, such as identity theft, the spread of computer viruses, cyberbullying, the distribution of pornographic material, and phone theft, ble carry them around and use them almost constantlyconstantly. The theory of routine activities postulates that behavioral shifts in society can reduce the likelihood of criminal activity. For instance, in order toto prevent injuries, many states have made it mandatory to wear a helmet when riding a motorcycle. This has also decreased the likelihood that a motorcycle will be stolen. That is, when stealing a motorcycle, the thief needs to have his own helmet or else he runs the risk of being stopped—not for stealing, but for wearing an improper helmet.

From the standpoint of this theory, crime analysts inquire about broad behavioral patterns and how those patterns affect the likelihood of crimes. Because crime analysis typically focuses on smaller subsets of society, such as one city or a specific region, local patterns of behavior, such as the prevalence of a particular type of drug in a community or the tendency of teenagers in an area to use drinking and driving as their primary form of entertainment on weekends, are particularly important.

1.6.6. Law of Crime Concentration

The "place" side of the problem analysis triangle is a crucial component of environmental criminology for crime analysts. Studies conducted over the past three decades have demonstrated that strategies aimed at reducing crime that prioritize "place" outperform those that prioritize people (Telep and Weisburd, 2012). Thus, a new criminological law has emerged from the fields of place-based policing and criminology research. A conclusion we reach about "how the world works" based on data and research findings is referred to as a criminological law. Since criminology is a social science, criminological laws relate to more general patterns of crime and behavior rather than specific instances. The age-crime curve, which holds that most people "age out" of crime but that offenders' criminality is not constant and stable throughout their livesne such law that has been established through many years of research (Laub and Sampson, 2003). Since most of the research on criminology lacks consistent and conclusive answers to criminological questions, there aren'tare not many "laws" in the field.

The "law of crime concentration" is a new criminological law that was developed in 2014 by Professor David Weisburd. He gives the following definition of it: "The concentration of crime will fall within a narrow bandwidth of percentages for a defined cumulative proportion of crime for a defined measure of crime at a specific microgeographic unit" (Weisburd, 2015). This indicates that not only do we know that certain locations are associated with higher crime rates, but these clusters can also be precisely identified and are stable and predictable over time. The importance of place in the problem analysis triangle, criminal opportunity, activity space, and people's daily activities are all fully supported by this law.

In terms of implications for crime analysts, this suggests that they should devote most of their time to applying the theories covered here and concentrate their analysis on understanding crime at places. Places are far more reliable units of analysis, according to this law and the research, even though understanding offenders and their decisions to commit crimes in the present are crucial. The most straightforward explanation for this is that while criminals are mobile and shift locations to carry out their crimes, locations remain stationary, and their regular activities and functions remain constant. For police departments and, consequently, crime analysts, the most promising approach is to analyze, comprehend, and respond to crime at the scene.

1.6.7. Repeat Victimization, Near Repeats, and the 80/20 Rule

The term "repeated victimization" refers to crimes committed against the same victims or in the same locations. A significant discovery in the literature on recurrent victimization is that individuals and locations with a history of victimization are more likely to experience victimization in the future than individuals and locations with no history of victimization (Farrell and Pease, 1993). Actually, prior victimization of the individual or location is the best indicator of future victimization (Grove, Farrell, Farrington, and Johnson, 2012; Weisel, 2005). According to the law of crime concentration, crime clusters are created when certain locations are repeatedly targeted for criminal activity.

Because it makes it easier to identify patterns of opportunity and because recurrent victimization is a common occurrence, this is an important theoretical consideration in crime analysis. The opportunity to identify common characteristics among crime events and gain insight into the reasons behind crime to a particular group or setting arises when the same people, location, or type of target is repeatedly victimized in different situations. Since those who have previously experienced victimization should be the primary target of preventative efforts, the phenomenon of repeat victimization also serves as a focal point for prevention. Since police have few resources and must prioritize preventing crimes, this is especially crucial for them. ..

Repeat victimization is broken down into the following four types (Weisel, 2005):

1. **True Repeat Victims:** These are the exact same individuals or places that were previously victimized. For example, the same residents are living in the same house, which is burglarized twice.

2. **Near Victims:** These are victims or targets that are physically close to and share characteristics with the original victim. Burglary of several condos in the same community is an example, not only because they are physically close but also because they may have the same door locks and physical design.
3. **Virtual Repeats:** These are victims or targets that are virtually identical to the original victim and share some of the same characteristics. For example, electronics retail stores of the same name that are victimized across cities or states are considered virtual repeats because they have similar, if not identical, store layouts, policies, and types of property. Also, new occupants (e.g., owners of a store or residents of a home) in places victimized in the past are considered virtual repeats.
4. **Chronic Victims:** These are individuals who are repeatedly victimized over time by various offenders for various types of crimes (e.g., assault, robbery, theft). This is also called multiple victimization.

Repeat victimization is also related to other ways in which crime clusters:

- **Repeat Offenders:** Individuals or types of individuals who commit multiple crimes. These can be individuals who specialize in one type of crime (e.g., robbery) or commit a variety of crimes (e.g., theft, robbery, assault).
- **Hot Spots:** Areas that suffer from proportionately large amounts of crime (Sherman, Gartin, and Buerger, 1989). Areas can be hot spots based on one type of crime or a variety of crimes. The size of the hot spot area depends on both the amount of crime and the relative size of the jurisdiction.
- **Risky Facilities:** Individual locations that attract or generate a disproportionate amount of crime (Eck, Clarke, and Guerette, 2007). Examples include a large retail plaza or mall, a low-budget motel, and a high school. Also, these include types of places that are frequently victimized but not necessarily in the same area. Examples include beauty salons, ctores, day care centers, bars, and fast-food restaurants.
- **Hot Products:** Types of property that are repeatedly targeted or, as Clarke (1999) puts it, "those consumer items that are most attractive to thieves." In order forFor an item to be a hot product, it must fit the following criteria: It must be "concealable, removable, available, valuable, enjoyable, and disposable." Examples include precious metal (e.g., gold, copper, platinum from catalytic converters), smartphones and tablets, and handguns.

Under the concepts of repeat victimization and the law of crime concentration, near repeat victimization is a very particular kind of repeat victimization that is particularly significant for crime analysis. According to Bowers and Johnson (2005), "near repeats" are areas that have not been victimized but are close to areas that have. Police crime analysts have actually been identifying near-repeat crime clusters for decades as crime patterns to help police with their tactical responses (Austin et al., 1973; Gwinn, Cooper, Hick, and Bruce, 2008). For this reason, a summary of the near repeat research is presented here, serving as a basis for the subsequent strategies discussed in the tactical crime analysis chapters.

- Research has established that near repeats occur regularly and that they have been shown to occur rapidly (i.e., one right after another; Johnson and Bowers, 2004; Johnson, Summers, and Pease, 2007, 2009; Townsley, Homel, and Chaseling, 2003). Most of the research on near repeats has been conducted for residential burglary and theft from vehicle crimes, which are two crime types often analyzed by crime analysts. Thus, these findings from the research have direct relevance for crime analysts (Bernasco, 2010; Coupe and Blake, 2006; Johnson, Lab, and Bowers, 2008):
- Houses next to a burgled home have been found to be at a substantially higher risk of being burglarized.
- Most near repeats occur within 1 week of the initial burglary.
- The increased risk is caused by offenders returning to the area of a prior successful burglary. If the previous house is still vulnerable, a "true repeat" will occur, but if that house has been hardened (e.g., posted alarm signs in the front yard, locked windows and doors), a near repeat will occur.
- Short-term clusters of crime occur within, but also outside of, long-term clusters. One study showed that most 2-week periods had little risk of repeat victimization, but there were 2-week periods here and there with very high risk. Thus, simply examining crime for long-term hot spots can make it seem that a stable hot spot exists when it does not and ignore crime flare-ups that occur in isolation.
- Offenders are tightly coupled to place in that burglars are most likely to commit crimes that require the least amount of effort and energy by choosing targets that are most convenient to them.
- The near repeat research has three implications for crime analysis: (i) crime analysts should search for more burglaries in the same area shortly after one; (ii) they should search for short-term crime clusters

within long-term clusters, as well as throughout the jurisdiction; and (iii) they should take into account the possibility that the same offender is committing the crimes within a cluster of near repeats.

The Pareto principle, also known as the 80/20 rule, is another crucial idea regarding recurrent victimization. This idea generally stems from the observation that only 20% of related causes account for 80% of certain types of outcomes. This is true for many natural phenomena as well. For instance, a very large percentage of earthquake-related damage worldwide is caused by a small percentage of actual earthquakes. The same is true for many of the phenomena that are studied in crime analysis: a small percentage of people and places are consistently targeted by a large proportion of offenders; a small percentage of offenders are responsible for a large percentage of offenses; and a small percentage of locations are the source of a large number of crime events (Clarke and Eck, 2005).

An 80/20 analysis enables us to examine the phenomenon of repeat victimization or offending from a wider perspective. However, the terms "large" and "small" amounts are only used here to denote amounts of 80 and 20, respectively; the actual proportions vary with each analysis based on the nature of the community and the type of activity. According to the 80/20 rule, police can maximize the effectiveness of their crime prevention efforts by pinpointing the tiny percentage of locations, victims, and offenders where a high concentration of activity occurs (i.e., they can solve 80% of the crime problem by focusing on crimes in particular areas, like 20% of the community.

1.6.8. Situational Crime Prevention

The concept of environmental criminology, which addresses why crime occurs in particular settings and looks for solutions that reflect those settings, forms the basis of situational crime prevention, a practice that was first implemented in England in the 1980s (Cornish and Clarke, 1986). Based on the crime analysis of those problems, situational crime prevention offers police targeted measures to address crime issues in local contexts. Based on the problem analysis triangle and the theories covered thus far, Clarke first proposed a system for categorizing the methods that individuals and communities can employ to lessen the likelihood of crime in an article that was published in 1980. In 2003, Cornish and Clarke revised this classification scheme. The classification system's outline is shown in Table 1.1, and each technique's examples are given below.

The first category of tactics in the system consists of those that deter crime by making the offender think that it would take more work to commit the offense. To put it simply, these strategies address the offender's motivation and expected rewards by making it more difficult for them to carry out the crime. There are five broad categories of prevention techniques: (i) target hardening (e.g., locks, deadbolts, and unique locks on sliding glass doors); (ii) managing facility access (e.g., putting up gated barriers, minimizing the number of entrances and exits); (iii) screening exits (e.g., employing electronic product tags and requiring a ticket to exit); (iv) diverting violators (e.g., blocking off roads, setting up a police beat office); and (v) managing instruments and weaponry (e.g., limiting spray paint sales to adults).

Table 1.1. *Techniques to Situational Prevention*

Increase the Effort	Increase the Risks	Reduce the Rewards	Reduce Provocations	Remove Excuses
1. Harden targets	6. Extend guardianship	11. Conceal targets	16. Reduce frustrations and stress	21. Set rules
2. Control access to facilities	7. Assist natural surveillance	12. Remove targets	17. Avoid disputes	22. Post instructions
3. Screen exits	8. Reduce anonymity	13. Identify property	18. Reduce emotional arousal	23. Alert conscience
4. Deflect offenders	9. Use place managers	14. Disrupt markets	19. Neutralize peer pressure	24. Assist compliance
5. Control tools/ weapons	10. Strengthen formal surveillance	15. Deny benefits	20. Discourage imitation	25. Control drugs and alcohol

Techniques that raise the offender's perceived risk of committing a crime make up the second category. Stated differently, these tactics cause criminals to "think twice" because they realize there's a chance they'll be discovered. There are five broad categories of prevention strategies: (i) expanding guardianship (e.g., taking up walking alone, carrying a phone, and joining a neighborhood watch group); (ii) supporting natural surveillance (e.g., upholding landscaping, and enhancing street lighting); (iii) lowering anonymity (e.g., mandating taxi drivers to show identification, requiring school uniforms); (iv) making use of place managers (e.g., convenience stores employing two clerks for each shift); and (v) making use of official surveillance (e.g., putting in burglar alarms and video cameras).

Methods that lessen the expected benefits of the crime for the perpetrator are included in the third classification category. Stated differently, these tactics lessen the value of the crime itself to the perpetrator. These preventive methods can be divided into five broad categories: (i) hiding targets (e.g., leaving valuables in the trunk of the car rather than on the street, parking cars in garages rather than on the street); (ii) eliminating targets (e.g., leaving no more than $50 in cash in the register of a convenience store); (iii) identifying property (e.g., granting bicycle licenses, adding a car's VIN to spare parts); (iv) upending markets (e.g., keeping an eye out for stolen goods at street vendors and pawn shops); and (v) refusing benefits (e.g., putting interchangeable faces on automobile stereos, putting ink tags on apparel).

Techniques that lessen the provocation of the offender to commit the crime comprise the fourth category in the system. Stated differently, the goal of these strategies is to alter the social and environmental factors that contribute to stress, conflict, and the desire to offend. These preventative methods can be categorized into five broad categories: (i) lowering tension and frustration (e.g., effectively handling lines, offering cozy seating, music, or other entertainment to patrons waiting for service); (ii) preventing conflicts (e.g., setting fixed taxi fares, lessening bar crowding); (iii) lowering emotional arousal (e.g., banning a bikini competition at a bar, regulating the amount of alcohol served); (iv) counteracting peer pressure (e.g., scattering groups at athletic events and schools); and (v) preventing imitation (e.g., swiftly fixing damaged property, hiding information about crimes when supplying the media).

The methods that address the offender's motivation by concentrating on eliminating justifications for the offense make up the last category of the classification system. Stated differently, the goal of these strategies is to influence social norms in order to promote legal compliance. These preventative strategies fall into five categories: (i) rule-making (e.g., requiring rental agreements in writing, or requiring registration to enter a hotel); (ii) posting guidelines (e.g., placing signs that state "No Parking" or "Private Property"); (iii) raising awareness (e.g., putting up a speed limit sign by the side of the road, alerts on social media platforms about requesting sex from minors); (iv) supporting compliance (e.g., supplying recycling bins and trash cans in public spaces); and (v) regulating alcohol and drugs (e.g., putting Breathalyzers in bars and declining to serve alcohol to intoxicated people).

Situational crime prevention aims to offer interventions that are specifically tailored to the current crime environments. Just as the opportunities that give rise to criminal activity may be distinct, so too may the interventions required to keep those opportunities from materializing. The aim is to choose crime prevention measures that have the greatest impact because a given action may address multiple opportunities or problematic behaviors. For instance, school uniforms increase compliance with rules requiring students to wear appropriate clothing in class, which may reduce provocations for inappropriate behavior. However, they also lessen students' anonymity in public. An additional illustration would be the imposition of a juvenile curfew, which not only raises the perceived risk of juveniles being apprehended after curfew but also eliminates potential victims (e.g., of abuse and/or sexual assault) during that period. Although they do not carry out these crime prevention measures directly, recommending them and assessing their efficacy after implementation are crucial components of crime analysis.

1.7. DISPLACEMENT AND DIFFUSION OF BENEFITS

Crime analysts employ theory to comprehend how and why crime phenomena change when crime prevention measures are implemented, in addition to using theory to identify opportunities for crime and disorder (problem analysis triangle) and to choose and implement particular techniques to prevent crime (situational crime prevention). Displacement is the term used to describe how a crime phenomenon can change by moving to a different location or time, or by taking on a different form. Another way to change the issue is to get rid of it completely or partially. In certain cases, stopping one kind of criminal activity has an impact on other kinds of crime as well (e.g., when prostitution is eradicated from a community, female assaults and traffic issues also decline. We refer to this as "diffusion of benefits.." Since crime analysts are responsible for regularly examining changes in crime phenomena, it is imperative that they have an understanding of how these changes occur. e.g., a decline in home invasions at a residential complex) and to assess the results of particular crime prevention initiatives (e.g., a scheme that limits access to residential complexes).

1.7.1. Displacement of Crime

Displacement happens when criminal activity or other forms of criminal activity change to new forms, times, and places rather than disappearing. Crime analysts need to consider the following four types of displacement (Clarke and Eck, 2005):

- Spatial displacement is the shifting of an activity from targets in one area to those in another area. For example, when the police address prostitution in one area, the activity moves to another area of the city.
- Temporal displacement is the shifting of an activity from one time to another. This can include changes in the time of day of the week, and season of the year. For example, if police routinely patrol a particular area between 8:00 p.m. and 10:00 p.m. looking for gang members hanging out on the street, the gang members may shift their behavior and hang out in the area either later or earlier in the day.
- Target displacement is the shifting of the choice of one victim/target to a more vulnerable victim/target. That is, when place managers harden one type of target, offenders may focus on other types of

targets. For instance, if officials change the pay phones in a bus station so they take only credit cards and no coins, they become poor targets for offenders who want to obtain cash. Offenders in the bus station may shift from breaking into pay phones to breaking into coin-operated vending machines.

- Tactical displacement is the shifting of tactics by offenders. This can happen when offenders find that their usual methods are no longer working or if they become more confident and reckless in committing crime. Offenders might shift from conning their way into someone's home to steal valuables to breaking into the home, or an offender who has previously gone no further than exposing himself to women at a bus stop may shift to touching his victims.

Extensive analyses of studies on crime reduction (Guerette and Bowers, 2009; Hesseling, 1994; Johnson, Guerette, and Bowers, 2014) revealed that, in the few instances where spatial displacement was observed, it was almost never one-to-one. This means that only 75 or 50 crimes, for instance, would be moved to another location if there were 100 crimes at one location. To help police agencies understand how crime activity changes and whether any changes observed are the result of their strategies or other factors, crime analysts should consider the likelihood of displacement when examining the effects of crime reduction strategies, as these studies indicate that displacement of activity is possible.

1.7.2. Diffusion of Benefits

According to research, situational crime prevention principles—which try to lessen or eliminate opportunities for crime—can be applied to solve crime problems (Clarke, 1992). Furthermore, studies show that when specific problems are successfully resolved, other issues are frequently resolved as well; this phenomenon is known as the distortion of benefits (Clarke and Weisburd, 1994). For instance, when police shut down a hotel that has functioned as a center for drug sales and prostitution, other undesirable activities that have been occurring nearby, like theft, robberies, assaults, vandalism, and traffic issues, either decrease or stop completely. When the hotel closes, it removes opportunities for offense, so offenders leave the area. This stops drug users from robbing people in the area so they can buy drugs at the hotel, and it also stops traffic jams caused by men driving slowly past the hotel in search of prostitutes (Sampson, 2003).

Using crime mapping, analysts can ascertain whether a change in opportunity for a crime or a specific crime prevention effort has resulted in a diffusion of benefits or a spatial displacement of crime or other activity. If an analyst were to look at the results of the hotel's closure in the previous example, they would pinpoint the 500–1,000 feet surrounding the hotel and see if there had been a decrease in crime and disorder activity.

1.7.3. Opportunity

The main focus of this chapter's explanation of how crime analysts identify and handle patterns in criminal incidents is opportunity. Felson and Clarke (1998, pp.) synthesized the ideas of environmental criminology, situational crime prevention, displacement, the 80/20 rule, and diffusion of benefits. v and vi), two of the first scholars in this field, outline ten important ideas about opportunity and crime:.

1. Opportunities play a role in causing all crime.
2. Crime opportunities are highly specific.
3. Crime opportunities are concentrated in time and space.
4. Crime opportunities depend on everyday movements of activity.
5. One crime produces opportunities for another.
6. Some products offer more tempting crime opportunities than do others.
7. Social and technological changes produce new crime opportunities.
8. Crime can be prevented through the reduction of opportunities.
9. Reducing opportunities does not usually result in the displacement of crime.
10. Focused opportunity reduction can produce wider declines in crime.

REFERENCES

1. Austin, R., Cooper, G., Gagnon, D., Hodges, J., Martensen, K., & O'Neal, M. (1973). *Police Crime Analysis Unit Handbook*. U.S. Department of Justice, National Institute of Law Enforcement and Criminal Justice.
2. Baker, T. E. (2004). *Introductory Criminal Analysis: Crime Prevention and Intervention Strategies*. Prentice-Hall.
3. Baltaci, H. (2010). *Crime Analysis: An Empirical Analysis of its Effectiveness as a Crime Fighting Tool* (Doctoral dissertation). The University of Texas at Dallas, Richardson.
4. Barthe, E. (2006). *Crime Prevention Publicity Campaigns* [Monograph]. Office of Community Oriented Policing Services.
5. Beck, C., & McCue, C. (2009). Predictive policing: What can we learn from Wal-Mart and Amazon about fighting crime in a recession? *Police Chief Magazine, 76*, 18–20, 22–24.
6. Bernasco, W. (2010). A sentimental journey to crime: Effects of residential history on crime location choice. *Criminology, 48*(2), 389–416.
7. Bichler, G., & Gaines, L. (2005). An examination of police officers' insights into problem identification and problem solving. *Crime & Delinquency, 51*(1), 53–74.
8. Block, R. C., Dabdoub, M., & Fregly, S. (1995). *Crime Analysis Through Computer Mapping*. Police Executive Research Forum.
9. Boba, R. (2003). *Problem Analysis in Policing*. Police Foundation.
10. Boba, R. (2010). A practice-based evidence approach in Florida. *Police Practice and Research, 11*(2), 122–128.
11. Boba, R., & Crank, J. (2008). Institutionalizing problem-oriented policing: Rethinking problem identification, analysis, and accountability. *Police Practice and Research, 9*(5), 379–393.
12. Boba, R., & Santos, R. G. (2007). Single-family home construction site theft: A crime prevention case study. *International Journal of Construction Education and Research, 3*, 217–236.
13. Boba, R., & Santos, R. G. (2011). *A Police Organizational Model for Crime Reduction: Institutionalizing Problem Solving, Analysis, and Accountability*. Office of Community Oriented Policing Services.
14. Booth, W. L. (1979). Management function of a crime analysis unit. *Law and Order, 27*(5), 28–33.
15. Bowers, K. J., & Johnson, S. D. (2005). Domestic burglary repeats and space–time clusters: The dimensions of risk. *European Journal of Criminology, 2*, 67–92.

16. Braga, A. (2013). *Ideas in American Policing: Embedded Criminologists in Police Departments*. Police Foundation.
17. Braga, A. A., & Weisburd, D. (2010). *Policing Problem Places: Crime Hot Spots and Effective Prevention*. Oxford University Press.
18. Braga, A. A., Papachristos, A. V., & Hureau, D. M. (2014). The effects of hot spots policing on crime: An updated systematic review and meta-analysis. *Justice Quarterly, 31*(4), 633–663.
19. Braga, A., & Weisburd, D. (2012). The effects of focused deterrence strategies on crime: A systematic review and meta-analysis of the empirical evidence. *Journal of Research in Crime and Delinquency, 49*(3), 323–358.
20. Braga, A., & Weisburd, D. L. (2006). Problem-oriented policing: The disconnect between principles and practice. In D. L. Weisburd & A. Braga (Eds.), *Police Innovation: Contrasting Perspectives* (pp. 133–154). Cambridge University Press.
21. Brantingham, P. J., & Brantingham, P. L. (1981). *Environmental Criminology*. Sage.
22. Brantingham, P. L., & Brantingham, P. J. (1990). Situational crime prevention in practice. *Canadian Journal of Criminology, 32*, 17–40.
23. Brantingham, P. L., & Brantingham, P. J. (1993). Nodes, paths and edges: Considerations on the complexity of crime and the physical environment. *Journal of Environmental Psychology, 13*(1), 3–28.
24. Bruce, C. (2008a). Fundamentals of crime analysis. In S. Gwinn, C. Bruce, J. Cooper, & S. Hick (Eds.), *Exploring Crime Analysis: Readings on Essential Skills* (2nd ed., pp. 11–36). BookSurge.
25. Bureau of Justice Assistance (BJA). (2005). *Why Law Enforcement Agencies Need an Analytical Function*. United States Department of Justice.
26. Bureau of Justice Statistics. (2016). *Law Enforcement Management and Administrative Statistics (LEMAS), 2013*. Retrieved from: http://www.icpsr.umich.edu/icpsrweb/NACJD/studies/36164 (accessed on 14 October 2024).
27. Burrell, A., & Bull, R. (2011). A preliminary examination of crime analysts' views and experiences of comparative case analysis. *International Journal of Police Science and Management, 13*, 2–15.
28. Center for Problem-Oriented Policing. (2016). Retrieved from: http://www.popcenter.org (accessed on 14 October 2024).
29. Chainey, S., & Ratcliffe, J. (2005). *GIS and Crime Mapping*. John Wiley & Sons.

30. Chamard, S. E. (2003). *Innovation-Diffusion Networks and The Adoption and Discontinuance of Computerized Crime Mapping by Municipal Police Departments in New Jersey* (Doctoral dissertation). Rutgers, The State University of New Jersey, Newark.
31. Chammah, M. (n.d.). Policing the future: In the aftermath of Ferguson, St. Louis cops embrace crime-predicting software. *The Verge, 2*(3). Retrieved from: http://www.theverge.com/2016/2/3/10895804/st-louis-police (accessed on 14 October 2024).
32. Chang, S. K., Simms, W. H., Makres, C. M., & Bodnar, A. (1979). *Crime Analysis System Support: Descriptive Report of Manual and Automated Crime Analysis Functions*. National Criminal Justice Information and Statistics Service.
33. Chula Vista (California) Police Department. (2009). *Reducing Crime and Disorder at Motels and Hotels in Chula Vista, California*. Submission for the 2009 Herman Goldstein Problem-Oriented Policing Award. Retrieved from: http://www.popcenter.org (accessed on 14 October 2024).
34. Clarke, R. V. (1983). Situational crime prevention: Its theoretical basis and practical scope. In M. Tonry & N. Morris (Eds.), *Crime and Justice: An Annual Review of Research* (Vol. 4, pp. 225–256). University of Chicago Press.
35. Clarke, R. V. (1992). *Situational Crime Prevention: Successful Case Studies*. Harrow & Heston.
36. Clarke, R. V. (1999). *Hot Products: Understanding, Anticipating, and Reducing Demand for Stolen Goods* (Police Research Series Paper 112). Home Office, Research, Development and Statistics Directorate, Policing and Reducing Crime Unit.
37. Clarke, R. V., & Eck, J. (2005). *Crime Analysis for Problem Solvers: In 60 Small Steps*. Office of Community Oriented Policing Services.
38. Clarke, R. V., & Schultze, P. A. (2005). *Researching a Problem*. Office of Community Oriented Policing Services.
39. Clarke, R. V., & Weisburd, D. (1994). Diffusion of crime control benefits: Observations on the reverse of displacement. In R. V. Clarke (Ed.), *Crime Prevention Studies* (Vol. 2, pp. 165–183). Criminal Justice Press.
40. Commission on Accreditation for Law Enforcement Agencies. (2016). About CALEA. Retrieved from: https://www.clarksvilletn.gov/940/CALEA-Accreditation#:~:text=The%20Commission%20on%20Accreditation%20for,Of%20Chiefs%20Of%20Police%20(IACP).
41. Cope, N. (2004). Intelligence-led policing or policing led intelligence? *The British Journal of Criminology, 44*, 188–203.

42. Cornish, D. B., & Clarke, R. V. (1986). *The Reasoning Criminal*. Springer-Verlag.
43. Cornish, D. B., & Clarke, R. V. (2003). Opportunities, precipitators, and criminal decisions: A reply to Wortley's critique of situational crime prevention. In M. J. Smith & D. B. Cornish (Eds.), *Theory for Practice in Situational Crime Prevention* (pp. 41–96). Criminal Justice Press.
44. Coupe, T., & Blake, L. (2006). Daylight and darkness targeting strategies and the risks of being seen at residential burglaries. *Criminology, 44*, 431–464.
45. Dabney, D. (2010). Observations regarding key operational realities in a Compstat model of policing. *Justice Quarterly, 27*, 28–51.
46. Darroch, S., & Mazerolle, L. (2012). Intelligence-led policing: A comparative analysis of organizational factors influencing innovation uptake. *Police Quarterly, 16*(1), 3–37.
47. Demir, S. (2009). *Diffusion of Police Technology Across Time and Space and the Impact of Technology use on Police Effectiveness and its Contribution to Decision-Making* (Doctoral dissertation). Kent State University.
48. Eck, J. (2002). *Assessing Responses to Problems: An Introductory Guide for Police Problem-Solvers*. Office of Community Oriented Policing Services.
49. Eck, J., & Spelman, W. (1987). *Problem Solving: Problem-Oriented Policing in Newport News*. Police Executive Research Forum.
50. Eck, J., & Weisburd, D. (1995). Crime places in crime theory. In J. Eck & D. Weisburd (Eds.), *Crime and Place* (pp. 1–34). Criminal Justice Press.
51. Eck, J., Chainey, S., Cameron, J., Leitner, M., & Wilson, R. (2005). *Mapping Crime: Understanding Hot Spots*. National Institute of Justice.
52. Eck, J., Clarke, R. V., & Guerette, R. T. (2007). Risky facilities: Crime concentration in homogeneous sets of establishments and facilities. In G. Farrell, K. J. Bowers, S. D. Johnson, & M. Townsley (Eds.), *Imagination for Crime Prevention: Essays in Honor of Ken Pease* (pp. 225–264). Willan.
53. Emig, M., Heck, R., & Kravitz, M. (1980). *Crime Analysis: A Selected Bibliography*. U.S. National Criminal Justice Reference Service.
54. Farrell, G., & Pease, K. (1993). Once bitten, twice bitten: Repeat victimization and its implications for crime prevention (Crime Prevention Unit Series Paper 46). Home Office, Police Research Group.

55. Federal Bureau of Investigation (FBI). (2004). *UCR: Uniform Crime Reporting—Handbook*. US Department of Justice.

56. Federal Bureau of Investigation (FBI). (2016). 2014 Crime in the United States. Retrieved from: https://ucr.fbi.gov/crime-in-the-u.s/2014/crime-in-the-u.s.-2014/resource-pages/fbi-releases-2014-crime-statistics#:~:text=In%202014%2C%20there%20were%20an,percent%20and%202.0%20percent%2C%20respectively..

57. Felson, M. (2006). *Crime and Nature*. Sage.

58. Felson, M., & Boba, R. (2010). *Crime and Everyday Life*. Sage.

59. Felson, M., & Clarke, R. V. (1998). Opportunity makes the thief: Practical theory for crime prevention (Police Research Series Paper 98). Home Office, Research, Development and Statistics Directorate, Policing and Reducing Crime Unit.

60. Giblin, M. J. (2006). Structural elaboration and institutional isomorphism: The case of crime analysis units. *Policing: An International Journal of Police Strategies & Management, 29*(4), 643–664.

61. Gill, C., Weisburd, D., Telep, C., Vitter, Z., & Bennett, T. (2014). Community-oriented policing to reduce crime, disorder and fear and increase satisfaction and legitimacy among citizens: A systematic review. *Journal of Experimental Criminology, 10*, 399–428.

62. Goldstein, H. (1979). Improving policing: A problem-oriented approach. *Crime & Delinquency, 24*, 236–258.

63. Goldstein, H. (1990). *Problem-Oriented Policing*. McGraw-Hill.

64. Gottlieb, S., Arenberg, S., & Singh, R. (1994). *Crime Analysis: From First Report to Final Arrest*. Alpha.

65. Groff, E. R., & La Vigne, N. G. (2002). Forecasting the future of predictive crime mapping. In N. Tilley (Ed.), *Analysis for Crime Prevention* (pp. 29–58). Criminal Justice Press.

66. Grove, L., Farrell, G., Farrington, D. P., & Johnson, S. D. (2012). *Preventing Repeat Victimization: A Systematic Review*. Swedish National Council for Crime Prevention.

67. Guerette, R. T., & Bowers, K. J. (2009). Assessing the extent of crime displacement and diffusion of benefits: A review of situational crime prevention evaluations. *Criminology, 47*(4), 1331–1368.

68. Gwinn, S., Bruce, D., Cooper, J., & Hick, S. (2008). *Exploring Crime Analysis: Readings on Essential Skills* (2nd ed.). BookSurge.

69. Haberman, C., & Ratcliffe, J. (2012). The predictive policing challenges of near repeat armed street robberies. *Policing, 6*(2), 151–166.

70. Harries, K. D. (1980). *Crime and the Environment*. Charles C Thomas.
71. Harries, K. D. (1999). *Crime Mapping: Principles and Practice*. National Institute of Justice.
72. Harris, S. (2014). Product feature: Predictive policing helps law enforcement: See around the corners. *The Police Chief, LXXXI*(11). Retrieved from: https://www.policechiefmagazine.org/product-feature-predictive-policing-helps-law-enforcement-see-around-the-corners/.
73. Helms, D. (2004). Temporal analysis. In C. Bruce, S. Hick, & J. Cooper (Eds.), *Exploring Crime Analysis: Readings on Essential Skills* (pp. 220–262). BookSurge.
74. Henry, V. (2002). *The COMPSTAT Paradigm*. Looseleaf Law.
75. Hesseling, R. (1994). Displacement: A review of the empirical literature. In R. V. Clarke (Ed.), *Crime Prevention Studies* (Vol. 3, pp. 197–230). Criminal Justice Press.
76. Hick, S., Bair, S., Fritz, N., & Helms, D. (2004). Crime mapping. In C. Bruce, S. Hick, & J. Cooper (Eds.), *Exploring Crime Analysis: Readings on Essential Skills* (pp. 314–339). BookSurge.
77. Hollywood, J., & Winkelman, Z. (2015). Improving information-sharing across law enforcement: Why we can't know. RAND.
78. Hollywood, J., Smith, S., Price, C., McInnis, B., & Perry, W. (2012). Predictive policing: What it is, what it isn't, and where it can be useful (PowerPoint presentation). RAND.
79. International Association of Crime Analysts (IACA). (2011a). Certified Law Enforcement Analyst program (CLEA). Retrieved from: http://www.iaca.net/certification.asp (accessed on 14 October 2024).
80. International Association of Crime Analysts (IACA). (2011b). Crime pattern definitions for tactical analysis (White Paper 2011–01). Overland Park, KS: Author.
81. International Association of Crime Analysts. (2013). RMS technical requirements of crime analysis (White Paper 2013-01). Overland Park, KS: Author.
82. International Association of Crime Analysts. (2014a). Information-sharing platforms (White Paper 2014-01). Overland Park, KS: Author.
83. International Association of Crime Analysts. (2014b). Definition and types of crime analysis (White Paper 2014-02). Overland Park, KS: Author.
84. INTERPOL. (2014). Intelligence analysis. Retrieved from: http://www.interpol.int/INTERPOLexpertise/Intelligence-analysis (accessed on 14 October 2024).

85. Jang, H., Hoover, L., & Joo, H. (2010). An evaluation of Compstat's effect on crime: The Fort Worth experience. *Police Quarterly, 13*, 387–412.

86. Johnson, S. D., & Bowers, K. J. (2004). The burglary as a clue to the future: The beginnings of prospective hot-spotting. *European Journal of Criminology, 1*, 237–255.

87. Johnson, S. D., Guerette, R. T., & Bowers, K. (2014). Crime displacement: What we know, what we don't know, and what it means for crime reduction. *Journal of Experimental Criminology, 10*(4), 549–571.

88. Johnson, S. D., Lab, S., & Bowers, K. J. (2008). Stable and fluid hot spots of crime: Differentiation and identification. *Built Environment, 34*(1), 32–46.

89. Johnson, S. D., Summers, L., & Pease, K. (2007). *Vehicle Crime: Communicating Spatial and Temporal Patterns*. Jill Dando Institute of Crime Science.

90. Johnson, S. D., Summers, L., & Pease, K. (2009). Offenders as foragers: A direct test of the boost account of victimization. *Journal of Quantitative Criminology, 25*, 181–200.

91. Johnson, S., & Bowers, K. (2003). Opportunity is in the eye of the beholder: The role of publicity in crime prevention. *Criminology & Public Policy, 2*(3), 497–524.

92. Kelling, G. L. (2015). An author's brief history of an idea. *Journal of Research in Crime and Delinquency, 52*, 626–629.

93. Kennedy, D. M., Braga, A. A., & Piehl, A. M. (1998). The (un)known universe: Mapping gangs and gang violence in Boston. In D. Weisburd & T. McEwen (Eds.), *Crime Mapping and Crime Prevention* (Crime Prevention Studies, Vol. 8, pp. 219–262). Criminal Justice Press.

94. Kennedy, D. M., Braga, A. A., & Piehl, A. M. (2001). *Reducing Gun Violence: The Boston Gun Project's Operation Ceasefire*. National Institute of Justice.

95. Koper, C. S., Lum, C., Willis, J. J., Woods, D. J., & Hibdon, J. (2015). *Realizing the Potential of Technology in Policing*. George Mason University and Washington, DC Police Executive Research Forum.

96. Laub, J., & Sampson, R. (2003). *Shared Beginnings, Divergent Lives: Delinquent Boys to Age 70*. Harvard University Press.

97. LeBeau, J. L. (1987). The methods and measures of centrography and the spatial dynamics of rape. *Journal of Quantitative Criminology, 3*, 125–141.

98. Lynch, J. P., & Jarvis, J. P. (2008). Missing data and imputation in the Uniform Crime Reports and the effects on national estimates. *Journal of Contemporary Criminal Justice, 24*, 69–85.

99. Maltz, M. (1999). *Bridging Gaps in Police Crime Data*. Bureau of Justice Statistics.

100. McLaughlin, L., Johnson, S. D., Bowers, K. J., Birks, D. J., & Pease, K. (2006). Police perceptions of the long- and short-term spatial distribution of residential burglary. *International Journal of Police Science & Management, 9*(2), 99–111.

101. Mohler, G., Shorty, M., Malinowskiz, S., Johnson, M., Tita, G., Bertozzik, A., & Brantingham, J. (2015). Randomized controlled field trials of predictive policing. *Journal of the American Statistical Association*. https://doi.org/10.1080/01621459.2015.1077710.

102. Newman, G. (2007). *Sting Operations* [Monograph]. Washington, DC: Office of Community Oriented Policing Services.

103. O'Shea, T. C., & Nicholls, K. (2003). Police crime analysis: A survey of U.S. police departments with 100 or more sworn personnel. *Police Practice and Research, 4*, 233–250.

104. Office of Community Oriented Policing Services. (2014). *Community Policing Defined*. Washington, DC: Author.

105. Omnibus Crime Control and Safe Streets Act of 1968, Pub. L. No. 90-351, 82 Stat. 197 (codified as amended in scattered sections of 18 U.S.C.A.).

106. Pace, E. (1972). Fifty-seven slain in week, a record for city. *The New York Times*, p. 1.

107. Paulsen, D. J., Bair, S., & Helms, D. (2009). *Tactical Crime Analysis: Research and Investigation*. Boca Raton, FL: CRC Press.

108. Petersen, M. (1994). *Applications in Criminal Analysis: A Sourcebook*. Westport, CT: Greenwood.

109. Petersillia, J. (2008). Influencing public policy: An embedded criminologist reflects on California prison reform. *Journal of Experimental Criminology, 4*, 335–356.

110. Police Executive Research Forum. (2013). *Compstat: Its Origins, Evolution, and Future in Law Enforcement Agencies*. Washington, DC: Author.

111. Pomrenke, N. E. (1969). Police selection, training and education action grant programs in 1969: State law enforcement plans submitted under Title I, Omnibus Crime Control and Safe Streets Act of 1968–1969 state plan analysis. Washington, DC: National Sheriffs' Association.

112. Ratcliffe, J. H. (2002). Aoristic signatures and the spatiotemporal analysis of high-volume crime patterns. *Journal of Quantitative Criminology, 18*, 23–43.
113. Ratcliffe, J. H. (2004a). Crime mapping and the training needs of law enforcement. *European Journal of Criminal Policy and Research, 10*, 65–83.
114. Ratcliffe, J. H. (2004b). The hotspot matrix: A framework for the spatiotemporal targeting of crime reduction. *Police Practice and Research, 5*(1), 5–23.
115. Ratcliffe, J. H. (2008). *Intelligence-Led Policing*. Cullompton, UK: Willan.
116. Ratcliffe, J. H. (2011). Jerry's top ten PowerPoint tips. Retrieved from: http://jratcliffe.net (accessed on 14 October 2024).
117. Ratcliffe, J. H., & Guidetti, R. (2008). State police investigative structure and the adoption of intelligence-led policing. *Policing: An International Journal of Police Strategies & Management, 31*, 109–128.
118. Ratcliffe, J. H., & McCullagh, M. (2001). Chasing ghosts? Police perception of high crime areas. *British Journal of Criminology, 41*, 330–341.
119. Reiner, G. H., Greenlee, M. R., & Gibbens, M. H. (1976). *Crime Analysis in Support of Patrol: National Evaluation Program, Phase I Summary Report*. Washington, DC: Law Enforcement Assistance Administration.
120. Rengert, G., & Wasilchick, J. (1985). *Suburban Burglary: A Time and a Place for Everything*. Springfield, IL: Charles C Thomas.
121. Rossmo, D. K. (2000). *Geographic Profiling*. Boca Raton, FL: CRC Press.
122. Sampson, R. (2003). Crime analysis in the United States: What it's accomplished, where it's going. Paper presented at the annual training meeting of the International Association of Crime Analysts, Kansas City, MO.
123. Santos, R. B. (2013). Implementation of a police organizational model for crime reduction. *Policing: An International Journal of Police Strategies and Management, 32*(2), 295–311.
124. Santos, R. B. (2014). The effectiveness of crime analysis for crime reduction: Cure or diagnosis? *Journal of Contemporary Criminal Justice, 30*(2), 147–168.
125. Santos, R. B., & Santos, R. G. (2015). Examination of police dosage in residential burglary and theft from vehicle micro-time hot spots. *Crime Science, 4*(27), 1–12. https://doi.org/10.1186/s40163-015-0041-6.

126. Santos, R. B., & Taylor, B. (2014). The integration of crime analysis into police patrol work: Results from a national survey of law enforcement. *Policing: An International Journal of Police Strategies and Management, 37*(3), 501–520.
127. Santos, R. G. (2011). Systematic pattern response strategy: Protecting the beehive. *FBI Law Enforcement Bulletin*. Retrieved from: https://leb.fbi.gov/articles/featured-articles/systematic-pattern-response-strategy-protecting-the-beehive.
128. Santos, R. G., & Santos, R. B. (2015a). An ex post facto evaluation of tactical police response in residential theft from vehicle micro-time hot spots. *Journal of Quantitative Criminology, 31*(4), 679–698.
129. Santos, R. G., & Santos, R. B. (2015b). Evidence-based policing, "What works" and stratified policing, "How to make it work." *Translational Criminology, 8*, 20–22.
130. Santos, R. G., & Santos, R. B. (2015c). Practice-based research: Ex post facto evaluation of evidence-based police practices implemented in residential burglary micro-time hot spots. *Evaluation Review*. https://doi.org/10.1177/0193841X15602818.
131. Schaible, L. M., & Sheffield, J. (2012). Intelligence-led policing and change in state law enforcement agencies. *Policing: An International Journal of Police Strategies and Management, 35*(4), 761–784.
132. Schmerler, K., & Velasco, M. (2002). Primary data collection: A problem-solving necessity. *Crime Mapping News, 4*(2), 4–8.
133. Scott, M. (2000). *Problem-Oriented Policing: Reflections on the First 20 Years* [Monograph]. Washington, DC: U.S. Department of Justice, Office of Community Oriented Policing Services.
134. Scott, M. (2004). *The Benefits and Consequences of Police Crackdowns* [Monograph]. Washington, DC: Office of Community Oriented Policing Services.
135. Sever, B., Garcia, V., & Tsiandi, A. (2008). Municipal police departments' attention to crime analysis: Essential or impractical? *Police Practice & Research, 9*, 323–340.
136. Shaw, C. R., & McKay, H. D. (1969). *Juvenile Delinquency and Urban Areas* (Rev. ed.). Chicago, IL: University of Chicago Press.
137. Sherman, L. W. (1998). *Evidence-Based Policing: American Ideas in Policing*. Washington, DC: Police Foundation.
138. Sherman, L. W., Gartin, P. R., & Buerger, M. E. (1989). Hot spots of predatory crime: Routine activities and the criminology of place. *Criminology, 27*, 27–55.

139. Sherman, L. W., Gottfredson, D., MacKenzie, D. L., Eck, J., Reuter, P., & Bushway, S. (1997). *Preventing Crime: What Works, What Doesn't, What's Promising: A Report to the Attorney General of the United States*. Washington, DC: U.S. Department of Justice, Office of Justice Programs.
140. Silverman, E. (2006). Compstat's innovation. In D. L. Weisburd & A. Braga (Eds.), *Police Innovation: Contrasting Perspectives* (pp. 267–283). Cambridge, UK: Cambridge University Press.
141. Skogan, W., & Frydl, K. (2004). *Fairness and Effectiveness in Policing: The Evidence*. Washington, DC: The National Academies Press.
142. Smith, M. J., Clarke, R. V., & Pease, K. (2002). Anticipatory benefit in crime prevention. In N. Tilley (Ed.), *Analysis for Crime Prevention: Crime Prevention Studies* (Vol. 13, pp. 71–88). Monsey, NY: Criminal Justice Press.
143. Sousa, W., & Kelling, G. (2006). Of "broken windows," criminology, and criminal justice. In D. L. Weisburd & A. Braga (Eds.), *Police Innovation: Contrasting Perspectives* (pp. 77–97). Cambridge, UK: Cambridge University Press.
144. Taxman, F. S., & McEwen, T. (1997). Using geographical tools with interagency work groups to develop and implement crime control strategies. In D. Weisburd & T. McEwen (Eds.), *Crime Mapping and Crime Prevention* (pp. 83–111). Monsey, NY: Criminal Justice Press.
145. Taylor, B., & Boba, R. (2011). *The Integration of Crime Analysis into Patrol Work: A Guidebook*. Washington, DC: Office of Community Oriented Policing Services.
146. Taylor, B., Kowalyk, A., & Boba, R. (2007). The integration of crime analysis into law enforcement agencies: An exploratory study into the perceptions of crime analysts. *Police Quarterly, 10*(2), 154–169.
147. Telep, C. W., & Weisburd, D. (2012). What is known about the effectiveness of police practices in reducing crime and disorder? *Police Quarterly, 15*(4), 331–357.
148. The SMT Mission. (n.d.). Standards, methods and technology committee. *iaca.net*. Retrieved from: http://www.iaca.net/committee_smt.asp (accessed on 14 October 2024).
149. Theodore, J. (2001). Crime mapping goes Hollywood: CBS's *The District* demonstrates crime mapping to millions of TV viewers. *Crime Mapping News, 3*(3), 7.
150. Tompson, L., & Townsley, M. (2010). (Looking) Back to the future: Using space–time patterns to better predict the location of street crime. *International Journal of Police Science and Management, 12*, 23–40.

151. Townsley, M., Homel, R., & Chaseling, J. (2003). Infectious burglaries: A test of the near repeat hypothesis. *British Journal of Criminology, 43*, 615–633.

152. Truman, J. L., & Langton, L. (2014). *Criminal Victimization, 2013*. Washington, DC: Bureau of Justice Statistics.

153. Uchida, C. (2010). A national discussion on predictive policing: Defining our terms and mapping successful implementation strategies. Washington, DC: National Institute of Justice.

154. Weisburd, D. (2015). The 2014 Sutherland Address: The law of crime concentration and the criminology of place. *Criminology, 53*(2), 133–157.

155. Weisburd, D. L., & Braga, A. (2006). *Police Innovation: Contrasting Perspectives*. Cambridge, UK: Cambridge University Press.

156. Weisburd, D., & Eck, J. (2004). What can police do to reduce crime, disorder, and fear? *The Annals of the American Academy of Political and Social Science, 593*, 42–65.

157. Weisburd, D., & Lum, C. (2005). The diffusion of computerized crime mapping in policing: Linking research and practice. *Police Practice and Research, 6*(5), 419–434.

158. Weisburd, D., & McEwen, T. (1997). Crime mapping and crime prevention. In D. Weisburd & T. McEwen (Eds.), *Crime Mapping and Crime Prevention* (pp. 1–26). Monsey, NY: Criminal Justice Press.

159. Weisburd, D., Mastrofski, S. D., McNally, A. M., Greenspan, R., & Willis, J. J. (2003). Reforming to preserve: Compstat and strategic problem solving in American policing. *Criminology and Public Policy, 2*, 421–456.

160. Weisburd, D., Mastrofski, S., Willis, J., & Greenspan, R. (2006). Changing everything so that everything can remain the same: Compstat and American policing. In D. L. Weisburd & A. Braga (Eds.), *Police Innovation: Contrasting Perspectives* (pp. 284–304). Cambridge, UK: Cambridge University Press.

161. Weisburd, D., Telep, C. W., Hinkle, J. C., & Eck, J. (2010). Is problem-oriented policing effective in reducing crime and disorder? Findings from a Campbell systematic review. *Criminology & Public Policy, 9*(1), 139–172.

162. Weisel, D. L. (2004). *Street Prostitution in Raleigh, North Carolina: A Final Report for the Field Applications of Problem-Oriented Guides for Police project*. Washington, DC: Office of Community Oriented Policing Services.

163. Weisel, D. L. (2005). *Analyzing Repeat Victimization*. Washington, DC: Office of Community Oriented Policing Services.

164. Welsh, B., Braga, A., & Bruinsma, G. (2015). Reimagining broken windows: From theory to policy. *Journal of Research in Crime and Delinquency, 52*(4), 447–463.

165. Willis, J. J. (2011). Enhancing police legitimacy by integrating Compstat with community policing. *Policing: An International Journal of Police Strategies & Management, 34*, 654–673.

166. Willis, J. J., Mastrofski, S. D., & Kochel, T. R. (2010). The co-implementation of Compstat and community policing. *Journal of Criminal Justice, 38*, 969–980.

167. Willis, J. J., Mastrofski, S. D., & Weisburd, D. (2007). Making sense of COMPSTAT: A theory-based analysis of organizational change in three police departments. *Law & Society Review, 41*(1), 147–188.

168. Wilson, J., & Kelling, G. (1982). Broken windows: The police and neighborhood safety. *Atlantic Monthly, 24*(9), 29–38.

169. Wilson, O. W. (1957). *Police Planning* (2nd ed.). Springfield, IL: Charles C Thomas.

170. Wilson, O. W. (1963). *Police Administration* (2nd ed.). New York, NY: McGraw-Hill.

171. Wilson, O. W., & McLaren, R. C. (1977). *Police Administration* (4th ed.). New York, NY: McGraw-Hill.

172. Wright, R., & Decker, S. (1997). *Armed Robbers in Action: Stickups and Street Culture*. Boston, MA: Northeastern University Press.

Chapter 2

Crime Analysis and Evidence-Based Policing

Contents

Introduction 56
2.1. Research on Crime Analysis and Crime Reduction 56
2.2. Stratified Policing: Framework for Crime Analysis 70
2.3. Evidence-Based Policing 79
2.4. Crime Analysis and Evidence-Based Policing Strategies 87
2.5. The Role of Crime Analysts in Evidence-Based Policing 98
References 104

INTRODUCTION

Crime analysis and evidence-based policing are two interconnected approaches that play a crucial role in modern law enforcement, focusing on the use of data, research, and systematic analysis to enhance public safety and improve the effectiveness of policing strategies.

Crime analysis involvticsystematic examination of crime data to identify patterns, trends, and correlations that can inform law enforcement strategies. By analyzing data related to criminal activity—such as locations, times, types of crimes, and characteristics of offenders and victims—analysts can uncover valuable insights that help predict and prevent future crimes. This process often includes the use of advanced tools like geographic information systems (GIS) for crime mapping, statistical analysis for identifying trends, and predictive analytics to forecast where and when crimes are likely to occur.

The insights gained from crime analysis form the foundation of evidence-based policing, a practice that emphasizes the use of empirical evidence and research to guide policing decisions. Unlike traditional approaches, which may rely heavily on intuition or historical precedent, evidence-based policing prioritizes strategies that have been proven effective through rigorous evaluation. This could include targeting resources in crime hotspots identified through analysis, implementing community-based interventions that have demonstrated success in reducing crime, or adopting new technologies based on their proven impact in similar contexts.

Evidence-based policing also involves continuous assessment and adjustment of strategies, ensuring that policing efforts remain responsive to changing crime dynamics and community needs. By grounding decisions in solid evidence, law enforcement agencies can allocate resources more efficiently, enhance the effectiveness of their operations, and ultimately improve public trust and safety.

Together, crime analysis and evidence-based policing represent a shift towards more scientific, data-driven approaches in law enforcement. These methods not only enhance the ability to prevent and combat crime but also contribute to the development of more just and effective policing practices that are responsive to both current challenges and future threats.

2.1. RESEARCH ON CRIME ANALYSIS AND CRIME REDUCTION

The amount of information regarding the prevalence and application of crime analysis is expanding, but little is known about the connection between crime analysis and crime reduction (Santos, 2014). The question of whether crime analysis lowers crime has only been investigated in two studies—both doctoral dissertations—by looking at the characteristics of police agencies that use crime analysis in relation to crime and clearance rates.

Demir (2009) investigated whether agencies with crime analysis also cleared more crimes than those without crime analysis by analyzing data from a national survey carried out by the National Institute of Justice (NIJ) in 1997. The study looked at the relationship between the crime mapping and analysis functions of over 2,000 agencies and their crime clearance rates. The investigator discovered some proof that agencies with higher crime mapping and analysis activity had lower clearance rates. Baltaci (2010) investigated the impact of crime analysis activity on crime and clearance rates of police agencies using the national survey data gathered by O'Shea and Nicholls in 2000 (O'Shea and Nicholls, 2003). The findings from a sample of about 800 agencies with more than 100 officers demonstrated that an agency's violent crime rates would decrease and its rates of property, violent, and overall clearance would increase with the breadth of its crime analysis activities.

Despite looking at crime statistics and crime analysis, these two studies are correlational in nature rather than causative, so it is impossible to draw conclusions about the "effect" of crime analysis on crime levels. Specifically, while the research indicated a connection between crime analysis and crime clearance rates, it lacks proof that crime analysis "caused" the decline or whether other variables (e.g., The disparity in crime and clearance rates among the agencies was explained by factors such as police response, evidence collection, and economic downturn.

"Does crime analysis reduce crime?" is a question that is frequently posed by researchers and practitioners. It is challenginause there isn'tis not a clear correlation between the two. Crime analysis is the process of looking through data and drawing conclusions; on its own, it is not a method for reducing crime. The connection between crime analysis and crime reduction can be better understood by drawing an analogy from the mstry.

In order toTo diagnose a disease or injury, a magnetic resonance imaging (MRI) machine examines the entire body or a specific body part. The software on the machine is used by the MRI technician to create a series of images, which represent the data. Following that, the radiologist (i.e., a physician) who analyzes the pictures to identify any concerns or problems with the patient. Based on what the data indicate, the radiologist draws both firm and tentative conclusions. The patient's doctor, who is frequently not the same person, receives the radiologist's report. Based on the radiologist's report, best medical practices, and the patient's characteristics, this physician evaluates the report and determines a course of treatment for the patient's illness. Depending on factors like the patient's age, gender, or level of illness, different approaches may be chosen for different patients with the same illness. As a result, the patient's final plan is determined by a multi-step procedure involving several specialists. Furthermore, even though the MRI and the analysis reports are precise and of the highest caliber, the effectiveness of the plan (i.e., treatment) that the patient's physician chooses will rely on the physician's comprehension of the MRI data analysis, the caliber of the radiologists report, the suitability of the treatment, and—most importantly—the correct administration of the treatment.

Would you conclude, after reading this explanation, that a radiologist or even an MRI analysis can heal a patient? Probably not. As a diagnostic tool, magnetic resonance imaging (MRI) is critical and indispensable for physicians. It can idlness in its early stagespreliminary stages and recommend the best course of treatment. But the MRI technology, the information generated, and the report from the radiologist only deal with one part of the procedure. The process of "diagnosing" a disease is significant and frequently required, but it does not "cure" a patient's illness on its own. This medical procedure is depicted in Figure 2.1.

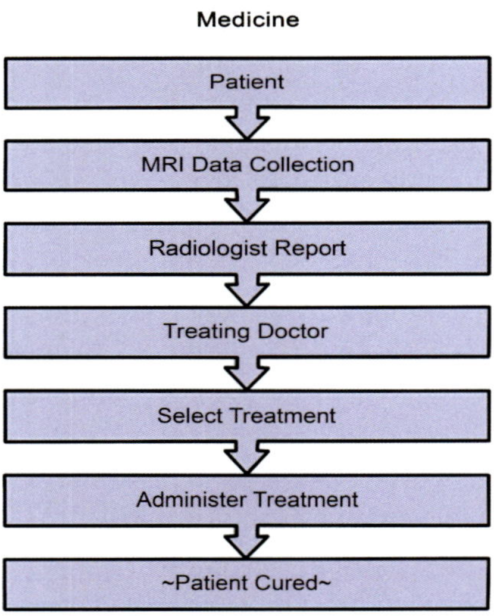

Figure 2.1. *Process for diagnosing and curing a patient.*

Source: Rachel Boba Santos, Crime Analysis With Crime Mapping, ISBN: 9781506331034.

The MRI procedure in medicine is comparable to the crime analysis process in crime reduction. A crime analyst has access to computer software and data, just like a radiologist does. g., crime data from a police record management system) and applies particular methods to the data's analysis and interpretation in order to create a "diagnosis" of a specific crime issue. Similar to how a doctor administers treatment, another doctor receives the report (in this case, the sworn police officers), who choose an evidence-based course of action and supervise its execution. Therefore, it is impossible for crime analysis to "cause" crime to decrease or to have a direct correlation with it. The relationship is indirect, and the police's ability to use the crime analyst's findings to select and implement an efficient strategy will have a major impact on reducing crime. A similar flow chart of the crime analysis process in crime reduction is shown in Figure 2.2.

The process is initiated on the left by the crime analysis results (i.e., as reported by the radiologists). The quality of the data, the methods employed, and the analyst's interpretation all affect the outcome. The outcomes will also be flawed if any of these components are weak or inaccurate. Sworn police officers receive this information, and they should ideally choose an efficient, evidence-based response before supervising and funding it (i.e., deciding on and executing the course of treatment). There is only a chance that crime can be reduced if these two actions are carried out successfully. In the ario, the response's final resultresult is a decrease in crime (i.e., healing the ailment). Naturally, to ascertain whether the police response was the real factor influencing crime or if other factors also played a role, this effect necessitates careful examination and rigorous evaluation techniques. The figures and the analogy demonstrate how crime analysis and crime reduction are not directly correlated. But just as an MRI aids in medical diagnosis, crime analysis also contributes to a decrease in crime.

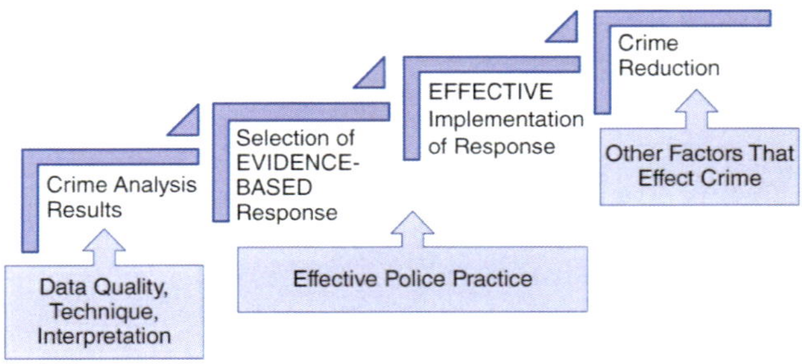

Figure 2.2. *Crime analysis process in crime reduction.*

Source: Rachel Boba Santos, Crime Analysis With Crime Mapping, ISBN: 9781506331034.

Since there is no direct connection between crime analysis and crime reduction, the latter can only be understood by looking at the police's most successful approaches to crime reduction (i.e., the function of crime analysis, and evidence-based policing. The essential elements of popular crime reduction policing strategies, the findings of research regarding their efficacy in lowering crime, and the function of crime analysis in each are covered in the sections that follow. The main conclusions drawn from the discussion conclude each section. By the end of this section, a distinct pattern emerges, showing that crime analysis is essential to newer, untested approaches, successful strategies, and promising strategies. This conclusion holds great significance as it indicates a promising future for the application of crime analysis in law enforcement.

2.1.1. Standard Model of Policing

The conventional policing model includes tactics that are commonly associated with the duties that the general public associates with law enforcement. The main component of the conventional policing model is the extensive and responsive application of the law, mostly through the use of police resources (Weisburd and Eck, 2004). In particular, the following are some of the tactics used in the conventional police model (Sherman et al., 1997; Eck and Weisburd, 2004):

- Increased number of police officers (to increase the ability to detect crime and arrest offenders);
- Unfocused, random motorized patrols (to create a perception of a police "omnipresence" to deter crime in public places);
- Rapid response to calls for service (to increase the likelihood of catching offenders);
- Follow-up investigations by detectives (to increase the solvability of the crimes);
- General reactive arrest policies (to deter and punish specific offenders as well as deter the general public from committing crimes).

Research on the efficacy of these strategies has generally concluded that each of these widely used enforcement initiatives has had varying degrees of success (Sherman et al., Weisburd and Eck, 2004; Telep and Weisburd, 2012; Skogan and Frydl, 1997).

The standard model of policing uses crime analysis to help determine future optimal staffing levels and estimate the number of officers that may be required to staff the required number of crimes and calls for service. The agency evaluates its own procedures, including how employees, funds, assets, and other resources are distributed across organizational, temporal, and geographic boundaries. This kind of analysis favors the agency's resource management over the decrease of crime. By looking at the different kinds of calls, priorities, the routes officers take to respond to calls, and the geographic assignment of officers, analysis is also used in the standard model of policing to evaluate and enhance the quick response to calls for service. In particular, criminal investigation work includes conducting investigative database searches and identifying suspects and individual offenders (O'Shea and Nicholls, 2003). Although some crime analysts might perform this task, it is more accurately classified as investigative support, which is carried out by an investigative technician or crime analyst. The total amount of crime and whether it has increased or decreased are ascertained using crime statistics generated by crime analysis for the conventional model of policing. However, since reactive arrests and random patrols are typically used, the statistics are not used to guide strategies for reducing crime. Because proactivity is so severely limited in the standard model, crime analysis is therefore primarily used as information so that sworn personnel, from patrol officers to the chief, have an idea of when and where crime has occurred as well as overall how much has occurred. However, it does not directly inform their proactive crime reduction strategies. (Weisburd and Eck, 2004). According to O'Shea and Nicholls (2003), a large portion of crime analysis in this method is devoted to identifying specific offenders and carrying out investigative support.

2.1.2. Community Policing

Community policing has been hailed by police academics as one of the most extensively used police tactics in recent decades (Weisburd and Eck, 2004). It is challenging to define, though, because its concepts are nebulous and its definition has evolved over time. As stated by the U. S. Community policing, according to the Department of Justice's Office of Community Oriented Policing (the COPS Office; 2014), is described as follows: An organizational strategy that encourages the methodical application of partnerships and problem-solving techniques in order to proactively address the immediate conditions that give rise to public safety issues like crime, social disorder, and fear of crime.

The first essential element of community policing is building relationships and partnerships with the community in order to comprehend issues and address them, as well as to encourage police cooperation and legitimacy in order to make partnerships meaningful. The process of problem solving is the second essential element of community policing (i.e., The process of SARA (scanning, analysis, response, and assessment) is also employed in problem-oriented policing.

A number of particular tactics that are categorized as community policing have undergone evaluation. One tactic is "neighborhood watch," also known as "block watch," which is one of the most popular community policing initiatives. Its objective is to increase neighborhood surveillance by locals and residents. Additional tactics include utilizing storefront beat offices, community meetings, officers walking the "beat" and conversing with residents, increasing the flow of information from the community to the police, and giving the public access to crime data via the Internet, crime maps, letters, and "reverse 911" phone calls so they can protect themselves (Sherman et al., 1997). Nevertheless, studies reveal that newsletters, community gatherings, storefront offices, and neighborhood watch programs do not lower crime (Weisburd and Eck, 2004). Although police door-to-door visits have been shown to lower crime, it has not been demonstrated that merely informing the public about crime can deter crime (Sherman et al., 1997; Eck and Weisburd, 2004).

A survey of the literature on community policing's efficacy reveals a range of outcomes, but ultimately comes to the "ambiguous" conclusion (Gill, Weisburd, Telep, Vitter, and Bennett, 2014). The researchers come to the conclusion that while community policing tactics do have some effect on reducing property crime, the most compelling evidence suggests that they also improve citizens' perceptions of disorder, aspects of police legitimacy, and citizen satisfaction with the police. In other words, when successful community policing tactics are used, people have a more favorable opinion of the police, there is less chaos, and they are more inclined to collaborate with the police. Conversely, the researchers do not discover any proof that community policing lowers the number of crimes that are formally reported or lessens the fear of crime among the populace. Gill and associates. (2014) state that further data is required to draw firm conclusions regarding the efficacy of the program and that the research's conclusions are predicated on the police's imperfect execution of community policing. Returning to the medical analogy, this is akin to attempting to assess the efficacy of a medication that was not taken as directed.

In an effort to be open and take collective responsibility for community crime issues, police departments utilize crime analysis to provide information to the public as part of community policing. Historically, crime analysts have been essential in providing statistical data on crime to businesses, neighborhood and block watch groups, community groups, and newsletters that aim to inform the public about crime. The last 15 to 20 years have seen a shift in the distribution of crime and disorder data to the Internet. As a result, data analysis is now produced and disseminated through public Internet companies, to which police agencies provide data that citizens can access and search for themselves, rather than necessarily by crime analysts.

A police agency will also employ crime analysis methodology to gather and examine data from the public regarding victimization, perceptions of crime, fear, and safety, as well as satisfaction with the police. This process is sometimes managed by crime analysts, but other times it is handled by hired researchers and survey firms. Once more, the community's relationships are understood and common issues that need to be addressed are identified with the help of this information. Even though analysts might not be directly involved in gathering and distributing this data, the procedures are still regarded as part of a police department's crime analysis function.

2.1.3. Problem-Oriented Policing

The concept of problem-oriented policing (POP) was first presented by Herman Goldstein in his influential 1979 article "Improving Policing: A Problem-Oriented Approach." POP holds that police should be proactive in recognizing, comprehending, and addressing community problems rather than isolated incidents. According to Goldstein, the police were overly preoccupied with the ends (i.e., patrols and making arrests) and insufficient at the conclusion of their shifts (i.e., averting disorder and crime). He proposed that police might be more successful in addressing isses with disorder and crime if they adopted a more "problem-oriented focus.." Simultaneously, Goldstein contended that in order for the police to be "problem oriented," they need to adopt a new, more methodical strategy that requires them to gather fresh information, create fresh techniques for analysis, find creative solutions, and implement metrics for gauging the effectiveness of their work (Goldstein, 1990).

When John Eck and William Spelman (1987) created the SARA model for their problem-oriented policing program in Newport News, Virginia, they gave the approach a particular methodology. (S)canning and defining specific problems, (A)nalyzing data to understand the opportunities that create the problem, (R)esponding to the problem using both police and nonpolice methods, and (A)ssessing whether the response has worked are all part of the SARA model, which is covered in detail in Chapter 12. (Center for Problem-Oriented Policing, 2016). The theories of situational crime prevention and environmental criminology form the foundation of POP. The goal of POP's analysis and tactics is to pinpoint and lessen the likelihood of crime and disorder issues in particular contexts.

According to Weisburd, Telep, Hinkle, and Eck (2010), a systematic meta-analysis of the best POP research revealed that, in the few studies that were conducted, POP had a small but significant impact on reducing crime. Furthermore, even less thorough pre- and postevaluations showed that POP had a positive impact on lowering crime. Researchers found that employing the problem-solving process to address issues even superficially can have an impact on the levels of crime and disorder (Braga and Weisburd, 2006; Telep and Weisburd, 2012). POP initiatives require more thorough investigation, but the data available thus far indicates that it is the most promising police tactic (Skogan and Frydl, 2004; Weisburd and Eck, 2004, Weisburd et al., 2010).

It is obvious that crime analysis plays a part in problem solving for decreased crime. Notably, crime analysis is essential to every stage of problem solving, not just the apparent As and S of SARA (analysis and assess), but also the S and respond). In other words, analysis is necessary for scanning in order toto help identify and rank issues for selection. The particular responses that are deployed during the response stage of problem solving are determined by further analysise responses themselves being chosen based on the analysis. Essentially, crimeCrime analysis, also known as "problem analysis," is a necessary component of problem solving.

2.1.4. Hot Spots Policing

According to Braga, Papachristos, and Hureau (2014), Telep and Weisburd (2012), Weisburd and Eck (2004), and other scholars, hot spots policing is a place-based policing approach in which traditional police strategies, such as increased police presence and arrests, are implemented in areas or "hot spots" that have disproportionately more crime than other areas within a jurisdiction. There is a wealth of thorough research on the efficacy of hot spot policing. The findings demonstrate the effectiveness of police response to hot spots in lowering crime, whether they are single or multiple addresses, blocks, or sections of a street (Braga et al., 2014; Weisburd and Eck, 2004; Telep and Weisburd, 2012). While the evidence indicates that the interventions typically result in the diffusion of benefits rather than the displacement of crime, the sustainability of crime reduction is constrained by the fact that the effects are mainly transient (Braga et al., 2014). But according to Braga and Weisburd (2010), when hot spots policing is combined with more thorough problem solving, like in problem-oriented policing (i.e., Long-term effectiveness of the strategy can be achieved by not only recognizing the hot spots but also comprehending the reasons behind their "hotness.."

Finding the hotspots where policing tactics are most effective is made possible by crime analysis, especially when using spatial analysis and crime mapping. Since many researchers have discovered that police do not consistently agree on what constitutes a hot spot in their respective areas of responsibility or can accurately identify hot spots, analysis is a crucial component of properly identifying hot spots (Bichler and Gaines, 2005; McLaughlin, Johnson, Bowers, Birks, and Pease, 2006; Ratcliffe and McCullagh, 2001). As mentioned previously in the POP discussion, crime analysis becomes even more crucial in identifying and comprehending the nature of the hot spot in order to implement appropriate responses when hot spots policing is combined with in-depth problem solving. Crime analysis is crucial in determining whether traditional responses to hotspot policing, when combined with problem-solving techniques, have an impact on crime and whether the strategies lead to the displacement of crime or diffusion of benefits (Braga et al., 2014; Weisburd and Telep, 2012).

2.1.5. Focused Deterrence

Called the "pulling levers" strategy, focused deterrence is essentially a targeted approach to problem-solving that targets violent offenders in high-crime areas of a city (Braga and Weisburd, 2012). Drawing from deterrence theory, the responses should be decisive, harsh, and quick (Braga and Weisburd, 2012). Individual offenders are classified as high-risk or chronic offenders, and each offender receives a customized response meant to motivate them to give up their criminal activity. In an attempt to "pull" whatever "lever" is necessary to persuade and convince the offender that committing crimes is no longer a preferable way of life, police may bring in probation officers, prosecutors, family members, and other relevant parties. Although this strategy was first used as a POP project in Boston in the 1990s, it has since been applied in numerous communities all over the nation. According to the type of violent crime and offenses that occur in each community, particular deterrence tactics are put into place using a problem-solving approach (Braga and Weisburd, 2012; Telep and Weisburd, 2012).

Braga and Weisburd (2012) conducted a meta-analysis of the most comprehensive research on the focused deterrence approach and found that the strategies have a significant positive impact on crime reduction. Less thorough studies demonstrated large effect sizes, suggesting the approach is promising even though there is a dearth of systematic experimental research to support this conclusion. Similar to POP, this approach places a strong emphasis on problem-solving, which makes crime analysis a crucial component (Telep and Weisburd, 2012). While this approach focuses on individual responses, finding the right individuals requires identifying areas with disproportionately high crime rates (i.e., hot spots; Kennedy, Braga, and Piehl, 1998) as well as knowing the characteristics of crime and how offenders relate to it (Kennedy, Braga, and Piehl, 2001), all of which call for a thorough understanding of crime. ..

2.1.6. Disorder Policing

The concept of "broken windows policing," also known as disorder policing, dates back to the 1980s and draws a logical link between crime and disorder and the disorderly conditions of a neighborhood (Wilson and Kelling, 1982; Kelling, 2015). That is, people who live, work for companies, or are employed in neighborhoods with high rates of social ills (public drinking, loitering, drug use, and prostitution) along with physical ills (disrepair of streets, sidewalks, lighting), abandoned or dilapidated buildings, and overgrown, vacant lots grow afraid and either leave the area or take precautions to protect themselves by keeping to themselves and avoiding other people. When this occurs, people lose their social connections, and criminals who commit both minor and major crimes start to settle in and operate with little opposition (Welsh, Braga, and Bruinsma, 2015). Wilson and Kelling (1982) recommend that police should deal with the physical deterioration of the neighborhoods and engage in "order maintenance," even though they do not specifically outline any tactics to be used for disorder policing (Welsh et al., 2015). Therefore, a policing strategy grounded in this concept utilizes tactics aimed at "cleaning up" the social injustices (e.g., disorderly conduct and infractions) in order to deter the commission of more serious crimes (Sousa and Kelling, 2006).

The effectiveness of broken window policing has been the subject of conflicting research (Weisburd and Eck, 2004). However, Welsh and colleagues (2015) conducted a meta-analysis of 30 randomized and quasi-experiments and discovered a modest impact on crime from the disorder strategies used by the police. They discovered that the most successful approaches were community-based and focused on modifying both physical and social disorders through the use of problem-solving techniques. Aggressive order maintenance techniques, commonly known as "zero tolerance policing," on the other hand, proved to be completely ineffectual. Indeed, the investigators discovered that these combative tactics seemed to distance the police from the communities they served, leading to a rise in grievances against police personnel, racial discrepancies, and the criminalization of mentally ill and homeless people (Welsh et al., 2015). Furthermore, there isn't much proof that disorder policing improves community cohesion or lessens fear of crime (Welsh et al., 2015).

The way the tactics are applied determines how crime analysis fits into the disorder policing framework. Crime analysis is limited to the ex post facto evaluation of police order maintenance tactics if they are applied in an unfocused manner, meaning that no analysis is required to focus the tactics in any way. On the other hand, crime analysis is crucial in identifying the type and source of the issue as well as the appropriate time and location for the application of strategies when disorder policing tactics are implemented in particular neighborhoods through the process of problem solving.

2.1.7. Compstat

Compstat was developed and put into use by the NYPD in 1994 (Silverman, 2006). However, cops across the country have quickly adopted it, so it is no longer just a single agency's isolated tactic (Police Executive Research Forum, 2013; Weisburd, Mastrofski, McNally, Greenspan, and Willis, 2003). According to Weisburd et al., the Compstat model is an attempt to combine strategic problem solving with an accountability framework., 2003), and pressure to appear progressive and effective in decreasing crime has led many police departments to adopt it (Willis, Mastrofski, and Weisburd, 2007).

The four steps of the SARA problem-solving process are ideally directly correlated to the four guiding principles of the Compstat process. The goal of Compstat's initial step, "accurate and timely intelligence," is the same as that of SARA's scanning and analysis procedures, which examine crime and disorder data to provide insight into when, how, where, to whom, and by whom activity is taking place. The goal of Compstat's "rapid deployment of personnel and resources" and "effective tactics" is comparable to that of SARA's response stage. Lastly, "relentless follow up and assessment" is comparable to SARA's assessment phase. Compstat's implementation has not been as thorough or strategic as Goldstein's problem-solving methodology (Boba and Crank, 2008), but both approaches offer a framework for a dynamic process to address problems. Compstat's unique contribution is the creation of a formal accountability structure to guarantee the process is followed (Weisburd et al., (2003)).

Although many people credit Compstat for the significant drop in crime in New York City, the program's efficacy has not been thoroughly assessed. According to Jang, Hoover, and Joo's (2010) case study, Fort Worth, Texas, saw a decrease in property crime but not violent crime. Although the quick and widespread implementation of "Compstat-like" programs in American and international police agencies (Weisburd, Mastrofski, Willis, and Greenspan, 2006) may be seen as a success, there is no proof that these programs are any more effective at reducing crime. Much like research on crime analysis, the majority of studies conducted on Compstat to date have concentrated on the type and frequency of its use (e.g., Willis, 2011; Willis, Mastrofski, and Kochel, 2010); Dabney, 2010).

Crime analysis plays a big part in Compstat. It is noteworthy that while not all law enforcement agencies have adopted the same management model as the New York Police Department, crime analysis is typically the central element of most "Compstat-like" programs (Boba and Santos, 2011; Weisburd et al., 2003). Crime mapping serves as the primary means of communication in Compstat meetings, in addition to the routine analyses generated by crime analysts that are used to allocate resources and hold managers accountable (Ratcliffe, 2004a). Actually, a lot of police departments nowadays have technology for crime mapping and analysis just because they put in place a "Compstat-like" program.

2.1.8. Intelligence-Led Policing

According to Ratcliffe (2008), intelligence-led policing (ILP) is a modern police management model where the intelligence or analysis function plays a key role in the agency's efforts to prevent and reduce crime. The collection of intelligence and distribution of analysis products directly informs decision-makers as a top-down management philosophy and business model (Ratcliffe, 2008). ILP employs a problem-solving methodology along with traditional intelligence analysis, with a focus on persistent and severe offenders (Ratcliffe, 2008).ous organizations both domestically and internationally have adopted ILP. There have not haven't been any thorough analyses of its performance in lowering crime rates up to this point. Similar to Compstat, the majority of research focuses on various aspects of the business model's implementation (Darroch and Mazerolle, 2013; McGarrell, Freilich, and Chermak, 2007; Ratcliffe and GSchaible and Sheffield, 2012).

The ILP model's core component is crime analysis, particularly ofparticularly intelligence data, as the approach's name suggests. When it comes to creating and sharing analysis for crime reduction responses and decision-making, crime analysts play a crucial role (Ratcliffe, 2008). Since problem solving is a crucial aspect of ILP, analysis is also significant in that regard.

2.1.9. Predictive Policing

"Any policing strategy or tactic that develops and uses information and advanced analysis to inform forward-thinking crime prevention" is the definition of predictive policing, a recently developed approach (Beck and McCue, 2009; Uchida, 2010) and as "the process of anticipating risks of crime and informing actions to prevent crime through the use of computer models, supported by historical crime and environmental data" (Hollywood, Smith, Price, McInnis, and Perry, 2012). Predictive policing is an "advanced" analytical approach that is used to deploy patrol officers in the short and immediate term, rather than a predetermined set of tactics or police responses.

Numerous software applications with various statistical models are available to support predictive policing (Harris, 2014). The majority of these software applications seek to pinpoint narrow geographic regions (e.g., several hundred square feet) based on the probability of crime occurring there, where patrol officers can be assigned during their shift for that day. Predictive policing employs statistics that vary almost as much as the various software packages. Regrettably, many statistical models and algorithms are proprietary to the software providers, making it impossible to determine the precise techniques.

The use of predictive policing in all of its forms is spreading both domestically in the United States and abroad, including in South America, Europe, Canada, South Korea, and the Caribbean. There is no systematic evidence that suggests either 1) the statistical models' predictions are accurate in predicting crime events or 2) responding to the identified areas reduces crime, due to their relative newness, the variety of statistical approaches employed, and the variety of police tactics used in the identified areas. Still, scholars are starting to examine particular statistical techniques and reactions used by the Kent Police Department in the United Kingdom and in the anticipated areas of Los Angeles (Mohler et al., 2015), in Philadelphia, Pennsylvania (Haberman and Ratcliffe, 2012), and in Shreveport, Louisiana (Hunt, Saunders, and Hollywood, 2014). It is obvious that crime analysis plays a key role in predictive policing. Since predictive policing is more of an analytical approach than a police response, it is possible to argue that it is synonymous with crime analysis. Referring back to the analogy from medicine, predictive policing is the MRI scanner.

2.1.10. Police Effectiveness and Crime Analysis

As a result, after 30 years of research on policing, scholars have come to the conclusion that in order for policing strategies to be successful, they need to be methodical and problem-solving in nature (Braga and Weisburd, 2006; Sherman et al., 1997; Weisburd and Eck, 2004; Telep and Weisburd, 2012; Weisburd et al., 2010). Realizing that criminal activity opportunities and crime prevention tactics are specific and localized (i.e., occur in particular contexts for crimes). Researchers come to the conclusion that, in order for policing to play a preventive role, strategies for reducing crime must be targeted and applied methodically using the problem-solving approach (Sherman et al., 1997; Weisburd and Eck, 2004; Weisburd et al., 2006a, and 2002. 2010). Furthermore, as highlighted in Compstat, accountability is essential to institutionalizing successful crime reduction initiatives in police organizations, according to recent practice-based research (Boba, 2010; Santos, 2011). (Santos, 2013; Santos and Santos, 2015a; Taylor and Boba, 2011).

An overview of the usefulness and function of crime analysis in each policing strategy is provided in Table 2.1. The summary table and key takeaways make it evident that the most successful tactics (i.e., POP, hot spots, and targeted deterrence), crime analysis plays a crucial role in putting the strategy into practice. Crucially, crime analysis is involved in all policing strategies to some extent. This includes strategies like community policing and disorder policing, which have only modestly reduced crime. The traditional police model is ineffective at crime, but crime analysis can help allocate resources and inform different audiences about crime statistics—statistics, albeit to a limited extent. When examining the three strategies—compstat, integrated learning program, and predictive policing—for which there is a dearth of empirical data on police effectiveness, the importance of crime analysis as a fundamental element of each strategy becomes evident.

To return to the initial question, crime analysis is a necessary diagnostic tool for successful crime reduction, but it is not a cure for crime. But employing a crime analyst in law enforcement involves more than just "hiring one" or purchasing hardware or software. i.e., the MRI). An organization would first choose an efficient policing strategy that best fits the issues facing the community before hiring a crime analyst with effective "diagnosis" skills to start reducing crime. Finally, following the creation of the crime analysis, the agency would need to successfully apply the strategy (i.e., give the medication) in order for everything to go smoothly and the illness to be "cured."

Table 2.1. *Summary of Crime Analysis Assessment*

Policing Approach	Effectiveness	Role of Crime Analysis
Standard model	Not effective	Limited
Community policing	Ambiguous	Limited
Disorder policing	Modest effect	Essential when focused
Problem-oriented policing	Shows promise	Essential
Hot spots policing	Effective	Essential
Focused deterrence	Shows promise	Essential
Compstat	No evidence	Essential
Intelligence-led policing	No evidence	Essential
Predictive policing	No evidence	Synonymous

Source: Rachel Boba Santos, Crime Analysis With Crime Mapping, ISBN: 9781506331034.

To sum up, crime analysis is involved in all of the police strategies that have been covered here, though it is more involved in some than in others. It is impossible to exaggerate the significance of crime analysis in policing, but sadly, the field is still having difficulty gaining acceptance and making a successful application because crime analysts have only lately been integrated into police departments. The bulk of what is required for crime analysis to help police implement crime reduction will be described and explained in the remaining sections of this book. The crime analysis methods that are left out are mainly concerned with operational tasks that are better suited for an advanced crime analysis text, like staffing allocation, resource assessment, and performance measures.

2.2. STRATIFIED POLICING: FRAMEWORK FOR CRIME ANALYSIS

Its foundation is the organizational strategy known as stratified policing, which aims to reduce crime (Santos and Santos, 2015b). Rather than being a method of reducing crime like hot spots or community-oriented policing, stratified policing is a way for a police department to arrange its investigations and deterrent measures. It describes various categories of "problems" (i.e., strata) for which a framework comprising police tactics and strategies, accountability procedures, and crime analysis tools and techniques is supplied to establish a framework for the remainder of the book. It is noteworthy that this is the only policing strategy that aims to integrate crime analysis into the regular activities of the police force and that provides a detailed framework for the use of crime analysis products.

Police departments need a framework for "how" to apply evidence-based tactics and crime analysis together. For instance, as was previously covered in this chapter, law enforcement officials are aware of the effectiveness of hot spots policing, but they lack specific implementation guidelines. Hot spots with disproportionately high crime rates are identified, and police respond to those areas. This is known as hot spots policing. Before a police organization can implement hot spots policing, however, a number of organizational and operational questions need to be addressed. These include: What constitutes a hot spot? How often should police identify new hot spots? Who responds to hot spots? Which responses should be implemented—when and how? Who ensures that responses are sufficient and appropriate? How do we know when to stop responding, and who makes that decision? Stratified policing is a framework that standardizes the procedures that address these issues in terms of crime analysis, the tactics used to reduce crime, and the methods used to hold people accountable.

2.2.1. Problem Stratification

The foundation of stratified policing is the notion that the police apply evidence-based tactics to address various levels of activity related to crime, disorder, and quality of life issues. The levels range in complexity and temporal nature, and they typically comprise short-term clusters, long-term issues, and immediate incidents. The organization of the stratified policing structure is fundamental (i.e., arranged) around these kinds of undertakings. A stratified structure for addressing them is defined, organized, and carried out in an uniform manner within the organization by breaking down what police do into different levels.

The purpose of crime analysis is to look at problematic activity that happens at various levels rather than to comprehend and analyze one crime or incident at a time. Because of this, the concept of the "problem," which has numerous definitions, lies at the core of the stratification of crime and disorder activity. Herman Goldstein defines a problem as one of three things: (i) a unit of police business; (ii) a substantive community concern; or (iii) a cluster of similar, related, or recurring incidents rather than a single incident (1990). "A recurring set of related harmful events in a community that members of the public expect the police to address" (Step 14) is how Clarke and Eck (2005) define a problem. Unfortunately, it has proven difficult to put these conceptual definitions into practice. Police researchers have observed that the police have had trouble defining issues precisely, which has affected their capacity to solve problems and deter crime (Braga and Weisburd, 2006; Scott, 2000).

The complexity and temporal evolution of the crime and disorder activity categories make them the easiest to understand. In other words, more complex problems, like long-term problem locations, take longer to develop than simpler problems, like the combination of multiple incidents, which usually show symptoms very quickly. Although a particular problem can sit anywhere on this continuum, problems can be broken down into three categories (adapted from Boba and Santos, 2011):

1. Immediate Problems: Incidents and serious incidents (individual calls for service and crime reports);
2. Short-Term Problems: Repeat incidents and patterns;
3. Long-Term Problems: Problem locations, problem areas, problem offenders, problem victims, problem products, and compound problems.

2.2.2. Immediate Problems

Isolated incidents that happen and are fixed in a matter of minutes, hours, or sometimes even days are referred to as "immediate" problems. Patrol officers and detectives who have received more in-depth investigative training as well as basic police training respond to them using their investigative skills. This level is the most specialized stratum of crime and disorder problem, even though crime analysts don't usually look at specific immediate problems. Officers and detectives typically conduct what is known as an investigation, which is an analysis for immediate problems. Here, there are two categories of immediate crime and disorder activity: incidents and serious incidents.

Individual occurrences that an officer usually responds to or finds while on patrol are known as incidents. Crime, disorder, or service-related tasks like disturbances, robberies in progress, traffic crashes, subject stops, and traffic citations are all examples of incidents, which are calls for assistance generated by citizens and officers. These events typically transpire and are resolved in a matter of minutes or hours, usually within a single shift. In order to resolve each incident as fast and efficiently as possible in compliance with the laws and policies of the jurisdiction and the police agency, police officers usually carry out the preliminary investigation and respond to incidents.

Individual events that result from service calls that are classified as serious incidents under the laws and policies of the police department necessitate further investigation and/or a more comprehensive immediate response. They happen in a matter of minutes or hours and can take days, weeks, or even months to resolve. Examples of these include rapes, hostage negotiations, homicides, traffic fatalities, or armed robberies. Usually, investigators or individuals with specialized training (e.g., homicide detectives, and traffic crash investigators) carry out more thorough analyses and react to these grave incidents with the intention of solving the case in accordance with local laws and police agency policies and, most importantly, capturing the offender or offenders.

2.2.3. Short-Term Problems

The next stratum, known as short-term problems, consists of serious incidents and clusters of incidents. "Short-term" problems are ones that take place over a few days or weeks and usually call for quick fixes as opposed to long-term ones. Repeat incidents and patterns are the two categories into which short-term issues are divided.

2.2.3.1. Repeat Incidents

Repeat incidents happen when two or more distinct incidents occur at the same location (usually) or are of a similar nature and are committed by the same person. Since repeat incidents are collections of incidents, they happen less frequently than individual incidents.

These (typically) frequent noncriminal or interpersonal criminal incidents, which include traffic crashes, neighbor disputes, barking dogs, domestic violence, troublesome youth, and the like, may or may not lead to a crime report. A repeat incident is composed of several incidents that occur hours, days, and sometimes even weeks apart.

Because it indicates a transient pattern of opportunity that can concentrate crime analysis and problem-solving strategies, a repeat incident is a significant stratum. Finding an address with numerous service requests and fixing the underlying issue at hand are the main goals of the analysis and problem-solving process for a recurring incident. For example, a neighbor dispute over a barking dog may be the cause of two complaints for a disturbance and one for loud noise at a specific address. After the police have determined what the fundamental "problem" is with the recurring incident, they will formulate and carry out a plan of action to address the general disagreement between the neighbors (as opposed to each other). simply responding to each request for assistance).

2.2.3.2. Patterns

Groups of two or more crimes that are reported to the police or found by them are called patterns, and they are analyzed as a single unit because: (i) they have one or more notable characteristics in common; (ii) the victim and offender are not known to be related; and (iii) the criminal activity is usually short-lived (IACA, 2011b). Crimes such as stranger rape, indecent exposure, public indecency, robbery, burglary, theft from vehicle, auto theft, and grand theft are analyzed for patterns. Because they see crime patterns as the most direct threat to personal safety, the police, residents, businesses, the media, and every member of the community view them as critically important. i.e., criminals preying on unidentified victims).

Crucially, the kinds of data that are examined distinguish patterns from recurrent incidents. Both relate to short-term activity; however, patterns consist of reported crimes committed by strangers, while repeat incidents are caused by interpersonal problems or common "quality of life" issues. Through casual conversations and the examination of police reports, detectives and police officers have historically connected patterns on an as-needed basis. In recent times, analysts who have received specialized training have joined the central police force to carry out pattern analysis (i.e., tactical analysis of criminal activity (O'Shea and Nicholls, 2003).

2.2.4. Long-Term Problems

The next stratum is a long-term problem, which is a collection of related activities spanning several months, seasons, or years and resulting from regular opportunities brought about by environment and behavior. Issues may include typical disorder behavior (e.g., loud parties or driving too fast in residential areas) in addition to significant criminal activity (e.g., rape on a date, or bank heist). Three key differences are as follows (IACA, 2011b):

1. **Scope and Length:** Where a long-term problem is chronic in frequency and duration and may be characterized by acute spikes, a crime pattern is acute in its frequency and duration.
2. **Nature of Activity:** Where a long-term problem is related to "harmful events" that may include crime, safety, disorder, or quality of life concerns (Clarke and Eck, 2005), a crime pattern is limited to a specific set of reported crimes.
3. **Response:** Where a long-term problem requires specialized strategic responses that often involve multiagency and community collaboration, a crime pattern typically requires routine operational tactics carried out primarily by the police.

Repeated incidents and patterns may be a part of a series of related activities that eventually develop into a problem, even though they are not always a part of a larger issue. On the other hand, problems will have a lot of patterns or recurring incidents. By first figuring out these immediate problems and how well the solutions work, more can be discovered about the problem (e.g., interviews with criminals concerning their motivations for committing those crimes, as well as what works and doesn't work to stop recurrent incidents).

There are various long-term problem categories, which can be distinguished by the fact that police responses and analysis vary depending on the category. Because the three sides of the problem analysis triangle—place, offender, and victim/target—are the foundation for understanding the various long-term problem types, they are simple to comprehend.

The problem location (also known as a "risky place") is the first (Clarke and Eck, 2005; Eck, Clarke, and Guerette, 2007). Issue sites may be specific addresses (e.g., Convenience stores) or a certain kind of location (e.g., all convenience stores) where criminal activity or problematic behavior is concentrated. The problem location is the focus because different victims and offenders are involved in the activity there. In this instance, the analysis would concentrate on locating every activity, comprehending the creation and utilization of opportunities, and figuring out how that particular location or kind of place stacks up against other comparable, trouble-free locations.

Second, there is the issue area, also known as a "hot spot" (Eck, Chainey, Cameron, Leitner, and Wilson, 2005; Chainey and Ratcliffe, 2005). These are comparatively small geographic areas with a disproportionately high rate of disorderly conduct, including various forms of crime. Block faces and complete square block areas, groups of street segments, and defined police geographic areas like zones or beats can all be included in the areas. Crucially, trouble spots ought to be compact enough so that the chances of criminal activity are uniform throughout the region. For instance, a problem area for residential burglaries would mainly involve homes rather than commercial establishments. Similar to problem areas, the activity in the area involves a variety of victims and offenders. In this instance, the analysis would concentrate on figuring out what activities are taking place in the problematic areas, comprehending how opportunities are generated and taken advantage of, and figuring out how those areas relate to comparable, nonproblematic areas.

The problem offender represents the third category of persistent issue. These could be single individuals who commit a disproportionate number of crimes or groups of criminals with comparable traits. The crucial element for problem offenders is that an individual or group of individuals moves through various environments and preys on various victims. For instance, truancy in high school could be an issue for a city. These students have one thing in common: they don't go to school. When they aren't in class, they might be buying or selling drugs, breaking into homes, or loitering in public. Understanding and dealing with these offenders and their truancy, which has led to a variety of problematic behavior, would be the main focus of the analysis and response.

The problem victim is the fourth category of persistent problem. Like trouble spots and offenders, these can be specific individuals (e.g., a person whose vehicle has been taken three times) or clusters of victims with similar traits (e.g., robbery victims who are Hispanic migrant laborers. The essential element for problem victims is that an individual or group of individuals experiences victimization from various offenders in a variety of settings. The reasons behind these people's victimization and the aspects of their behavior that make them susceptible are the main topics of analysis and response. For instance, the fact that Hispanic migrant workers don't use banks and carry all of their cash on them makes them susceptible to robbery, as does the fact that they walk rather than drive from place to place.

The problem property represents the fifth category of long-term problems. Problem property is typically not a single item that is taken frequently, but rather a group of goods that have similar qualities that make them appealing to different kinds of thieves and expose them to different risks. For instance, copper wire poses a problem because different kinds of criminals steal copper from various sources (e.g., old houses, cell phone towers, building sites, etc.,) and exchange it for money. The environments in which the property is situated and the chances for criminal activity are the main subjects of analysis and response. Because copper wire is easy to turn into cash, it is common for the careless practices of scrap metal buyers to encourage theft by not requiring identification or questioning scrap metal sellers.

The last and most widespread kind is the compound problem, which typically affects an entire jurisdiction and involves a number of victims, offenders, and locations. For instance, an issue might be initially classified as a theft from vehicle issue, but additional investigation might reveal that the crime primarily happens in residential areas; nonetheless, no specific kind of location, small area, victim, or offender can be linked to this issue. This would turn the issue into a compound one. These types of problems require the most comprehensive analysis and response because a number of factors (e.g., perpetrators, sites, and victims) could be involved in the issue. Fortunately, these are fortunately the least common kinds of issues.

Specifically, the significance of the stratification lies in the fact that effectively managing current issues helps to keep repeat incidents and patterns (short-term problems) from occurring, and effectively managing these issues helps to keep long-term problems from developing into serious problems. Long-term problems are characterized by a high number of incidents, significant incidents, repeat incidents, and patterns. Police can prevent long-term problems by systematically identifying smaller, less complex problems and effectively addressing them. An easy way to understand this is to use the analogy of a fire: small sparks can be easily extinguished, but if they aren't, they can combine and become small fires. These tiny fires have the potential to combine and grow into larger, more complex, and challenging to put out fires if they are not extinguished. So, while firefighters concentrate on sparks, small fires, and big fires at the same time, police and crime analysts concentrate on various levels of issues.

The term "problem" has two meanings: generally (e.g., urgent, transient, and long-term issues) and particularly (e.g., the location of the issue). The term "problems" can refer to any kind of activity that the police handle, which is probably why there has been so much confusion around it. It is simpler to apply and comprehend the discussion of crime analysis methods and techniques when problems are categorized using distinct terms based on their temporal and complex nature.

2.2.5. Stratification of Police Responsibility

Stratified policing aligns the ranks within the police organization with the stratification of activity, because simply listing the different kinds of activities and standardizing the processes for analysis, response, and evaluation for each is insufficient to give a police agency a framework to continue operating. Higher ranks are tasked with handling increasingly complex tasks, such as handling calls for service and investigations, which are currently the responsibility of police officers and detectives. While organizations with fewer ranks must assign more responsibility to each rank, those with more ranks can distribute responsibility for crime reduction more widely and thinly. The fact that all agency ranks are accounlved, and responsible for crime reduction efforts is the most crucial feature. Comparablsis is stratified in that, in order toto facilitate response and evaluation, various product types are required at each level.

With regard toRegarding crime, disorder, and quality of life issues, this structure guarantees that everyone in the organization is moving in the same direction and that each person is assigned a specific and suitable role. This is comparable to a football team's offense. Every player has a task to complete and the same objetive of scoring points. The roles that the players play are determined by their skills, and they are expected to provide certain "responses.." Under this approach, a police agency does not ask line-level officers to perform crime reduction work that is outside the scope of their positions, just as the team would not regularly assign linemen to play wide receiver. This is not to argue that spec(or linemen) are incapable of doing their jobs; rather, it is to argue that each rank's responsibilities within the organization as a whole areare reasonable and appropriate given its scope, authority, experience, training, and skills. This is one of the most crucial elements of strating because it guarantees sustainability and uniformity since crime prevention and reduction are now considered duties that must be carried outconducted by all employees on a daily basis.

2.2.6. Stratification of Accountability and Evaluation

Stratified policing's accountability process is crucial because organizational change in a police department cannot happen without accountability. In the same way that sergeants inspect officers' weapons and gear to ensure they comply with agency policy, direct supervisors hold each rank's employees accountable for their work. The core components of the accountability system are setting reasonable goals for evidence-based strategies, monitoring their development, recording the work completed, and assessing the strategies' efficacy. Daily accountability is a feature of stratified policing, but it also uses a meeting structure that is divided into tiers based on activity levels. They include the following:

- Daily roll calls facilitate action-oriented accountability at the line level for evidence-based strategies implemented for immediate and short-term problems.
- Weekly accountability meetings facilitate action-oriented accountability because individuals from the various divisions of the organization (e.g., patrol, investigations, crime prevention, and media relations) come together to coordinate, track, and assess responses to short-term activity—repeat incidents and patterns. This meeting does not include a review of any statistics or crime counts since its focus is on "action" (i.e., response).
- Monthly accountability meetings facilitate evaluation-oriented accountability. Specifically produced crime analysis products and maps are used to assess whether short-term strategies are effective as well as to identify emerging long-term problems and to monitor ongoing long-term strategies. In addition, every 12 months, the monthly meeting facilitates evaluation-oriented accountability for the entire organization, based on the agency's crime reduction and prevention goals. The results of this meeting are shared with the agency as well as with city government to show how the chief is holding the entire agency accountable for crime reduction.

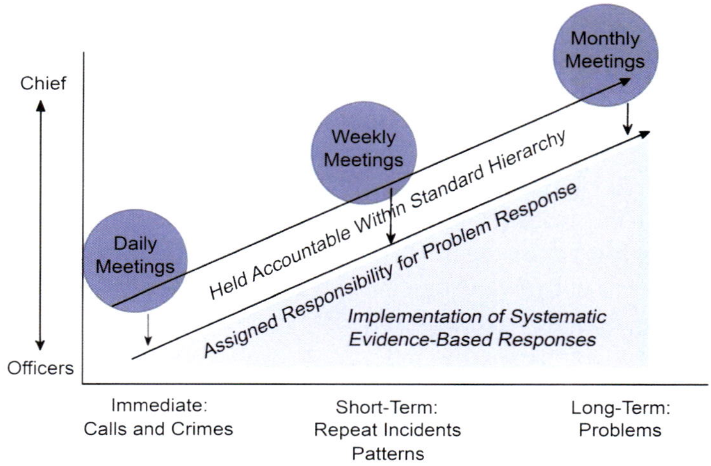

Figure 2.3. *Stratified policing structure.*

Source: Rachel Boba Santos, Crime Analysis With Crime Mapping, ISBN: 9781506331034.

Demonstrates every aspect of stratified policing, including the idea that higher ranks in the organization handle more complicated issues and that the structure of the organization makes sure that those in positions of authority hold subordinates accountable. The organization's rank is indicated by the y-axis, while the x-axis displays the various problem levels. Which rank is in charge of the problem response is indicated by the lower black arrow (i.e., cops to calls or crimes, sergeants to reoccurring incidents, and commanders to issues). The upper black line shows the manner in which those people are held responsible (i.e., by the position above them). The circles show which meetings are relevant to a given problem type and priority.

2.3. EVIDENCE-BASED POLICING

"The use of the best available research on the outcomes of police work to implement guidelines and evaluate agencies, units, and officers" is how Sherman (1998) defined evidence-based policing. Research, analysis, evaluation, and general science should all be considered when making these decisions, according to EBP (Lum and Koper, 2017). It does not, however, imply that the only factor that should influence decisions made in law enforcement is research evidence or minimize the importance of experience in the field (Lum et al., 2012). Asvidence-based policing improves resource allocation, increases transparency, and promotes better relationships with the community," EBP ultimately seeksseeks to increase the value of modern policing (Dolly and Shawver, 2018).

According to Huey et al., some, EBP is about forming partnerships between researchers and practitioners to learn more about t works" in policing. Sherman (1998), Keay and Kirby (2018), and others. According to Piza and Feng (2017) and Weisburd and Neyroud (2011), the philosophyphilosophy promotes police participation in the research process, including the development of internal capacity for high-level evaluations. This is difficult because, as crises arise, decision-makers usually want quick analyses and solutions, and policing is a fast-paced field (Belur and Johnson, 2018). But quality research frequently takes time, and methods used to determine "wat works" in policing must be carefully considered (Huey et al., 2017; Sherman and Eck, 2002; Sherman et al.; Keay and Kirby, 2018. (Piza and Feng, 2017;, 1997). Sadly, impact and process evaluations are still infrequently carried out in law enforcement, leaving the field ignorant of the reasons behind the success or failure of initiatives (Belur and Johnson, 2018; Santos and Taylor, 2014). Additionally, Sherman (2013) distinguished three key elements of EBP—tracking, testing, and targeting—that have an impact on the function of analysts in law enforcement. Targeting is the process of determining a high priority for law enforcement, testing is the act of putting an initiative into action and determining whether the intervention was successful, and tracking is the process of monitoring the initiative's impact—as well as any modifications made to it—over extended periods of time (Huey et al., 2017). There are unmistakable similarities to the SARA model of problem-oriented policing (Eck and Spelman, 1987), which entails root cause analysis, response implementation, impact assessment, and scanning (for problems). Analysts will undoubtedly be involved in scanning, analyzing, and evaluating the data, but they also have the power to influence the responses that are selected, which may necessitate further analysis (Santos, 2014). In his initial discussion of EBP, Sherman (1998) concentrated on the creation, utilization, and application of research to inform police decision-making. To this, Lum and Koper (2017) argue that institutionalizing the knowledge gained from research and translating it into a form that police agencies can use are equally important. There are chances for analysts to participate in the creation, application, and interpretation of research (Lum and Koper, 2017).

According to EBP, policing must change; it must now use research evidence to guide police practices rather than relying solely on gut feelings to make decisions. The role of the analyst has been defined as "challenging the established way of working and offering new options for consideration: to provide and recommend an [sic] variety of tactics for intervention that can and do challenge normal police tactics," so analysts are natural proponents of EBP

(Sissens, 2008). However, as previously indicated, despite the enormous benefits of EBP, there are obstacles that prevent the application of research findings in law enforcement, which is similar to the difficulties analysts encounter.

2.3.1. Receptivity of Research in Policing

The results of decades of evaluative research have not yet been completely integrated into standard police procedure (Lum et al., 2012; Rojek et al.; Lum and Koper, 2014; Lumsden and Goode, 2018. Sherman, 2015, 2020; Sherman, 2012). Regretfully, there aren't many recent studies that have looked at the receptivity of policing research and have identified the barriers and factors that influence receptivity (Cherney et al., 2020; Lum and others. Kalyal, 2020;, 2012). Much of policing still uses the traditional reactive model, which includes follow-up investigations, quick response to calls, and random patrols,f culture and tradition (Sherman et al., 1997; Lum et al.; Weisburd and Eck, 2004. 2012). Furthermore, experience and "gut" instinct continue to play a big rolea crucial decision-making. Although experience is valuable, opinions can be skewed and representative of specific situations. On the other hand, research makes an efforttries to take into consideration different viewpoints and methodically look at collective experiences.

Given the apparent benefits of EBP, what obstacles mightprevent research from moving forward? Lum et al. (2012) stated clearly that "political, organizational, or individual barriers to the use of research can exist.." It is crucial to stress that analysts might not hny control over these variables. Rather, to effect change and make EBP a routine procedure in their agency, progressive police leadership must be enlisted. We'llWe will talk about a few of these studies in this section to draw crisons with the obstacles faced by crime analysts. More importantly, it will teach analysts some new lessons.

2.3.1.1. Individual Factors

Numerous research havehas examined personal characteristics like educational attainment (Telep and Lum, 2014; Blaskovits et al., 2015) rank (Hunter et al., 2018; Telep, 2017; Kalyal, 2020)., as well as a host of additional individual characteristics, none of which would be pertinent to analysts' work. The officer's awareness of EBP, reliance on experience, exposure to research and research literature, interest in participating in policing research and evaluation, and familiarity with efficient police techniques are the main topics of discussion in this section. It is recommended that analysts comprehend these concepts in order to consider the implications for the relationship between officers and analysts, as well as their degree of acceptance of research lysis.

2.2.3.1.1. Officer Knowledge

The first survey to examine police receptivity to research was created by Telep and Lum (2014). Officers in three US cities—cities, Roanoke County, Virginia; Sacramento, California; and Richmond, Virginia—were given the survey as part of their study. One of the questions they posed was, "Are officers familiar with the term EBP?" Across all three sites, between 25.1% and 48.4% of respondents said they were. Receptivity studies, on the other hand, have just lately begun in Canada. Blaskovits and associates. (2018) conducted a replication of this study and discovered that Canadian respondents were more familiar with EBP than their US counterparts. It's crucial to remember, though, that familiarity does not always equate to a thorough comprehension of EBP concepts.

2.2.3.1.2. Reliance on Experience

Research is no longer a major factor in police decision-making; instead, police experience and public feedback are still highly valued (Palmer, 2011; Santos and Taylor, 2014; Telep and Lum, 2014). Having said that, officers welcome research (e.g., willingness to participate in pre- and post-evaluations, as well as an openness to working with researchers (Lum et al., 2012; Telep and Lum, 2014; Palmer, 2011). Palmer (2011) discovered that "the meaningfulness, cost, and perceived risk of the research, as well as on its alignment with an officer's own' sense'" are the factors that determine this openness (Lum et al., 2012). Blaskovits and associates. (2018) discovered that Canadian officers relied more on experience than scientific knowledge, just like their international counterparts. However, respondents from Canada were more open to accepting outside assistance, and more of them agreed that experience and scientific knowledge should be given equal weight when making decisions. The indirect networking that comes with becoming a member of the Canadian Society of Evidence-Based Policing (Can-SEBP) was another reason given by Canadian officers for their membership. This lends credence to the theory that Canadian officers, like their international counterparts, placed more trust in the expertise and experience of their peers than in science (Palmer, 2011; Lum et al., 2012). An important lesson for analysts is the prominence given to firsthand experience and the experiences of others over scholarly sources.

2.2.3.1.3. Exposure and Acceptance

Officers should certainly rely on their experience, the advice of their peers, and the community, but they can also learn about good police practices by reading scholarly journals and trade magazines. According to studies, officers typically read government publications or professional policing publications like the Police Chief instead of scholarly journals (Rojek et al., Blaskovits et al., 2012; Palmer, 2011; Telep and Lum, 2014. 2018). This could be because academic jargon or paywalls are obscuring research articles (Blaskovits et al., 2018). Officers are more open to EBP, nevertheless, when they do have access to government publications and read two or more of them (Palmer, 2011; Telep, 2017). When it came to the efficacy of police tactics, officers were more likely to turn to their own agencies for information and assistance than to turn to outside sources (Lum et al., (2012); Lum and Telep, 2014). This is an excellent chance for analysts to interpret, share, and apply research findings informally or through their analytical products (see Lum et al., 2012).

Researchers, crime analysts, and their work continue to be regarded with suspicion in spite of this opportunity (Lum et al., 2012). This was due to several distinct factors. First, how research is presented, especially by senior leadership, may influence officers' acceptance of it. If they believe it to be an academic exercise or a component of an accountability system like CompStat, they will be resistant (Lum et al., 2012). Additionally, it implies that officers may be resistant if they believe they no longer have autonomy; this is consistent with findings regarding certain officers' opinions of hot spot policing (Lum et al., 2012). Additionally, the experiences of officers are frequently derived from isolated, unrelated incidents (Evans and Kebbell, 2012). Regretfullnts are subjective and potentially biased as they only reflect the viewpoint of one individual (Cope, 2004). On the other hand, research and analysis make an efforttry to present phenomenon summaries (Cope, 2004). Officers do not reject scientific evidence per se, as Kalyal (2020) noted, but rather they feel that generalizations cannot be applied to police work, which varies from case to case (*see also* Lum et al., 2012). An internal culture that promotes and rewards single-case arrests may exacerbate this (Telep and Lum, 2014).

Police departments must first give priority to conducting internal research. It makes sense that officers believed findings from academic research would not apply to their day-to-day experiences, particularly if those findings ignore their perspective or the local context. Thus, it will be crucial for analysts to participate in studies that use the data from their agency. It's crucial to take the officers' experiences into account. Lum and associates. Researchers should take note of what (2012) suggests, as it can also apply to analysts: "Officers' professional experience should not be disregarded when conducting evaluation research. This is because officers can provide valuable insights that will enhance the project overall,also likely be more cooperative with researchers who acknowledge and value their knowledge and experience" (Lum et al., 2012). Finally, when analysts are involved inengage in project implementation, they should not only take into account the opinions of officers, but they should also make recommendations that respect officers' autonomy needs in order to gain support and acknowledge that police data and research have limitations. Officers who are exposed to research are more open to EBP in general and are more willing to participate in research evaluations in particular (Palmer, 2011). According to Koehle et al., officers tend to be more open to simpler qualitative methods as opposed to more complex qualitative and quantitative methods, which they perceive as being too abstract and disconnected from the realities of everyday police operations. 2010). Additionally, it was discovered that officers were more open to less thorough evaluations; they were more inclined to participate in pre- and post-studies and were less inclined to halt a police tactic for the sake of a controlled study (Palmer, 2011; Telep and Lum, 2014). As was already mentioned, receptivity was influenced by the level of risk (Lum et al., 2012) and the possible harm to regular law enforcement activities (Blaskovits et al., 2018). It's important for analysts to understand that, even though more thorough research methodologies have merit, police are more open to simpler approaches that are more in line with the realities of everyday policing—basically, keep it simple.

2.2.3.1.4. Knowledge of Effective Police Practices

It is also crucial to take into account the officers' familiarity with efficient police procedures. As mentioned earlier, if there is a culture that values arrests, officers could be hostile to ideas that contradict their values (Telep and Lum, 2014). When promoting evidence-based procedures and suggesting cutting-edge police techniques and strategies, analysts should keep this in mind. Officers in Telep and Lum (2014) and Blaskovits et al., for instance. Despite the evidence to the contrary, (2018) studies found that community policing was successful in lowering crime (Gill et al., 2014). Police still operate under what is thought of as the traditional model of policing, which places a strong emphasis on reactive investigations, quick call response times, and random patrols (Sherman et al., 1997; Eck and Weisburd, 2004). Weisburd (2008) in Lum and others., 2012) contended that the persistent use of random patrols as a standard policing strategy, despite research showing that it has no effect on crime, is a glaring example of the gap between evidence-based practice and reality (Kelling et al., 1974), but that focused and targeted methods work better (Braga et al., 2019). In fact, the officers in Blaskovits et(2014) as well as Telep and Lum (2014). According to (2018) studies, responding to crimes quickly is an effective strategy.

According to Lum et al. (2012) they found state that proactive, place-based, problem-specific, and deployment strategies are more likely to have an impact on preventing crime than general, reactive, and individual-based approaches (Telep and Lum, 2014). Once more, the lack of awareness regarding efficient police techniques might just be the result of how research is accessed or displayed (Blaskovits et al., 2018). For instance, while novel techniques like restorative justice and pulling levers may be well-known in academia, many of the officers in Telep and Lum's (2014) study were not. On the plus side, Telep (2016) discovered that police officers thought evidence-based strategies like hot spots policing and problem-oriented policing worked. This is significant because patrol support is needed for both strategies. And Blaskovits and others. (2018) discovered that compared to their US counterparts, respondents from Canada were more open to experimenting with novel ideas. These are crucial points because analysts are pushing evidence-based strategies that are more in line with officers' perceptions of what works.

2.2.3.1.5. Attitudes Towards Researchers and Police-Researcher Partnerships

Although there is still mistrust for analysts and researchers as well as their work (Lum et al., 2012), some fluctuation exists (Telep and Lum, 2014). Take Blaskovits et al. (2018) as an example discovered that most Canadian officers said the data they got from researchers and analysts was either very useful or helpful. According to studies, officers believe that working together with researchers was important (Telep and Lum, 2014; Telep and Winegar, 2016; Blaskovits et al., Blaskovits, 2018). Remember that when research did not contradict their beliefs or materially alter their daily operations, officers were more open to it. The relationship between the police and academics is complicated by the fact that they typically operate under different schedules, have different expectations, hold different worldviews, and disagree on how best to measure police effectiveness and what evaluation techniques to employ (Mastrofski, Willis, and Revier, 2011 in Lum et al., 2012). Police and researchers may also disagree on what constitutes "evidence" (Buerger, 2010). Academic research evidence may be viewed as too general to have any bearing on routine police work. Moreover, the purpose of an officer's work may not always be crime control, even though researchers may be assessing whether an initiative decreased crime and disorder (Sparrow, 2015; Telep and Lum, 2014).

Some insights are also offered by Kalyal's (2020) study, which involved officer interviews. First, responders pointed out that academic reports have a long history of failing to show that the authors have a thorough understanding of police issues or police operations. Similarly, the reports that are being generated don't show that the authors clearly comprehend the data and the context in which it is gathered, which could lead to findings being interpreted incorrectly. Police also encountered resistance when certain academics refused to accept criticism of their research. It was feared that working with academics would take police departments "down an academic route.." Concerns over sensitive data were also legitimate. One thing that analysts can learn from these remarks is that in order for their work to be more positively received, analysts must show that their products are useful and applicable to officers by incorporating their feedback.

2.2.3.1.6. Resourcing and Time

In contrast to the fast-paced world of law enforcement, where prompt resolutions are imperative, the production of rigorous academic research of the highest caliber requires time (Lum et al., 2012). The public's desire for prompt attention to their concerns contributes to some of this pressure, and even when improvements are made in the way police perform their duties, it can still be problematic. This is due to the fact that people are accustomed to police responding to service requests in a reactive manner (Kalyal, 2020). Aside from time, other research has indicated that financial, technologicalman resource costs are barriers to EBP adoption (Kalyal, 2020; Telep and Lum, 2014). Therefore, having analysts who are already compensated resources who can conduct researchresearch, and evaluation can be beneficial to police agencies (Piza and Feng, 2017; Piza et al., 2020).

2.2.3.1.7. External Factors

Since policing is a public institution, political will and public opinion can have an impact on whether or not EBP is adopted (Lum et al., 2012). When police agencies bargain for objectives and tactics that meet the needs of the public grants them legitimacy (and funding). In addition to funding and government policies, public opinion can influence advocacy group demands and policies that may run counter to scientific findings (Davies and Nutley, 2008; Frambach and Schillewaert, 2002; Greenhalgh et al., 2004, Lum et al., 2012). It's also possible that some legislators or oversight organizations won't be persuaded by or hostile to EBP (Kalyal, 2020). However, the need to justify operations or expenditures, as well as the need for police reform, may be the driving forces behind the adoption of EBP (Kalyal, 2019). Police leaders bear the responsibility of furnishing oversight bodies with context, perspective, and research evidence regarding police work in these forums and in gaining support. This is particularly important since, frequently, oversight bodies are merely presented with police statistics as a gauge of police outputs and outcomes (Kalyal, 2020). By offering objective analytical products that address political concerns and pressure, analysts can assist police leadership.

Though their acceptance of the research is limited by the risks associated with policing, daily operations disruptions, and resource constraints, officers were not entirely hostile to it. Despite decades of evaluative research, police practice continues to support a standard model of policing that emphasizes quick response to calls, random patrols, and reactive investigations. Nevertheless, they were unaware of effective police practices. This could be partly explained by the way that research is presented and made available. Translating and internalizing external research is a critical function of analysts. Supporting and developing the ideas of hot spots policing and problem-oriented policing would be one chance for analysts.

2.4. CRIME ANALYSIS AND EVIDENCE-BASED POLICING STRATEGIES

Modern law enforcement relies crime analysis and evidence-based policing, which provide tactics based on data and research to increase the efficacy of crime prevention and intervention initiatives. In order toTo increase public safety and community trust, these strategies concentrate on comprehending crime trends, assessing policing strategies, and putting tested ideas into practice.

The methodical examination of crime data to find trends, patterns, and correlations that can direct law enforcement efforts is known as crime analysis. Law enforcement can more efficiently allocate resources by using tools like predictive analytics to forecast potential criminal activity, statistical models to identify trends, and geographic information systems (GIS) to map crime hotspots. Police departments can target areas with higher crime rates, recognize new threats, and take proactive rather than reactive measures thanks to this data-driven approach.

Evidence-based policing prioritizes tactics that have been shown to work by empirical research, building on the understandings obtained from crime analysis. This approach emphasizes the use of research and data to determine the most effective policing methods, rather than depending on tradition or anecdotal evidence. For instance, research has shown that hot spot policing, which concentrates resources on areas with high crime concentrations, significantly lowers crime rates. In a similar vein, problem-oriented policing, which aims to pinpoint and deal with the root causes of crime, has demonstrated efficacy in a number of settings.

These strategies must be continuously evaluated and adjusted to ensure their success. Law enforcement organizations need to continually evaluate the results of their tactics, modify their plans in light of fresh information, and keep an open mind when it comes to implementing novel techniques. To improve these strategies and make sure they are receptive to community needs, cooperation with academic researchers, community stakeholders, and other law enforcement agencies is essential. Law enforcement agencies can improve their capacity to prevent and reduce crime by incorporating evidence-based policing and crime analysis into their daily operations. This will ultimately lead to safer communities and more effective policing practices.

Analysts and crime analysis play important roles in EBP, but analysts also need to be aware of the current role that crime analysis plays in law enforcement. Similar to criminology, crime analysis seeks to combine existing knowledge about crime from a decontextualized perspective (Peterson, 1990; Cope, 2004). Analysts target and track crime patterns and trends, providing decision makers with solutions at the tactical and strategic levels (Evans and Kebbell, 2012). They also convert information and data into actionable intelligence for operations (Cope, 2004).

2.4.1. Utilization and Weak Integration of Analysis in Policing

Numerous scholars worldwide have discovered that analysis is consistently underutilized and poorly integrated into policing (Sissens, 2008; Sanders et al., Sanders and Condon, 2017; Santos and Taylor, 2014; Belur and Johnson, 2018). There is still more to be done to guarantee that analysis forms the basis of modern policing (Telep and Lum, 2014). Studies have revealed organizational and structural barriers, such as mistrust of analytical work, police hierarchy (civilian vs. (O'Shea and Nicholls, 2003; MacVean and Harfeld, 2008; Sissens, 2008; Belur and Johnson, 2018; Taylor and Boba, 2011) include the traditional reactive model of policing, the standard reactive model, a lack of support for innovation, a lack of understanding of the role of analysts, poor relationships between analysts and sworn staff, limited or basic training, and a lack of promotion opportunities. Instead of being used for proactive goals, analytical work is still being used to support the traditional model of policing, which emphasizes statistical summaries and supports a predominate enforcement/reactive approach to policing.

Lum and Koper's audacious claim belies the body of research that shows analysts still endorse the traditional police model, which places a premium on reactive investigations, random patrols, and quick responses (Lum et al., 2012; Sherman and associates., 1997; Eck and Weisburd, 2004). Police departments that use conventional policing techniques will request work from their analysts in order to further this goal. But analysts will be working more pro-actively if a police department wants to be data-driven and proactive.

According to Santos (2014), analysts have a very small role in a typical policing model. For management meetings such as CompStat (Lum, 2013; Lum and Koper, 2017; Sanders and Condon, 2017; Sanders, Weston, and Schott, 2015), analysts are typically tasked with tracking police activity and counting crimes. They also provide information about offenders to support investigations for arrests and case clearance for short-term, tactical purposes (O'Shea and Nicholls, 2003; Lum and Koper, 2017). In order to enable quick responses to calls, it might also entail determining the appropriate staffing levels based on the volume of calls and crimes (Santos, 2014). This includes the creation of weekly crime statistics, crime maps, and charts, as well as regular administrative reports about the quantity, location, and timing of crimes (Cope, 2004; Weisburd and Eck, 2004; Santos, 2014; Belur and Johnson, 2018). Analysis is primarily descriptive and summarizes what has already happened; it is not used to reduce crime (Cope, 2004; Santos, 2014). Importantly, analysts are too busy gathering and purging data to devote much time to a deeper comprehension of crime issues. As a result, they are unable to supply information that would enable targeted, specialized responses to crime issues (O'Shea and Nicholls, 2003; Keay and Kirby, 2017; Belur and Johnson, 2018). Therefore, it is not unexpected that some members of the sworn staff might not think analytical products are helpful (Lum et al., 2017). Rather, the work on crime analysis ought to be useful in directing efforts towards reducing crime (Boba and Santos, 2011; Taylor and Boba, 2011).

In addition, a typical police model heavily depends on the enforcement of the law and reactive arrests as a means of controlling crime (Weisburd and Eck, 2004; Cope, 2004; Taylor et al., 2008). In fact, Chan (2001) discovered that when analytical work aided in an arrest, police officers valued it. Additionally, the primary users of analytical work are police managers, who typically prioritize making quick arrests over longer-term strategic decisions by relying more often on tactical analysis (O'Shea and Nicholls, 2003; Taylor and Boba, 2011; Santos and Taylor, 2014). O'Shea and Nicholls (2003) discovered, surprisingly, that crime analysts preferred tactical analysis over strategic analysis. This finding may indicate that analysts have integrated themselves into police culture and now see the success of their work as directly related to the number of arrests it results in.

According to O'Shea and Nicholls (2003), "if police operations and management are designed to identify and apprehend offenders, then the demand for data analysis will confirm to that limited philosophy," which is similar to Lum and Koper's (2017) statement regarding the use of analysts as reflective of its function and purpose. The nature of data analysis and the need for it will change, as will the role of crime analysts, if, on the other hand, a more expansive goal and vision is created that aims to comprehend the complexity of the criminal incident.

Similarly, O'Shea and Nicholls's (2003) research demonstrated that crime analysis studies did not delve deeper into issues to identify the root causes of community issues. Sanders and Condon (2017) even went so far as to say that crime analysts provide police with crime data by synthesizing, articulating, and visualizing it. Crime analysis, therefore, does not alter or question conventional police practices or ways of knowing, but rather reinforces them. Analysts' analytical output does not instruct police on how to handle the issue or explain why it is occurring.

Police departments can benefit from the assistance of crime analysts in carrying out proactive, focused, and preventive work. Crime analysis hasn't, however, fully realized its potential to direct operations, help police agencies be proactive, or aid in problem solving (Cope, 2004; Santos and Taylor, 2014; Koper et al.). As a result, it hasn't yet become essential to policing operations (Cope, 2004). 2015; Lum and associates. 2017). Research on analysis usually helps managers make decisions that aim to defend their current course of action (Cope, 2004; MacVean and Harfeld, 2008; Sanders et al., 2015). Sanders and Condon (2017) conducted field research and found that analysts are often asked to confirm information that officers already know, and that their work is guided by officers who may not always know what they need or how to use an analyst: "The field note expert above illustrates how analytical knowledge provided to police officers both constrains analytical development and impedes the integration of analysis.."

2.4.2. Barriers to Integrating Crime Analysis Into Policing

In addition to a number of structural and cultural barriers, "poor working conditions, a lack of management support, inadequately trained staff to fill positions, and inadequate renumeration to attract the right staff" are additional factors contributing to this lack of integration (Evans and Kebbell, 2012b).

2.4.2.1. Structural Barriers

Let's concentrate on time and resources when addressing structural barriers. To guarantee that sufficient analysis is being done, police agencies must have a sufficient number of analysts. Budget cuts may have an impact on recruiting or retaining analysts; if there are fewer analysts, this may lead to analyses that are less in-depth and analysts who perform routine administrative work (Belur and Johnson, 2018; Wartell and Gallagher, 2012). Increasing data volumes that call for speedy analyses may exacerbate this (Belur and Johnson, 2018). In addition, analysts require support in the form of adequate time and tools to enable them to perform their duties effectively (MacVean and Harfeld, 2008).

Good analytical work in policing requires time, much like good research (Ratcliffe, 2016; Belur and Johnson, 2018). This can be contrasted with the inclination of law enforcement to concentrate on immediate, tactical issues and hastily assembled reactive solutions, rather than appreciating the complexity of issues through thorough investigation (Belur and Johnson, 2018). According to an analyst who was interviewed, "the police are very impatient culturally" (Belur and Johnson, 2018). Analysts may encounter unjustifiable demands from upper management regarding the time and resources required to fulfill requests (Belur and Johnson, 2018). Like researchers, analysts work in a time-consuming, rigorous manner, which may not always align with the quick fixes that law enforcement officials need (Lum et al., 2012). Regretfully, this implies that analysts are performing cursory analyses when they would prefer to have more time to complete quality work (Cope, 2004). Additionally, some analysts believe their time and effort are undervalued despite the fact that they put forth great effort in producing their work (Belur and Johnson, 2018). Analysts are occasionally just extracting data rather than interpreting it due to the growing volume of data and the added pressure to find quick fixes (Belur and Johnson, 2018). According to Keay and Kirby (2018), an analyst would be better able to comprehend crime issues if they were given more time to conduct in-depth analysis, including developing and testing hypotheses, gathering larger data sets, and using appropriate research methods.

2.4.2.2. Cultural Barriers

There are cultural barriers in addition to structural ones. We will talk about two main topics: (i) failing to recognize the importance of analysis in policing (inadvertent resistance) and (ii) failing to recognize the importance of analysis in policing (intentional resistance). A portion of the inadequate incorporation of crime analysis can be attributed to a culture of policing that is unreceptive to change and innovative methods of enforcement (Chan, 2001; Boba Santos and Taylor, 2014; Belur and Johnson, 2018).

2.4.2.3. Failing to Understand the Role of Analysis in Policing (Unintentional Resistance)

Numerous academics have suggested that a general lack of knowledge about analysis, its function in policing, the analyst's role in policing, and the analyst's capabilities may be the cause of this lack of integration (Cope, 2004; Belur and Johnson, 2018; Burcher and Whelan, 2018). Most importantly for analysts, a breakdown in communication can occur when officers do not comprehend the role of analysts and analysis in policing (MacVean and Harfeld, 2008; Santos and Taylor, 2014; Belur and Johnson, 2018; Cope, 2004). In addition to a "lack of agreed methodologies, techniques, and even definitions of what intelligence is," this is complicated by the diversity and conceptual ambiguity of the role of analysts in policing (Belur and Johnson, 2018). This misunderstanding may result in managers assigning analysts to tasks that are not suitable for them. It is crucial to be clear about tasking because it can cause analysts to feel overworked or underutilized, which can lead to subpar analytical output and a lack of confidence in the validity of the analyst's work and analysis. The simple fact that managers and senior leadership lack training is a significant factor in subpar tasking (Ratcliffe, 2009). Because they are unsure of what their analysts are capable of and how sophisticated of an analysis they can perform, some managers believe that they are not giving their analysts enough work (Belur and Johnson, 2018). As a result, analysts are merely restating what officers already know and are not offering products that can be put into practice (Cope, 2004; MacVean and Harfeld, 2008; Santos and Taylor, 2014; Sanders and Condon, 2017; Belur and Johnson, 2018). It is the duty of managers to make sure that the requests that analysts receive have purpose and will result in action (Cope, 2004).

The quality of the data analysts receive, the lack of task clarity, and the incapacity of some analysts to speak up when requests are unclear due to police hierarchy all contribute to this negative cycle of tasking that results in subpar analytical work, which in turn leads to a lack of trust and legitimacy (Belur and Johnson, 2018; Cope, 2004; Evans and Kebbell, 2012b). As a result, analysts might not have the chance to fully comprehend what officers require (Cope, 2004). For analysts and officers, this results in a "no-win situation" (Cope, 2004; Santos and Taylor, 2014). Then, one might wonder, "Why not have the analyst lead the process if officers and managers are not knowledgeable about analytical work or what their analysts actually do?" While this has some merit, unsolicited products, no matter how well done, have no operational value if they are not actionable or do not meet operational needs (Cope, 2004; Taylor and Boba, 2011; Santos and Taylor, 2014).

2.4.2.4. Failing to Appreciate the Role of Analysis in Policing (Intentional Resistance)

Regretfully, there are instances in which police deliberately obstruct analysis (Cope, 2004; Sissens, 2008; Atkinson, 2016). For instance, according to Cope (2004), O'Shea and Nicholls (2002), Sanders et al., some analysts have stated that they feel ignored or unsupported by their sworn colleagues. 2015; Taylor and others. 2008). We will talk about a few topics that highlight this point: (i) the undervaluation of analysts in a police hierarchy just because they are considered "civilians"; (ii) the idea that police expertise is the only kind of expertise that counts in policing; and (iii) the challenges analysts encounter when making recommendations based on their analysis.

Researchers have noted that a police hierarchy that minimizes the work of analysts—who are usually civilians—has contributed to the underappreciation of analysts and their analytical work (Cope, 2004; Lum, 2013; Santos and Taylor, 2014; Taylor et al., 2008). Cope (2004) discovered that sworn analysts' work was valued more highly than comparable work produced by civilian analysts. According to Atkinson (2016), analysts who are viewed as 'infantilized,' that is, as unsophisticated and immature, are subjected to even greater deprofessionalization. Because of the "need to know" mentality in law enforcement, this can occasionally lead to the witing of important information from them (Cope, 2004).

The concept of "infantilization" may have originated in a society that valued police experience more highly than other viewpoints. But "street" experience isn'tis not the only experience that police deave access to, nor is it the only experience that modern police departments can benefit from (Ericson and Haggerty, 1997 in Cope, 2004). Police agencies need to be progressive, effective, and efficient in order toto operate in the fast-paced, complex social world of today. This calls for a diversity of perspectives and experiences to be incorporated into their own organizations. This might necessitate a dramatic shift in the way that "expertise" is understood in law enforcement and the recognition of people according to their roles rather than their rank (Cope, 2004).

When analysts are brought in to translate external knowledge into police operations, they may become resistant to the emphasis on policing experience. Analytical work may put more pressure on analysts' specialization and challenge officers' discretion and autonomy as policing becomes more data-driven (Chan, 2001). In contrast to officers' firsthand accounts, analytical work aims to present a more comprehensive, objective picture of crime and police data (Cope, 2004). As we've seen, anything that seems to deviate from experiences should be viewed with suspicion (Belur and Johnson, 2018; Cope, 2004; Crank, 1998; Lum et al.). Offcer autonomy is a crucial component of policing culture. as well as Sissens (2008) and Telep and Lum (2014). Nonetheless, sworn employees will respect and legitimize analysts if they recognize the complementary potential between leveraging officer experience and the demands of analytical work (Dolly and Shawver, 2018), and this will produce "a new generation of crime experts" (Cope, 2004). By promoting the knowledge of analysts, pracademics—offcers with advanced training and research abilities—play a crucial role in establishing legitimacy and trust within the police hierarchy (Braga, 2016; Santos and Taylor, 2014).

Analytical work must explain the what, so what, and now what—that is, why a problem exists, why it matters, and what can be done about it—in order to be considered actionable. It cannot just be descriptive. The importance of the latter cannot be overstated: analysts can include research findings in the range of options they provide to decision makers regarding possible courses of action. For analysts, describing and analyzing a problem, identifying its main contributing factors, and then providing decision makers with relevant options based on that analysis, research evidence, and police experience should be a logical and natural next step.

According to certain studies (Cope, 2004; Sissens, 2008; Weston, Bennett-Moses, and Sanders, 2020; Weston, Bennett-Moses, and Sanders, 2019), there may be opposition to the idea of analysts making recommendations, even though some officers do (Belur and Johnson, 2018). For instance, "a supervisory intelligence manager said that it can be quite demoralizing for analysts to get knocked back by senior officers when they get creative and make original recommendations in their reports" (Belur and Johnson, 2018).

Analysts are typically expected to perform analysis only; they are not expected to choose or help implement solutions (Santos, 2012; Belur and Johnson, 2018). Remember that there are a few reasons for this: (i) officers were more comfortable with research as long as it aligned with their experiences than with research/analysis; (ii) officers were skeptical of analysis because it tries to find novel solutions. Analysts are supposed to be "identifying trends and predicting problems" instead (Belur and Johnson, 2018). Once more, this compels analysts to forego more in-depth problem solving in favor of cursory and descriptive analysis. A portion of this opposition stems from the idea that analysts and analysis pose a threat to the status quo in law enforcement by offering creative substitutes for established tactics (Sissens, 2008). This supports the opposition that solutions are rejected if they do not align well with experience (Belur and Johnson, 2018).

Officers' perception that analysts lack the necessary operational knowledge and experience—given that they are primarily civilian—is a major contributing factor to skepticism and resistance to analytical recommendations (Cope, 2004; Belur and Johnson, 2017).

As stated by analysts themselves (Cope, 2004; Sissens, 2008), they would concur with this. However, it's probable that the hierarchical structure of law enforcement, which prohibits analysts from questioning officers, particularly those in higher positions (Cope, 2004), is molding analysts' perceptions of this and directing their "value" toward supporting the police (even if that means endorsing conventional policing methods). Alternatively, EBP gives analysts the chance to use results from previous studies as a remedy and include that in their suggestions.

2.4.3. The Need for Change

We have looked over the research that shows how poorly crime analysis is integrated into policing. It is still based on an antiquated policing model, which restricts analysts' ability to successfully integrate into operations. Arrests are the main focus, and analysts aren't asked to solve more complex problems; instead, they are only required to administratively count crimes and identify people who police can detain. We observed both structural and cultural barriers. The impact of not having enough time and resources for high-quality analytical work was discussed in relation to structural barriers. When there is a perception that police are always dealing with crises and thus require quick fixes, poor analysis can be influenced by police culture. We looked at cultural barriers in terms of circumstances where inadvertent resistance arises from inadequate tasking, a lack of managerial training regarding analysis, and general ignorance regarding analysts' capabilities. As a result, there is a lack of legitimacy and trust in analysts and their work, which feeds a vicious cycle of analysts performing pointless, superficial analyses. While it is evident that this kind of resistance is unintentional, instances of deliberate resistance against analysts and their work have also been documented. This includes the devaluation of analysts due to their status as mere citizens, the overemphasis placed on police experience at the expense of other skills required for modern policing to be effective and efficient, and the opposition analysts encounter when they offer recommendations. As the last section of this chapter will demonstrate, EBP presents a fresh chance for analysis to become a pillar of modern policing.

2.4.3.1. Shifting Police Culture to be Evidence Based

It must be recognized that analysis is a specialty with numerous obstacles to be surmounted before it can be regarded as a tool essential to the policing function in an organizational culture that has not historically relied on evidence-based analysis to guide decision-making. Analysis provides a crucial and worthwhile function that cannot be carried out "in the heads or mindsets" of police officers. This is especially true of strategic and volume crime analysis. Before analysis can truly have an impact, there must be a shift in culture. Although there is evidence that this is occurring, the integration of these two very different cultures will need to happen gradually because analysis runs counter to long-standing, customary policing procedures (Sissens, 2008).

Sissens (2008) contends that a substantial cultural shift is necessary before the gap between research evidence (and analysis) and practice can be closed. One could argue that external social and political pressures are forcing police agencies to operate more effectively and efficiently. Analysis must play a central role in policing in order to implement effective evidence-based practices (Lum,

2009, 2013; Santos, 2014). Reiterating Lum and Koper's (2017) compelling claim that "how analysts are deployed reflects how an agency views its function and purpose" is crucial (also see Sanders and Condon, 2017). Analysts who work for police departments that support evidence-based practice (EBP) should be involved in "the development, implementation, and evaluation of tactics and strategies...that are evidence based," as analytical work ultimately supports the agency's policing approach (Lum, 2013; Lum and Koper, 2017). Because they possess the skills necessary for their jobs, such as critical thinking abilities, knowledge of research methodology, problem solving abilities, and effective communication, effective crime analysts are well-positioned to be strong and effective proponents of EBP (Evans and Kebbell, 2012). Crucially, an internal mechanism that can support the implementation of EBP is the active use of crime analysis products (Lum, 2009; Telep and Lum, 2014).

Regretfully, Lum and Koper (2017) draw attention to the fact that analysts frequently receive greater support when generating standard crime statistics than when participating in EBP-supporting activities. Crime analysis is essential to EBP, and in order for EBP to be sustained, police culture and sworn personnel need to understand what analysis is, what an analyst does, and how EBP works. All of this, though, depends on the senior leadership, who establish the organization's direction and culture. Effective police techniques that are "focused, targeted, place based (when appropriate), and problem oriented" must be unambiguously endorsed by the leadership (Lum and Koper, 2017). To support EBP, leadership must also make investments in crime analysis (Lum, 2013; Lum and Koper, 2017). This entails giving analysis top priority by helping analysts advance professionally and by hiring more analysts (Lum et al., (2012); Kirby and Keay (2018)). Since analysts are frequently pulled in different directions, having more analysts will help EBP continue because it will free up more time for high-caliber research and analysis (Lum and Koper, 2017; Piza et al., 2020).

2.4.3.2. Redefining the Role of Analysts in Policing

The idea that analysts support police operations is one that is frequently brought up in discussions about their role in law enforcement. Analysts have an unofficial leadership opportunity. This calls for a respect for various policing specializations (rather than just police experience), but as previously indicated, it also calls for a recognition of an individual's role in relation to their rank, which would necessitate a profound cultural shift. While crime analysis is an active supporting component of policing approaches such as CompStat, intelligence-led policing, and EBP, analysts who support the standard model of policing play a passive supportive role. The fact that the majority of analysts are not asked to participate in problem-solving discussions or the planning of solutions, let alone attend management meetings, amply illustrates a passive role (Lum, 2013). There are those who contend that analysts, especially those in senior positions, ought to be considered exceptionally skilled experts who should be regarded as professional peers of sworn managers. They should collaborate closely with command staff and help to steer these gatherings (Lum, 2013; Lum and Koper, 2017).

Analysts should actively assist with policing. They ought to offer suggestions for action to those in charge (MacVean and Harfeld, 2008). Studies indicate that the traditional view of analysts as technicians is gradually beginning to shift, with analysts now considered to be "part of a support structure for decision-makers" (Evans and Kebbell, 2012). As a problem solver, consultant, and "decision-makers' associate," they are perceived in various ways (Evans and Kebbell, 2012; additionally, see Keay and Kirby, 2018). Analysts should be involved in more than just counting crimes; their work should encompass "developing strategies for crime prevention and community engagement, working with line-level staff to solve problems, tracking and investigating problematic locations and individuals, conducting evaluations and other research projects, and analyzing community and organizational issues that go beyond crime prevention" (Lum and Koper, 2017; see also Lum, 2013 and Piza et al., 2020).

2.4.3.3. Analysts as Informal Leaders in Policing

With this newfound chance, analysts must take initiative, intentionally influence others, and, in some cases, assume the role of unofficial police leaders. Despite lacking a formal leadership title, informal leaders possess the ability to motivate teams to take action, cultivate relationships, take initiative, and assist others by drawing on their knowledge (Smart, 2010). Proficient analysts exhibit traits of leadership. In their research, Evans and Kebbell (2012) discovered that having leadership skills is essential for an effective analyst. These analysts are not merely technicians; rather, they are problem-solving associates who assist decision makers. They are well-known for being "do-ers," self-starters, and deeply dedicated to their work (Evans and Kebbell, 2012). Information that sparks discussion on original and creative solutions is what analysts should be producing (O'Shea and Nicholls, 2003). Proactive analysts help decision makers allocate resources and prioritize issues (Belur and Johnson, 2018). As a police chief introduced EBP to their agency, a case study found tht crime analysts played a crucial role in the culture shift. According to Dolly and Shawver (2018), "their enthusiasm for using data and evidence to solve problems was contagious, creating excitement to use their services for projects.."

2.5. THE ROLE OF CRIME ANALYSTS IN EVIDENCE-BASED POLICING

There is a lot of potential for analysts to play a more active role than previously mentioned within an EBP framework. In addition to assisting police departments with research generation, translation, and dissemination, crime analysts can also assist them in identifying crime issues, gathering community opinion, and assessing initiatives (Lum and Koper, 2017; Piza et al., 2020; Feng and Piza, 2017). Crime analysts can assist law enforcement organizations in implementing evidence-based strategies like hotspot policing or focusing on people who are most likely to commit crimes (Lum and Koper, 2017).

2.5.1. Crime Analysts' Role in Generating Research Evidence

There are many instances where analysts contribute to the creation of research evidence. Indeed, as Lum and Koper (2017) note, researchers at George Mason University's Center for Evidence-Based Crime Policy worked with crime analysts to conduct a number of the studies included in the Evidence-Based Policing Matrix. But more significantly, some academics have discussed what has to be done to better equip crime analysts to support EBP in addition to offering pertinent criticisms of the analytical methods used today.

According to some academics, analytical work reflects past events rather than accurately reflecting the state of crime today (Innes et al., 2005). Moreover, some people think that analytical work is low quality, unreliable, merely descriptive, and superficial (Belur and Johnson, 2018; Cope, 2004; Chainey, 2012; Innes et al., 2005). Additionally, keep in mind that analysts frequently prefer to support administrative duties over conducting analysis (Sissens, 2008).

Researchers need to improve their research skills if they are interested in producing research. Evans and Kebbell (2012) pointed out that strong academic research abilities are a prerequisite for effective analysis, and analysts have not received enough training in this area (Sissens, 2008; Townsley et al., 2011; Johnson and Belur, 2018).

Current theory and research are also important for analysts to be aware of (Evans, 2008 in Keay and Kirby, 2018; Weston, Bennett-Moses, and Sanders, 2020). Some (O'Shea and Nicholls, 2003; Cope, 2004; see also Piza et al.) have noted that if analytical processes could be improved by incorporating scientific rigor and advanced data analysis, analytical work could be more consistent and reliable. 2020). This might be achieved by fostering more collaborations between academics and practitioners or by making evaluation a core component of analyst training (Piza et al., 2020; Feng and Piza, 2017).

2.5.2. Contributing to the Evidence Base

In the past, police have relied on academic expertise to evaluate their own tactics and strategies, but this is one of the most important ways that police can contribute to the creation of research evidence (Piza et al. (Piza and Feng, 2017; 2020). In contrast, academics and crime analysts have recently made the case that police ought to play a larger role in the creation of policing research and evaluation (Huey and Mitchell, 2016; Sparrow, 2011; Piza and Feng, 2017; Piza et al., 2020; Neyroud and Weisburd, 2011). Academics and crime analysts are more likely to be completing advanced degrees or have already obtained one, and they are also competent to conduct internal assessments on their own (Evans and Kebbell, 2012; Huey and Mitchell, 2016; Piza and Feng, 2017). More importantly, having internal staff members involved in evaluations is advantageous because they will increase the actionability of research findings and have "insider" contextual knowledge of policing (Piza et al., 2020). Crime analysts are therefore ideal candidates for producing police research because of their expertise in police operations and their analytical skills (Piza and Feng, 2017).

Piza and associates. (2020) examined how police personnel perceived different "roles" in EBP and discovered that analysts of criminal justice were thought to be "easier to incorporate into police program evaluation activities than pracademics" (It is possible to adapt a large portion of the work analysts currently perform for tactical and strategic goals to serve evaluative purposes (Piza et al., 2020). Since analytical products are meant to support efforts to reduce crime, it makes sense to measure this reduction in addition to identifying strategies to do so (Piza and Feng, 2017).

The fact that analysts can devote their entire attention to this kind of work, unlike academics who might have to take time away from other possible responsibilities, is another advantage of having analysts involved in the generation of evidence (Piza and Feng, 2017). Regretfully, studies have shown that analysts only spend a small percentage of their time evaluating, and when they do, it's mostly for managerial objectives (Santos and Taylor, 2014; Piza and Feng, 2017). In fact, according to Evans and Kebbell (2012), police personnel hardly ever cited "evaluation" as a crucial ability for skilled analysts.

It is plausible that the low frequency of evaluations in policing is the reason why analysts are not participating in them as frequently (Evans and Kebbell, 2012). Even though it is well recognized that having crime analysts participate in evaluations is beneficial, analysts might not possess the necessary abilities (Cope, 2004; Boba, 2013). Piza and associates. (2020) discovered that when it came to research and evaluation skills, analysts received the lowest scores from their respondents (compared to pracademics and academics). Lum and Koper (2017) contend that while this may not be true for all analysts or agencies, some do possess the necessary scientific background to produce thorough evaluations. Furthermore, training or partnerships between academics and practitioners could improve these abilities (Piza et al., 2020; Feng and Piza, 2017).

2.5.3. Implementing the Evidence Base

One of the main forces behind the implementation of EBP can also be analysts (Lum and Koper, 2017). They can help police departments locate hotspots, target persistent and serious offenders, investigate the underlying causes of trends and patterns, and subsequently support ongoing efforts to prevent crime (Lum and Koper, 2017). In addition to bolstering intelligence-led strategies, focusing on persistent and severe offenders may also entail risk assessments of offenders or be coupled with hotspot policing (Ratcliffe, 2016; Egge, 2011; Lum and Koper, 2017). Additionally, analysts can delve deeper into police issues and practice problem solving, which combines social science methods with standard crime analysis approaches and criminological theory (Eck, 1998; O'Shea and Nicholls, 2003; Lum and Koper, 2017). Analysts can help decision makers understand the causes and facilitators of crime and disorder by solving problems (Reuland, 1997 in O'Shea and Nicholls, 2003). While analysts help with the implementation of EBP, they must remember that in the end, EBP needs to be implemented at different organizational levels; their work cannot simply stay with management. This exact concept is actually put forth by Boba and Santos (2011) in their model of stratified policing, which describes a methodical approach to applying EBP and crime analysis. According to this approach, EBP and related crime analysis products are customized for various ranks and roles.

2.5.4. Translating the Evidence Base

Since directed hotspot policing has been shown to be effective through years of research, the use of random patrols is one of the most glaring examples of the disconnect between research and practice (Weisburd, 2008 in Lum et al., 2012). Remember that there were two obstacles that prevented better integration of EBP in law enforcement: (i) a large portion of research is restricted by paywalls; and (ii) research papers are long and laden with technical terms. It could be argued that because crime analysts are required to produce work products that are easily assimilated, actionable, and quick to read, they have a unique advantage over other researchers in terms of exposure to research. As a result, crime analysts may play a significant part in interpreting research and putting it to use in law enforcement.

In addition to participating in the integration of external research into law enforcement, analysts may also have the opportunity to contribute internal knowledge to external research initiatives (Piza et al., 2020). Lum and associates. (2012) noted that if familiar and internal mechanisms of information dissemination are used to present research findings, "research and researchers may be better received in police agencies." They also suggested that researchers need to be more creative if they want to reach police audiences, and that working with crime analysts may be one way to do so.

In addition to producing research, police leaders, researchers, and analysts should consider how to "package" their findings and processes to make them relevant to police audiences and officers' daily experiences (Lum et al., 2012).

Because they have both technical expertise and "insider police" knowledge from their interactions with officers, analysts can be useful in knowledge translation (Boba, 2010 in Piza and Feng, 2017). They can assist police leadership in determining whether their tactics and strategies are in line with research by using their understanding of EBP to instruct officers. Piza and associates. (2020) discovered that crime analysts were the next most suitable group to translate research for police, after pracademics. Finally, in spite of these beneficial chances for analysts to participate in the translation of research, Piza et al. (2020) also note that role clarity and analysts' position within the police hierarchy may present challenges, as analysts are frequently pulled in different directions that do not always align with EBP.

2.5.5. Providing Recommendations

The contentious nature of analysts making recommendations to sworn staff was covered earlier. According to Sissens (2008), implementing recommendations is a key strategy for enhancing the use of analysts. Police leadership is crucial to the success of these recommendations because without it, the analysis's value may be compromised (Belur and Johnson, 2018). When analytical work is done well, it clarifies the issue more, which logically leads to suggestions and possible solutions (Cope, 2004). Opportunities for intervention should be presented by analytical work (MacVean and Harfeld, 2008). Good analysts offer suggestions that are supported by the data (Evans and Kebbell, 2012). Cope (2004) highlights a crucial distinction: "It is necessary to emphasize the distinction between the capacity to make recommendations based on research and analysis with the capacity to make decisions about adopting recommendations and directing action," despite the fact that some officers are reluctant to accept recommendations from analysts. Stated differently, the ability to make recommendations and the decision to act upon them are two different things; analysts are primarily responsible for the former, while sworn staff is in charge of the latter. Maintaining open lines of communication with officers to learn about their needs, issues, and pressure points is a crucial part of making recommendations. By doing this, analysts have the chance to build and preserve trust with officers (Belur and Johnson, 2018).

2.5.6. Effective Communication

Analysts must be skilled communicators if they are to be trusted and their recommendations to be accepted as genuine. These abilities are essential for analysts to effectively communicate information to a variety of audiences (IACA, 2018 in Weston, Bennett-Moses, and Sanders, 2020). With the possibility of counterarguments, analysts need to be able to speak confidently about their work in communication (Evans and Kebbell, 2012). This may also require analysts to have effective communication skills in more casual contexts where they must exhibit strong interpersonal skills (Evans and Kebbell, 2012; Weston et al., 2020) or in formal settings where they must instruct sworn staff about analysis (IACA, 2018 in Weston, Bennett-Moses, and Sanders, 2020).

Studies have indicated that analysts are frequently not given clear instructions about what is expected of them, and that this, along with police hierarchy that prevents analysts from "pushing back" against sworn requestors, results in analysts producing products that are useless for the requestor (Cope, 2004; Chainey, 2012; Belur and Johnson, 2018). This feeds a vicious cycle of mistrust that eventually results in analysts being underutilized (Evans and Kebbell, 2012b). When it comes to task clarity, analysts' (and analytical managers') interpersonal and informal communication skills are crucial more than anywhere else (Belur and Johnson, 2018). This is used to describe a situation in which an analyst is assigned by a requestor, and the analyst then negotiates the "terms of reference" with the requestor, outlining what can and will be done. In order to ensure that the request is fulfilled, this should be a cooperative effort in which the requestor gives background information about the issue they are bringing to the analyst, and the analyst uses their analytical skills to suggest the best way to show the requestor what they are looking for. Senior analysts may collaborate directly with the requestor in order to ensure that the "development of the product is organic," even though analytical managers can help with this (Belur and Johnson, 2018).

2.5.7. Collaboration with Officers

The goal of EBP is to combine police experience and academia (Piza et al., 2020). Seeking their expertise to inform research ideas, giving them feedback on the process and results of the research, and, if they are interested, involving them in research projects are some possible strategies for encouraging officers to support research (Lum et al., 2012). According to Cope (2004), "what analysts and officers need to strive for is a balance between their words: reconciling the grounded, contextual knowledge with overviews of data" also applies to the officer-analyst partnership. Analysts must establish credibility and trust with officers in order for their analysis and recommendations to be well-received (Belur and Johnson, 2018). Because police problems are intricate and multifaceted, it is essential that analysts and officers collaborate to create win-win situations (*see* Burcher and Whelan, 2018). When these relationships give analysts the priceless context for their analysis, they can enhance the receptivity of their work. Officers gain from these connections by being exposed to fresh viewpoints and having the chance to express their own (Boba, 2013; Evans and Kebbell, 2012; Lum et al., 2012; Sanders, Weston, and Bennett-Moses, 2020).

Partnerships between officers and analysts also have certain additional advantages. First, we talked about how, unless it was actionable, even excellent unsolicited analytical work can be met with resistance (Belur and Johnson, 2018; Santos and Taylor, 2014; Taylor and Boba, 2011; Taylor et al., 2008). Analysts would be more likely to produce work that matches operational experience and becomes more actionable if they included officers and their perspectives in the development process. According to Taylor et al., it aids analysts in comprehending operational realities and available resources. (2008); Johnson and Belur, 2018). Furthermore, by supporting crime analysts, pracademics can help them integrate more deeply into real-world police operations and possibly build credibility and trust through collaboration (Braga, 2016; Huey and Mitchell, 2016; Piza et al., 2020). In general, receiving input from sworn employees can help to enhance analytical work in the future (Belur and Johnson, 2018). Regular interaction between analysts and sworn staff can lead to increased task clarity and, ultimately, higher-quality analytical outputs. According to Belur and Johnson (2018), these products have the potential to enhance the credibility and trustworthiness of analysis, thereby driving up demand for analytical work. On the other hand, strengthening this bond can aid in enlightening sworn members about analysis and the benefits analysts can provide (Telep and Lum, 2014). EBP can be advantageous in that it can aid in debunking stereotypes that are ingrained in police culture. g. concerning efficient police procedures) (Lum et al., 2012). Lum and Koper (2017) highlight that in order to fully utilize crime analysis within an evidence-based framework, there is a need to prioritize long-term strategic planning, develop analytical products that are useful to officers, and ensure that all levels of the agency receive the necessary training, coaching, support, and reinforcement.

REFERENCES

1. Atkinson, C. (2016). Patriarchy, gender, infantilisation: A cultural account of police intelligence work in Scotland. *Australian & New Zealand Journal of Criminology, 50*(2), 234–251.
2. Belur, J., & Johnson, S. (2018). Is crime analysis at the heart of policing practice? A case study. *Policing and Society, 28*(7), 768–786.
3. Blaskovits, B., Bennell, C., Huey, L., Kalyal, H., Walker, T., & Javala, S. (2018). A Canadian replication of Telep and Lum's (2014) examination of police officers' receptivity to empirical research. *Policing and Society,* 1–19.
4. Boba Santos, R., & Taylor, B. (2014). The integration of crime analysis into police patrol work: Results from a national survey of law enforcement agencies. *Policing: An International Journal, 37*(3), 501–520.
5. Boba, R. (2010). A practice-based evidence approach in Florida. *Police Practice and Research: An International Journal, 11*(2), 122–128.
6. Boba, R. (2013). *Crime Analysis and Crime Mapping.* Sage Publications, Inc.
7. Boba, R., & Santos, R. (2011). A police organizational model for crime reduction: Institutionalizing problem solving, analysis, and accountability. U.S. Dept. of Justice, Office of Community Oriented Policing Services.
8. Braga, A. A. (2016). The value of 'pracademics' in enhancing crime analysis in police departments. *Policing: A Journal of Policy and Practice, 10*(3), 308–314.
9. Braga, A., Turchan, B., Papachristos, A., & Hureau, D. (2019). Hot spots policing of small geographic areas effects on crime. *Campbell Systematic Reviews.* Retrieved from: https://onlinelibrary.wiley.com/doi/full/10.1002/cl2.1046 (accessed on 14 October 2024).
10. Buerger, M. E. (2010). Policing and research: Two cultures separated by an almost-common language. *Police Practice and Research: An International Journal, 11,* 135–143.
11. Burcher, M., & Whelan, C. (2018). Intelligence-led policing in practice: Reflections from intelligence analysts. *Police Quarterly, 22*(2), 139–160. https://doi.org/10.1177%2F1098611118796890.
12. Chainey, S. (2012). Improving the explanatory content of analysis products using hypothesis testing. *Policing: A Journal of Policy and Practice, 6*(2), 108–121.
13. Chan, J. (2001). The technology game: How information technology is transforming police practice. *Criminal Justice, 1*(2), 139–159.

14. Cherney, A., Antrobus, E., Bennett, S., Bevan, M., & Newman, M. (2018). *Evidence Based Policing: Queensland Police Technical Report.* The University of Queensland School of Social Sciences.
15. Cope, N. (2004). Integrating volume crime analysis into policing. *The British Journal of Criminology, 44,* 188–203.
16. Crank, J. P. (1998). *Understanding Police Culture.* Anderson Publishing Company.
17. Davies, H. T., & Nutley, S. (2008). Learning more about how research-based knowledge gets used. *Unpublished Working Paper.* William T. Grant Foundation.
18. Dolly, C., & Shawver, B. (2018). The organizational and practical considerations of starting a crime analysis unit: A case study of a midwestern police department. *Policing: A Journal of Policy and Practice, 12*(3), 255–264.
19. Eck, J. E. (1998). What do those dots mean? Mapping theories with data. In D. Weisburd & T. McEwen (Eds.), *Crime Mapping and Crime Prevention* (pp. 379–406). Criminal Justice Press.
20. Eck, J. E., & Spelman, W. (1987). *Problem Solving: Problem-Oriented Policing in Newport News.* Police Executive Research Forum.
21. Egge, J. (2011). Experimenting with future-oriented analysis at crime hot spots in Minneapolis. *Geography and Public Safety, 2*(4). National Institute of Justice.
22. Evans, J., & Kebbell, M. (2012). The effective analyst: A study of what makes an effective crime and intelligence analyst. *Policing and Society, 22*(2), 204–219.
23. Evans, J., & Kebbell, M. (2012b). Integrating intelligence into policing practice. In T. Prenzler (Ed.), *Policing and Security in Practice: Challenges and Achievements.* Palgrave Macmillan.
24. Frambach, R. T., & Schillewaert, N. (2002). Organizational innovation adoption: A multi-level framework of determinants and opportunities for future research. *Journal of Business Research, 55*(2), 163–176.
25. Gill, C., Weisburd, D., Telep, C., Vitter, Z., & Bennett. (2014). Community-oriented policing to reduce crime, disorder, and fear and increase satisfaction and legitimacy among citizens: A systematic review. *Journal of Experimental Criminology, 10,* 399–428.
26. Greenhalgh, T., Robert, G., Macfarlane, F., Bate, P., & Kyriakidou, O. (2004). Diffusion of innovations in service organizations: Systematic review and recommendations. *Milbank Quarterly, 82*(4), 581–629.

27. Griffiths, C. (2014). *Economics of Policing: Baseline for Policing Research in Canada.* Report commissioned by Public Safety Canada. Retrieved from: http://www.publicsafety.gc.ca/cnt/rsrcs/pblctns/bsln-plcng-rsrch/index-eng.aspx (accessed on 14 October 2024).
28. Huey, L., & Mitchell, R. J. (2016). Unearthing hidden keys: Why pracademics are an invaluable (if underutilized) resource in policing research. *Policing: A Journal of Policy and Practice, 10*(3), 300–307.
29. Huey, L., Blaskovits, B., Bennell, C., Kalyal, H., & Walker, T. J. (2017). To what extent do Canadian police professionals think that their agencies are 'targeting, testing, and tracking' new police strategies and programs? *Police Practice and Research: An International Journal, 18,* 544–555.
30. Hunter, G., May, T., & Hough, M. (2015). An evaluation of the "What Works Centre for Crime Reduction" final report. Institute for Criminal Policy Research. Retrieved from: https://whatworks.college.police.uk/About/Documents/ICPR_Final_Evaluation_WWCCR.pdf (accessed on 14 October 2024).
31. Innes, M., Fielding, N., & Cope, N. (2005). The appliance of science? The theory and practice of criminal intelligence analysis. *The British Journal of Criminology, 45*(1), 39–57.
32. Kalyal, H. (2019). "Well, there's a more scientific way to do it!": Factors influencing receptivity to evidence-based practices in police organizations. *Police Practice and Research, 21*(6), 609–623.
33. Kalyal, H. (2020). One person's evidence is another person's nonsense: Why police organizations resist evidence-based practices. *Policing: A Journal of Policy and Practice, 14*(4), 1151–1165.
34. Kalyal, H., Peladeau, H., & Huey, L. (2017). Senior officer and recruiter views on "big topics" in policing for new recruits. *Journal of Community Safety and Well-Being, 2*(3), 112–115.
35. Keay, S., & Kirby, S. (2018). The evolution of the police analyst and the influence of evidence-based policing. *Policing: A Journal of Policy and Practice, 12*(3), 265–276.
36. Kelling, G. L., Pate, A. M., Dieckman, D., & Brown, C. (1974). *The Kansas City Preventive Patrol Experiment: Technical Report.* Police Foundation.
37. Koehle, G., Six, T., & Hanrahan, K. J. (2010). Citizen concerns and approval of police performance. *Professional Issues in Criminal Justice, 5*(1), 9–24.
38. Lum, C. (2013). Is crime analysis evidence-based? *Translational Criminology, 5,* 12–14.

39. Lum, C., & Koper, C. (2014). Evidence-based policing. In G. Bruinsma & D. Weisburd (Eds.), *The Encyclopedia of Criminology and Criminal Justice* (pp. 1426–1437). Springer-Verlag.
40. Lum, C., & Koper, C. S. (2017). *Evidence-Based Policing: Translating Research into Practice.* Oxford University Press.
41. Lum, C., Koper, C. S., & Willis, J. (2017). Understanding the limits of technology's impact on police effectiveness. *Police Quarterly, 20*(2), 135–163.
42. Lum, C., Telep, C. W., Koper, C. S., & Grieco, J. (2012). Receptivity to research in policing. *Justice Research and Policy, 14*(1), 61–95.
43. Lumsden, K., & Goode, J. (2018). Policing research and the rise of the 'evidence-base': Police officer and staff understandings of research, its implementation, and 'what works'. *Sociology, 52*(4), 813–829.
44. Palmer, I. (2011). Is the United Kingdom police service receptive to evidence–based policing? Testing attitudes towards experimentation (Unpublished master's thesis; Supervisor: Cynthia Lum). Cambridge University.
45. Piza, E., & Feng, S. (2017). The current and potential role of crime analysts in evaluations of police interventions: Results from a survey of the International Association of Crime Analysts. *Police Quarterly, 20*(4), 339–366.
46. Piza, E., Szokla, J., & Blount-Hill. (2020). How can embedded criminologists, police pracademics, and crime analysts help increase police-led program evaluations? A survey of authors cited in the evidence-based policing matrix. *Policing: A Journal of Policy & Practice.* https://papers.ssrn.com/sol3/papers.cfm?abstract_id=3571391 (accessed on 14 October 2024).
47. Public Safety Canada. (2013). *Summit on the Economics of Policing: Strengthening Canada's Policing Advantage.* Government of Canada.
48. Rojek, J., Alpert, G., & Smith, H. (2012). The utilization of research by the police. *Police Practice and Research, 13*(4), 329–341.
49. Santos, R. (2014). The effectiveness of crime analysis for crime reduction: Cure or diagnosis? *Journal of Contemporary Criminal Justice, 30,* 147–168.
50. Santos, R. (2016). *Crime Analysis and Crime Mapping.* Sage Publications, Inc.
51. Santos, R. B. (2012). *Crime Analysis with Crime Mapping.* Sage.

52. Santos, R. B., & Taylor, B. G. (2014). The integration of crime analysis into police patrol work: Results from a national survey of law enforcement agencies. *Policing: An International Journal of Police Strategies and Management, 37*(3), 501–520.
53. Sherman, L. W. (1998). *Evidence-Based Policing.* Ideas in American policing series. Police Foundation. https://www.policinginstitute.org/wp-content/uploads/2015/06/Sherman-1998-Evidence-Based-Policing.pdf.
54. Sherman, L. W. (2013). The rise of evidence-based policing: Targeting, testing, and tracking. *Crime and Justice, 42*(1), 377–451.
55. Sherman, L. W. (2015). A tipping point for "totally evidenced policing": Ten ideas for building an evidence-based police agency. *International Criminal Justice Review, 25*(1), 11–29.
56. Sherman, L. W., & Eck, J. E. (2002). Policing for crime prevention. In D. P. Farrington, D. L. MacKenzie, L. W. Sherman, & B. C. Welsh (Eds.), *Evidence-Based Crime Prevention* (pp. 295–330). Routledge.
57. Sherman, L. W., Gottfredson, D., MacKenzie, D., Eck, J., Reuter, P., & Bushway, S. (1997). *Preventing Crime: What Works, What Doesn't, What's Promising: A Report to the United States Congress.* U.S. Department of Justice, Office of Justice Programs.
58. Sissens, J. (2008). An evaluation of the role of intelligence analysts within the national intelligence model. In C. Hartfeld, A. MacVean, J. Grieve, & D. Phillips (Eds.), *The Handbook of Intelligent Policing: Consilience, Crime Control and Community Safety* (pp. 121–130). Oxford University Press.
59. Sparrow, M. K. (2015). Measuring performance in a modern police organization. *Psychosociological Issues in Human Resource Management, 3*(2), 17–52.
60. Taylor, B., & Boba, R. (2011). *The Integration of Crime Analysis into Police Work: A Guidebook.* Office of Community Oriented Police Services.
61. Taylor, B., Kowalyk, A., & Boba, R. (2008). The integration of crime analysis into law enforcement agencies: An exploratory study into the perceptions of crime analysts. *Police Quarterly, 10*(2), 154–169.
62. Telep, C. W. (2016). Expanding the scope of evidence-based policing. *Criminology and Public Policy, 15*(1), 243–252. https://onlinelibrary.wiley.com/doi/10.1111/1745-9133.12188 (accessed on 14 October 2024).
63. Telep, C. W. (2017). Police officer receptivity to research and evidence-based policing: Examining variability within and across agencies. *Crime & Delinquency, 63*(8), 976–999.

64. Telep, C. W., & Lum, C. (2014). The receptivity of officers to empirical research and evidence-based policing: An examination of survey data from three agencies. *Police Quarterly, 17*(4), 359–385.
65. Telep, C. W., & Winegar, S. (2016). Police executive receptivity to research: A survey of chiefs and sheriffs in Oregon. *Policing: A Journal of Policy and Practice, 10*(3), 241–249. https://academic.oup.com/policing/article-abstract/10/3/241/1753480 (accessed on 14 October 2024).
66. Townsley, M., Mann, M., & Garrett, K. (2011). The missing link of crime analysis: A systematic approach to testing competing hypotheses. *Policing: A Journal of Policy and Practice, 5*(2), 158–171.
67. Wartell, J., & Gallagher, K. (2012). Translating environmental criminology theory into crime analysis practice. *Policing: A Journal of Policy and Practice, 6*(4), 377–387.
68. Weisburd, D., & Eck, J. (2004). What can police do to reduce crime, disorder, and fear? *The Annals of the American Academy of Political and Social Science, 593*(1), 42–65.
69. Weisburd, D., & Neyroud, P. (2011). Police science: Toward a new paradigm. New perspectives in policing. Executive session on policing and public safety. U.S. Department of Justice, Office of Justice Programs.
70. Weston, C., Bennett-Moses, L., & Sanders, C. (2020). The changing role of the law enforcement analyst: Clarifying core competencies for analysts and supervisors through empirical research. *Policing and Society, 30*(5), 532–547. https://doi.org/10.1080/10439463.2018.1564751.

Chapter 3

Analyzing Reading Cases and Statutes

Contents

Introduction 112

3.1. Analyzing by Reading 112

3.2. The Science of Observation 126

3.3. Analyzing by Asking and Listening 136

3.4. Sources of Statutes 153

References 158

INTRODUCTION

Analyzing crime cases and statutes is a critical aspect of the legal field, requiring a deep understanding of both the facts of individual cases and the broader legal frameworks that govern them. This analysis is essential for legal professionals, scholars, and law enforcement, as it informs decisions in criminal investigations, prosecutions, and defenses.

Crime cases are the practical applications of criminal law, showcasing how statutes are interpreted and enforced in real-life situations. Analyzing these cases involves examining the facts, the actions of the parties involved, and the legal arguments presented. This process often reveals how courts interpret statutes, set precedents, and apply legal principles to specific circumstances. Understanding the nuances of case law is crucial for predicting how future cases might be decided and for formulating effective legal strategies.

Statutes, on the other hand, are the written laws enacted by legislative bodies that define criminal conduct and prescribe penalties. Analyzing statutes requires not only understanding the literal text but also interpreting the intent behind the law, its historical context, and how it fits within the broader legal system. Statutory analysis is essential for determining the applicability of laws to various situations and for identifying potential ambiguities or conflicts within the legal code.

In criminal law, the intersection of case analysis and statutory interpretation is where legal arguments are crafted and contested. Lawyers must skillfully navigate both to build strong cases, whether they are prosecuting or defending. For instance, understanding how a particular statute has been applied in previous cases can be pivotal in arguing for a specific interpretation in court.

Analyzing crime cases and statutes is a foundational skill in the legal profession. It involves a detailed examination of the facts, legal principles, and legislative intent, all of which are critical for achieving just outcomes in criminal law. This analytical process not only shapes the application of law in individual cases but also contributes to the evolution of legal standards over time.

3.1. ANALYZING BY READING

The processes of gathering and analyzing various forms of information from a variety of sources, such as personal experience, rumors, political discourse, scientific data, and the media, are how we as researchers and regular members of the public learn about crime. One of the most fundamental ways to collect and evaluate data in a variety of fields is through reading research. In order to gain knowledge and insights on a particular topic, it entails a methodical approach to reading written materials, including books, academic journals, articles, reports, and other documents. The first step in the process is to identify and define the research question or interest topic. The choice of pertinent materials and sources is guided by this focus. Separating primary from secondary sources is necessary for conducting effective research. Original research articles, court documents, and historical records are examples of primary sources that provide firsthand information or proof. Critical essays, textbooks, and review articles are examples of primary sources that are analyzed, interpreted, or commented upon by secondary sources. We will be examining the various approaches we take to gaining knowledge about crime, and we will accomplish this by concentrating on the ways in which researchers collect and evaluate data through "reading," "seeing," and "talking/listening" about crime. Much of our authoritative knowledge about crime comes from reading, which makes sense for this section of the book to start with when we start working as researchers. We're going to talk about research methodologies that use previously published research findings that have been documented and made accessible. Although some materials (e.g., studies, reports, statistics, books written by academics or government agencies) may be created specifically with the intention of increasing our understanding of crime, we also want to think about other uses for these materials news, entertainment, which could still advance our knowledge of crime.

3.1.1. Reading and Reviewing the Literature Critically

The literature review is arguably the most crucial component of any research project. We should emphasize right away that before beginning any research project, a researcher has an obligation to gain a thorough understanding of the body of literature in the field in which they are interested. The literature review is a crucial first step in the majority of research projects, but it's important to understand that it's more than just a brainstorming session for research design. At several stages of the research process, including before a topic is chosen, when formulating a research question, during the stage of methodology design, and during data analysis, it may very well be required to refer to and expand the literature review. As researchers, we also need to be aware of the chance that new information could be released during a project that conflicts with, overlaps, or changes the course of the ongoing work. To put it simply, the majority of the work used by researchers is published in the form of books, reports, and articles in academic jerhaps itIt would be worthwhile to take a moment to clarify what we mean exactly by "literature" in the context of reseat there'sthere is also another category of sources that O'Leary (2004) refers to as "grey literature," which comprises sources like unpublished conference papers, newspaper articles, and student theses. The multidisciplinary and policy-driven nature of criminology means that there is an especially large body of literature available to criminological researchers. It is often necessary to read literature from other disciplines, such as sociology, psychology, law, and geography. We also need to familiarize ourselves with pertinent research conducted by a variety of entities, including academic researchers, government departments, public and private sector agencies, and interest groups.

Therefore, there is a very broad potential range of sources, and finding and reviewing the literature can be a difficult and time-consuming process. The research design needs to take into account the substantial time and effort that a researcher will need to devote to reading and evaluating the work of other researchers in the field. Since a lot of time is spent working alone at computers and/or libraries, it is important to incorporate some variety into the workday and make an effort to engage with colleagues about research problems or recent discoveries. It is worth noting that this can be an isolating task. It also necessitates a high degree of organization because multiple lines of inquiry must be pursued concurrently to develop a comprehensive picture of the work in a given area. A literature review can be approached in a variety of ways, so it's critical to start with a well-defined plan. Getting started is often the hardest part, but once you've located a few initial sources, more will appear and start to accumulate (kind of like a snowball effect). To get things going, it might be necessary to use a few different search tactics. For instance, using a bibliographical database—many of which are now accessible online—is a good way to locate journal articles; however, for books, it might be more effective to look up local bookshop databases and library catalogues. Furthermore, searching the websites of these organizations or, if needed, using an internet search engine might be the best way to locate reports and studies that are published by interest groups and agencies in the public and private sectors. Creating a strong set of search terms that can be derived from the topic, subtopics, main ideas, theories, and named authors is essential to success in all of these search strategies. Thus, for instance, your search terms might be "fraud" and "credit card" if you were looking for literature about techniques used by credit card fraudsters. Subsequently, as you become familiar with the relevant literature, you'll find that the terms "plastic card" and "payment card" are frequently used; you'll use these new terms in subsequent searches. More search terms will surface as you go on; using identity fraud, card-not-present fraud, skimming, and counterfeis examples, you'llyou will see that these are all techniques used in credit card fraud. It's also possible to identify theories or use the names of the authors as search terms. After locating and identifying each piece of literature, the researcher needs to organize and assess the data. As previously mentioned, it is typical for a researcher to amass a sizable collection of literature for a project.

There are two problems to be solved: first, how to organize the sources into a catalog, and second, how to document the data that is contained in them. Building a catalogue or bibliographic database required the use of card indexes and manual filing systems in the past, but computers have made this task much simpler today. Although many people prefer to use their own personal system of cataloguing, there are several excellent bibliographic computer programmes that are especially helpful because they are automatically formatted and particularly simple to search. Whatever method you choose, the most crucial thing to keep in mind is to make sure you record a complete reference for every item when you acquire it. Nothing is worse than realizing later that you have forgotten where or how you found anecause you haven'thave not recorded a reference. You will need to select which category of information you will use to organize the materials and decide which details—such as author names, year of publication, article/book title, journal title, page numbers, ISBN/ISSN, http address, date source was recorded, where it was found/how it was acquired, and whether a copy is held on file—are important to record.

After you have located and accurately recorded an item in the catalogue, the next step is to actually sit down and read it! Because reading involves critical analysis, this is probably the most difficult part of the literature review process. Obviously, one cannot memorize everything that they have read, so they must maintain some sort of record of the information found in each source. However, recording a brief synopsis of the source's content is neither productive nor efficient; these summaries are typically long and have little meaning when consulted later. Rather, it is preferable to evaluate a source and distill its "contribution to the field" through critical analysis. By doing this, the investigator can formulate research questions by identifying gaps or inconsistencies and creating a meaningful picture of the state of knowledge regarding a specific subject. Critical analysis is not an easy process, though; it takes confidence and eence. While we won'twill not go into great detail here, O'Leary (2004) offers some very helpful advice, particularly for those who are unfamiliar with research methodology. In addition, we believe that one last note regarding context is necessary, which is especially significant for those of us who conduct research on crime and crime policy. Periodically taking a step back to examine the environments in which the literature has developed is crucial. In our work as crime researchers, we typically address current social issues that have their roots in particular political, economic, and legal environments. The arguments surrounding ASBOs are one example. It is best to understand the emerging litehis field in light ofconsidering the public discussions surrounding knife possession, binge drinking, and the "respect agenda." Similarly, it's best to consider the contentious identity card proposals in the light of the post-9/11 terrorism concerns and the status of illegal immigration. If the larger context is not known, we can imagine that in ten years, researchers reviewing today's literature on identity cards or anti-social behavior may not fully comprehend the significance of its conclusions and recognize its contribution to criminology and policy.

3.1.2. Analyzing other People's Data

We covered how published research—articles, books, reports, etc.—is obtained in the section before this one.) should be examined in order to develop a knowledgeable and critical understanding of the suggested field of study. You will frequently be reading and reviewing data that has been summarized and analyzed by researchers (as there is a limit to the number of points that can be covered in a publication!). You'llYou will have moments when you wish the information was in your possession. Maybe you can think of alternative lines of inquiry beyond those that are offered, or maybe you just want to learn more about the connections between sets of variables that you find interesting. Should the latter scenario hold true, you might be able to envision a whole research project that could be completed with data that has already been gathered by someone else! In certain circumstances, such as when the data is provided by a government agency, a significant survey series, or a project supported by a Research Council, it might be feasible to obtain access to other people's datasets and carry out original analysis on the raw data. In criminological research, this strategy—known as secondary analysis—is frequently employed. To put it simply, secondary analysis is the process of having a "independent" researcher (i.e., who was not involved in the data collection process or who was not initially intended to be the main "user" of the data) analyzing the data and making inferences from it. Secondary analysis typically entails a fresh interpretation of the data, making it an innovative and fascinating method of conducting research. It is appealing as a research methodology for several useful reasons as well. First, there is a strong incentive to use data that has already been gathered by someone else because the process of gathering and evaluating empirical data is frequently costly and time-consuming. Data analysis can take up more time, which is a luxury that empirical work does not always afford. Access to high-quality datasets is also getting easier. In the UK, this is undoubtedly the case, but it's also getting simpler to access data from abroad. The UK is lucky to have the UK Data Archive, which serves as the "curator" of the country's largest digital data collection in the humanities and social sciences.

3.1.3. Secondary Analysis of Qualitative Data

The utilization of secondary analysis for qualitative data is growing in popularity, particularly with the expansion of data availability via the Economic and Social

Data Service (ESDS) offered by Essex University's UK Data Archive (UKDA). The service contains digital data sets from modern mixed-methods and entirely qualitative research, including all pertinent ESRC-funded studies. For the purpose of managing research projects, providing data creators and depositors with specialized advice on matters of consent and confidentiality, as well as data documentation for archiving, general guidelines are offered. Analyzing qualitative data that has been gathered by another person can be challenging. Unlike quantitative analysis, qualitative analysis is not subject to the same set of regulations and guidelines. As a result, it is crucial that the researcher create a unique analytical approach, guaranteeing high standards of validity and reliability all along the way. This necessitates a thorough comprehension of the project's methodology as well as the circumstances surrounding the data collection. Indeed, some contend that secondary analysis of qualitative data is impractical due to the impossibility of a third party understanding the data completely, such as an observer or interviewee. But the fact that there is so much space for investigation and conceptual development, along with the potential for a fresh analyst to offer an insightful, unbiased viewpoint to the data, seems to outweigh the possible drawbacks.

3.1.4. Secondary Analysis of Quantitative Data

The secondary analyst can access a wider variety of quantitative datasets, including official statistics gathered and generated by government agencies as well as significant survey series carried out by research organizations. Someof these quantitative datasets are managed by specialized research institutions, but the majority are held by the UKDA and accessible for secondary analysis. Because the data are gathered by large, reputable research organizations using carefully thought-out sampling techniques, they are typically of exceptionally high quality. The datasets are frequently repeated (either annually or less frequently), which makes them appropriate for longitudinal or trend analysis. However, te also a lot of drawbacks. You have tomust take a lot of time to fully comprehend the data before you can start analyzing it because you were not involved in the operationalization of the measures, the data collection, or the dataset preparation. This is especially troublesome when it comes to big datasets like the British Crime Survey. Additionally, there will be several limitations on what you can do with the information. For instance, you might have data that only functions at the individual level (as opposed to the household, local, or national levels). It's also possible that some important variables are absent, either because they weren't there in the first place or because they were eliminated to anonymize the data (for instance, postcode variables are occasionally eliminated from datasets, which can be annoying if you want to try area-level analysis). Arber (2001) concludes with a great point: creating theoretically grounded research questions and exercising sociological imagination are both necessary for secondary analysis. You will find value in two different forms of quantitative data as a criminological researcher. Firstly, we will take a quick look at the main survey series that are currently accessible. These are not specifically "crime surveys," but they frequently include data on social traits and markers of social change that criminologists find interesting (such as political views, unemployment, poverty, and health). Subsequently, we examine the set of data gathered by the government, which we commonly refer to as official statistics.

3.1.4.1. Major Survey Series

Numerous extensive surveys and long-term studies that have been conducted over many years offer a more comprehensive and in-depth picture on a range of subjects. While some of these are funded and conducted by independent organizations, others are government surveys. They include:

- **The OPCS Longitudinal Study:** It is based on records of significant events pertaining to 1% of the people in England and Wales who were born on four different dates every year beginning in 1971 (roughly 500,000 individuals). Rather than being a sample taken at a specific moment in time, it represents a continuous sample of the population.
- **The National Child Development Study (NCDS):** A long-term study involving 17,000 people who were born in Great Britain between March 3 and March 9, 1958 intended initially to look into infant health and perinatal mortality. The sample has undergone seven primary follow-ups to date to track its development; the most recent one was conducted in 2004 at the age of 46 by the Social Statistics Research Unit, which is now known as the Centre for Longitudinal Studies (CLS).
- **The 1970 British Cohort Study:** This is similar to the NCDS, based on a cohort of 17,000 people born in the UK between 5th and 11th April 1970. Also being carried out by SSRU and was last followed up in 1999/2000.
- **The Millennium Cohort Study:** All live births in the UK during a 12-month period, beginning on September 1, 2000, in England and Wales and December 1, 2000, in Scotland and Northern Ireland, comprised the sample population for the study. The goal is to investigate the crucial first year of life and possibly find answers to

many of the questions regarding its long-term effects. These include matters of fundamental interest to policy, such as the underpinnings of cohesiveness and social capital. To date, the survey has been swept three times; the most recent one took place in 2006, the year the kids began primary school.

- **Labor Force Survey:** An 80,000-person quarterly survey with a primary focus on employment and training activities. Its definition of unemployment is founded on an internationally accepted definition, in contrast to the monthly claimant count, and its findings are frequently contrasted with the claimant count.
- **General Household Survey:** A yearly survey that was started in 1971 and surveyed roughly 10,000 households was used to track the impact of different government policy areas over time.
- **British Social Attitudes Survey:** An annual survey that tracks how British social, political, economic, and moral values have changed and remained consistent with other societal shifts. Newspaper readership, political parties and trust, public spending, welfare benefits, health care, child care, poverty, the workplace and labor market, education, charitable giving, rural areas, transportation and the environment, Europe, economic prospects, immigration, sentencing, prisons, and race and religion are just a few of the topics covered.

3.1.4.2. Official Statistics

A broad range of statistics produced by government departments and agencies are referred to as "official statistics." When you stop to consider it, the majority of a person's life's significant occurrences and activities are documented by government organizations. As a result, the government gathers an enormous quantity of data about its citizens. An individual's contacts with state organizations, including the NHS, Benefits Agency, Passport Office, HM Revenue and Customs, Land Registry, and criminal justice system, are documented as soon as their birth is registered. Naturally, in the contemporary era of potent electronic data exchange and storage systems, this is becoming more and more true. While each government department is in charge of gathering and producing statistics on subjects falling under its purview, the Office for National Statistics (ONS) has served as the central government organization in charge of organizing government statistics since 1996. Naturally, the criminological researcher is most interested in the Crime Statistics, which are a subset of the Official Statistics. As demonstrated previously in this chapter, it is imperative to construct an overview of existing knowledge regarding a particular topic or research idea prior to delving deeper into it. A summary of the pertinent official statistics is frequently included in literature reviews, and this is helpful for creating the theoretical framework and context. Policy-makers, the public, the media, and researchers are interested in finding answers to questions like: How much crime is there? Is crime rising or falling? Are the police doing their jobs? How do criminals get punished for their crimes? The data has been used as a kind of barometer of the moral health of the country for more than a century (Maguire, 2007). Researchers may also be able to access the datasets and use them for secondary data analysis. The Scottish Executive and the Police Service of Northern Ireland, respectively, independently collect and publish crime statistics for Scotland and Wales; the Home Office is currently in charge of these statistics. Historically, the data have been disseminated through three primary statistical reports or series, each with well-established advantages and disadvantages are:

- **The Criminal Statistics:** The government has been producing criminal statistics for over 150 years. They are a national compilation of local police and court records that are produced at the national level. They concentrate on the number of police-recorded notifiable offenses, the number of cautions issued, and the number of offenders found guilty of particular offenses. The Criminal Statistics were the primary metrics used for many years to track changes in crime throughout the nation. However, a shift in criminological theory in the 1970s led to requests for new types of data. After police and court records came under fire for serving as more of an indicator of institutional needs than a neutral source of information about crime, new research on victims and situational crime prevention was initiated. Formerly, the Criminal Statistics served as the exclusive official source of information about crime; today, however, they are only one piece in a larger "kaleidoscope" (Maguire, 2007).
- **The Recorded Crime Statistics:** A nationwide compilation of crimes reported to the police and maintained since 1876 is known as the Recorded Crime Statistics (RCS). The Home Office compiles and disseminates the information supplied by various forces and establishes regulations that dictate the manner and timing of crime reporting. By comparing different crime types and trends, the statistics can be used to identify changes in crime issues. For instance, they can show whether property crime is more common than violent crime or whether auto crime is on the rise. The statistics are helpful in providing overall totals of all recorded crimes). You must interpret the data with extreme caution, though, as the

RCS have drawn a lot of criticism for their validity and reliability. Maguire notes that there are three main factors which need to be taken into consideration:

- **Conceptual Consistency:** The definitions of offenses are subject to change over time as new laws and policies are introduced. Therefore, you need to be cautious that the crime you are looking at now meant the same thing to people who were employed, say, in the 1950s. The most recent significant modifications were made in 1998 to introduce a whole new range of recordable offenses and alter the guidelines for recording multiple offenses in an effort to promote uniformity amongst police forces. The result was a sharp increase in the number of crimes reported, which has made historical comparisons extremely challenging.
- **Consistency in Recording Practice:** Despite the Home Office's regulations controlling recording procedures, police discretion remains an option, potentially leading to disparities in the methods employed by different units. Numerous people contend that the attitudes and actions of the police have a big impact on the statistics. It is still concerning that the police have the capacity and, in an increasingly managerial and performance-driven culture, the motivation to conceal certain offenses and/or over record others, despite the fact that adjustments have been made to help assure consistency. Therefore, you still need to be aware of potential differences both within and between forces.
- **Reporting of Crime by the Public:** It is common knowledge that individuals report crimes to the police or not for a variety of reasons, such as ignorance, trust, apathy, or accessibility. When interpreting the statistics, you should always keep in mind that the RCS are subject to any changes in reporting behavior.

- **The British Crime Survey:** The British Crime Survey (BCS) was launched in 1982, during a period of growing criminologists' interest in the victim perspective and harsh criticism of official statistics based on police and court work. The BCS is a nationwide household survey that aims to find out if any household members have ever been victims of crime and, in the event that they have, to learn more about that experience. It is therefore claimed to give a more accurate picture of crime as it captures all crimes that are either not reported to the police or wind up in court. Along with self-completion questionnaires for drug use and domestic violence, it also includes questions measuring attitudes toward the police and the criminal justice system. It used to be done on a four-year cycle, but it is currently done on a continuous annual cycle with 40,000 respondents as the sample size each year. The questionnaire's content has not changed significantly from its original format, and maintaining it is highly valued in order to enable precise trend analysis. This has, however, drawn a great deal of criticism because it has made it difficult to make adjustments to certain measures that have been acknowledged as being conceptually weak or badly designed. Additionally, the BCS only covers a narrow subset of crimes, which complicates comparisons with RCS data. Researchers and the media have most frequently used the RCS and BCS statistics as measures of crime over the last 20 years. They were previously released separately as different but complementary data sources, but the Home Office decided to combine the two in an annual report titled "Crime in England and Wales" recently. This choice has drawn a lot of criticism because it seems to have produced "analysis with political spin" rather than an objective presentation of the available facts. The most severe criticism may have come from the Statistics Commission's 2006 review of crime statistics (Statistics Commission, 2006), which suggested that the distinction between BCS data and Recorded Crime Statistics be restored as soon as feasible. The Criminal Statistics, the British Crime Survey, and the Recorded Crime Statistics are still undoubtedly three of the most significant sources of data for criminological researchers, despite the clear shortcomings in all three methods. Nonetheless, there are regular reviews of the crime statistics, and it is crucial for criminological researchers to remain up to date with the modifications that are made. There are variations in the amount and variety of data gathered, as well as in the methods used for conducting and sharing analysis. In fact, Maguire (2007) speaks of a "data explosion" that has recently taken place in the field of crime statistics. This explosion has been fueled by a new managerialism and performance management culture in government departments and agencies, as well as notable technological advancements that have revolutionized the ways in which we can store and analyze electronic data. He notes that more data—both quantitative and qualitative—is currently being gathered in a variety of new areas, such as crimes that go unreported or are not recorded, the circumstances surrounding the crime, the geographic distribution of crimes, the improvement of concepts like "street crime," the amount of information on hidden crimes and hidden offenders, victims, and public perceptions. Additionally, it appears that there is a willingness to consider crime statistics in a more creative way and that the idea that crime is a social construct rather than one based on "legal definitions" of crime is becoming more prevalent.

The Simmons Report proposed a 'national index' of crime which would focus on the most serious and high volume crimes, for example. However, it would appear that we are some way from developing a meaningful 'index' of crime. Therefore, it is evident that utilizing the official crime statistics can lead to confusion. In fact, there has been increasing criticism that the public is given confusing statistics, and it has been suggested that the general misinformation about crime rates and distributions is undermining public confidence. How these issues are resolved remains to be seen but it is perhaps worth concluding by reflecting on the six key recommendations made by the Statistics Commission aimed at improving the availability, usability and accuracy of official crime statistics:

1. The structure of the Home Office should be changed to separate the policy-making and information provision/publication functions.
2. Improved communication with users.
3. Better data at the small area level.
4. Furthering of research opportunities.
5. Improvements to the comparability of data (especially with Scotland and Northern Ireland).
6. Further work on index measures of 'total crime.'

3.1.4.3. Criminological Research, Policy and Politics

We believe it is necessary to discuss the connection between criminological research and politics before moving on from the subject of official crime statistics. A wide range of individuals functioning in various capacities actually use crime statistics. Statistics are used, for instance, by the government and local delivery organizations to manage performance, create policies regarding criminal justice and crime reduction, and inform the public about crime. Crime statistics are used by the general public to assess risk in their daily lives, to understand the justification for government policy, to hold local delivery organizations accountable, and to learn about the experiences and perceptions of others regarding crime and disorder. As a result, public concern about crime, where crime is on the political agenda, and government investment in data collection are closely related (Maguire, 2007), and research must always take this relationship into account.

It is difficult to recall a period in which criminological research did not some bearing on politics. For instance, The New Criminology (Taylor et al., 1970s).) embodied a radical critique of criminology, which waught of as a branch of the criminal justice system. However, there was a period of timea period before the 1980s when issues related to party politics did not include crime and the treatment of offenders. But in recent decades, criminological research has inevitably become more politicized due to changes in criminal justice policy. Parallel to this (though we do not necessarily propose a direct causal relationship), discussions concerning the methodology of criminological research and its applicability to policy have emerged. These have addressed the two primary criminological fields of assessment and criminal statistics. The so-called "paradigm wars" were a discussion about the nature of evaluation that took place in the 1990s. That being said, this was primarily a disagreement about various assessment models rather than something obviously political. Nonetheless, the Labor Government's announcement in the late 1990s that it was dedicated to "evidence-based" research increased the importance of evaluation. Later, this commitment was called into question when it appeared that some of the evidence did not support the government's claims. As a result, Tim Newburn, President of the British Society of Criminology, spoke of "the rise and fall of evidence-based research."

Tim Hope, a former Home Office researcher, has been one of the Home Office's most scathing critics. Hope addresses the role of "scientific" evidence in politics within the framework of a contentious project he worked on (Hope, 2004). He points out that the conventional Enlightenment paradigm views science as distinct from policy. On the other hand, more contemporary scholars—such as Beck in his 1992 analysis of the Risk Society—have contended that when scientific data serves as the foundation for policy choices, "science itself becomes a site for politics." The methodology of science is no longer the only thing that gives it value; it now also has the promise of application and utility. The emergence of a purportedly new "crime science" that aims to apply methods in ways that could improve the work of criminal justice agencies and views research as primarily something that is intended for policy utilization has added to this promise in recent years. The previously held belief that criminology is primarily concerned with comprehending and explaining crime and criminality, with policy relevance being incidental, is in contrast to the "reflexive" role of science. The Treasury's role is another aspect of the relationship between research and politics. Government departments must provide evidence of the cost-effectiveness of their programs to HM Treasury, in accordance with guidelines provided by the Treasury in the form of The Green Book, which lays out a framework for project appraisal. The government social research context is enhanced by the addition of the Magenta Book, which provides guidelines for policy analysis and evaluation. While it makes sense that a government would want to show that its expenditures are worthwhile, doing so can limit the scope and speed of research. Raynor and Robinson have argued that:

- The policy of recruiting as many offenders as possible to programmes to meet Treasury targets has probably tended to undermine the fit between offenders' needs and programmes and contributed to increasing attrition and non-completion, which in turn reduces the overall impact of the programmes if non-completers reconvict more.

Furthermore, a frequent grievance expressed by researchers is that meticulously planned and developed programs are expedited to yield outcomes before they have had adequate time to settle in. In conclusion, the Home Office does contribute significantly to funding criminological research and sets the research agenda, even though it is not the only authority on the field. The point we are trying to make here is that these issues should alert criminological researchers to the fact that their field of study does involve politics, disagreements, and values, all of which must be taken into account before beginning any new project.

3.1.5. Analyzing Documents

The last research strategy through reading that we would like to discuss in this chapter is the content analysis method of document analysis. A multi-method strategy frequently includes content analysis as an auxiliary method. Both quantitative and qualitative data—such as the quantity of pertinent words or paragraphs or the style of the pictures—may be gathered and analyzed in this process. The majority of criminological studies that have employed a content analysis approach have concentrated on official policy documents and printed news media. However, as a reading-based research method, we should talk briefly about content analysis here. Finding a specific research question and, when appropriate, developing hypotheses are the first steps in the process. Formulating a strategy for sampling is the next step. The selection of the sample frame will be contingent upon the specific research question. For instance, if the objective is to investigate the correlation between news reports of criminal activity and public perceptions of crime rates, then the sampling frame would be comprised of pertinent national and local newspapers, as well as news programs broadcast on radio and/or television. Once more, the nature of the research question will dictate how the sample is drawn. Some possible criteria include time, publication, author, and reference to specific events. Content analysis has advantages and disadvantages, just like any other research methodology. The documents that are being examined have typically been produced for a different reason, which content analysis clearly has a strength in being non-reactive and unobtrusive (though not for the research'sresearch' purpose). The document may be structured in an inefficient manner, which leaves the researcher with the difficult task of organizing the data, which can also cause issues for the researcher. Ensuring the validity of the research is one of the main challenges, particularly when the analyst needs to discern between "witting evidence," or information that the document's author intended to convey, and "unwitting evidence," or any additional information that the analyst learns from reading the document. Finally, even though computers have made the process somewhat easier, content analysis is still known for being a very time-consuming and laborious process.

3.2. THE SCIENCE OF OBSERVATION

Natural scientists who follow positivist principles acknowledge that repeated, methodical, and objective observations of naturally occurring phenomena are the best ways to learn about the natural world. Thus, for instance, by heating a piece of glass to various temperatures and noting any changes in color or texture, we may be able to learn more about the physical characteristics of glass. In this case, formal, structured, and objective observational methods would be used, and the experiment would be managed with the use of instruments like thermometers, stopwatches, and pre-made tables for recording data. Can these techniques be applied to the study of social phenomena, though? Social observation techniques were first created in the British Empire's colonial era. British anthropologists developed a research approach that included methods of observation, document collection, and interviewing because they were eager to learn about and comprehend the "exotic" cultures that existed in the recently established colonies. This method was later called ethnography. Even though the first anthropologists truly went on scientific expeditions into uncharted territory, the "armchair approach" became the norm and was more common. Instead of working in the field, they would use the notes that the teams of colonial administrators sent back to create a picture of life in the colonies while based in their libraries in London. The colonial administrators were guided in their actions by a manual that was first released in 1874 and gave the local district commissioners a list of inquiries to make of aboriginal informants.

Following the colonial era, American sociologists from the Chicago School of Sociology in the 1920s and 1930s revolutionized ethnographic methods. Notably, the researchers from the Chicago School added two essential components to the British anthropological approach. Initially, they added a pragmatist component to an otherwise highly positivistic approach. They embraced the idea that social life is dynamic and ever-changing rather than a static, unchangeable phenomenon (the kind of thing positivists like to study with their fixed measuring instruments). Formalism constituted element number two. This is the notion that social relationships represent underlying forms that can have similarities even though they will always differ in content. Therefore, rather than the individuals themselves, the interactions between people will be the main focus of any social setting. As a result, the Chicago School researchers' methodologies differed greatly from the anthropological one. They rejected positivism's rigid precepts and held the view that knowledge cannot come from a methodical process of hypothesis testing. Rather, they contended that one needs to make thorough and in-depth observations before drawing conclusions from the information. The researchers were then urged to map the layout of the city's streets using blank notebooks rather than clipboards and questionnaires, which asked fixed, static questions. Their goal was to make an effort to document and comprehend urban change.

Importantly, the Chicago researchers did not begin with a predetermined hypothesis that they intended to investigate. Instead, after gathering and analyzing the data, they came up with a theory. One of the main characteristics of ethnography is that the theory is developed from the data (instead of gathering data to support a theory). As the research develops, the researcher typically reformulates the research question. However, Hammersley and Atkinson (1983) point out that "substantive" or "topical" theory constantly interacts with one another theory created for particular empirical investigations) and "formal" or "generic" theory (i.e., more comprehensive conceptual theory). From the formal to the substantive, an ethnographic study can transition (see Hargreaves et al., study on classroom deviance). (1975), where label theory was used as a springboard and developed into a "shopping list" of topics specifically pertinent to educational institutions, or the other way around (Atkinson's study of industrial training units (1981) is a good illustration of this), wherein specific, topical research questions were connected to abstract ideas like stigma and labeling. Anyone thinking about using an ethnographic approach should understand that observation and ethnography are two different things; an observation study can be conducted without being an ethnography. Considering ethnography as a research strategy and observation as a research method may be the most beneficial approach.

Thus, an ethnographic study may use a variety of techniques, such as interviews, observation, and documentary research. Consider a study by Tomsen (1997), for instance, which examined the culture of drinking violence in Newcastle, Australia, by combining observations made in pubs and bars, interviews with bouncers, and the examination of police data. An ethnography's theoretical/epistemological foundation (the creation of theory from data) and the researcher's prolonged "immersion" in the social context are its distinguishing characteristics. Then, a "grounded theory" approach is used, in which the observer approaches the environment with an entirely open mind to whatever conclusions may be drawn. This method works especially well when the researcher wants to investigate and comprehend a situation or phenomenon that is unknown. An observer who takes an open observation approach assumes a neutral starting point and becomes more receptive to the relationships and surroundings that emerge in front of them. Making a list of concepts to observe or formulating theories in advance of the observation are not necessary. Rather, as the process progresses, the ideas, theories, and hypotheses become apparent. The observer has total control over what gets noticed and recorded right away and can let the process of observation take its natural course. Nonetheless, as we have previously highlighted, observation can be conducted independently as a research method and need not be a component of an ethnography. Research strategies of various kinds, including strongly positivistic ones, can incorporate an observation. In fact, there are study situations where a more structured and prescriptive approach to observation is more appropriate. For instance, if the objectives of the research project involved measuring pre-identified concepts and testing particular hypotheses, the observer would need to create a research tool or instrument to be used during the observation process as well as predetermine the concepts that are to be measured. In these kinds of studies, it is common for the observer to take on the role of a detached/non-participant observer and there are a number of good examples of this approach in criminology, including a street observation study by Shapland et al. (1994).

3.2.1. Role of the Observer

In an observation study, choosing the observer's role during the observation may be the most crucial choice you have to make. Two types of roles can be distinguished, broadly speaking: one in which the observer participates in the group and environment and another in which the observer is not involved in the group and is not attached to the environment. When it comes to the two roles, Robson points out that the main distinction is whether the participant observer acts as the instrument or the non-participant observer typically uses some sort of observation tool. Numerous factors, such as the nature of the research question and the researcher's chosen epistemological stance, will influence the decision. The participant role is standard practice in ethnographic research. In other scenarios, a non-participant role is taken, particularly when preventing the "observer effect" is crucial. The decision to assume a covert or overt role will have been made by the observer. As we've already seen, there are obvious ethical concerns with taking on a covert role, so this is not a decision that should be made lightly. The benefit is that people are more likely to behave naturally because they are unaware that they are being watched. While it is typical to see the clear division between participant and non-participant observation, there is actually a range of observational roles that fall in between total detachment and full participation. The most helpful analysis of observational roles is frequently attributed to Gold's scheme of classification of participant observer roles (1958) in textbooks. Within it, he identifies four key roles:

1. *Complete Participant:* The full participant is an active participant in the situation and does not disclose to the other group members that they are an observer. Naturally, it is simpler in situations where the observer already plays a part in the group. Holdaway's work (Holdaway, 1983), which was mentioned earlier in the chapter, is a good example. Because Holdaway was a police officer at the time of his study, he was able to carry out his investigation discreetly from the other officers. The benefit in this case is that the observer can fully immerse themselves in the "real" social environment without worrying about how the research may affect group members' behavior. Even though it might seem like the "perfect" research environment, this requires a great deal of dishonesty, and it can be very taxing for the observer—both physically and psychologically. Additionally, there is a risk of "going native," a term used to characterize the circumstance in which a researcher loses their ability to remain objective because they become too emotionally invested in the setting, endangering the validity of their work. While it is difficult to find examples of this in the literature, there are instances where researchers have had difficulty remaining impartial.
2. *Participant-As-Observer:* In this capacity, the observer engages in full group participation, just like a full participant, but the other group members are aware that the observer is conducting research. It is not required—in fact, it is frequently preferable—that the group members be aware of the subject of the researcher's observation. Ditton's study of fiddling and pilfering in a bakery provides an illustration of this role. While his coworkers were aware that he was a research student, they were unaware that he was specifically observing their dishonest behavior (Ditton, 1977). If they had known, they might have acted differently.
3. *Observer-As-Participant:* The participant-observer does not genuinely take part in the group activities. Despite being able to be in

the room, s/he does not contribute completely as a productive group member. In this capacity, the researcher is essentially conducting interviews, as noted by Bryman (2004). He or she must question people as those acts or decisions happen to find out why they act in particular ways or make particular decisions because they have no say in the situation itself. Punch's study on police operations in Amsterdam serves as one example. He was unable to fully engage in police activities because he was not a trained police officer, but he was still allowed to go on patrol with officers and ask them questions (Punch, 1979). Robson (2002) raises concerns about whether individuals who engage in such interactions with group members can truly be classified as "not taking part" in the context. Consequently, caution must be exercised in evaluating the validity of the findings.

4. *Complete Observer:* The complete participant is at one end of the spectrum; at the other is the complete observer. He or she does not communicate in any way with the other members of the group and is totally cut off from them. Loftland's 1973 study, which examined street behavior through a window, is a classic example. Sampson and Raudenbush (1999) took an intriguing modern approach to this role, observing disorder on the streets of Chicago by driving slowly and methodically through the streets while covertly filming their surroundings with two cameras attached to each side of the car. Without trespassing into the areas they were observing, they were able to gather and examine their data.

5. Each of the four roles has distinct benefits and drawbacks, which the researcher must carefully weigh before selecting one to assume. Interestingly, despite being at opposite ends of the spectrum, Hammersley and Atkinson (1983) point out that there are certain benefits and drawbacks to both the complete participant and complete observer roles. Since the researcher does not engage with the subjects in the course of performing their research, both approaches minimize reactivity. However, it is unlikely that direct questioning will occur, so the researcher is forced to rely solely on his or her own interpretations of the observed interactions, exchanges, and events. They come to the conclusion that taking on a role at either extreme of the spectrum can make it challenging to develop and test theory in a rigorous manner. They do, however, raise a legitimate concern regarding whether there is a meaningful distinction between the observer and the participant.

3.2.2. Data Collection

The numerous methodological, ethical, and epistemological choices that must be made prior to starting an observation study underscored the significance of a carefully considered research plan. The observation can then start after these choices have been made. One last question remains to be answered, though, and that is how the data will be recorded and analyzed. The answer to this will vary depending on whether the observation is open-ended or structured, as well as whether the data is quantitative or qualitative. It is crucial for the observer to keep a record of their observations in all observational work because it can be very challenging to look back on an event days, weeks, or months later and remember every significant event. However, there are various approaches to data recording, which are discussed below.

3.2.2.1. Open/Unstructured Observation Studies

The notebook is the primary tool of the observer in unstructured, open observation studies. The ability to take notes is one that the observer must develop; there is a delicate balance between taking too many and too few notes. On the one hand, as Hammersley and Atkinson note:

- A research project can be as well organized and as theoretically well informed as you like, but with inadequate note taking, the experience will be like using an expensive camera with poor quality film. In both cases, the resolution will prove unsatisfactory and the results will be poor. Only foggy pictures result.

But you can't capture everything on camera. Despite the fact that it may seem apparent, this is a crucial point to remember. For ten minutes, try to observe a television show (dramas or soap operas work best), noting everything you see, including the environment, people, and events. Try to note down your observations in a notebook and use a stopwatch to keep track of the time. You'll probably feel worn out at the end of the ten minutes, and your notes will probably be long and disorganized. If you looked back on your notes six months later, would they still make sense to you? Even if something is not immediately understood, it is still important to document it. The majority of seasoned observers will concur that the best time to record events is as soon as possible after the action or event has occurred. If the observation is hidden, it will obviously be difficult to carry it out because the constant scribbler will undoubtedly raise suspicions (unless writing is part of the role being adopted, perhaps). While taking notes in an overt setting is easier when done in an open manner, it is still important to ensure that note-taking does not look strange or distracting in the context.

Though there are general guidelines to follow, the specific study will determine what should be recorded and what should be omitted from notes. In general, field notes ought to include specific accounts of social processes as well as contexts. According to Robson (2002), an observer can pose three different kinds of questions during an observation: what, how, and why. What are the simple facts and contexts that can be discovered through other means in addition to being observed and possibly recorded during the observation? records). Thus, for instance, if we were to observe a courtroom, we may ask about the cases scheduled for hearing that day, the number of witnesses called in a particular case, and a description of the court staff, including the names of the judges and barristers. The how questions address exchanges and occurrences that take place throughout the observation procedure. We may then inquire as to how the judge addresses the defendant (words used, tone adopted, facial expression) or how barristers present a legal argument (using statutes and cases to support their case), to return to the example of the courtroom. Investigating the causes of the behaviors being seen is frequently required to move things along a bit further. Perhaps the hardest questions to answer are the "why" ones since they call for the observer to make assumptions based on what is said or done. By genuinely questioning the participants about the circumstances, the observer who has taken on a participatory role will be able to expand on these deductions.

3.2.2.2. Structured Observation Studies

An observation schedule or coding scheme is typically used by the researcher to document his or her observations during a structured observation. All that is needed for a coding scheme is a list of pre-established elements that will be tallied or graded throughout the observation. Either a straightforward counting of items or events or a more intricate recording of behavioral sequences can be part of the coding scheme. It is true that careful planning and application of coding schemes are necessary to guarantee validity and reliability. Researchers frequently modify coding schemes that have already been employed in other studies. The categories that are employed ought to be precise, objective, comprehensive, non-exclusive, and simple to document. The purpose of this study was to investigate the patterns of crime in various parts of a city. They contend that it's critical to determine how people use various areas of a community and what opportunities there are for crime in order to investigate these patterns in the context of the physical environment in which they arise. Thus, an observation schedule was used for the street observations that were used in this study. To focus crime reduction efforts, the observation's findings were combined with information gathered from police data analysis and interviews.

Mapping an area gave the observers the ability to identify possible crime targets during the first observational phase. They paid special attention to mapping public spaces and properties, including those used for residential, commercial, and industrial purposes; routes for pedestrians and cars; parking; potential crime hotspots, such as car parks, pubs, and amusement arcades; potential issues, such as litter, poorly maintained roads, abandoned buildings, and graffiti; and crime prevention measures, such as burglar alarms, security lighting, CCTV, etc.,). The observation proceeded to a series of 10-minute observations of street activity at various times of the day. Prior to commencing the observation, observers were mandated to record the overall environmental conditions, including the weather, lighting, overall atmosphere of the area, ongoing activities, etc. Every movement in the area, including traffic flow and social use, had to be recorded by observers during the ten-minute observation period (totals of each type of vehicle and pedestrian counted). The observation schedule was created in a way that allowed for the clear and individual logging of every item of interest, including pedestrians (women alone, families, or groups of children) and vehicles (cars, taxis, buses, or lorries).

Therefore, well thought-out observation schedules were employed in both phases of the study, which made it possible to gather valuable quantitative data. However, a coding scheme or schedule can be helpful in a variety of situations and is not always limited to gathering only quantitative data. It is especially helpful in situations where there are numerous distinct sample periods or when a team of observers is engaged to ensure consistency across observations.

3.2.2.3. Alternatives to Note-taking

Using a tape recorder is the most efficient way to maintain an accurate record of circumstances in which a lot of speech is used. On the other hand, tape recording has a lot of drawbacks. People may become uncomfortable when they see a tape recorder; in fact, some may refuse to allow it to be there in the first place. Additionally, this method generates a lot of data that must be meticulously sorted through later. It might not be feasible to tape record and transcribe every observation study if it is going to take place over an extended period of time. Hammersley and Atkinson (1983) suggest that it could be more suitable to record only particular formal meetings or interviews using one method and use a different technique for other, less formal settings. An alternative method that has been effectively employed in certain research studies is video-taping (refer to Sampson and Raudenbush (1999), who drove through Chicago's streets and recorded people's behavior on camera to create social disorder scales, and Shrum and Kilburn (1996), who recorded the Mardi Gras festival in New Orleans on video to investigate instances of ritual exchange and nudity. Additionally, some researchers advise keeping a fieldwork journal to document the research process. It can be used in "de-briefing" sessions as a stress-reduction strategy and allows the observer to document methodological issues and developmental concepts (Johnson, 1975).

3.2.3. Data Analysis

After the data collection process has started, you need to give careful consideration to how to store and catalog the data. There are various methods to go about this. One option would be to organize the data in a chronological fashion. Nonetheless, it is frequently preferable to create a cataloging system based on theoretical ideas and themes that have been determined both before and during the study. Thus, for instance, you could arrange based on individuals, locations, or occasions.

Making the choice to maintain computerized or manual records is another decision. Indexes, file annotations, and occasionally duplicate entries (when observations fall into more than one category) will be required. Some find it easier to operate a manual system, while others find it easier to use a computerized one. In contrast to other approaches, observation studies do not have a discrete phase for analysis. Rather, analysis happens all along the way in the research process. The precise methods of data analysis in an observation study will vary, depending upon the amounts of quantitative and qualitative data collected, but there are some basic principles which should be followed. All observation studies should start with the process of descriptive observation – a 'painting the picture' exercise (Robson, 2002). We saw an example of this in the street observation study where the observers 'mapped' what they could see before the 10-minute observation period began.

The next stage is to go beyond the descriptive and identify concepts and develop theoretical frameworks. To give an example, in a study of the ways in which the police deal with disputes, Kemp et al. (1992) identified a series of different concepts which together form an 'incident': the arrival of the police at the scene, contact (when the police physically restrain someone), information-gathering, decision-taking and implementation, the conclusion and the aftermath.

You should be able to formulate some hypotheses by considering the relationships between various concepts and potential definitions for emergent "problems." The next step of the analysis is to test the initial hypotheses and determine the frequency and distribution of these observed concepts. The theories are revised and retested if they turn out to be false, which is often the case. The theories are reformulated until they are conclusively demonstrated. The more intricate modeling of relationships (and relationships between relationships) is required for the final analysis. This entails the development of "roles" and the relationships that link them so that they can eventually be expanded into comprehensive descriptions of social environments and lifestyles.

3.2.4. The Disadvantages of Observation

Despite some serious criticism over the years, observational methods are still widely used in criminological research. Thus, before starting any observational work, it's critical that you are aware of the possible objections. The process of observation requires a lot of time and resources, first and foremost. A participant observation study should last at least a year, according to Goffman (1961). Although we don't want to establish strict upper or lower bounds on this time frame, we must carefully weigh the demands of sufficient data collection against the constraints imposed by limited resources. Serious concerns have also been expressed by some observers regarding the moral dilemmas presented by both overt and covert observation (Bulmer, 1982; Norris, 1993). An additional prevalent critique is that observation is inherently subjective, thereby posing a substantial risk of the researcher's personal opinions influencing the study's conclusion. This occurs in the context of structured observations when the group or environment you are observing is given a conceptual framework that is wholly inappropriate.

This is especially troublesome in cases where the goal of the study is to be exploratory and find new information. According to Bryman (2004), one way to approach this issue might be to begin with some unstructured observations and use the information gathered to create an observation schedule. This is not to argue that unstructured observations are less subject to subjectivity, though. Analytical induction may be argued to be a helpful tool in theoretical development, particularly in the context of grounded theory studies. However, we would join critics in challenging the notion that a researcher can approach a research study without contributing any theoretical ideas at all. Therefore, we believe it's critical to stress how important it is that the researcher incorporates validity checks into the research methodology whenever feasible.

Understanding the boundaries of what can be learned from observation is also crucial. The fact that you can only record what is "directly observable" is one of the main limitations of structured observation. This implies that you might not be able to gather much information about people's intentions or motivations and that you might miss the context in which an event or interaction takes place. Particularly participant observation has come under fire since it is primarily limited to working-class environments as a result of serious access problems, making it incapable of producing any meaningful analysis of power dynamics. This is especially frustrating for criminological researchers because it closes off intriguing research directions (such as examining the work habits of top criminal justice system officials or the ways in which executives in large corporations commit crimes and corruption).

3.3. ANALYZING BY ASKING AND LISTENING

The approach of listening to what people have to say has arguably produced the most criminological research of any other method. Because we include questionnaires, which occasionally but not always result in non-verbal responses, we use the term "listening" in a colloquial sense here. However, we believe that answering questionnaires in writing is a means of listening to what is being said. This article covers three primary methods of listening: semi-structured interviews, questionnaires, and focus groups, which are a type of group interview. The fact that there is interaction of some kind between the researcher and participants unites them all. This is significant because it involves a reciprocal relationship. It is simple for a researcher to view the people they are interacting with as passive partners who are only there to provide them with the information they need in order to continue their studies. There are various reasons why this would be a grave error. One is that it involves objectifying participants, which makes it easier for unethical research practices to occur afterward. The second rationale is more practical in nature: you are more likely to obtain trustworthy and significant insights if you are cognizant of how others react. It's also critical to consider the potential uses of researchers by participants. This can occur in a number of ways. One is that the researcher might end up acting as an entirely unqualified, on-demand counselor.

People who participate in research have the chance to be heard, which they might not otherwise have, to express their opinions and feelings as well as perhaps to discuss some very private topics. A competent and skilled researcher will develop the ability to elicit information from subjects—victims, offenders, members of the public, or members of the legal system, depending on the situation. It's possible that a victim is confiding in someone about their experiences for the first time. It's possible that an offender is disclosing actions they regret taking. In this way, the researcher is being employed almost exactly as a listening post. This makes perfect sense, but in order to avoid unreal expectations, it's crucial to keep in mind and remind respondents of your true role as well as its limitations. Speaking with representatives of different branches of the criminal justice system may be part of the researcher's strategy to get their opinions heard by research consumers, such as the Home Office, which is funding the project, or by a larger audience that will read the research output. When interviewing court officials, for instance, about the impact of recent legislation or changes to criminal justice procedures, you should be mindful that the information you receive may represent the agency's "party line" on the matter. It could be that you are accepting of the agency's "party line" after learning what it is, or it could be that this is hiding what is actually going on. A competent researcher must make numerous decisions regarding the type of data they obtain and how to interpret it in the context of their own intervention.

Listening can take place in various methodological settings. A survey is typically far more structured than ethnography or participant observation, which are likely to involve the least structured types of research encounters. Multiple listening techniques may be used in a research project, such as semi-structured interviews and structured questionnaires. This could be the result of various techniques complementing one another or because various techniques are appropriate in various contexts. For instance, relatively unstructured conversations with important figures and representatives of different groups of people could be the first step in a study of crime and law enforcement patterns in a given area. The findings from these could be added to a more formal questionnaire that is distributed to a greater number of individuals in order to determine whether the conclusions drawn from the small-scale investigations are applicable to a wider audience.

3.3.1. Interviewing

A questionnaire can be used to conduct a much more highly structured interview than one with very little structure. Three types of interviews:

- The schedule standardized interview;
- The non-schedule standardized interview;
- The non-standardized interview.

The scheduled standardized interview is extremely structured, with the same questions asked in the same order to each respondent. Nonetheless, thorough initial research, development, and pre-testing are necessary; the latter may initially require less structured interviewing techniques. A list of details that each respondent must provide is part of the non-schedule standardized interview, also known as the focused interview. The questions may be asked in any order or with different wording. It necessitates competent interviewing and acknowledges the unique nature of each interviewee's contribution. There are no predetermined questions in a non-standardized interview. As the interview goes on, the interviewer can delve into different topics and explore a variety of theories. It also implies that the interviewee is free to explore areas during the interview that the researcher had not previously thought of. The goal of unstructured, non-standardized interviews is typically to extract information from respondents with as little researcher intervention as possible. However, the researcher is probably going to follow an agenda even in this situation. Usually, the researcher enters a situation with some expectations and emergent theories.

Each of the three interview formats has a distinct purpose. For instance, the standardized interview allows for more generalizable hypothesis testing, while the non-standardized interview is better for exploratory work that aims to determine the meanings and definitions used by respondents. It's critical to understand which function is being used when throughout the investigation. Every interview format has drawbacks, and how best to use them depends on the goal you want to achieve, the interviewers' experience, and the time and resources you have available.

3.3.1.1. Semi-structured Interviews

In socio-legal research, this approach is widely used, particularly by individuals without prior training in social research. It is attractive because it seems less complicated than creating a questionnaire, but it should only be utilized when necessary because it is appropriate and not just handy. Instead of just "fishing" for information, the theoretical requirements of a study should be the primary factor in deciding whether to use such a data collection technique. To make the most of an interview without coming across as naïve, you must have done enough preliminary research and informal inquiries to gain sufficient knowledge about the subject. Semi-structured interviews are not a reliable way to learn about a problem. Semi-structured interviews can be utilized when comprehensive research is the primary goal, particularly when understanding the significance of particular items to individuals or when examining a procedure or series of events is desired. Semi-structured interviews are probably going to be especially beneficial when examining complicated phenomena that might have evolved over time. For instance, asking people about their activities during specific times after they left school or some other period of time could be helpful if you were trying to figure out the connection between employment and criminality. Likewise, a study examining the relationship between fine default and other debt issues may require that participants recall their debt status through a meticulous reconstruction of their circumstances (Crow et al., 1993). Examining the experiences that members of ethnic minorities have had with the criminal justice system could be another application for semi-structured interviews. In this case, walking people through the process step-by-step could be beneficial.

When conducting what are known as "elite" studies, semi-structured interviews are also appropriate in certain situations (Moyser and Wagstaffe, 1987). A large portion of social science research targets "ordinary" people, or the weakest and least powerful members of society. Elite studies focus on the more powerful members of society, including senior police officers, judges, magistrates, and organization executives. If you are able to reach someone like that, they probably won't think filling out a questionnaire is for them. Making the most of the chance to interact with influential people is important, as is their desire to have some standing during the research process. These are probably circumstances that the researcher will need to handle carefully.

Semi-structured interviews can also be used when researching sensitive topics, which is a frequent occurrence in the field of criminology. These could include histories of abuse, mental illness, and both victimization and offense. Though not all situations can benefit from semi-structured interviewing, these examples should help illustrate some of the situations in which it may be suitable.

3.3.1.1.1. The Interview Schedule

The important aspect of the semi-structured interview is that the questions and their sequence are not entirely preset; we will address question construction in the context of questionnaire design in a moment. As a result, pre-planned "prompts" may come after the main questions, or the interviewer may use general prompts like "Could you tell me more about that?" or "Can you tell me what you mean by that?" to encourage the respondent to elaborate on a topic. This does not imply that questions in semi-structured interviews can be answered freely. The research process has produced hypotheses, which will influence the interview; however, the development of hypotheses is more likely to be aided by the interview than by testing them. The generalizability of the interviews determines how much of this occurs. Interviews can provide insight into a broader group of people, such as a bench of magistrates, when the interviewees are part of that group. However, the interviewees won't help you assess whether the information you learn from them is accurate in general unless they make up a trustworthy sample. For this to occur, a more methodical approach to data collection—such as distributing a questionnaire to every magistrate—might be required. What they say may be more conclusive, though, if you were interviewing people who are crucial to the topic of the study, like a chief constable, a judge at the Crown Court, or a senior civil servant in charge of a particular area of criminal justice policy.

3.3.1.1.2. ConInterview

Depending on the situation, the interview will be conducted in a different manner. The interview will probably take place in the respondent'srespondents' office if they work for a criminal justice system or another organization. It could be in their house, your office, or a mutually agreed-upon public place if they are a victim, an offender, or a member of the public. In any case, it's critical to make arrangements for both privacy and an uninterrupted interview (e.g., through phone calls). Cafés and bars are bad ideas. It is necessary to inform the interviewee ahead of time of things like the expected duration of the interview. The duration of the interview will depend on the specifics, and in some cases, it may be desirable and feasible to conduct multiple interviews with the same subject (for example, when attempting to piece together the subject's life history). If you are conducting an interview with a busy criminal justice practitioner, allow 45 to 60 minutes. One may be fortunate to receive 20 to 30 minutes if the respondent is an adolescent who has appeared in court. Even though most people dislike the idea of an interview going longer than planned, it is common for the interviewee to get carried away and talk for longer than planned. As such, you should be patient and ready to hear some things that will later turn out to be irrelevant.

The interview's recording method is a crucial factor to take into account. Ideally, a recorder will be used; however, this wil the interviewee's consent. If at all possible, seek permission ahead of time rather than putting them on the spot during the interview. In the event thatIf a recorder is being used, make sure the recording is clear and noise-free. Verify that the batteries are fully charged (or that there is a mains supply) and that there is adequate tape, disc, or memory on the recording medium being used for each interview. All of these might seem apparent, but tapes or batteries dying have ruined many a good interview. Taking notes is the best course of action he interview is not being electronically recorded, but managing the rapport required to conduct an interview, pay close attention to the answers, and taketaking notes at the same time is challengIt might be better to have some very brief aide-memories because respondents won't open up if they have to wait for you to write things down. If you don'tdo not know shorthand, try creating your own shorthand codes. It is occasionally feasible to conduct an interview with a fellow researcher present, which facilitates the sharing of the interviewing and note-taking tasks as well as the subsequent note-comparing. Even taking notes may not be feasible in some circumstances; in these cases, your best option is to jot down as much information as you can as soon as the interview is over. One of us experienced this while researching drug users and dealers. It is a good idea to write it up as soon as possible, if not the same day, even after taking notes and recording the interview. After an interview, words and concepts stick in your head until the next night when you sleep. Writing a summary of the findings from a group of interviews at regular intervals is beneficial when conducting a series of interviews. It's also critical to consider the insights you are gaining and how they relate to the theories you are researching.

It might be necessary for your design that the interview's agenda or timetable be the same each time. This allows you to draw general conclusions about all respondents, but it can also be annoying because, once you've spoken with a few people, you might come up with additional questions. However, if you keep changing the interview, you won't be able to find out how previous interviewees might have responded.

3.3.1.1.3. Analytic Induction

The method referred to as analytical induction represents an alternative. By employing this method, the objective is to gradually advance your understanding and concepts from one respondent to the next rather than asking the same or comparable questions of every respondent. In order to accomplish this, you formulate a preliminary hypothesis before conducting an interview with the first respondent based on it. After that, you take into account what you've discovered from this respondent and adjust your hypothesis as necessary. Based on this revised hypothesis, the next respondent is interviewed, and the information gleaned from the second interview is utilized to further refine the hypothesis so that it is applicable to both respondents. Until diminishing returns are attained, this process is repeated. Denzin proposes that participant observation can be used to demonstrate causality through analytical induction. The participant observer looks to refute a hypothesis until every case in the study can be explained, whereas quantitative analysis using survey techniques can manipulate variables statistically to control factors that might affect the relationship between the dependent variable and independent variables.

Lindesmith employed this method to explain how opiate addiction started in 1947. As an illustration, one of us employed this method several years ago while conducting exploratory research to determine why some users of illegal substances, like cannabis and LSD, were reporting negative side effects. One first theory could be that there was some sort of contamination with the medication. While the respondent had a negative experience, friends who had taken the same drug had not, according to the first interview. The first theory was disproved, which gave rise to the theory that some of his friends were to blame for the unpleasant experience. Additional interviews uncovered a number of additional details, such as the environment in which the drug was used and any personal issues that were going on at the time. After conducting several dozen interviews, it became clear that negative drug experiences could be the product of a specific set of circumstances that differ from person to person. This allows for the provision of guidance to users regarding ways to lower their chance of experiencing negative effects. Although analytical induction is a valuable technique, it is crucial to consider its limitations. The first relates to case selection, and the question of how far one can extrapolate from the cases interviewed remains relevant to social science research to this day. Denzin proposes that the maximization of the likelihood of finding a conclusive negative case should be the guiding principle when choosing cases to test a theory. A single instance is adequate to disprove or alter a hypothesis. That being said, a lot relies on the specific context of the research being conducted. Developing and improving hypotheses through analytical induction can be highly beneficial, as they can subsequently be verified on a larger and more representative sample. In a manner that is not possible with purely correlational analysis, it also offers the benefit of helping the researcher comprehend the mechanisms that influence the relationships between variables.

3.3.2. Group Interviews and Focus Groups

The second way to gather information through listening and asking is with groups of people. These come in two primary forms. It is helpful to start by defining the differences between the two methods—one uses focus groups, and the other employs group interviews. In its most basic form, group interviewing is simply conducting interviews with multiple subjects at once. You can record responses based on what each person says, you can use a schedule similar to one for a semi-structured interview, and you can analyze the data both quantitatively and qualitatively. It is more complex than doing interviews one by one, but the key features are:

- Group interviews are a way of saving time and resources;
- Several topics are usually discussed;
- The researcher is interested in the responses of the individuals involved.

Conversely, focus groups are typically employed to delve deeper into a particular subject, with the primary focus being on group dynamics. While there are some similarities between the two approaches, we will primarily focus on focus groups, with references to group interviews made when necessary.

3.3.2.1. When are Focus Groups Appropriate?

The sociologist Robert Merton created focus groups in the 1940s to assess the impact of propaganda during World War II (Merton et al., 1956). In the 1990s, they gained popularity once more as a research methodology and as a social and political policy instrument (Morgan, 1992; Morgan and Krueger, 1993). In semi-structured or unstructured interviews as well estionnaires, people are questioned and listened to. However, opinions and perceptions, as well as actions within organizations, are socially constructed and don'tdo not happen in a vacuum. People frequently interpret their experiences, even the most intimate ones, in relation to other people. People's interactions with their neighbors, coworkers, family, and friends shape their ideas and the way they express them. Thus, gathering a group of them together is one way to find out how they feel about things like safety and crime in their neighborhood, for example. This allows you to become more familiar with the back-and-forth social interactions that occur in daily life. Also, the image is livelier.

Individual interviews yield unchanging outcomes, suggesting that the subject has always thought or done this; however, communication alters people's understanding, perceptions, and conclusions.

People are constantly creating their own theories and testing them in light of their surroundings in a (non-scientific) manner. Though limited in scope, focus groups offer some insight into this process. For this reason, focus groups are helpful when we want to learn how people solve problems or come to decisions. They enable us to learn how different groups of people interpret and give meaning to a phenomenon, and they aid in our understanding of why people feel the way they do.

3.3.2.2. Limitations of Focus Groups

However, opinions that one person may voice alone are likely to face opposition when discussed in a group setting, and people may become uncomfortable if the subject is very delicate. One disadvantage of gathering material from groups of people is that they might be reluctant to discuss personal experiences, like being victimized, in front of others and might not say what's really going on. For instance, it is less likely that someone in a mixed-race group will be truthful if we are investigating people's opinions and experiences regarding how the criminal justice system handles individuals from various ethnic backgrounds. In a mixed-sex group, there are topics that both men and women might find less interesting to discuss.

Moreover, a group's dynamics and interactions can influence the direction of a discussion. We might see a very different picture than we would if the first, third, fifth, seventh, and ninth people were in one group and the second, fourth, sixth, eighth, and tenth people were in another group if ten people are divided into two groups based on the first ten in one group and the second ten in another.

Group interviewing, including focus groups and group interviews, is a much more involved process than collecting data one-on-one.

The researcher must be well-versed in interpersonal skills and has less control than in a single interview. A careful balance must be struck between enforcing just enough control to prevent the group from taking over and deviating from the subject and overly controlling the other. Should the latter occur, the researcher's influence might have an excessive amount of control over the group's responses. When multiple people are involved, the material is also more challenging to record and analyze.

3.3.2.3. Forming the Groups

It is usually necessary to conduct multiple focus groups in order to ensure that the discussions that emerge are not specific to that group. The number of groups you hold will rely on the resources at your disposal, but as a general rule, you should hold groups until you believe you can predict the topics the group will discuss (a process known as "category saturation"). A group will usually have six or eight people in it. Predicting how many people will actually show up on the day is a common challenge. The topic will determine how candidates are chosen. The idea behind focus groups is that, like any other type of social research, they should be as representative as possible of the subject matter being studied. This is where the sampling principles come in. Nonetheless, a fantastic advantage of focus groups is that they encourage conversation about shared interests (e.g., Judges discussing sentences or prostitutes discussing topics they'd prefer not to bring up in public. Asking a group of young offenders about their experiences with the criminal justice system is one example of the very purposeful sampling that is occasionally required. Morgan (2006) makes the case that homogeneous groups are better suited for discussing subjects that would be taboo in other settings.

3.3.2.4. Running the Groups

One way to encourage people to listen to what they have to say is to use a structured set of questions or to start with a few general questions that can be followed up with more specific inquiries and prompts (e.g., "What do you mean when you say that?" and "Can you give me any examples?"). Likewise, with regard to focus groups. An agenda is essential, even if the questions are not structured, to make sure that everyone stays on topic and that, in the event that multiple groups are being used, everyone is covering the same ground. The moderator's role is very important. He or she might be a researcher, but if funds allow, it might also be beneficial to have someone whose only responsibility is to facilitate. This frees up the researcher or researchers to focus on the action, both visually and verbally. The drawback of this is that a facilitator who isn't a researcher might not be as familiar with the demands of the study and less likely to lead participants in the right path. Two researchers should be present if there isn't an independent facilitator; one should moderate and the other should record, though this isn't as important if the session is being filmed.

The moderator should strike a balance between encouraging conversation and maintaining attention on the topics that will allow the study hypotheses to be investigated without being overly controlling. In addition to introducing themselves and outlining the goal of the study, he or she should also go over the session structure, recording methods, confidentiality policies, and what to do in the event that any participants have questions. In closing, the moderator will express gratitude to everyone present and explain what will happen to the data. Making sure there is a sufficient balance of participation in focus groups—both inviting more reserved participants and preventing more assertive individuals from becoming overly dominant—is one of the main concerns. However, there may be situations when sensitive topics are being discussed (e.g., family violence) when it is appropriate to offer participants the choice to stay silent. It is also important to note that focus groups may, whether on purpose or not, have an impact on participants. This is particularly important because criminological research frequently addresses difficult topics like victimization and crime. Sessions have the power to arouse memories or bring about shifts in attitude and perception.

It is a matter of good ethical practice to provide for handling this by carrying out any repercussions and, if necessary, directing participants to get assistance. Ideally, focus groups should be videotaped and/or audio recorded with a voice recorder. It's crucial to keep in mind that visual responses and reactions can teach us a lot in addition to what people say. In addition to eye contact and body language, people's expressions of anger, concern, and disgust can also be telling. This is especially crucial in situations where specific types of groups are being utilized. If, for instance, you were to gather a group of criminal justice professionals—judges, police, and probation officers—to discuss how local crime problems are being addressed, which members of the group seem more self-assured than others? Similarly, if the focus group consisted of young people, it would be intriguing to observe which members are more outspoken than others. This could reveal a lot about the influences of peer groups.

3.3.3. Questionnaires

A systematic approach to creating questions intended to elicit particular information, attitudes, behaviors, or opinions is required when creating questionnaires, which are crucial tools for effectively collecting data from large groups. To help with the development of pertinent and targeted questions, the process starts with precisely defining the study objectives. These questions can be left open-ended, allowing for more individualized responses and qualitative insights, or closed-ended, offering predetermined response options for quantitative analysis. To ensure clarity and prevent bias, questions should be formulated effectively and logically arranged to maintain a natural flow. Before a large-scale rollout, pretesting the questionnaire on a small sample size aids in identifying possible problems. The distribution strategy—online, offline, over the phone, or in person—should be determined by the study's objectives and target audience. It is crucial to take ethical issues—like getting informed consent and maintaining confidentiality—into account. After the data is gathered, it is cleaned to remove any inconsistencies before being analyzed to look at both the qualitative and quantitative responses thematically and statistically. The last stage entails presenting the results in their entirety, interpreting the data and coming to relevant conclusions through the use of narrative and suitable visual aids. All things considered, well-crafted questionnaires are effective tools for gathering thorough and trustworthy data in a variety of study domains.

3.3.3.1. Strengths and Weaknesses of Questionnaires

Firstly, they facilitate the relatively easy and quick collection of data about a large number of people, or whatever it is you are studying. Asking people to complete questionnaires at conferences, meetings, schools, colleges, or any other place where people are gathered can result in the collection of hundreds of completed forms in a comparatively short amount of time. You can achieve the same thing in a few days by sending people questionnaires. As a result, you can quickly obtain a vast quantity of information at your disposal. This seeming simplicity, though, could be misleading because there is no assurance that the method of administration you have chosen will yield consistent outcomes or a high rete.

Second, it can be quite simple and quick to produce at least some of the results after you have your completed questionnaires. A software package can be used to carry outct numerical analysis. Currently, it is relatively simple to enter data directly into a computer or set up a pre-coded questionnaire so that the responses can be scanned in tointo the computer. Entering data by hand can take some time. Once more, a word of caution: data errors can cause issues, and advanced statistical knowledge and data manipulation are frequently needed to produce more complex and valuable results.

Third, generalizations to a larger population are possible as long as the sample is a well-founded probability sample with a reasonable response rate. This is one of the survey's main advantages over alternative research methods. These factors have led to the widespread use of questionnaires as a method of inquiry. However, they also have disadvantages. One is that because they are now so popular, people may get "questionnaire fatigue" and find it difficult to fill them out. They are also a very stilted way to do research. They tend to simplify things because of the same characteristics that make them relatively simple to finish. A questionnaire can be a handy tool for gathering factual data, classifying information, and creating rankings and scales, but it is less helpful for examining intricate processes and shades of meaning. Another issue is validity: it's hard to guarantee that every respondent understands a question in the same way. Therefore, it is probably best to use questionnaires when you know exactly what you want to know—possibly from prior fieldwork—and you want to be able to extrapolate the findings to a much larger population. Due to their limitations, questionnaires should only be created after a fair amount of planning and preliminary work has been done. It is also best to avoid attempting to use them in an attempt to accomplish an impossible task. Examples of when a questionnaire might be appropriate in criminology are:

- Crime surveys, where a study is being undertaken of people's experiences of, or views about, crime-related matters;
- Questionnaires for criminal justice personnel about some aspect of their work.

3.3.3.2. Collecting the Data

Actually, the word "questionnaire" refers to a wide range of data gathering methods. These differ based on the information's source and the manner of collection (Table 3.1). The most common image that people have when they think of a questionnaire survey is that of a researcher interviewing a respondent in-person from a sample using a clipboard. It's not the only way of administration, even though it's fairly popular. It is among the best because it allows for both visual and verbal interaction, allowing the participants to express themselves most effectively. A popular substitute is the quick and reasonably priced phone interview. The fact that not everyone had access to a phone in the past made telephone interviews problematic and resulted in a skewed sample. Landlines helped to lessen this issue, but the proliferation of cell phones in recent years has made things more difficult because people are more likely to rely on their phones, which make it more difficult for researchers to get in touch with them. Given that telephone surveys frequently rely on landlines, they may leave out specific populations that don't have access to personal landlines, such as those who are homeless, live in hostels, or don't have a place of their own. In addition, conducting interviews over the phone lacks the personal touch of in-person interviews and has lost value due to its increased use in marketing campaigns. However, it might still be helpful when interviewing individuals who are speaking on behalf of companies or organizations.

The internet has also been utilized to collect online questionnaire responses, which has the benefit of anonymity. When an organization wants information from its employees, students, clients, and so on, it is probably especially helpful;

that is, if the person making the inquiry has access to a database or sample frame. Nonetheless, its applicability to general population surveys is restricted due to the greater challenge of obtaining a feasible sample frame. Moreover, a 2003 study discovered that even "even after very considerable weighting of the results has been undertaken or care exercised to ensure that those who are asked to complete an internet poll are demographically and politically representative of the whole population," results from online surveys are not always representative of the population as a whole. A convenient and reasonably priced method of surveying a large number of individuals or organizations is through postal questionnaires. However, response rates may be low, particularly if the questionnaire is received "out of the blue" by the recipient. Additionally, the researcher has very little control over how the questionnaire is completed, and there is no chance to clarify any questions that the respondent might interpret in an unclear way.

Table 3.1. *Data Collection*

Methods of collection	*Who produces the information*
Face-to-face	Researcher
Telephone	Researcher's assistants
Internet	Agency staff
Postal	Respondent

Source: http://ndl.ethernet.edu.et/bitstream/123456789/23015/1/228.pdf.

3.3.3.3. Who Produces the Information?

Who participates in the collection process is an additional crucial factor to take into account. When respondents choose self-completion, you have less control over how the questions are interpreted and must take care to ensure they understand what is expected of them. Self-completion involves respondents providing the data directly. If interviews are being used for collection, who is conducting the interviews? If assistants are being used, they must receive training to guarantee consistency in the process. Workers in an organization that assists the individuals under investigation may occasionally be able to gather or supply information. For instance, the mediators will probably be interviewing referrals anyhow if you are studying a victim-offender mediation program, and they can explain that they wish to ask questions that will also be used for research. Similarly, a large portion of the data for a study on offenders participating in employment and training programs may come from forms filled out by project staff members when participants join and discontinue the program. People may be reluctant to tell project workers certain things in such circumstances, so it's important to keep in mind that the relationship between the worker and client differs from that between the researcher and respondent. It is important to remember that although these employees might be skilled in their field, they may not have received training as researchers or be aware of the demands of the field.

Information extracted from agency records is one type of data collection that follows a similar principle. Data gathered for court or medical records is gathered to satisfy the needs of the relevant agency, not research needs. There might be a lot of material to sort through, and some important pieces of information might not be available or might not be in the best format for researchers. For instance, the prior convictions of offenders may be a crucial piece of information in a study on sentencing in magistrate's courts. It is possible, though, that this information was kept by the Crown Prosecution Service or the police after the case was resolved, and is not currently in the court files. It may therefore be necessary to contact these agencies as well.

Apart from the aforementioned, it is imperative to take into account the conditions under which data is gathered. Which people will be interviewed, if a family, agency, or business is involved, for example? The mode of collection has an impact on the validity and reliability of the data as well as the expected response rate. Will it be in the street, on the doorstep, in offices? If respondents are not guaranteed privacy and confidentiality, it is unlikely that the information gathered is reliable. The information is unlikely to be trustworthy if different people ask the same questions in different ways. Response rates are significant because they can skew the results because individuals who choose not to answer a questionnaire might differ from those who do in some way. You will be less able to extrapolate from your chosen sample to the entire population if the response rate is low.

Responses to surveys about one's intention to vote are one instance of this. Any extrapolation from the survey to likely election results may be incorrect if those who are likely to vote for a specific party also dislike being asked how they will vote. This is what happened during the General Election of 1991. It is inevitable that those who have broken the law will be reluctant to tell a stranger about it, which makes it challenging, but not impossible, to conduct reliable surveys of the offending rates based on self-report. If respondents are unprepared for postal questionnaires, they are especially likely to receive low response rates. Offering to pay respondents or rewarding participants with coupons or prizes has been one strategy used to address the response rate issue. This gives rise to accusations that people who accept these offers will respond in an untrustworthy manner because they are acting for the "wrong" reason or may provide information in an atempt to appease the person wo is calling the shots. The question that inevitably arises is, "What constitutes an acceptable response rate?" To which the inevitable response is, "tThere is no definitive answer.." It is customary in social science research that, for a general population survey employing in-person interactions based on a reliable sampling frame, a minimum of 60% of respondents would be considered acceptable. However, this implies that four out of ten sample participants are disregarded, which introduces a significant degree of uncertainty. Because you might be working with populations that are difficult to establish contact with, the circumstances for getting a good response in criminology aren't always ideal. Instead of accepting a low response rate, though, the solution to this is to minimize the possibility of non-response when designing the study. This can entail reaching out to individuals via a middleman, like an organization they are already in contact with. For instance, you could get in touch with known offenders by using the probation or jail services. An alternative route to access could be through organizations that assist victims or offenders.

3.3.3.4. Drafting the Questionnaire

3.3.3.4.1. Content

The theoretical underpinnings of the investigation and the hypotheses being investigated or tested dictate what goes into a questionnaire in any empirical study. Thus, you begin by enquiring as to what data is required in order to test or formulate hypotheses. Every question should ideally be considered a variable, with some variables serving as independent, some as dependent, and some as intervening factors. A few of the variables will be classificatory or demographic information, like marital status, age, sex, and ethnicity. These are probably going to be the independent factors that the dependent variables are measured against. The topics you are most interested in learning more about will be covered by additional questions, and these will probably make up the dependent variables. Thus, for instance, a very basic survey might be interested in learning what people think about different facets of crime and associated issues. This might lead to hypotheses such as:

- Whether younger people are more in favor of legalizing cannabis than older people;
- Whether people from higher income groups are more liberal towards convicted offenders than those from lower income groups;
- Whether men have more confidence in the police than women.

The respondent's attributes (gender, income, and age) serve as independent variables in each of these cases, while their opinions on various subjects serve as dependent variables. Additionally, there might be some intervening factors that are considered. For instance, when comparing people's opinions on whether cannabis should be legalized, it may be crucial to take into account respondents' personal cannabis use histories and examine the impact of these factors in addition to age differences – a three-way analysis. It is also important to keep in mind that an item may be a dependent or intervening variable in relation to one hypothesis while acting as an independent variable in the context of another. For instance, income is the independent variable in the second hypothesis mentioned above regarding income and perceptions of offenders. However, gender would be the independent variable and income would be the dependent variable if our hypothesis were true—that is, that men generally make more money than women. When creating a questionnaire, take into account the purpose of each question. Regardless of the topic, it is generally a good idea to go over the final draft and consider the purpose of each and every question, how you plan to use it in the analysis, and what you want to do with the findings. This involves several considerations: theoretical (every question should have a theoretical justification somewhere along the line), pragmatic (having an excessively lengthy questionnaire that wastes a lot of material is pointless), and ethical (why are you asking someone something if it's not really necessary?).

3.3.3.4.2. Sequence

When drafting a questionnaire, it is quite important to think about the order in which questions will be asked. There are a variety of reasons for this:

- One of them is to just consider what order will make the most sense and be most cozy for the responders. One of the issues with this is that you shouldn't start off by asking a lot of personal questions to people you don't know well. Conversely, it might be crucial to find out people's age and background to determine if they fit into any specific categories that are relevant to the discussion that follows. In addition, it's a good idea to record some important information in case the questionnairpleted for any reason.
- Another reason for giving careful thought to the sequence of questions is what is referred to as routing. Some questions may be not applicable to all respondentsrespondents, and they need to be directed to the next question that is appropriate for them, for example:
  - Have you been burgled within the last six months?
  - I, go to Question X; If no, go to Question Y.

These are loop-related filter questions. To ensure that respondents will be guided through the questionnaire in the correct order and won'twill not be left stuck, it could be helpful to create a flow chart.

- The timing of events. If, as an example, you are interviewing someone about their history of employment and offending, it may be necessary to have a question sequence that takes them through a sequence of time, such as since they left school, or over the past three years. This could bedone diagrammatically by showing them a dated timeline. Remember that you also need to think about how it is going to be analyzed subsequently.
- Multiple events. It's possible that some people have had multiple experiences. Some people may have experienced multiple instances of victimization or a string of fines that preceded them becoming defaulters, for instance, if you are asking about their experiences. It might be necessary to ask someone the same set of questions multiple times, once for each experience that is to be recorded. It might be worthwhile to think about whether information is required regarding all of the incidents, those that occurred within a specific time frame (like the last year), the last three incidents, or just the most recent one. Even though you might overlook significant experiences for specific people, a well-sized probability sample will ensure that the overall picture is representative of the sample. Once more, careful consideration should be given to the analysis of a sequence of incidents.
- Lastly, the sequence in which questions are posed may have an impact on the responses that are received. If you were to ask people, for instance, what sentences they believe burglars should receive after asking them about the effects burglaries have on their victims, you might get different answers than if you asked people first what sentences they believe burglars should receive before asking them about the effects burglaries have on victims.

3.3.3.4.3. Question Construction

There are a number of important rules about question composition:

- **Avoid Leading or Biased Questions:** A research inquiry is rarely, if ever, truly "objective," as asking certain questions instead of others implies that you are approaching the subject from a specific angle. But every effort should be made to ensure that the questions are as impartial as possible. Therefore, it is better to ask, "Are you for or against hanging?" as opposed to, "Are you in favor of hanging?"
- **One Idea Per Question:** Attempting to squeeze too much information out of each question is a common mistake made when attempting to keep questionnaires as short as possible. This may

lead to an excessively complicated query. Asking someone how they typically get to and from work, for instance, is inappropriate because different people may have different commutes. Here, two questions are required as opposed to one.

- **Use Simple Sentence Construction:** clearly defined terms, and avoid jargon. The more complex a question is, the more chance of a misunderstanding occurring.
- **Beware of 'Social Desirability' Effects:** For instance, asking someone, "Are you in favor of recycling?" is unlikely to cause them to disagree, but it might not accurately represent their actual opinions or actions. According to one study, kids learn how to control their reactions so they don't openly display their ethnic prejudices. In a similar vein, steer clear of questions that have "obvious" answers, like "Are you against cruelty to children?" or "Are you afraid of crime?" Instead, ask hypothetical questions, be more specific, or list potential concerns and ask respondents to rank the top two.

It is a good idea to put yourself in the position of the respondent and think about how you might answer a question.

3.4. SOURCES OF STATUTES

Statutes come from a variety of sources and are essential to a jurisdiction's legal system and legislative process. Gaining an understanding of these sources is crucial to understanding the creation, interpretation, and application of laws. The primary sources of statutes include:

- **Legislatures:** The legislature—whether federal, state, or local—is the main source of statutes. State legislatures pass state laws in the US, whereas Congress enacts federal statutes. Ordinances are imposed by local governments, such as county boards and city councils. These legislative bodies draft, discuss, and decide on bills that, once signed into law by the executive branch (e.g., either the mayor, governor, or president).
- **Executive Orders:** Executive orders signed by the president or state governors may have legal authority even though they are not statutes in the conventional sense. These directives are frequently used to carry out policies that fall under the purview of the executive branch and to guide the activities of government agencies. Executive orders may occasionally have an impact on how current laws are interpreted and applied.

- **Administrative Agencies:** Statutory-created administrative agencies are empowered to promulgate regulations with legal force behind them. These rules interpret and carry out legislative directives. In addition, agencies possess quasi-legislative authority, which enables them to address matters not specifically mentioned in the statute. Particularly in intricate and specialized fields like labor laws, securities regulation, and environmental regulation, the ensuing rules and regulations are crucial sources of law.
- **Constitutions:** Both the U.S. Constitution and state constitutions are fundamental sources of statutory law. They establish the framework for government authority and set forth the basic rights and principles that statutes must adhere to. Constitutional provisions often require legislative action to be fully implemented and can also limit the scope of statutory law.
- **International Treaties and Agreements:** After they are ratified, international treaties and agreements are included in the statutes. Legislative action may be necessary to fully implement the provisions of these agreements, which have the potential to impact domestic statutes. Trade, human rights, and environmental protection are just a few of the many topics that treaties may address.
- **Judicial Decisions:** Statutory law is derived from judicial interpretations of statutes, not the statutes themselves. Court decisions have the power to effectively establish new legal principles or clarify those that already exist. Courts are crucial in interpreting the meaning and application of statutes. The interpretation and application of future statutes are guided by this corpus of case law.

Each of these sources contributes to the dynamic and evolving nature of statutory law, shaping the legal landscape and ensuring that laws remain relevant and effective in addressing societal needs and challenges.

3.4.1. Case Laws and its Sources

Judicial precedent, or case law, is a corpus of law that is created by judges making decisions in court rather than by legislative acts or executive branch directives. It is an essential source of law, especially in common law jurisdictions where the interpretation and application of the law are determined by earlier court rulings. The opinions and decisions rendered by trial, appellate, and supreme courts constitute the main source of case law. These rulings interpret laws, rules, and constitutional clauses; they frequently close legislative gaps and shed light on murky legal matters. Furthermore, case law can originate from several judicial levels, with rulings from higher courts usually carrying greater weight and serving as legally binding precedent for lesser courts operating under the same jurisdiction. Legal principles established by common law, which is derived from enduring customs and judicial practices, are another source of case law. Judicial rulings continuously mold this corpus of unwritten laws, mirroring the changing social mores and customs. Additionally, case law is influenced by international judicial bodies like the European Court of Human Rights and the International Court of Justice, especially when it comes to issues pertaining to human rights and international law. All things considered, case law acts as a dynamic and interpretive source of law, making sure that legal systemso be adaptable to changing social norms and new situations.

3.4.2. Foreign Cases and Statutes

Statutes and court rulings from foreign jurisdictions are referred to as "foreign cases" and "enactments..enactments." These legal resources are essential for international legal practice and comparative law studies because they show how various legal systems handle related problems. International treaties, customary international law, and domestic laws as interpreted by foreign courts are all included in the category of foreign cases. When examining the ways in which various legal traditions—such as common law, civil law, or mixed legal systems—resolve legal disputes, these cases are especially helpful. International collaboration and harmonization are crucial in fields like commercial law, environmental law, and human rights, where foreign court rulings can have a significant impact on domestic case law. Legislative enactments from other countries are known as foreign statutes. Local governments, regional legislatures, and national parliaments have all passed laws that fall under this category. Legal academics and practitioners can compare legislative strategies, comprehend various regulatory frameworks, and find best practices that could be modified for their own legal systems by studying foreign statutes. Examining foreign labor laws, health laws, or environmental policies, for example, can provide fresh insights and creative solutions to typical legal problems. Foreign statutes are important for guaranteeing adherence to international obligations because international treaties and agreements frequently demand the implementation of particular statutes in participating countries. Furthermore, international business operations, immigration, and cross-border transactions may be impacted by foreign statutes, so a comprehensive understanding is necessary for efficient legal practice in a globalized society. All things considered, international cases and statutes contribute to the advancement of cross-jurisdictional understanding, legal innovation, and the creation of coherent international legal norms.

3.4.3. Importance of Case Laws

Since "neither a judge nor a lawyer knows more than a relatively tiny part of the law," the legal professional, judge, and researcher all search for the law to be applied to a particular case. However, they must be aware of where and how to locate the law. Attorneys obtain pertinent legal propositions to utilize in a given case from two primary sources: rulings rendered by superior courts, etc., the laws, and the precedents.

A fact situation covered by one source of law does not always correspond to a single law. Frequently, one cannot infer the legal conclusion to be applied in a given factual scenario from a specific body of law. A lawyer who is well-versed in both substantive and procedural laws can sift through a client's mountain of information to find the pertinent facts for a case. A lawyer employs reasoning to establish a correlation between pertinent facts and the law that must be applied to them.

A precedent is essentially a body of case law that directs the resolution of a case that is similar to it. Case laws have frequently been crucial in determining how to interpret statutes. Case law is the set of guidelines and precepts that judges articulate and apply when rendering judgments. In a case-law-based system, a judge must render a decision in a subsequent case in the same manner as the previous case, unless there is a valid reason why they cannot. This implies that when cases have identical material facts, they must be decided in the same manner.

Naturally, this does not mean that every fact must be the same. Case law is the set of guidelines and precepts that judges have articulated and applied when rendering judgments. The case laws are an essential component of any doctrinal investigation since the decisions made by the High Court and Supreme Court bind the lower courts.

ruling in a specific case sets "precedent." The precedent doctrine states that a judge's decision when rendering a judgment does not necessarily set a precedent. However, the judgment's justification for the ruling is the only thing that makes it precedent. Thus, the justification given in the decision of an appeal case becomes an essential topic for a lawyer to research and evaluate. The researchers' secondary source of data is case laws. A legal issue may arise while the researcher is reading case laws. In this situation, he can formulate a hypothesis, carry out an empirical investigation, and conduct research. The arguments in deductive analysis are supported by case laws as the evidentiary source. Case laws are used by judges, attorneys, and researchers to support their logical arguments. As a result, case laws serve as legal studies' official source of data.

3.4.4. Analysis of Cases and Statutes

Investigation of cases in a designated problem area constitutes the majority of legal research. Setting legal trends is a difficult undertaking. Helping with the precise fact and its nature are very difficult issues. The proceedings in Coasts typically center on factual issues related to specific criminal trials. Court battles are won and lost according to which party can provide more evidence to support its claims. As stated by William J. Grode and Paul K. Hatt" an observation is considered an empirically verifiable fact. The fact could be a law, a behavior, or an attitude. What is the rationale behind accepting or rejecting something as fact? This aspect is criminal to the electric is a criminal case is the central question of doctrinal research on criminal justice.

How are facts established? There are three common bases for establishing facts:

- Authority;
- infusion; and
- logic

But these methods may lead us to false conclusion.

Therefore, a scientific method has developed for establishing facts.

Systematically collects data, undertake tests for their internal consistency and subjects them to empirical examination. Thus, scientific information is based on reliable and valid observation.

The researcher must undertake case interpretation following the verification of facts. However, prior to that, the data must be broken down into its component parts in order to answer the research question or hypothesis. Using the legal system as an example, let's say a researcher believes there is a link between poverty and criminality. He gathers sociological information about the individuals found guilty in court cases over time from court records, and he then has to arrange, panic, and manipulate the information in order to find the answer to the research question or conjecture. Using the legal system as an example, let's say a researcher believes there is a link between poverty and criminality. He gathers sociological data from court records and case files about individuals found guilty of theft over time. He then has to arrange, deconstruct, and manipulate the information to find the answer to the research question. A study may also examine the judges' attitudes. While rendering a decision in a given case, a judge attempts to make generalizations (ratios) by connecting the case to more general social and historical concerns concerning that specific society in addition to discussing the land and circumstances (facts) of that particular case. He might make obiter dicta that have an impact on how people behave in social situations and how big-picture issues are handled.

REFERENCES

1. Arber, S. (2001). Secondary analysis of survey data. In N. Gilbert (Ed.), *Researching Social Life* (pp. 86–100). London: Sage Publications.
2. Atkinson, P. (1981). Transition from school to working life. Sociological Research Unit, Cardiff (Unpublished memorandum).
3. Atkinson, R., & Flint, J. (2001). Accessing hidden and hard-to-reach populations: Snowball research strategies. *University of Surrey, Social Research Update*, (33).
4. Crow, I., Howells, G., & Moroney, M. (1993). Credit and debt: Choices for poorer consumers. In G. Howells, I. Crow, & M. Moroney (Eds.), *Aspects of Credit and Debt* (pp. 31–48). London: Sweet and Maxwell.
5. Denzin, N. K. (1988). *The Research Act: A Theoretical Introduction to Sociological Methods* (2nd ed.). Englewood Cliffs, N.J.: Prentice Hall.
6. Goode, W. J., & Hatt, P. K. (1952). *Methods of Social Research*. New York: McGraw Hill.
7. Kershaw, C. (1998). Interpreting reconviction rates. In *The Use and Impact of Community Supervision, Research Bulletin No. 39, Special Edition* (pp. 9–16). London: Home Office Research and Statistics Directorate.
8. Lewins, A. (2001). Computer assisted qualitative data analysis. In N. Gilbert (Ed.), *Researching Social Life* (pp. 205–221). London: Sage Publications.
9. Maguire, M. (2002). Crime statistics: The 'data explosion' and its implications. In M. Maguire, R. Morgan, & R. Reiner (Eds.), *The Oxford Handbook of Criminology* (3rd ed., pp. 201–234). Oxford: Oxford University Press.
10. Morgan, D. L. (1992). Designing focus group research. In M. Stewart (Ed.), *Tools for Primary Care Research* (pp. 105–114). Thousand Oaks, CA: Sage.
11. Morgan, D. L. (2006). Focus groups. In V. Jupp (Ed.), *The Sage Dictionary of Social Research Methods* (pp. 83–85). London: Sage.
12. Morgan, D. L., & Krueger, R. A. (1993). When to use focus groups and why. In D. L. Morgan (Ed.), *Successful Focus Groups: Advancing the State of the Art* (pp. 3–19). Newbury Park, CA: Sage.
13. Moyser, G., & Wagstaffe, M. (1987). *Research Methods for Elite Studies*. London: Allen and Unwin.
14. O'Leary, Z. (2004). *The Essential Guide to Doing Research*. London: Sage Publications.

15. Oppenheim, A. N. (2000). *Questionnaire Design, Interviewing and Attitude Measurement*. London: Continuum.
16. Rutland, A., Cameron, L., Milne, A., & McGeorge, P. (2005). Social norms and self-presentation: Children's implicit and explicit intergroup attitudes. *Child Development, 76*(2), 451–466.
17. Sampson, R. J., & Raudenbush, S. W. (1999). Systematic social observation of public spaces: A new look at disorder in urban neighborhoods. *American Journal of Sociology, 105*(3), 603–651.
18. Schuman, H., & Presser, S. (1996). *Questions and Answers in Attitude Surveys: Experiments on Question Form, Wording, and Context*. London: Sage.
19. Selltiz, C., Jahoda, M., Deutsch, M., & Cook, S. W. (1964). *Research Methods in Social Relations*. New York: Holt, Rinehart & Winston.
20. Sherman, L. W., Gottfredson, D. C., MacKenzie, D. L., Eck, J., Reuter, P., & Bushway, S. D. (1998). *Preventing Crime: What Works, What Doesn't, and What's Promising*. Washington, DC: U.S. Department of Justice, National Institute of Justice.
21. Smith, J. K. (1983). Quantitative versus qualitative research: An attempt to clarify the issue. *Educational Researcher, 12*(3), 6–13.
22. Spalek, B. (1995). Trust as an ideology: Exploring fear of white collar crime. Paper presented at the British Criminology Conference, Loughborough University, 18–21 July 1995.

Chapter **4**

Crime Analysis Process, Application, and Data

Contents

Introduction **162**

4.1. The Crime Analysis Process **162**

4.2. Types of Crime Analysis **168**

4.3. Crime Mapping by Type of Analysis **177**

4.4. Crime Analysis Data and Technology **179**

4.5. Databases Used in Crime Analysis **185**

4.6. Using Calls-for-Service Data to Study Crime Problems **199**

References **205**

INTRODUCTION

Crime analysis is a systematic process used by law enforcement agencies to identify patterns and trends in criminal activity. This analytical approach is essential for developing effective strategies for crime prevention, resource allocation, and tactical decision-making.

The crime analysis process begins with data collection. Law enforcement agencies gather a wide range of data, including incident reports, arrest records, calls for service, and more. This data is then cleaned and standardized to ensure accuracy and consistency. Advanced analytical tools and software are often employed to manage and process this vast amount of information efficiently.

Once the data is prepared, analysts apply various techniques to uncover meaningful patterns. These techniques can include spatial analysis, which examines the geographic distribution of crimes; temporal analysis, which looks at crime trends over time; and social network analysis, which explores the relationships between individuals involved in criminal activities. By employing these methods, analysts can identify hotspots of criminal activity, predict potential crime occurrences, and understand the underlying factors contributing to crime. The application of crime analysis extends beyond mere data examination. It plays a crucial role in strategic planning, helping law enforcement agencies allocate resources more effectively. For instance, by identifying crime hotspots, police departments can deploy officers to areas where they are most needed, thereby enhancing their presence and deterrence capabilities. Additionally, crime analysis supports community policing efforts by fostering a data-driven approach to addressing public safety concerns. The data used in crime analysis is diverse and extensive. It includes not only traditional law enforcement records but also data from other sources such as social media, public records, and surveillance systems. This comprehensive approach ensures that analysts have a holistic view of the crime landscape, enabling them to make more informed decisions. Crime analysis is a vital process that leverages data and analytical techniques to enhance law enforcement strategies. Its applications range from tactical operations to strategic planning, all aimed at improving public safety and reducing crime.

4.1. THE CRIME ANALYSIS PROCESS

The crime analysis process, a technique unique to the field that is used in all of the work that crime analysts do, is covered in this section. The crime analysis process, however, is an outline of the methodology and approach a crime analyst uses to conduct crime analysis and produce crime analysis products rather than a predetermined set of tasks and techniques or hardware and software used by crime analysts. The crime analysis process won't change regardless of the technology an analyst uses today or in the future. The crime analysis process, as it is generally carried out and refined over time, is depicted in Figure 4.1. Data collection, data collation, analysis, results distribution, and user feedback incorporation are the steps in this process (Gottlieb, Arenberg, and Singh, 1994). Data, or observations, are the first step in the crime process. Data originateoriginates from a variety of sources, most frequently from outside sources of crime analysis. Crime analysts review information that has been seen and gathered by other professionals, including police, 911 dispatchers, community service coordinators, census takers, and geographers.

4.1.1. Collection

Data collection, which is closely related to data storage, is the first step in the crime analysis process. As was previously mentioned, the crime analysis function has no direct control over this step. Officers or non-political staff members input crime reports and other data into a computer system in the majority of police departments. While many police departments now write their reports entirely on computers, some still require officers to write portions of them by hand or to call in reports over the phone for data entry clerks to type. Police dispatchers input every call for service's specifics straight into the computer system in almost all agencies. Crime analysis depends on the policies that govern data entry procedures and the diligence of those who carry them out. These factors influence the amount and quality of data that is entered into the system and the analysis that follows.

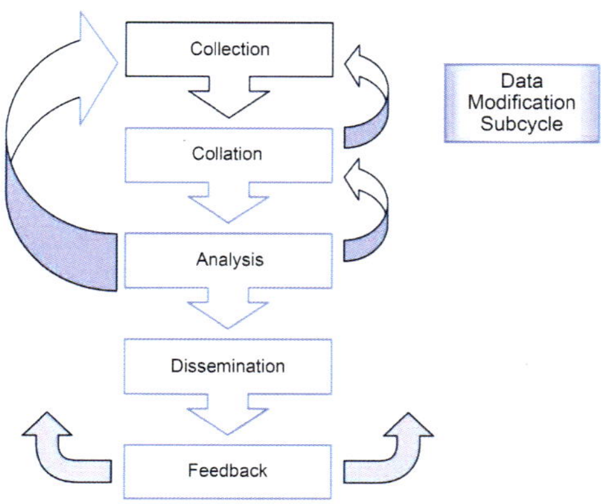

Figure 4.1. *The crime analysis process.*

Source: Rachel Boba Santos, Crime Analysis with Crime Mapping, ISBN: 9781506331034.

Subsets of the data that police departments gather are compiled for analysis because some of the information is not directly relevant to crime analysis. Police officers create diagrams of traffic accidents, for instance, in order to file insurance claims and handle other legal matters. Crime analysts are typically not concerned with the specifics of each event, even though this data is kept to comprehend the nature of each crash. Instead, they are focused on gathering information about the times, dates, places, and types of all crashes. Because this information can aid in their understanding of this kind of activity more broadly, only the pertinent information—not every diagram—is made available and downloaded for crime analysis.

The quantity and format of data stored also play a significant role in crime analysis and can affect how applicable and valuable the findings are. Data must be routinely collected in an electronic format (e.g., weekly or daily), and preserved for a long period of time (e.g., for a number of years) to be beneficial for the study of crime.

Crime analysts find that using paper copies of reports and other information is inefficient because it takes too long and is difficult to analyze the data. For crime analysis to be effective, information must be coded into an electronic database. In the past ten or so years, police departments have increasingly tended to make their reports and other vital information available electronically, not just for crime analysis but for all purposes. This is despite the fact that, in certain departments, crime analysts still manually enter specific data into a computer system.

For data to be useful for crime analysis, especially for immediate and short-term problems, there must be a reasonable amount of time between observation or data collection and the availability of the data. For instance, the information is useless for determining current crime trends if electronic crime report data are not accessible for several weeks after the reports are written by the officers. Additionally, a sufficient quantity of data must be archived (e.g., several years' worth) in order for crime analysts to gather sufficient data to perform adequate analyses, particularly for persistent issues. For instance, two months' worth of data would not paint a picture of a burglary problem that would be as complete as one or two years' worth.

Ultimately, crime analysts require the ability to work with substantial volumes of uncooked data. Often, police computer systems are limited to retrieving singular records or generating statistical summaries and lists. However, crime analysts necessitate the capacity to export digital data and specific parameters into numerous analytical software applications to carry out investigations employing diverse analytical methods.

To summarize, the crime analysis data collection process requires the following:

1. The data must be collected accurately and consistently.
2. Only data relevant for crime analysis are compiled.
3. The data must be collected in a timely manner.
4. The data must be archived for an adequate amount of time to allow for effective analysis.
5. The data must be accessible in electronic raw form to be queried and downloaded.

All data used in crime analysis, including information gathered from sources other than the police department (e.g., data on parole and probation, geographical data, and census data).

4.1.2. Collation

The primary data sources (e.g., general police data collection systems, such as a record management system and a computer-aided dispatch system are used in crime analysis (crime reports and calls for service). Many of these systems are still not made to collect and store data that makes effective crime analysis possible, despite technological advancements. As a result, before utilizing data for analysis, crime analysts frequently find that it is necessary to query, reformat, and compile it. This can involve choosing particular data sets, generating new variables, and carrying out quality control (i.e., clearing the data). Data collation entails a number of different tasks, but generally it takes three forms:

1. Cleaning is the process of identifying then correcting mistakes and inconsistencies in the data.
2. Geocoding is the process of bringing crime analysis data together with geographic data so they can be analyzed spatially.
3. Creating new variables is the process of recoding or computing new variables from existing variables for more effective analysis. For example, the time it takes for an officer to respond to a call for service after being dispatched (i.e., response time) is computed by subtracting the time the call came in to the call center from when the officer arrived on the scene.

4.1.3. Analysis

Following the collection and preparation of the data, analysis is performed using a variety of statistical and visual aids. Unfortunately, problems with the data are frequently unknown to a crime analyst (e.g., until the analysis process is started, the data do not measure what needs to be studied or were not collected correctly. When this happens, the analyst frequently has to go back and revisit the steps related to data collection and collation in order to enhance or modify the methods used in data collection, archiving, and collation in order to finish the analysis and produce the crime analysis products. This procedure, known as the data modification subcycle, is essential to the crime analysis process and helps every police department that uses it to improve the process as a whole.

4.1.4. Data Modification Subcycle

Figure 4.2's arrows show how the data modification subcycle works. Data collection and collation in this crime analysis subprocess are modified in accordance with the crime analysis process itself. The steps in the crime analysis process are not sequential; first comes collection, then collation, then analysis. The analyst will typically discover that each of these steps can influence the one after it or necessitate going back and reviewing an earlier step. For instance, the analyst may discover new methods for gathering data while cleaning the data for collation; the demands of the analysis may lead the analyst to suggest adjustments for both police department data collection and collation. The following gives some specific examples of this interplay:

- An examination of the nature of loud parties in a particular area reveals that calls-for-service data contain only a "loud noise" call type, so the analyst cannot distinguish reports of loud parties from reports of general loud noises. The analyst must go back to the data collection step and recommend a new call type labeled loud party for police officers and dispatchers to use.
- The chief of police requests that an analyst examine crime data for the past 10 years, but there is a departmental policy that requires storage for only 5 years. The analyst examines the existing 5 years of crime data and recommends the adoption of a new policy for data storage that will allow for the preservation of 10 years' worth of data.
- Through analysis, a crime analyst determines that there are inconsistencies in the crime location variable (e.g., addresses are assigned to incorrect police beats); this leads to the development of a more comprehensive data cleaning process.

It is an indisputable fact of crime analysis that the process of crime analysis and the enhancement of data collection and collation require ongoing attention for improvement, even though problems like those outlined here might not arise in every analysis scenario. Analysts should never presume that a database is reliable or that using it for crime analysis will happen right away. Unexpected issues frequently come up, and new information on crime, disorder, and policing may not be gathered yet. Since some problems with the data are not found until the data are analyzed, the data modification subcycle is a crucial part of the crime analysis process and a crucial quality control mechanism for the entire police department. As a result, a large portion of crime analysts' time and resources are dedicated to resolving such problems.

4.1.5. Dissemination

The crime analyst must convey the findings to a variety of audiences after the data analysis is finished. Actually, until data and information are successfully conveyed, they do not qualify as analysis (Bruce, 2008a). Results of crime analyses can be shared via phone calls, emails, Internet documents, presentations, reports, and maps on paper and electronic media. Information on crime analysis is intended for a variety of audiences, including the news media, police management, citizens, students, and other analysts.

When communicating the findings of a crime analysis, analysts must bear in mind two crucial points. First and foremost, the presentation needs to be customized to the audience's level of knowledge. For instance, analysts may need to define various types of crimes more clearly for a citizen audience (e.g., theft versus. burglary) prior to sharing the findings of the analysis. Second, only the most essential informated when the results are presented. A significant portionA massive portion of crime analysis's work is done in the background (e.g., data collection), and details about all that labor don't have to be included in the results presentation.

Crime analysts should only share information that is pertinent to the subject at hand when sharing their findings, but they should also maintain documentation of all the work they have done. When the results of an analysis project can be succinctly summarized in one or two key points, analysts do not need to go into detail. In order to verify that the right procedures have been followed and for their own replication, analysts should also document the methods they used for gathering, compiling, and analyzing data. However, when disseminating results, they should only highlight the information that is most relevant to a given audience.

By sharing the findings of their analyses with other analysts, researchers, and police practitioners, crime analysts can help police departments as well as advance knowledge regarding disorder issues, crime, and general police practices. These findings can guide police procedures (e.g., enforcement or prevention initiatives) and techniques for crime analysis (e.g., replication of effective data collection and analytical strategies), as well as contribute to the general public's understanding of crime and other matters pertaining to law enforcement (e.g., the characteristics of prostitution in rural regions). That being said, over time, the dissemination of crime analysis results from multiple police agencies can start to form a body of knowledge and improve the discipline. It is not likely that a single report from a single crime analyst will produce a substantial amount of knowledge about a given topic.

4.1.6. Feedback

Following the dissemination of their analysis' findings, crime analysts must ask for and accept input from the people they supplied the data to. Similar to the subcycle for data modification, input from the application of an analysis's results can guide and enhance the overall procedure. Feedback regarding the caliber of specific reports or analyses, the type of data analyzed, or the applicability of the analyses for making decisions can all be given to analysts.

Since each step in the process can inform subsequent steps as the analyst gains insight and receives feedback, the crime analysis process is cyclical rather than linear. The process of changing data is a time-consuming and labor-intensive task for crime analysts. Nevertheless, as policies, technologies, databases, training, and successful analyses become more prevalent, so do the tools and methods used in the crime analysis process.

4.2. TYPES OF CRIME ANALYSIS

This section has been taken from the International Association of Crime Analysts (IACA) white paper titled Definition and Types of Crime Analysis (IACA, 2014b) to ensure consistency in definitions and the discussion of crime analysis types within the discipline, as with the definition of crime analysis generally. As a participant in the IACA Standards Committee that created these definitions, I can attest that the committee members were initially committed to beginning from scratch because they were not bound by the accepted definition and published types in the field (such as the ones utilized in the first three editions of this book). The objective was to deconstruct the components of crime analysis, such as the types and sources of data used, the methods utilized, the analysis's outcomes, its regularity and frequency, and its intended use and audience. Subsequently, the committee divided the work into different categories and created the definitions.

It is crucial that the various forms of crime analysis give the field, analysts' jobs, and criminal analysis instruction and training a framework. They ought to offure for roles, duties, and job descriptions as well. In order toTo make sure the analyst is performing each type of analysis; they should support police departments looking to implement or enhance their crime analysis functions.

They should also help crime analysts arrange their workload into daily, weekly, monthly, and annual tasks and classify products for their clients. The IACA (2014b) identifies four categories of crime analysis that are arranged in a continuum: 1) crime intelligence analysis, 2) tactical crime analysis, 3) strategic crime analysis, and 4) administrative crime analysis. The categories start with detailed data and analysis for individuals and groups and progress to aggregate data and analysis of locations, areas, and problems.

4.2.1. Crime Intelligence Analysis

The IACA (2014b) defines crime intelligence analysis as the examination of information regarding individuals who are involved in criminal activities, with a focus on repeat offenders, repeat victims, and criminal organizations and networks. Based on the context of offenders' lives, jobs, activities, motives, and plans, as well as those of their criminal networks, conclusions are drawn from crime intelligence analysis. A wide range of data is taken into consideration in addition to known police crimes and arrests, since the conclusions are based not only on the criminal activity of offenders but also on their social, financial, and routine activities. Information may be obtained, for instance, from an offender's phone conversations, financial records, itinerary, social media activity, and relationships with friends and family. Police data is the starting point for crime intelligence analysis, and gathering secret information, or "intelligence," forms the core of this kind of analysis. When performing this kind of analysis, there are particular issues with data security, data access, and personal privacy. The data obtained frequently needs a court order (e.g., acquiring phone logs, securing a search warrant). Processes and techniques of crime intelligence analysis include:

- **Repeat Offender and Victim Analysis:** This is using data to identify and prioritize (i.e., put in a rank order) individual offenders by the number, type, and seriousness of their crimes, and individual victims by the number, type, and seriousness of their victimizations.
- **Criminal History Analysis:** This analytical product is more than just running a person's name in a database and retrieving his or her criminal history; it is a report compiled by an analyst on an individual that includes personal identification information (driver's license, social security number, birthdate, work and home addresses), aliases, financial information, criminal and arrest activity, correctional status, social media activity, and other relevant information. While this is listed here as crime intelligence analysis, this is also produced as part of strategic offender approaches where it is called a "criminal résumé."

- **Link Analysis:** This is typically done for a criminal network but may also be conducted for one individual with significant criminal activity. It is a visual representation of individuals, their relationships with one another as criminal associates, spouses, friends, and "enemies," as well as relevant addresses (e.g., home, work, hangouts), and other information relevant to a particular person or case. The link analysis is used to visualize the nature and strength of "links" between people (i.e., relationships) and their activity. They are used for investigation to guide intelligence gathering or to "make the case" or to visualize a large criminal case or network for court purposes.
- **Commodity Flow Analysis:** This is a specific type of link analysis in which the focus is on the "flow" of money and other financial information. This is useful in cases involving individuals and networks of drug trafficking, illicit weapons sales, human trafficking, and money laundering, among others.
- **Communication Analysis:** This is a specific type of link analysis in which the focus is on the relationships and "flow" of communication through different types of media, including but not limited to in-person interaction, phone calls, e-mail, Internet, intranet, and social media. For example, in days before the Internet, child pornography sharing networks distributed hard copy photos and videos through stores, in-person delivery, and post office mail. Today, these networks share computerized images and video through e-mail and the Internet. Understanding how this network of communication is carried out is important for apprehending individuals and stopping the activity.
- **Social Media Analysis:** Many people, especially those who are young, have a presence on social media (e.g., Facebook, Twitter, Snapchat). By the time this book is published, there are likely to be new popular media apps, but overall, social media has become a very large part of communication between and among individuals, including people committing crimes. Thus, crime analysts have begun systematically analyzing social media sources to identify information on suspects, such as where they are staying if they are not at home, who their associates are, and, believe it or not, a description of their actual criminal activity (e.g., some criminals brag about their criminal exploits in public forums!). In addition, crime analysts examine social media to prevent crimes as well, looking for events or activity that have not yet happened. Some examples from city police departments are the advertising of large

house parties with a DJ and illegal drugs and discussions by one or more individuals who talk about "shooting up" a school. In addition to local activity, analysis at the FBI and other federal agencies look for patterns and discussions of potential terrorist activity.

Crucially, one category of analysis that falls under the purview of crime analysis is criminal intelligence analysis, as it is defined here. Regarding this distinction, the IACA clarifies the following (2014b):

Drawing from a heritage of military intelligence and applying its methods to domestic "enemies" like organized crime groups, "criminal intelligence analysis" historically emerged as a profession in parallel to crime analysis. It has thrived in national, international, and special-interest groups like the U.S. The FBI, the U.S. Interpol and the Security Service are two U.S. Fusion Centers; additionally, in sizable local law enforcement agencies. These other agencies, with the exception of the major local police departments, are typically limited by mandate to analyzing individuals, groups, and criminal activities. This in turn supports the need for criminal intelligence analysis to continue evolving as a specialized field of study. It makes sense for analysts who specialize in intelligence analysis to identify as a different profession from crime analysis. However, we [the members of the IACA] believe that the division of intelligence analysis from the broader profession of crime analysis is artificial, even detrimental, to a comprehensive understanding of the crime dynamic of a jurisdiction, since local-level police organizations require all types of crime analysis.

4.2.2. Tactical Crime Analysis

The definition of tactical crime analysis is as follows (IACA, 2014b): tactical crime analysis is the examination of police data with the goal of determining the priorities for patrol and investigation in the short term and allocating resources accordingly. With a focus on crime series in particular, its subject areas include the analysis of space, time, offender, victim, and modus operandi for individual high-profile crimes, repeat incidents, and crime patterns.

Tactical crime analysis, as opposed to crime intelligence analysis, uses police databases as its primary source of data, which includes field data, arrests, police crime reports, and calls for service. Finding short-term patterns is the aim of tactical crime analysis; since a series is one kind of pattern, the term [sic] is used in the IACA's definition. Various patterns are connected based on the type of activity, location, perpetrator, victim, property, and MO (i.e., modus operandi, or the criminal's technique). The following are some tactical crime analysis procedures and methods.

- **Repeat Incident Analysis:** This is using calls-for-service data to identify locations in which similar types of calls have occurred over a short period of time to direct police resources to "repeat call" locations.
- **Crime Pattern Analysis:** This is using crime report data to identify groups of crimes that are related in some way to direct police resources to prevent future crime and/or apprehend the offender(s).
- **Linking Known of Enders to Past Crimes:** This is using data of individuals who have been arrested for and/or convicted for a particular crime to link these known offenders to individual crimes or patterns that have occurred recently to direct police resources to apprehend the individual again and/or to clear one or more cases by arrest.
- **Criminal Investigative Analysis:** In the 1970s and 1980s, this type of analysis was referred to as criminal profiling, but overuse by television shows and movies led the FBI to change the term. It entails the process of constructing "profiles" of offenders who have committed serious crimes against strangers, primarily rape and/or murder. Analysis of the elements of the linked crimes (i.e., pattern) infers the characteristics of the unknown offender, such as drug addiction, social habits, and work habits with the purpose of identifying and prioritizing suspects for the crimes. According to the IACA (2014b), "To the extent that criminal 'profiling' or criminal investigative analysis occurs within local police agencies, we [IACA members] regard it as inherent in the tactical analysis process, as its focus is almost always on a series of crimes."
- **Geographic Profiling:** This is a subset of criminal investigative analysis, thus also falls under the purview of tactical crime analysis. Here, the analyst uses geographic locations of an offender's crimes (such as body dump sites or encounter sites) to identify and prioritize areas where the offender is likely to live (Paulsen, Bair, and Helms, 2009; Rossmo, 2000). Once again, the goal is to identify and capture an unknown offender.

4.2.3. Strategic Crime Analysis

The definition of strategic crime analysis is as follows (IACA, 2014b): strategic crime analysis is the analysis of data aimed at long-term strategies, policies, and prevention techniques development and evaluation. Long-term statistical trends, hotspots, and issues are among its topics.

Police databases provide the data for strategic crime analysis, just like they do for tactical crime analysis. However, in addition to primary data obtained through both quantitative and qualitative methods, strategic crime analysis frequently incorporates data from a range of other sources, including census, geographic zoning, and city data. Additionally, the same crime data is examined over a longer time period and in aggregate form in strategic crime analysis. For instance, a strategic crime analysis would reveal that, in the 1,000 cars stolen from vehicles in the city last year, 85% of them were unlocked, whereas a tactical crime analysis would find that, in a neighborhood, four out of every five cars were unlocked in car thefts last week. Strategic crime analysis aims to pinpoint persistent issues and comprehend their causes in order to allocate police resources toward creating long-term fixes. Processes and techniques of strategic crime analysis include the following:

- **Trend Analysis:** This includes the aggregation of data, typically by time period (e.g., month) and by geographic area (e.g., police district) to identify increases or decreases in crime. The statistics are relatively simple and straightforward in this analysis, but the analysis technique is aggregating the data into categories that make sense for crime reduction. Most trend analyses examine many different categories (e.g., robbery by year; street robbery by month; street robbery with a firearm by month for District 4).
- **Hot Spot (i.e., Problem Area) Analysis:** This is the identification of areas within a jurisdiction with a disproportionate amount of crime compared to other areas both temporally and spatially. Similar to trend analysis, how the data are aggregated will determine the findings and usefulness of the problem areas identified in the analysis.
- **Problem Analysis:** This is "an approach/method/process conducted within the police agency in which formal criminal justice theory, research methods, and comprehensive data collection and analysis procedures are used in a systematic way to conduct in-depth examination of, develop informed responses to, and evaluate crime and disorder problems" (Boba, 2003). It includes identifying and prioritizing long-term problems for police to address; understanding how, when, where, who, and why the problem is occurring; guiding the response to the problem; and assessing the effectives of the response.

4.2.4. Administrative Crime Analysis

According to IACA (2014b), administrative crime analysis is defined as analysis focused on the administrative requirements of the police department, the community, and the government. A wide range of methods and tools are used in this kind of crime analysis to cater to different audiences and goals. Administrative crime analysis supports the agency's internal operations, decision-making, efficiency, and accountability, whereas tactical and strategic crime analysis are primarily focused on supporting the external crime reduction efforts of officers, detectives, and supervisors (e.g., Compstat). Operations analysis, a term used in other texts and defined as follows by Bruce (2008a), has been incorporated into the IACA (2014b).

The investigation of whether a police department's operations and policies have the greatest impact on crime and disturbance in the area. This includes examining how staff, funds, equipment, and other resources are distributed geographically, organizationally, and chronologically. Administrative crime analysis also helps the police department communicate with other governmental bodies and the community.

Products designed for tactical and strategic analysis are frequently modified for use with other audiences. Administrative crime analysis is a useful kind of crime analysis even though it is not specifically focused on reducing crime because it helps with grant work, community engagement, decision-making and planning within the agency, accountability procedures for reducing crime, and other areas. Keep in mind that the term "administrative" excludes both technological duties like providing police officers with basic technological support and secretarial or nonanalytical tasks like creating brochures and taking notes during meetings. Processes and techniques of administrative crime analysis include, but are not limited to the following:

- **Crime Analysis for Accountability:** This includes creating original statistics and regular reports that support an agency's crime reduction accountability processes. Several products depict statistics and trends about the police crime reduction responses (i.e., how much directed patrol was conducted in a hot spot) and the amount of crime. While this type of analysis may overlap strategic crime analysis, its main purpose is to support accountability meetings held by agency command staff. The products for accountability tend to be slightly different than those used for identifying, understanding, and evaluating individual problems
- **Districting and Redistricting Analysis:** There are specific methods and software that crime analysts use to determine the best geographic boundaries of districts and beats within a jurisdiction. This analysis is meant to maximize efficiency by determining the best size and location of these areas to reduce the response time of officers to calls and equalize the number of calls and crime across the areas. This

type of analysis is conducted only rarely (e.g., every 5–10 years) because any changes made are resource intensive (e.g., all maps used to dispatch officers must change, and officer deployment must be adjusted).

- **Patrol Staffing Analysis:** This includes examining calls-for-service and unit history data to conduct workload calculations by area and shift. That is, based on the data, recommendations for an optimal patrol schedule are made. Unlike districting analysis, this is often conducted each year to ensure that how officers are deployed during the day and during the week is most efficient. Similar to districting analysis, there are relatively sophisticated methods, statistics, and software that analysts use for this process.
- **Community-Focused Analysis:** Many of the analysis products that are created for tactical and strategic crime analysis might also be useful for community members, community groups, businesses, and other external police entities. However, often those products contain information that cannot be released to the public. So, a large part of community-focused analysis is taking what has been produced and "sanitizing" it for the public. In addition, crime analysts also create products specifically for the community and/or individual community or neighborhood groups. This is an important part of transparency and partnerships developed as part of community policing.
- **Cost-Benefit Analysis:** This is an assessment of the relative cost of a particular program or initiative in the police department in comparison with the benefit or impact of that program or initiative. The results are used by police decision-makers to decide whether the particular program was "worth it." Oftentimes, the costs are fairly straightforward to assess, but the benefits are not so clear to estimate. For example, the cost of a police officer assigned to a high school is simple to compute, but how would the benefit of that officer be assessed? This analysis process often involves qualitative data collection and assessment of potential benefits based on research.
- **Support for the Agency's Grant Work:** Analysts often conduct specific trend or other types of analysis to provide statistics and support for requests for grant funding from state or federal organizations. Once the grant is received by the police department, additional crime analysis reports are required for quarterly progress reports and the final grant report.

- **Media Requests:** Similar to community-focused analysis, the media is often provided products by crime analysts that have been adapted for the public. Crime analysts typically do not work directly with the media but provide this information to the public information officer within the department.

4.2.5. Not Types of Crime Analysis

Crime analysis categories that have been used in the past or are being used by others are expressly rejected by the IACA. Every category is covered in detail in the following white paper (IACA, 2014b):

- **Compstat Analysis:** Depending on agencies' approaches, Compstat models can be tactical, strategic, administrative, or intelligence-oriented, and thus, analysis for Compstat can take on any or all of these characteristics. Compstat is an outlet for many types of analysis but is not a unique type of analysis itself.
- **Crime Mapping:** This is a set of skills and technologies useful to all types of crime analysis, not a unique category of crime analysis.
- **Criminal Analysis:** This term has gained favor in some sources (e.g., Baker, 2004; Petersen, 1994) that use it in an attempt to unify crime analysis and criminal intelligence analysis. It has not generally been embraced by practitioners, and we find the term unsatisfying to describe any aspect of crime analysis, which almost always involves more than just the criminal.
- **Criminal Investigative Analysis:** To the extent that criminal investigative analysis, which is also sometimes called profiling, is performed within police agencies by crime analysts, it is almost always part of the tactical crime analysis process. We therefore include it as a technique there and not a separate type.
- **Evidence Analysis or Crime Scene Investigation:** There will be no confusion in this area among actual professionals in the field, but for other readers, we must emphasize that crime analysis has nothing to do with the analysis of crime scene evidence, including blood spatters, DNA, fingerprints, and ballistics. Crime analysis is wholly unrelated to forensic science.
- **Investigative, Clerical, and Administrative Support:** Particularly given their computer skills, crime analysts are often called upon to provide various types of support unrelated to analysis, including preparing "wanted" or "BOLO" posters for an investigative unit, creating facial lineups, performing information technology duties, and running basic searches in common databases. Although such

tasks might be vital to a police agency (and we don't specifically discourage analysts from helping in these areas when necessary), they are not analysis tasks, and we see no need to codify them under any typology of crime analysis.

- **Operational Analysis:** The term appears in some European typologies (e.g., INTERPOL, 2014), almost always synonymous with tactical crime analysis. Between the two terms, we prefer tactical crime analysis as holding a more secure historical foothold in the profession. Also, the term is easy to confuse with operations analysis, described next.
- **Operations Analysis:** Operations analysis is often defined in literature as "the analysis of police operations, including workload distribution by area and shift" (e.g., Gwinn et al., 2008). The techniques associated with these processes are too limited and the literature too scant for the practice to merit a separate category of crime analysis. We enfold it in administrative crime analysis for this reason, as well as because it is too easy to confuse with operational analysis, which is used by some international agencies.
- **Police Planning:** Although aspects of budget, equipment, and personnel analysis are sometimes part of administrative crime analysis, we do not seek to extend the crime analysis profession to encompass all types of research and analysis that go into the profession of police planning.
- **Predictive Analysis:** Tactical crime analysis, strategic crime analysis, and crime intelligence analysis are all inherently predictive; the only point in analyzing any of their subjects is the likelihood that they will continue to present a threat in the future. There are techniques within all of these analysis types that help improve the accuracy and precision of predictions, but predictive analysis is not otherwise a unique type of analysis.

4.3. CRIME MAPPING BY TYPE OF ANALYSIS

Lastly, even though it isn't included in every crime analysis product, crime mapping is a valuable addition to and part of all types of analysis. Crime mapping is a technique used in the broader process of crime analysis that focuses specifically on geography, as stated by IACA in the previous list. It is not a stand-alone subcategory of analysis. The following are some examples of how crime mapping is used within the types of crime analysis discussed in this chapter:

- In crime intelligence analysis, crime mapping is used to display crime and relationships of individuals within networks in terms of where they live, work, and frequent (i.e., activity space). These maps can be of local communities or of states and regions of the country. One example is a map of gang territories along with gang-related crimes. Another is a map of gang members' home, work, and hangout locations, as well as the same for their associates, which may be used to help identify a gang territory or help build a case by connecting individuals in the gang.
- In tactical crime analysis, crime mapping is used to identify patterns that are linked by the proximity of the incidents. Crime mapping is particularly useful in identifying property crime and street robbery patterns. For example, spatial analysis of auto theft incidents may reveal clusters of activity at specific locations that might indicate a crime pattern. Crime mapping is also used to illustrate the locations of crimes in any crime pattern. In the case of geographic profiling, crime mapping and spatial analysis of crime and other locations are central.
- In strategic crime analysis, crime mapping is used in long-term applications, such as (i) to analyze the relationship between criminal activity and indicators of disorder, such as a high volume of vacant property or disorder calls for service; (ii) to examine patterns of crime at or around specific locations, such as schools, bars, or drug treatment centers; (iii) to calculate crime rate information, such as numbers of residential burglaries per household; and (iv) to incorporate crime data with qualitative geographic information, such as information on teenage hangouts, student pathways to school, or drug and prostitution markets.
- In administrative crime analysis, crime mapping is used in accountability meetings to evaluate the effectiveness of crime reduction activities by area. It is used to examine dispatched calls for service to determine geographic allocation of resources (i.e., patrol scheduling), as well as the best design of patrol beats and locations of beat offices. For example, spatial statistics are used to estimate area boundaries that distribute calls evenly among police beats and determine locations for beat offices that minimize the distance of travel for officers. It is also a valuable tool used by police, researchers, and media organizations to convey criminal activity information to the public. Websites operated by police departments and news organizations routinely post maps that depict areas of

crime, along with corresponding tables and definitions. For example, a police agency can reduce citizen requests for neighborhood crime information by placing monthly or weekly crime maps on a website that members of the public can access using computers in their homes or at the local library.

4.4. CRIME ANALYSIS DATA AND TECHNOLOGY

Analysts dedicate a significant portion of their time and effort to gathering and preparing data for crime analysis purposes. Data collection and collation are important steps in the crime analysis process. For analysts to save time and be able to perform the required procedures and produce the required products, technology use is vital. Because police departments employ a wide range of hardware and collection techniques, analysts have to deal with data that comes in a wide range of formats and quality levels. To work with data and produce products, analysts can also employ a range of software programs.

4.4.1. Data Matrix

A collection of organized information gathered from experience, observation, experimentation, or a collection of concepts is referred to as data. The values of a variable (i.e., numbers, words, or images) can be represented by data. e.g., a quantifiable attribute of a person or a system that is subject to change). The type of crime, the time, the date, and the location are a few examples of the variables gathered for crime data. Then, a data matrix is a rectangular table with rows and columns of variables and units—such as people, organizations, and crimes—from which data have been gathered. Variables are always shown in rows in a data matrix, while units, also known as cases or records, are shown in columns (also called fields). A crime report, a report on a vehicle accident, or an arrest report would all be considered records or cases in crime analysis. Matrices can be stored electronically or on paper. A basic data matrix of crimes (cases in rows) and their type, report date, and location (variables in columns) is shown in Table 4.1.

4.4.2. Database

An organized data matrix used for computer-assisted data retrieval, analysis, and search is called a database. Databases have the capacity to hold an almost limitless quantity of cases or records. Most contemporary databases (e.g., Relational databases (such as Microsoft Access, SQL Server, and Oracle) enable users to explore intricate connections between different tables.

Table 4.1. *Data Matrix Example*

Incident No.	Type	Date of Report	Location
2017-0001	Residential burglary	01/01/17	15 Exchange Pl
2017-0002	Grand theft	01/01/17	169 York St
2017-0003	Robbery	01/01/17	111 1st St
2017-0004	Commercial burglary	01/01/17	685 Grand St
2017-0005	Robbery	01/05/17	344 Pacific Ave
2017-0006	Rape	01/05/17	49 Fisk St
2017-0007	Auto theft	01/05/17	26 Journal Sq
2017-0008	Theft from vehicle	01/11/17	920 Bergen Ave
2017-0009	Auto theft	01/12/17	438 Summit Ave
2017-0010	Arson	01/13/17	921 Bergen Ave
2017-0011	Robbery	01/13/17	234 16th St

Source: Rachel Boba Santos, Crime Analysis with Crime Mapping, ISBN: 9781506331034.

4.4.3. Geographic Data

Crime analysts enter information about the geographic characteristics connected to crime and other activities into geographic information systems (GIS) for analysis purposes, much like police agencies enter crime reports into computer systems. Point, line, and polygon geographic data types, as well as the features and data linked to them, referred to as tabular (or attribute) data, are the three forms of geographic data or features that a GIS uses to represent objects or locations.

4.4.4. Tabular Data

Events that may contain geographic variables but are not intrinsically geographic are described by tabular data. Tabular data includes things like student information, crime reports, and crash reports.

4.4.5. Secondary Data

Data classified as secondary are those that have already been gathered and are often continuously collected; they are usually stored in electronic databases. Because police departments, city departments, and other government agencies regularly gather and store data relevant to the issues crime analysts study, secondary data is frequently used in crime analysis. Police departments, for instance, gather and keep data from arrest, crash, and crime reports in an RMS (records management system) and from service calls in a computer-aided dispatch system. City agencies maintain business registries, gather data on utility usage, gather tax and license information, and gather and store street network data in geographic data systems. The U.S. The Bureau of the Census gathers sociodemographic data, which includes details on age, race, education level, and income. Secondary information can be qualitative (i.e., mostly narrative) or numerical (i.e., numerical).

4.4.6. Primary Data

The secondary data used by crime analysts are sometimes insufficient to allow for a thorough examination of a topic because they were gathered for purposes other than crime analysis. In that situation, the crime analyst must gather primary data, or information gathered especially for the current analysis. Through surveys, interviews, fieldwork, and direct observation, analysts gather primary data. This data can then be coded, entered into a database, or left in narrative form. The crime analyst must make a deliberate effort to gather primary data in order for it to be accurate and relevant to the analysis.

4.4.7. Computer-Aided Dispatch System

A computer-aided dispatch (CAD) system is a highly specialized system that supports public safety agencies like fire and ambulance services as well as police dispatch response operations. It does this by using telecommunications and geographic display. Police agencies track officers' whereabouts and activities, dispatch officers in response to a "call for service," and monitor officer-initiated activity (e.g., traffic halts). Every action pertaining to service calls is documented in the CAD. The data contains specifics regarding the dispatched or officer-initiated call, including the officers who were sent to the scene, the location of the call, the time of officers' arrival, and the call's outcome (i.e., the way it concluded). Furthermore, the CAD records correspondence between dispatchers and officers (e.g., tag and registration checks, lunch breaks for officers), which is commonly referred to as unit history since it documents the actions of every police unit during a call (as opposed to... regarding the call as a whole). It is crucial to remember that a CAD system might only log calls that an officer answers or initiates. It might not record every call that enters the dispatch center. Information is frequently removed from CAD systems after a predetermined period of time due to the large amount of information they hold. For crime analysis purposes, police departments typically keep a snapshot or summary of a call for service on file for an extended amount of time. This CAD data may be downloaded or linked, depending on the system, into a records management system for retrieval.

4.4.8. Records Management System

The informational center of any police department's operations is its records management system (RMS). It is a computer hardware and software system for data entry and storage created specifically for police activity records. While some police agencies download data from other software programs, like CAD or crime report writing software, to the RMS, others enter data directly into the system. All pertinent information held by the police department should ideally be included in the RMS, which may also include other databases containing information on individuals, vehicles, crashes, field information, calls for assistance, property and evidence, arrest records, crime reports, and case investigations. While an agency's RMS may contain different information than another, all police departments and software companies use the same system to store crime incident data and connect it to relevant data.

As the primary source of data for crime analysis, the IACA offers a number of recommendations that police agencies should take into account to make sure their RMS system is appropriate for crime analysis. An overview of the recommendations is provided below (for a more thorough discussion, refer to IACA (2013)'s "RMS Technical Requirements for Crime Analysis").

- Analysts should be involved with the procurement and implementation of the RMS.
- The RMS should allow for third-party technology tools and open architecture for accessing data.
- The RMS should provide a detailed data dictionary describing all data elements and how they relate.
- The RMS should provide the ability to see database tables and fields within the system.
- Analysts should be involved with importing legacy data (i.e., data from a previous system).
- If not directly linked, CAD data should be imported into the RMS once the CAD event is complete.
- Data entry should be clear, understandable, and customizable to account for an agency's needs.
- The RMS should include validation rules to assist with data entry and quality control of the data.
- To support the quality control, agencies should employ specific personnel to verify the RMS data.
- The RMS should store historical data in the current data format so those records are accessible.

- The RMS should include geographic coordinates for every address in the system.
- The RMS should be flexible to be integrated into external systems.
- The RMS should allow attachment of files to records in the system with searchable text.
- The RMS should use a relational database management systems technology.
- Analysts should have access to data that is not yet finalized in order to have immediate access.
- The RMS should have a single search function that queries both variables, narratives, and attachments.
- RMS with reporting functions should provide metadata for the reports.
- Agencies should consider an RMS vendor that partners with companies specializing in crime analysis.
- In lieu of a crime analysis module, the RMS should provide replicated data for crime analysis purposes.

4.4.9. Agency Management System

An intranet web-based hardware and software system called an agency management system (AMS) simplifies internal police operations and promotes communication and transparency within the police department. Fundamentally, an AMS safely oversees an agency's business operations, administration, and official communications. Modules for reviewing policies and general orders, keeping track of internal investigations and use-of-force incidents, sharing crime analysis products, and facilitating communication about operational activities and crime reduction can all be included. It makes it possible to search and archive data and documents stored in the system. An agency management system can help with the regional exchange of data and bulletins related to homeland security and crime analysis. The AMS is an agency's communications, administrative, and business management system, much like the RMS is its central repository for official records. An AMS makes it possible for departments, partner organizations, and community organizations to collaborate and share information about crime analysis.

4.4.10. Information-Sharing Platforms

An information-sharing platform "is a centralized computer system that allows authenticated users to collect, manage, and share structured and unstructured data sets from a variety of sources," according to the International Association of Crime Analysts (2014a) (Although this is a broad category that could include many different hardware and software setups, the information-sharing platform's main goal is to provide a way to gather, arrange, and centralize the enormous amount of data produced by contemporary police forces. Information-sharing systems hold both traditional data, like calls for service and crimes, and new technology-collected data, like images from closed-circuit television systems (CCTVs), license plate readers, and body-worn cameras. The platform's objective is to give particular users a simplified method for gaining access to and conducting searches on data using common terms.

4.4.11. Jail Management System (JMS)

An electronic system called a jail management system (JMS) keeps track of all the individuals who have been booked into a detention facility, both those who are currently incarcerated and those who have already been released. The arrestee's most recent booking photo and personal details (e.g., weight, eye and hair colors), address, driver's license, identifying numbers, place of employment, and, if available, emergency contact details. It's possible to record distinguishing features like scars, glasses, tattoos, gang affiliation, and health issues. Every arrest's booking details, including the offense charge, statute, and, if relevant, warrant information, are also included in the JMS. The date of issuance, charge(s), and bond amount of an active warrant are all searchable and available. The ability to view a suspect's past arrest history information is one of a JMS's features. Even though they might not use it frequently, crime analysts frequently have direct access to the system or its data through jail staff.

4.4.12. Criminal Justice Information Services (CJIS)

The Federal Bureau of Investigation's largest division, Criminal Justice Information Services (CJIS), is also the hub for all of its crime services and initiatives. The National Crime Information Center (NCIC), the National Incident-Based Reporting System (NIBRS), the Integrated Automated Fingerprint Identification System (IAFIS), Uniform Crime Reporting (UCR), and NCIC 2000 are all included under CJIS. The criminal justice organization within a district, state, territory, or federal agency that is in charge of overseeing the use of NCIC is also referred to as CJIS. Records are protected because the information is delicate. Only authorized users are allowed access, the FBI keeps track of every login and search, and the system is periodically audited to ensure that no pointless searches are carried out (e.g., an uncle researching his new son-in-law).

4.4.13. National Crime Information Center (NCIC)

The National Crime Information Center (NCIC) is an electronic database that contains criminal justice information about individuals, including past criminal records, fugitives, stolen goods, and missing people across the country. It is a single location where the FBI has collected and categorized information related to law enforcement. The FBI and other local, state, and federal law enforcement organizations collaborate with the system's operation. Law enforcement officials from the federal, state, and local levels can access the database whenever and whenever they want to obtain up-to-date information about crimes and offenders within the system. Access to NCIC is limited because it is a CJIS program, and system searches are continuously monitored. Furthermore, the majority of states have a database comparable to this one that includes data on criminal activity and offenders within their borders (e.g., Arizona has ACIC, while Florida has FCIC.

4.4.14. Geographic Data System

Geospatial data is created, maintained, and stored by a geographic data system. Geographic data systems are typically used by city or county agencies to generate and manage data about parcels, buildings, streets, roads, and highways as well as to store aerial photos and other geographic information for use by different departments and agencies (e.g., scheduling, and utilities). Furthermore, these organizations frequently store local geographic data in addition to tabular and geographic data gathered from other sources, including census, demographic, and typological data. It is crucial to remember that crime analysts and police departments only borrow and utilize the data stored in geographic data systems for analysis purposes; they do not create or maintain the data themselves.

4.5. DATABASES USED IN CRIME ANALYSIS

Databases are essential for performing crime analysis because they let analysts utilize computers to quickly and effectively evaluate a lot of cases. Although crime analysts utilize a wide variety of databases, only the most popular kinds are covered in detail in this section in order to keep things concise. Data on crime incidents, arrests, calls for service, and traffic crashes are the four categories of secondary data that crime analysts use most frequently.

4.5.1. Crime Incidents

Crime reports that are taken by police officers or other law enforcement personnel provide the information about crime incidents that is used in crime analysis. These reports are typically kept in an RMS. A crime incident database, also known as a crime report database, is connected to various kinds of databases through the use of information from crime reports. These consist of databases for vehicles, property, witnesses, suspects, and victims. Every crime report's details, including the type of crime and its whereabouts, method, and time of occurrence, are included in the crime incident database. Since the criminal incident report serves as the unit of analysis, each criminal incident report in the database corresponds to a single case. Crime incident databases contain many variables; however, the following variables are typically used in crime analysis:

- **Record Number:** A unique number used to identify the crime incident and related information. (Nearly all databases assign a unique number to each case to distinguish it from the other cases.)
- **Date of Report:** The date the crime was reported to the police. Crime statistics are tallied based on when crimes were reported to the police rather than when they actually occurred.
- **Type of Crime (State and Federal):** The type of crime the officer assigned to the event as dictated by the laws of the state and/or the police jurisdiction. Often, there are corresponding federal (Uniform Crime Report or National Incident-Based Report) codes included as well.
- **Location of the Crime:** The address where the crime occurred as well as the area, such as police district or beat and census tract. Some databases also include the type of location, such as vacant lot, single-family home, or commercial business.
- **Date and Time of Occurrence:** The date and time when the crime occurred. This is often different from the date of report and can also be a range of time if the exact time of the crime is not known (e.g., burglary, auto theft). Military time is used in most police agencies when capturing temporal data and is always used in crime analysis (times are converted to military time, if necessary). It is important for analysis and statistical purposes that there is a unique value for each time of the day.
- **Method of the Crime (Also Called "MO" or Modus Operandi):** How the crime occurred, such as the point of entry, method of entry, weapon used, and suspect's actions. Numerous variables are used to capture this information. (For further discussion of MO [modus operandi] information.
- **Disposition:** The outcome of the incident (e.g., cleared by arrest, pending). A disposition is assigned when the initial report is written and is then updated if and when an investigation leads to arrest or another status.

Table 4.2, which shows an example of a section of a crime incidents database, has rows that represent crime incident reports and columns that detail specific attributes like date, address, and disposition.

4.5.2. Arrests

An officer fills out an arrest report after making an arrest, which contains details unique to that person's arrest. These details are connected, if relevant, to the initial crime report. Since there is only one record for each arrest, the arrest serves as the unit of analysis. There will be multiple arrest records for a person if they are arrested more than once on different days. Officers create three arrest records—one for each person—if they make three arrests for the same offense. As such, there is no one-to-one relationship between the arrest database and the crime incident database. Crime analysts typically use the following variables found in arrest databases:

- **Arrest Number:** A unique number used to identify the arrest;
- **Date and Time of Arrest:** May vary from both the date of the report and the date and time of the crime occurrence.

Table 4.2. *Sample Crime Incidents Data Table*

Incident No.	Report Date	Crime Type	Address	Beat	First Date	Last Date	Disposition
2017141524	11/15/2017	Burglary	1350 Allesandro Rd	24	11/15/2017	11/15/2017	Arrest
2017142640	11/18/2017	Burglary	1528 Calle Constancia	21	11/17/2017	11/18/2017	Pending
2017142676	11/18/2017	Burglary	953 Mendocino Way	16	11/17/2017	11/18/2017	Pending
2017142509	11/23/2017	Criminal trespass	1065 W Colton Ave	12	11/20/2017	11/21/2017	Pending
2017143275	11/23/2017	Burglary	996 E Colton Ave	16	11/19/2017	11/23/2017	Arrest
2017143496	11/26/2017	Burglary	298 5th St	19	11/15/2017	11/15/2017	Unfounded
2017144169	11/26/2017	Burglary	3235 Greenspot Rd	11	11/23/2017	11/25/2017	Pending
2017142878	11/27/2017	Criminal trespass	857 W Lugonia Ave	13	11/23/2017	11/23/2017	Pending
2017013294	12/20/2017	Burglary	210 Anita Ct	11	12/11/2017	12/19/2017	Pending

Source: Rachel Boba Santos, Crime Analysis with Crime Mapping, ISBN: 9781506331034.

- **Charge(s):** The specific crime(s) for which the arrestee is charged for one arrest
- **Location of Arrest:** The address and area where the arrestee was at the time of the arrest; may not match the location of the crime

- **Location of Residence:** The address of the residence of the arrestee
- **Physical Description:** A description of the arrestee's physical characteristics, including height, weight, hair color, and eye color
- **Date of Birth:** The arrestee's date of birth; note that date of birth, rather than age, is collected for identification purposes (age often computed from this variable)

An example of a section of an arrest database can be found in Table 4.3, where each row records an arrest of a single person and the columns detail the arrest's features.

Table 4.3. *Sample Arrest Data Table*

Arrest No.	Date	Hour	Charge	Address of Arrest	First Name	Last Name	Race	Sex	DOB
20164615	7/20/2016	0235	14-269	254 W 1st St	John	Patters	B	M	02/11/62
20169395	12/11/2016	1400	14-269	988 N Sunset Dr	Robert	Haars	W	M	06/09/44
20165518	10/5/2016	2325	14-269	51 S Martin L King Jr Dr	Kevin	White	B	M	01/02/65
20172213	1/12/2017	2130	14-269	1500 E 1st St	Rodney	Powers	W	M	07/18/82
20176639	3/4/2017	0800	14-269.2	12 S University Dr	Karim	Williams	B	M	11/15/78

Source: Rachel Boba Santos, Crime Analysis with Crime Mapping, ISBN: 9781506331034.

4.5.3. Calls for Service

Police respond to a variety of non-criminal activities, including loud parties, traffic accidents, neighbor disputes, disturbances, and burglar alarm calls. These calls are stored in a calls-for-service database. Residents dial the emergency number of a police department (i.e., 911) or a number that isn't emergency (e.g., the primary line of the police department) to make a police service request. Certain calls to the department don't require a police officer to answer, and some calls from citizens are handled in another way. Citizens' calls for service are any calls from citizens to which an officer answers, regardless of whether they are related to criminal activity or not. Police classifications for such calls for service include, but are not limited to, the following:

- Robbery in progress;
- Burglary in progress;
- Rape in progress;
- Theft;
- Homicide;

- Shoplifting;
- Family fight;
- Assault;
- Suspicious person;
- Suspicious vehicle;
- Loud noise;
- Dog barking;
- Collision;
- Assist motorist;
- 911 hang-up;
- Burglar alarm;
- Narcotics activity;
- Welfare check;
- Neighbor dispute;
- Loud party;
- Shots fired;
- Criminal trespassing;
- Speeding in neighborhood.

When police officers proactively spot troubling activity in the field, they also result in calls for assistance. An officer notifies the dispatcher of a call for assistance, recording it. These calls are classified differently by the police depending on the agency, but in general, they are called officer-generated calls for service.

Calls for service from citizens are more frequently used in crime analysis than calls from officers because the former show the community's need for police assistance while the latter show the officers' own initiative. Furthermore, the amount of citizen-generated calls for service has a significant impact on the volume of officer-generated calls for service because it determines how much time officers have to generate calls themselves. For instance, an officer may not have enough time to start calls like traffic stops if they are dispatched from one citizen-generated call to the next during a shift. As a result, crime analysts use calls from officers to look into officer activity and calls from citizens to look into citizen demands for assistance and community concerns about crime and disturbance. In other words, the police department prioritizes addressing community concerns before addressing other issues and problems when time permits.

The unit of analysis is a call for service, since each record in the database corresponds to a single call for service.

Similar variables apply to both citizen- and officer-generated calls for service in crime analysis; they are based on a snapshot of the entire call. The variables include the following:

- **Incident Number:** A unique number assigned by the computer system and used to track the call for service. In many cases, this number is the same for any subsequent reports (e.g., crime, traffic crashes, or information reports) written based on a call for service. This is done for tracking purposes, so a call for service and its resulting reports are linked together.
- **Dates and Times:** A measurement that displays particular dates and times of importance for a call. They include when the call was received by police call takers, when it was dispatched to an officer, when the first officer arrived at the scene, and when the call was closed or cleared. These variables are used to compute other variables, such as response time (i.e., how much time elapses between a person's call to the police and an officer's arrival at the scene).
- **Type of Call:** This is either an arbitrary number (e.g., 459, which signifies burglary) or descriptive term (e.g., burglar alarm call) specifying the type of call.
- **Priority:** A number showing the call's level of importance. To manage the order in which officers respond to calls for service, police assign priorities to calls as they are received. A call's priority is correlated to its seriousness and is dictated by the individual agency's policies. Calls with an "emergency" priority are dispatched first.
- **Disposition:** A description of the outcome of the call (e.g., no action taken, arrest, crime report, collision report, unable to locate). A call can have multiple dispositions.
- **Location of Call:** The address and area from which the call came. This is not necessarily the address where the problem is occurring, but only where the call is being made since a citizen may not be able to provide that information (e.g., loud noise coming from the next apartment building).

An example of a section of a call for service database is shown in Table 4.4, where each row represents the summary data from a single call for service and the columns contain the call's attributes.

4.5.4. Traffic Crashes

When a vehicle collides with an object, a person, or another vehicle, the event is known as a traffic crash or collision. Most communities are concerned about traffic crashes, and since responding to crashes takes up a significant portion of police officers' time, collision data is crucial for crime analysis. Officers typically gather and report crash data using a state form in accordance with the procedures specified by state law. The unit of analysis is a crash because every record in a traffic crash or collision database includes details about a single traffic crash. The following variables from traffic crash databases are commonly used by crime analysts.

Table 4.4. *Sample Call for Service Data Table*

Event No.	Date	Day	Call Type	Receive Time	Dispatch Time	Arrive Time	Complete Time	Priority	Location
201710621	10/1/2017	Sun	Robbery in progress	0015	0016	0018	0129	1	16 Morton Pl
201703160	10/2/2017	Mon	Suspicious person	0015	0020	0025	0045	2	238 Carbon St
201739616	10/2/2017	Mon	Disturbance	0015	0030	0039	0052	3	253 Stegman St
201714600	10/2/2017	Mon	Domestic dispute	0100	0101	0105	0312	1	48 Lienau Pl
201764094	10/3/2017	Tue	Burglar alarm	0130	0132	0137	0345	1	560 Bramhall Ave
201749640	10/3/2017	Tue	Burglary report	0130	0139	0145	0201	3	608 Bramhall Ave
201731049	10/4/2017	Wed	Traffic crash	0130	0142	0159	0235	3	68 Milk Dr

Source: Rachel Boba Santos, Crime Analysis with Crime Mapping, ISBN: 9781506331034.

- **Report Number:** A unique number used to track the traffic crash, which is often provided to an insurance company as well
- **Date of Report:** The date on which the traffic crash was reported to the police
- **Date and Time of Occurrence:** The date and time when the traffic crash occurred
- **Location of the Crash:** The address at which the traffic crash took place (in many cases, at an intersection); this information often is recoded into one variable from two others (e.g., street the traffic crash "occurred on" and street the traffic crash "occurred at")
- **Violation(s):** Description of what traffic law(s) were violated, if any (e.g., speed too fast for conditions or improper left turn); in many cases, multiple violations are listed in the data

Table 4.5 shows an example of a section of a traffic crash database, where the columns contain the characteristics of each crash and the rows represent individual crashes.

Table 4.5. *Sample traffic Crash Data Table*

Report No.	Date	Time	Location	Violation 1	Violation 2
2017009877	1/5/2017	0730	E Main Ave & S Center St	Improper left turn	None
2017009878	1/7/2017	1544	W Main Ave & N Cherry Ave	No signal	None
2017009882	1/12/2017	0845	E Elliot Dr & S Apple St	Speed too fast for conditions	No signal
2017009883	1/15/2017	0921	E Main Ave & S Center St	Improper left turn	Speed too fast for conditions
2017009879	1/28/2017	1623	E Main Ave & S Center St	Speed too fast for conditions	None

Source: Rachel Boba Santos, Crime Analysis with Crime Mapping, ISBN: 9781506331034.

4.5.5. Other Databases

In addition to the types of databases discussed so far, the following kinds are also used in crime analysis:

- **Persons Database:** This database contains information about all individuals involved in criminal incidents, including witnesses, victims, investigative leads, suspects (some police agencies have suspect databases that are separate from their persons and arrest databases), and arrestees. In this database, the unit of analysis is the individual. Each record contains information about the individual (name, birth date, address, physical description, aliases) and the nature of the contact (e.g., suspect, arrestee, witness, or victim). These data are normally linked relationally to the crime incidents database in the RMS.
- **Property Database:** This database contains information about individual pieces of property that have been stolen, found, or used in the commission of crimes. The unit of analysis is the piece of property, so multiple records for property can result from one criminal incident. These data are normally linked relationally to the crime incidents database in the RMS, and variables often include a description, type of property (e.g., jewelry, electronics), and value in dollars.
- **Vehicle Database:** This database contains information about vehicles stolen, recovered, or used in the commission of crimes. The unit of analysis is the vehicle, and each record includes information

about the vehicle (VIN [vehicle identification number], make, model, color, and year) and the nature of the incident (date, time, and location). These data are normally linked relationally to the crime incidents database in the RMS.

- **Field Information Database:** Many police agencies collect information from the field (also called field intelligence) through field interview cards filled out by officers. This information is collected when an officer determines that a crime report is not necessary, but the agency would like to document specific information that may not be able to be captured in a call-for-service record. This database is often a part of the RMS, but stands alone (i.e., is not linked to the crime database).
- **Traffic Database:** In addition to crash data, police agencies collect data on traffic citations and vehicle stops (one type of officer-generated calls for service). In recent years, because of racial profiling concerns, vehicle stop data have been examined more often by both researchers and crime analysts in order to more thoroughly understand the issue. This database is often a part of the RMS, but stands alone (i.e., is not linked to the crime database).
- **Known-Offender Database:** This database contains information about individuals who have been convicted, not just arrested, for crimes in the local jurisdiction. Typically, police agencies have their own known-offender databases that are obtained through local jail/prison release records and court/prosecution databases. However, there is a current trend to develop statewide databases with this information for use by crime analysts. Each record contains information about an individual (name, birth date, address, physical description, aliases), the crimes for which she or he has been convicted, and his or her correctional status (e.g., probation, parole, etc.,). This database is normally a stand-alone database in that it is not directly linked to an agency's crime database.
- **Pawn Database:** In many states, pawnbrokers are required to enter the property they receive along with the person's information into a database, so detectives can search for property that may have been stolen and pawned.
- **Gang Database:** This database contains information collected and validated by patrol officers and detectives about individuals who are both members and associates of gangs. Most states have specific guidelines for classifying whether a person is a gang member or an associate that are used for "validation."

- **Registered Sex Offender Database:** This database contains information about sex offenders who live in the local jurisdiction (or surrounding jurisdictions) and have registered as part of their sex offender status. Each record contains information about an individual (name, birth date, address, physical description, aliases), the sex crimes for which he or she has been convicted, her or his correctional status, and sex offender classification that varies by state. This database is normally a stand-alone database in that it is not directly linked to an agency's crime database.

4.5.6. Primary Data Collection

Crime analysts use secondary data—such as crime reports, information on service requests, and arrest records—to analyze problems related to crime, disorder, and other topics, but these data often leave out crucial details. As a result, gathering primary data—information obtained directly from people or locations for particular analysis purposes—is frequently necessary for crime analysts. Surveys, focus groups, and interviews are frequently used to obtain primary data from individuals. Because they are one-on-one and give the analyst the opportunity to clarify matters and ask follow-up questions of the interviewee, one-on-one interviews typically go deeper. In essence, focus groups are large-scale interviews. Focus groups are frequently used to gather information from a group of people, such as members of the community or police officers. One thing to keep in mind is that people might not speak up in a focus group setting as much as they would in a one-on-one interview. However, people might forget details or not "know the whole story" when a focus group would yield more thorough data collection. Finally, when time or resources prevent interviews, surveys are employed to gather data from a large number of people. It goes without saying that the kind of data collected depends on the analysis's goals and nature. Direct observation and environmental surveys are usually used to obtain primary data from locations. An environmental survey is used to methodically examine a location's physical attributes, like the amount of windows, parking spots, and lighting. In order to ascertain the social environment of a location—that is, how the area is used, what kinds of people are there, how they congregate, and so forth—direct observation entails watching the location for a predetermined period of time over several days or weeks. Researchers advise conducting 20-minute intervals of direct observation over a range of representative time periods (i.e., the crime analyst would visit a troubled bar on multiple occasions during the week to observe the issue (Schmerler, Wartell, and Weisel, 2004). Additionally, when conducting observation, the crime analyst should be discrete and establish a basic, standard protocol (i.e., items to pay attention to) in order to standardize the observations made at the same kind of location (Schmerler et al., 2004,).

The following are some practical examples of primary data collection techniques that crime analysts have used or might use:

- In analyzing a crime problem at local motels, analysts interview the maids who work at the motels to help determine how the rooms were used by patrons staying in them (e.g., determined by the condition of the room and the garbage left behind; Schmerler and Velasco, 2002).
- Crime analysts interview burglary victims to determine what prevention methods they employed before and after they were victimized (Schmerler and Velasco, 2002).
- A crime analyst conducts a focus group with construction site building supervisors to gather data on their building practices, current victimizations, crime prevention, and crime reporting methods (Boba and Santos, 2007).
- A crime analyst annually surveys citizens locally to determine their rates of victimization, attitudes toward police, quality of life, fear of crime, and crime prevention behaviors. The citizens are selected randomly, and the analyst uses the survey results to help determine problems that need attention and to contribute to current crime prevention efforts.
- After a safety problem is identified involving crimes occurring around schools, along pathways to and from schools used by elementary school children, and in areas where children hang out before and after school, crime analysts conduct an environmental survey to determine the exact locations of the children's hangouts and their pathways to and from school. The analysts then enter data about the locations of these pathways and hangouts into a GIS and analyze them in relation to crime in the area. They also use the information to scan for other problems and to identify intersections that are unsafe for children to cross.
- A crime analyst studying the problem of thefts from parking lots conducts an environmental survey to determine how many vehicles in particular parking lots are locked, how many have antitheft devices, how many have valuables left in view, and so on.
- A crime analyst directly observes a downtown area during the evening to determine the level of crowding, clustering of people at particular corners, and general attitude and behavior of individuals walking around.

Although analysts obtain primary data directly from people and locations, they frequently first quantify their findings by setting up databases, coding standards, and data entry before using the data to conduct analyses. The following example illustrates this process:

- **Problem:** You are a crime analyst who has been asked to help assess a chronic problem of thefts from autos and auto theft at several local apartment communities.

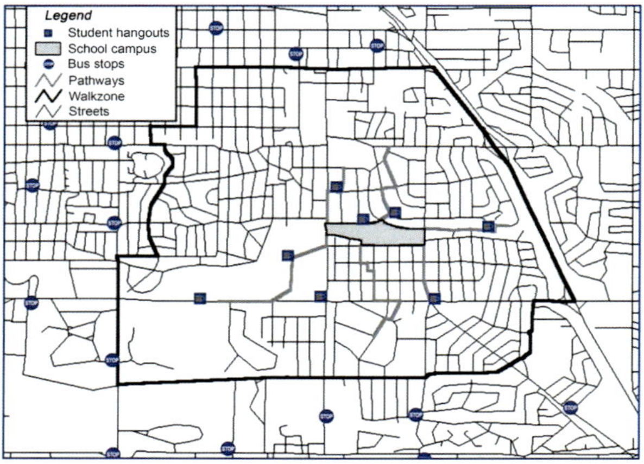

Figure 4.2. *Map of student pathways to school and hangouts.*

Source: Rachel Boba Santos, Crime Analysis with Crime Mapping, ISBN: 9781506331034.

- **Methodology:** In order to understand victim behavior, you decide to develop an environmental survey about the security habits of the residents who park at one of the affected communities. You use the following questions to guide your observation of cars in the parking lot:

1. Are any vehicle doors unlocked? Yes / No;
2. Are any vehicle windows open? Yes / No;
3. Are any valuables in view in the car (e.g., cash, smartphone, or purse)? Yes / No;
4. Is there an antitheft device? Yes / No.

You then code the results of 250 observations and enter them into a database. Table 4.6 shows several cases and some variables that you might include in the database for analysis.

- **Analysis:** By examining the data, you learn that although most people lock their car doors and close the windows when they park,

60% of the cars you observed had valuables in view, and few drivers used alarms. The results indicate that community residents should be advised not to leave valuables in view in their parked cars and to use their car alarms. You can conduct this same survey again later to determine whether the residents, in fact, changed their behavior.

Table 4.6. *Sample Database: Primary Data Collection*

Observation No.	Door	Window	Valuables	Anti-Theft	Type of Anti-Theft
1	Yes	No	Yes	No	None
2	No	No	Yes	Yes	Alarm
3	No	Yes	No	No	None
4	No	No	No	Yes	Other
5	Yes	Yes	No	Yes	Alarm

Source: Rachel Boba Santos, Crime Analysis with Crime Mapping, ISBN: 9781506331034.

4.5.7. Data Considerations

The data generated by all police agencies raises a number of significant issues regarding the inherent qualities of the data that is frequently used in crime analysis. These concerns include (i) the fact that the data are "reported" activities; (ii) the difference between federal and local data standards; (iii) whether call-for-service data should be used to study crime problems; (iv) whether arrest data should be used to study crime problems and offenders; and (v) the data's integrity. The ensuing sections address each of these concerns one after the other.

4.5.8. "Reported" Activity

The databases used for crime analysis show actions that have been "reported" or "known" by law enforcement (e.g., arrests, traffic accidents, crimes incidents, and calls for service) as opposed to the entirety of actual crimes or other activity. There are some activities that are more likely than others to be reported to the police or to come to their attention. For instance, there is a significant underreporting of rape, assault, and child abuse incidents, whereas the police are more likely to find evidence of prostitution, drunk driving, and gambling incidents than victim reports. Because victims of auto theft and arson require documentation for insurance purposes, these incidents are typically reported with a fair degree of accuracy.

When conducting analysis and interpretation of their findings, crime analysts must be aware of the limitations of the data on reported activity. According to victimization surveys, different types of crimes are reported at different levels and not all crimes are reported to law enforcement (Truman and Langton, 2014). Based on data from the National Crime Victimization Survey, the Bureau of Justice Statistics estimates that 45.6% of violent crimes in 2013, 44.2% of violent crimes in 2012, and 50.3 % of violent crimes in 2004 were reported to the police. According to Truman and Langton (2014), property crime was reported 36.1% of the time in 2013, 33.5% of the time in 2012, and 39.2% of the time in 2014. For instance, it is commonly known that police are notified of only a very small percentage of rapes that occur. It is important for analysts to recognize that variations in rape statistics might not necessarily indicate shifts in the incidence of rape; instead, they might stem from variations in the quantity of reports of this offense. This problem extends beyond crime statistics; call-for-service, crash, and other data types—including arrests and field information—also only show behavior that is reported to the police and might not give a complete picture of a given issue.

4.5.9. Local and Federal Crime Data Standards

Although police agencies' data have historically been similar, they actually differ by state, region, and even police agency. Because every agency has different policies and practices for documenting activity, it is challenging to compare crime counts, levels, and rates. As a result, the U. S. In 1930, the government created the Uniform Crime Reporting (UCR) program, a nationally based classification system, to maintain uniform crime statistics throughout the country. For a variety of research and planning purposes, law enforcement, criminologists, sociologists, legislators, municipal planners, and the media have all benefited from the UCR program's development of trustworthy crime report data. The UCR program, which establishes national standards for the consistent classification of crimes and arrests, is still used to measure crime today. Notably, UCR's definitions of crime are unique and don't follow those found in state or federal laws.

It is important to take into account the well-documented criticisms of the UCR data before using it for any kind of purpose. Although the limitations and nature of the data should be acknowledged, this does not mean that researchers, practitioners, and crime analysts cannot use the data to better understand crime and inform policy choices. While individual law enforcement agencies categorize reported crimes in accordance with the laws of their home states and jurisdictions, when reporting these crimes, these agencies reclassify the crimes in accordance with UCR definitions and provide aggregate counts of (i) specific crimes (also referred to as Part I crimes) such as motor vehicle theft, arson, rape, murder, robbery, aggravated assault, burglary, larceny/theft, and robbery. Be aware that the FBI only reports arrests made in relation to Part II crimes, such as simple assault, fraud, prostitution, and DUI, not the total counts of these offenses. As a result, only the eight Part I crimes are included in statistics regarding reported violent and property crime.

Furthermore, a hierarchical coding system must be used for UCR reporting; this means that only one crime is counted if two occur during a single incident. For instance, only the rape will be recorded if a single person is the victim of both the robbery and the rape; similarly, if a car is taken from a locked garage, it is classified as a burglary rather than both a burglary and an auto theft. The actual number of reported crimes may be understated because the UCR program uses specific coding guidelines that are not covered in this article. This is because the number of incidents reported is counted rather than the number of unique crimes that occur. While most police agencies choose to comply with UCR reporting on a voluntary basis, over 95% of the U.S. UCR statistics show representation of the population. The FBI receives reports from state agencies twice a year, which receives monthly counts from police agencies. Some criticisms of the UCR data include the following: the use of aggregate numbers that obscure other factors like time of day, location, and circumstances of the crime (e.g., Lynch and Jarvis, 2008; Maltz, 1999); inaccuracy due to inputting errors and handling of missing data. e.g., whether a family member or stranger is the one who committed the crime). Nonetheless, the UCR data on crime in the US are the most thorough and regularly gathered. The conversation usually starts with an analysis of UCR data, and to truly comprehend the nature and context of crime problems, more in-depth research of local crime is necessary.

In an effort to enhance the UCR, the federal government developed the National Incident Based Reporting System (NIBRS) more recently. Furthermore, this system solely serves to classify crimes—not to determine specific charges against individual offenders—and mandates the uniform classification of crimes, disregarding regional variations. It is optional to use the system. The FBI's annual national crime statistics are still based on UCR data because in 2012, 33% of law enforcement agencies provided electronic database forms to the FBI with individual records rather than aggregate counts.

4.6. USING CALLS-FOR-SERVICE DATA TO STUDY CRIME PROBLEMS

Occasionally, call-for-service data is used by crime analysts to research crime issues instead of crime incident data. In these situations, they portray crime incidents as calls for service, which are classified as criminal activity and result in police reports. Analysis of crime based on calls for service can be misleading for several reasons, which also highlight the differences between these two data sources:

- **Crime Type:** When a call comes in to a police department, the call taker assigns it a call type. In many cases, once on the scene an officer will discover that the incident is actually a different type. For example, a person calls the police department and says, "I've been robbedding officer finds that in reality the person's house has been burgled. In many calls-for-service databases, the original call types noted are never updated by the call takers, so these databases do not accurately represent the types of activities that actually occurredoccurred.
- **Date and Time:** The date and time variables in calls-for-service databases reflect when each call was received and dispatched to the officer, when the officer arrived, and when the call was cleared. Such databases do not accurately indicate when crimes occurred. For example, a victim can call on Monday morning about her car being stolen on Saturday night.
- **Location:** The location listed in a call-for-service database may not be the location of the crime incident but instead a nearby location or the location from which the call was made. The recording of apartment numbers in call-for-service data is often haphazard and depends on the amount of information available (e.g., "a loud fight coming from the next building") and the diligence of the call taker (e.g., in determining the apartment number at which the incident is occurring, not where the call originates).

It is more appropriate to use call-for-service databases in analyses of police disorder activity due to these limitations (e.g., code violations, noisy complaints, suspicious activity, disorderly conduct, public intoxication, and officer activity (e.g., calls made by officers) as opposed to crime incident analyses.

4.6.1. Using Arrest Data to Study Crime Problems and Offenders

Arrests take place when there is enough information, or probable cause, to believe that someone has committed a crime. Arrest data is used by crime analysts to comprehend specific es of crimes and perpetrators. There are three major concerns with using arrest data for this kind of analysis. Arrests typically correspond with police activity, to start. Only through arrests do police agencies record specific types of crimes (e.g., shopliftingshopping, prostitution, gaming, and drunk driving). For instance, an examination of prostitution arrests in February will reveal a sharp rise if law enforcement takes action against prostitution during that month. However, police action—rather than a real rise in prostitution activity—is what has caused this change. Therefore, police procedures that may have an impact on the number of arrests made for particular crimes must be known to crime analysts.

The second problem is that arrestees might not accurately represent offenders because caught offenders might vary (e.g., in knowledge and expertise) from those who evade capture.

The third concern is that certain crimes' arrest rates (e.g., property crimes) are incredibly rare, so it may be deceptive for analysts to use a small sample of offenders to understand the bigger issue. For instance, a study of people detained for auto theft may show that 60% of them are minors. Before analysts can make any inferences in this regard, they need to know the overall arrest rate for auto theft. Does that mean there is a problem with juvenile auto theft? Arrest rates for property crimes are usually low, ranging from 15% to 20%. Therefore, if the example has a 20% arrest rate, then 12% of the auto thefts involved juvenile arrests (60% of 20% is 12%). More generally, in this case, we are only examining 20% of the cases; in the remaining 80% of the cases, we do not know who is committing auto thefts. The answer to the question is that while we are unsure if minors are responsible for the majority of thefts, we do know that, "of the people who are arrested" for auto theft, minors make up the majority of offenders. These two conclusions are extremely dissimilar.

4.6.2. Data Integrity

A number of factors, including the following, may impact the accuracy of police data, which in turn may affect the findings of crime analyses.

- **Data Entry:** Crime analysis relies primarily on secondary data, and the individuals who enter data typically have little understanding of the importance of those data to crime analysis. In police agencies, these individuals include police officers, call takers, dispatchers, and records clerks. Their lack of awareness regarding the need for data accuracy can lead to carelessness and result in unreliable data. Data entry can be improved with technology (e.g., providing variable values, address-cleaning software) and proper training that includes information on the uses and importance of the data.
- **Timeliness:** A primary concern in crime analysis is that the data obtained are current and available in a timely manner. Missing or

old data can affect the quality of crime analysis. For example, it is difficult to analyze and identify immediate crime patterns using data that are several weeks old.

- **Validity:** Valid data accurately reflect the concepts they are meant to measure. Issues of validity include the facts that (i) as previously discussed, crime data do not reflect all crime that occurs, only crime reported to the police; (ii) calls for service do not represent crime incidents; and (iii) arrests are a better indicator of police activity than of criminal incidents.
- **Reliability:** Reliable data are data that are the same in repeated observations. Two reliability issues related to police data involve changes in policies or laws (e.g., mandatory arrest for domestic violence offenses) and the coding of similar activities in the same way (e.g., theft from building vs. residential burglary).
- **Data Transfer Process:** In many cases, crime analysts download, clean, and manipulate data before conducting their analyses. This process can affect data quality and integrity since data can be inadvertently or unavoidably lost or reformatted. An issue associated with the data transfer process is data compatibility. Police departments are notorious for having data in many different formats; converting and combining these data is often time-consuming and frustrating.
- **Data Confidentiality/Privacy:** Crime analysts are managers of police data; they are responsible for protecting the information and individuals represented within the data. Normally, the data used and created in crime analysis adhere to a jurisdiction's policies on privacy and confidentiality. In recent years, new ways of gathering and disseminating information have surfaced that require additional and more detailed policies, such as the use of the Internet and mapping. Consequently, police departments need to include specific crime analysis concerns in their data protection plans.
- **Data Management:** Every police department has its own set of procedures outlining how crime analysis data are to be collected and manipulated. However, many details regarding these procedures exist only in the memories of individual analysts. The term metadata refers to information about data. In the metadata process, this information is written down to ensure consistency in data handling and cleaning procedures, to provide guidelines for sharing work with others and keeping track of products and files created, and to reduce duplication of effort.

4.6.3. Hardware and Software Considerations

The data produced by computer-aided dispatch (CAD), records management (RMS), agency management systems (AMS), and geographic data systems are utilized in crime analysis. However, since their main function is data production and storage rather than analytical tool provision, these systems are not considered analysis systems. Software must therefore be used for crime analysis tasks. Four primary desktop software applications are utilized by crime analysts for data organization and analysis: database management system (DBMS) software, spreadsheet software, statistical software, and geographic information system (GIS) software. To create reports, publications, and presentations, crime analysts use six basic types of software applications, either separately or in combination: word processing software, spreadsheet software, graphics software, publication software, presentation software, and software for using the Internet and intranets.

While not designed with crime analysis in mind, all of these software kinds can be utilized for it. As a result, several software programs designed especially for crime analysis have been developed. These include more comprehensive programs that offer a wide range of features and techniques required for various types of crime analysis, as well as smaller applications for data entry and producing standardized crime analysis reports. The majority of programs made especially for crime analysis are made to carry out tasks that cannot be done by other programs currently in use. Apart from the federally funded and commercially produced programs, numerous police departments have developed their own software for conducting crime analysis. For instance, because his department did not yet have a records management system, one analyst built a database and data entry module in Microsoft Access because he had no other means of gaining access to electronic data for analysis. An additional analyst possessing sophisticated computer programming abilities devised a program to expedite the address cleaning procedure, reducing the duration from 4 hours to 30 seconds. Off-the-shelf software frequently proves to be an inadequate match for analysts' and law enforcement agencies' requirements for data, analysis, and presentation. Consequently, they employ computer professionals to modify pre-existing software or develop fresh software that fulfills their needs.

Finally, when it comes to crime analysts' use of hardware and software, automation of reports and information distribution is crucial. Software products are used by crime analysts to automate the creation of nearly identical crime analysis reports every day, week, or month. Once created, these reports require minimal analyst review. This frees up a significant amount of the crime analyst's time, which they can use to produce unique reports. There is an increasing amount of software available for this purpose, and many CAD and RMS systems already have the capacity to query data and generate reports automatically. Technology is also used by crime analysts to automate the distribution of information to various audiences. Depending on the situation, police personnel and others receive both automated and original crime analysis reports via email, an intranet site, or the Internet.

REFERENCES

1. Boba, R. (2005). *Crime Analysis and Crime Mapping* (pp. 5–6). Sage Publications.
2. Cramer, M. (2013). Cambridge police look at math to solve crimes. *Boston Globe*. Retrieved from: https://www.bostonglobe.com (accessed on 14 October 2024).
3. Osborne, D., & Wernicke, S. (2003). *Introduction to Crime Analysis: Basic Resources for Criminal Justice Practice*. Haworth Press.
4. Rudin, C. (2013). Predictive policing: Using machine learning to detect patterns of crime. *Wired*. Retrieved from: https://www.wired.com (accessed on 14 October 2024).

Chapter 5

Geographic Data and Crime Mapping

Contents

Introduction 208

5.1. Geographic Data 209

5.2. Crime Mapping Techniques 216

References 236

INTRODUCTION

Geographic data and crime mapping are pivotal components of modern law enforcement and public safety strategies. By utilizing geographic information systems (GIS), police departments and crime analysts can visualize and analyze spatial patterns of criminal activity, leading to more informed decision-making and effective crime prevention tactics.

At the core of crime mapping is the collection and integration of geographic data. This data includes precise locations of criminal incidents, often gathered from police reports, 911 calls, and other law enforcement databases. Additional geographic data, such as demographic information, land use, and infrastructure details, are also incorporated to provide context to the crime patterns. Advanced GIS software is used to manage, analyze, and display this data, transforming raw information into insightful maps and visualizations.

Crime mapping allows analysts to identify hotspots, which are areas with a high concentration of criminal activities. By pinpointing these hotspots, law enforcement agencies can allocate resources more effectively, deploying officers to areas where they are most needed and potentially preventing crimes before they occur. Additionally, temporal analysis within crime mapping can reveal patterns related to the timing of crimes, such as increases in certain types of crimes during specific times of the day, week, or year.

Moreover, crime mapping facilitates a deeper understanding of the relationships between various environmental factors and crime. For instance, analysts can examine how proximity to schools, parks, and transportation hubs influences crime rates. This spatial analysis helps in developing targeted interventions, such as improving lighting in high-crime areas or increasing patrols in vulnerable neighborhoods.

Community engagement is another significant benefit of crime mapping. By sharing crime maps with the public, law enforcement agencies can increase transparency, build trust, and encourage community members to participate in crime prevention efforts. Public access to crime maps also empowers citizens with information about their surroundings, enhancing their ability to take preventive measures.

Geographic data and crime mapping are essential tools in contemporary crime analysis. They enable law enforcement to visualize and interpret crime patterns, optimize resource deployment, and engage with the community effectively. Through these technologies, police departments can enhance public safety and work towards reducing crime more strategically.

5.1. GEOGRAPHIC DATA

Data and how they are portrayed on maps are referred to in crime mapping using a variety of special terms and components. A dedicated crime mapping text or an advanced crime analysis course would be a better place to learn about the components, which are not covered in this section, which focuses on and explains the most crucial ideas.

5.1.1. Vector Data

In the context of crime analysis, a geographic information system (GIS) converts real-world physical features like buildings, roads, lakes, and mountains into formats that can be displayed, altered, and examined alongside police data on crimes, arrests, and traffic accidents. The fundamental building blocks of spatial information for vector data, which is what a GIS uses to represent objects and locations in the real world, are points, lines, and polygons. These various features are shown independently in a GIS, and they are accompanied by attribute (or tabular) data that describes them.

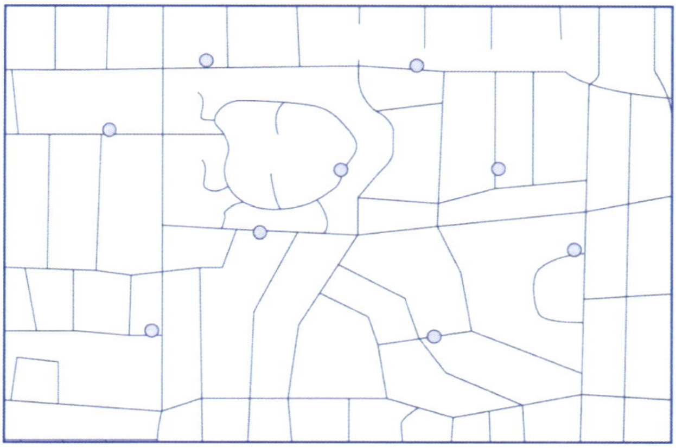

Figure 5.1. *Point and line feature map.*

Source: Rachel Boba Santos, Crime Analysis with Crime Mapping, ISBN: 9781506331034.

A label or symbol is typically used to represent a discrete location on a map created by a GIS. This is known as a point feature. A pin on a paper wall map is comparable to a point feature. The locations of data relevant to the analysis, such as crimes, auto accidents, traffic signs, buildings, police beat stations, and cell phone towers, are represented by various symbols in a GIS. Figure 5.1 depicts a map with circles that could stand in for any of these kinds of places. Table 5.1 shows the attribute data associated point as they wouldthey appear in a database. The points in this example stand for robberies. A record (row) in Table 5.1 corresponds to each point on the map in Figure 5.1. Additional details about that place, like the incident number, address, and kind of location where the robbery happened, are provided by the variables in the database. This is only a basic illustration; each point in geographic attribute data can have many more variables to describe it.

A line or collection of lines can be used to depict a real-world feature on a map. The street segments are represented by the lines in Figure 5.1. Rivers, streams, power lines, and bus routes are examples of addit features. Similar toLike points, every street segment has a corresponding record in the attribute data displayed in Table 5.2. The addresses at the start and finish of the street segment are contained in the variables, which also describe the characteristics of that specific street segment. The addresses on one side of the street segment's range are contained in the variables left from and left, and the addresses on the other side's range are contained in the variables right from and right. Additionally displayed are the street name, direction, and kind of street.

A polygon feature is a multi-sided figure with a closed set of lines that depicts a geographic area on a map. In maps created with a GIS, polygons can represent regions as big as continents or as small as buildings. They can be used to show police districts, parks, school campuses, and county or city borders. Figure 5.2's polygons depict police districts. Every district is associated with a record found in Table 5.3. Since the area is the unit of analysis for the polygon feature, only the area itself has attribute data; the polygon's lines, or borders, do not. Table 5.3's feature variable defines the kind of feature these data are, and the polygon's name or label is district.

Table 5.1. *Point Feature Attribute Data*

Incident No.	Address	Type of Location
2017-0025	15 Exchange Pl	Business
2017-0026	169 York St	Apartment
2017-0027	111 1st St	Business
2017-0028	685 Grand St	Street
2017-0029	344 Pacific Ave	Business
2017-0030	920 Bergen Ave	Park
2017-0031	438 Summit Ave	Apartment
2017-0032	921 Bergen Ave	Park
2017-0033	234 16th St	Street

Source: Rachel Boba Santos, Crime Analysis with Crime Mapping, ISBN: 9781506331034.

Table 5.2. *Line Feature Attribute Data*

Left From	Left To	Right From	Right To	Prefix	Street Name	Type
2201	2249	2200	2248	E	Columbia	Pl
2301	2399	2300	2398	E	Columbia	Pl
2101	2199	2100	2198	E	Columbia	Pl
2251	2271	2250	2270	E	Columbia	Pl
2273	2299	2272	2298	E	Columbia	Pl
2167	2231	2166	2208	E	Dartmouth	Cir
2101	2165	2100	2164	E	Dartmouth	Cir
2233	2299	2210	2298	E	Dartmouth	Cir
2999	2901	3030	2900	S	Fillmore	Way
3099	3001	3098	3032	S	Fillmore	Way
3099	2901	3124	2900	S	Milwaukee	Cir
2899	2701	2998	2700	S	Dallas	Way
2999	2901	3098	3000	S	Dallas	Way
2701	2899	2700	2898	E	Linvale	Pl
3081	3139	3074	3098	E	Yale	Way

Source: Rachel Boba Santos, Crime Analysis with Crime Mapping, ISBN: 9781506331034.

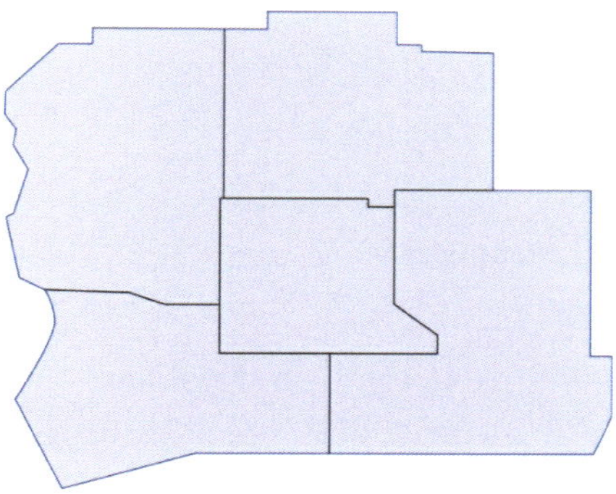

Figure 5.2. *Polygon feature map.*

Source: Rachel Boba Santos, Crime Analysis with Crime Mapping, ISBN: 9781506331034.

A wide variety of vector data types are used by crime analysts. Since many of these are representative of the real world and serve purposes other than crime analysis, most people are familiar with many of these. The following geographic feature-focused databases are among the many kinds of geographic databases frequently utilized in crime analysis:

- **Point Features:**
  - Police stations;
  - Schools;
  - Hospitals;
  - Businesses;
  - Retail stores/restaurants;
  - Offices;
  - Places of worship;
  - Government buildings;
  - Mass-transit stops and stations (e.g., bus stops, train stations).
- **Line Features:**
  - Streets;
  - Highways;
  - Rivers;
  - Railroads;
  - Mass-transit routes (e.g., subways).
- **Polygon Features:**
  - Parcels;
  - Buildings;
  - Census block groups and tracts;
  - Parking lots;
  - School campuses;
  - Airports;
  - City, county, and state boundaries;
  - Police areas (grid, beat, precinct, district);
  - Drug markets;
  - Gang territories;
  - Areas targeted for special policing efforts.

5.1.2. Raster Data

Raster data is another tool used by crime analysts to display features on the surface of the earth in addition to vector data. Raster data are collections of pixels or grid cells that cover a surface and are given attribute values, usually in the form of numbers. Satellite images and remote sensing photos are commonly stored in raster files, which are frequently shown in color (Chainey and Ratcliffe,

2005; Hick, Bair, Fritz, and Helms, 2004). Frequently, these pictures are taken with the right coordinates from an airplane or satellite (*refer to* Figure 5.3). In crime analysis, satellite images are usually used in conjunction with vector data to display the specifics of roads, buildings, parking lots, and surrounding landscapes. Crime analysis uses different kinds of raster data files for density mapping.

Table 5.3. *Polygon Feature Attribute Data*

Feature	District
Polygon	1
Polygon	2
Polygon	3
Polygon	4
Polygon	5

Source: Rachel Boba Santos, Crime Analysis with Crime Mapping, ISBN: 9781506331034.

Figure 5.3. *Satellite photo example.*

Source: Rachel Boba Santos, Crime Analysis with Crime Mapping, ISBN: 9781506331034.

5.1.3. Projections

The data files must be modified as they are integrated into the program and used for analysis when converting vector or raster data into a GIS. The earth is round, so these modifications, also known as project are required, even though a GISGIS presents geographic data in a flat manner. Projections, regrettably, distort the surface in some way because the data from a round surface can never be perfectly displayed on a flat surface. Prior to proceeding with the spatial analysis, the crime analyst chooses which kind of projection (e.g., conic, planar, or cylindrical), based on the area of interest's dimensions and location.

5.1.4. Coordinate Systems

Since coordinated systems are what analysts use to find data on a map, they are fundamental to Geographic Information Systems (GIS). X-Y coordinates, or latitude and longitude, are the universal reference system. They express data in degrees, minutes, and seconds spherical terminology that reflectreflects the spherical nature of the earth. Another system created for increased user convenience is the State Plane Coordinate System. The earth's surface is covered in a grid with coordinates expressed in yards, feet, or meters (Harries, 1999). The data and the analysis's goal determine the coordinate system that analysts employ. When analysts use multiple data sources, it is crucial that the sources have the same projection and coordinate system.

5.1.5. Scale

A map's scale indicates how small a given map actually is, as maps are tiny representations of the earth. A scale is defined as the ratio of the distance on a map to the actual distance (e.g., 1:10,000 feet). Large-scale maps display small areas, while small-scale maps display large areas (Harries, 1999).

5.1.6. Getting Events on a Map

The precise latitude and longitude coordinates of an event are the most reliable and accurate method for locatmap within a database. Almost everyEvery incident that needs to be mapped by crime analysts (i.e., offenses, requests for service, apprehensions, addresses of offenders, etc., are matched by an address. The corresponding x and y coordinates are entered into the database of records management systems (RMS) and computer-aided dispatch (CAD) systems when the address is entered using a GIS system. But not every incident takes place at a known address (e.g., parks or on undeveloped land), so occasionally police officers or detectives will have equipment with them that can provide the coordinates right away. The analyst can instantly plot the events on the map by using the x and y coordinates.

Data may occasionally lack the x and y coordinates connected to crimes or incidents involving calls-for-service, though. When this occurs, crime analysts have to use the addresses to locate the events on the map in order to geocode the data. The process of geocoding an address involves connecting it to its map coordinates so that the address can be shown on a map and recognized by the GIS in the future. Typically, a record's address (e.g., Street segment data (such as arrests, crimes, or calls for service) is geocoded. Less frequently, data are geocoded to various spatial precision levels, like the centroid, or middle, of a beat, grid, or zip code. Fortunately, as more and more CAD and RMS software automatically generates x and y coordinates, the need for crime analysts to geocode data has diminished over thst ten or so years. Even though it'sit is becoming less frequent, the crime analyst should still be familiar with the geocoding procedure.

The analyst sets up the geographic and tabular files, indicates the geocoding preferences, searches the GIS for matches, evaluates the findings, adjusts the parameters, and starts the process anew in five steps. Each of these steps is described briefly here:

- **Step 1:** Preparing the geographic and police data files. The analyst's task in this step includes making sure the addresses within the location variable of the database to be geocoded are accurate and consistent. To obtain accurate and complete geocoding results, the analyst must also ensure that geographic data (e.g., street segment file) are up-to-date and accurate. This can be challenging in cities that are growing rapidly and undergoing changing street development.
- **Step 2:** Specifying geocoding preferences. The analyst must determine and set the preferences for matching the reference data to the tabular data. Preferences include the spelling sensitivity of the matches (i.e., whether the police data street names and geographic street names are spelled exactly the same), address style (e.g., whether to match on "address only" or on "address and zip code"), and the acceptability of partial matches (i.e., whether to accept matches that are considered "close"). Geocoding produces a match score for each record that denotes how closely the address from the police data file matches the street segments in the geographic file, with a score of 100 signifying a perfect match.
- **Step 3:** Matching within the GIS. Once the preferences are set, the analyst's next step is simply the push of asoftware packages use a fairly simplesimple method to accomplish the placement of an address along a street segment. Each street segment contains a range of addresses, and the GIS places the point along the segment relative to its value within the range. For example, an address of "200 E Main St" would be placed halfway along a street segment that ranges from 100 to 300 East Main Street (*see* Figure 5.4).
- **Step 4:** Reviewing results. After the geocoding process is complete, GIS software programs generate statistics showing the numbers and percentages of addresses that were successfully matched, addresses

that were partially matched (i.e., with scores lower than 100), and addresses that were not geocoded (matched) at all. The ideal geocoding match rate is 100%, which means that all records from the police data file were matched to the geographic file. Depending on the number of cases and the purpose of the analysis, a score of 95% may be acceptable, provided there is a legitimate reason why perfection was not reached (e.g., cases that were not matched occurred outside the jurisdiction) and the missing cases will not compromise the analysis results. Whenever geocoding match rates are lower than 100%, analysts should reexamine and correct the data and go through the geocoding process again.

- **Step 5:** Respecifying parameters and geocoding again. Geocoding is a painstaking and often trying process, commonly requiring numerous adjustments and repetitions before a high enough match rate is achieved. The geocoding method uses a mathematical model to locate each address within an address range (e.g., "100 E Main St" is located halfwayain Street), but in reality, addressesbut addresses do not occur proportionally along street segments. Some addresses take up entire blocks, whereas others share space on a block, with one address behind another. Thus, there is an accuracy issue with this method, which is why having coordinates is ideal and most police data systems are now producing them for each record.

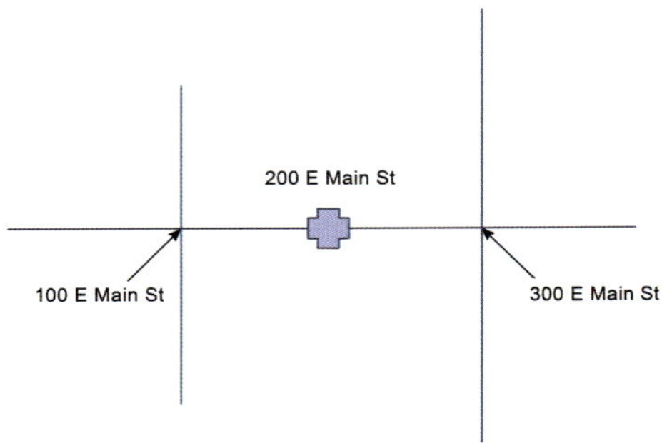

Figure 5.4. *Geocoding: street segment matching.*

Source: Rachel Boba Santos, Crime Analysis with Crime Mapping, ISBN: 9781506331034.

5.2. CRIME MAPPING TECHNIQUES

Crime mapping is used in policing in many different ways. Chainey and Ratcliffe (2005) outline some examples:

- Recording and mapping police activity;
- Supporting the briefing of operational police officers by identifying crimes that have occurred recently;
- Identifying crime problem areas or "hot spots" for implementing crime prevention responses;
- Helping to effectively understand crime distribution along with other local data;
- Monitoring the impact of crime prevention initiatives;
- Communicating crime statistics to the public.

When analyzing crime and disorder issues spatially, crime analysts employ two different methodologies. The first method, known as descriptive mapping, uses geographic units of analysis to display police data and statistics to illustrate the findings of the analysis. Using the second method, known as analytical mapping, analysts can identify problem areas or activity clusters by pinpointing the precise locations of incidents. This chapter explains how statistics are used to classify data in descriptive maps and gives an overview of the different kinds of descriptive mapping. Density mapping is one kind of analytical mapping that is covered at the end.

5.2.1. Types of Descriptive Crime Mapping

There are several varieties of crime mapping that are descriptive. The most common applications of those discussed here are in crime analysis. These consist of interactive Internet crime mapping, graduated mapping, single-symbol mapping, buffers, and chart mapping.

5.2.1.1. Single-Symbol Mapping

Stores, roads, states, and other features are represented by distinct, uniform symbols on single-symbol maps. An illustration of a single-symbol map that displays the streets and locations of homicides is Figure 5.5. When it comes to single-symbol maps, it's crucial to remember that a GIS stacks all of the points that have the same address directly on top of one another, making it impossible for the map to depict the actual number of points. There is no way for someone viewing this map to see every homicide because, for instance, in Figure 5.5, the GIS will have placed two gray circles in the same spot if two homicides occur at the same location. This disadvantage of single-symbol mapping is especially pertinent to the mapping of police data and crime because these events frequently recur at specific locatio, when analysts are working with large amountscopious amounts of data, single-symbol maps are also not helpful. Imagine the Figure 5.5 map, where 100 distinct crimes are marked with their locations. The map would be challenging to read because the points would overlap.

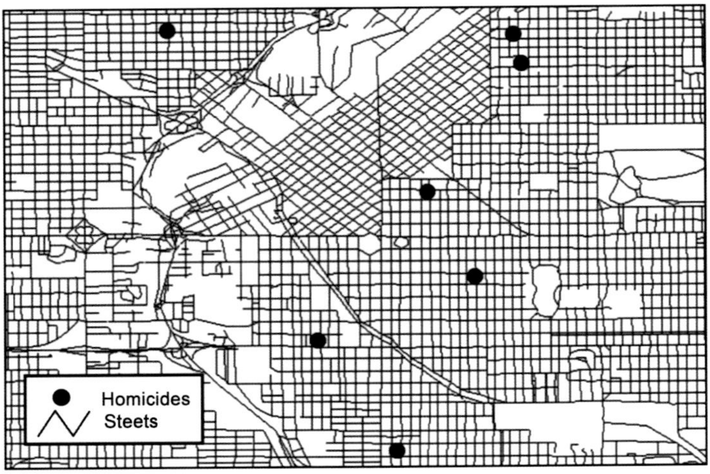

Figure 5.5. *Single-symbol mapping example.*

Source: Rachel Boba Santos, Crime Analysis with Crime Mapping, ISBN: 9781506331034.

Because of this, crime analysts use other types of maps to convey information about multiple incidents at specific locations; they primarily use single-symbol mapping to display small amounts of data as they are mapped for crime patterns and geographic information in which there is no overlap.

5.2.1.2. Buffers

A buffer on a map is the designated area that surrounds a feature. Depending on the goal and scale of the map, buffers can be set at smaller distances, like 50 feet, or larger distances, like 500 miles. By displaying the relative distances between features on a map, buffers aid in the analysis of crime. An elementary school (polygon feature) with a 1,000-foot buffer and one subject stop nearby is depicted on the example map in Figure 5.6. The map can be used to find the locations and numbers of stops as well as other activities (e.g., crimes, calls, and arrests) occurred in and around the school's 1,000 feet.

5.2.1.3. Graduated Mapping

Gradient maps, or maps with distinct feature sizes or colors designating different variable values, are frequently used by crime analysts. General examples of graduated-size and graduated-color maps are shown in Figures 5.7 and 5.8, respectively. The sizes of the symbols used for point and line features in a graduated-size map correspond to their value, which is usually the number of incidents that happened at that address or on that street. Single-symbol maps are inappropriate for displaying data about crimes that recur at the same locations, as was previously mentioned. Since graduated-size maps can account for multiple incidents at the same location, analysts use them for this purpose. Gradient-size maps, like single-symbol maps, can have overlapping points, though, if an excessive number of data points are examined at once. Figure 5.7 is a map where the number of crimes at each location is represented by a graduated point system. A graduated-color map uses points (in a single-symbol map only), two lines, and polygons, with the colors of the symbols representing their values. A color-coded map, shown in Figure 5.8, indicates the total number o in specific areas with lighter shading indicateindicates fewer crimes, and areas with darker shading indicate more crimes.

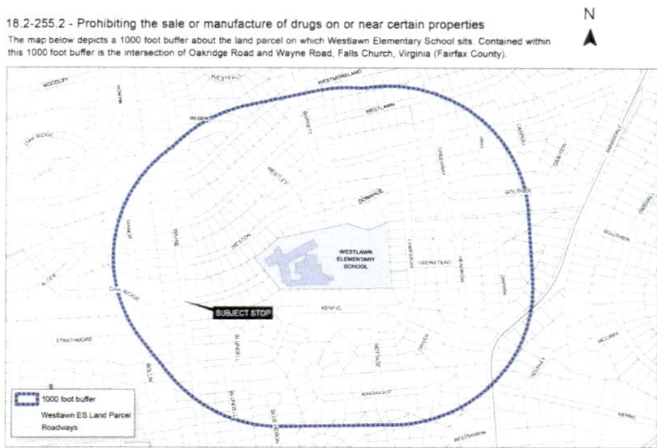

Figure 5.6. *Buffer map example.*

Source: Rachel Boba Santos, Crime Analysis with Crime Mapping, ISBN: 9781506331034.

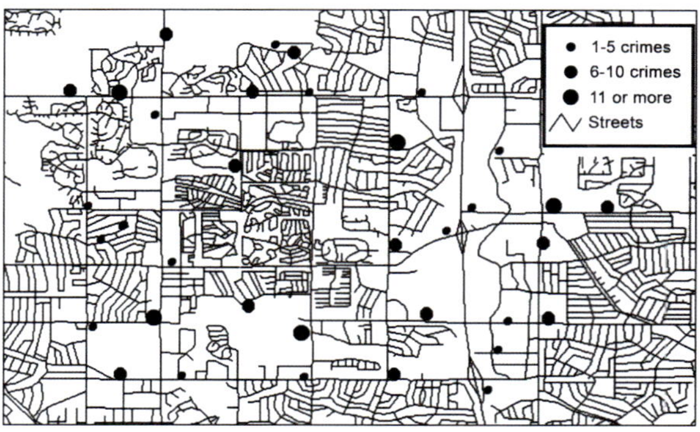

Figure 5.7. *Graduated-size map example.*

Source: Rachel Boba Santos, Crime Analysis with Crime Mapping, ISBN: 9781506331034.

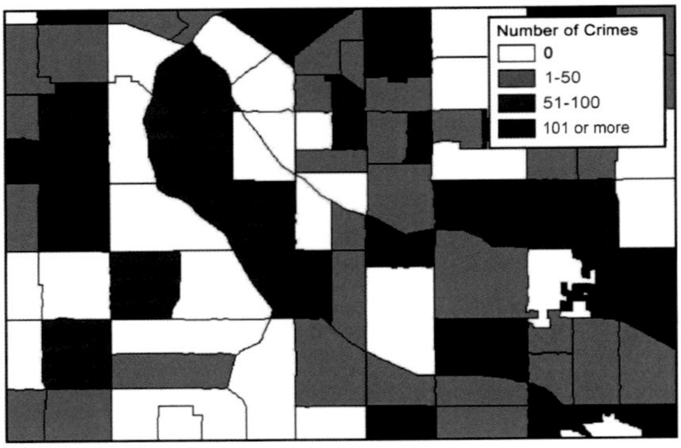

Figure 5.8. *Graduated-color map example.*

Source: Rachel Boba Santos, Crime Analysis with Crime Mapping, ISBN: 9781506331034.

5.2.1.4. Chart Mapping

Chart mapping enables the crime analyst to simultaneously display multiple values within a given variable (e.g., values = robbery, assault, and rape; variable = crime). Pie and bar charts are the two varieties of chart mapping. Pie chart mapping shows the relative percentages of values within a variable, represented by pie slices.

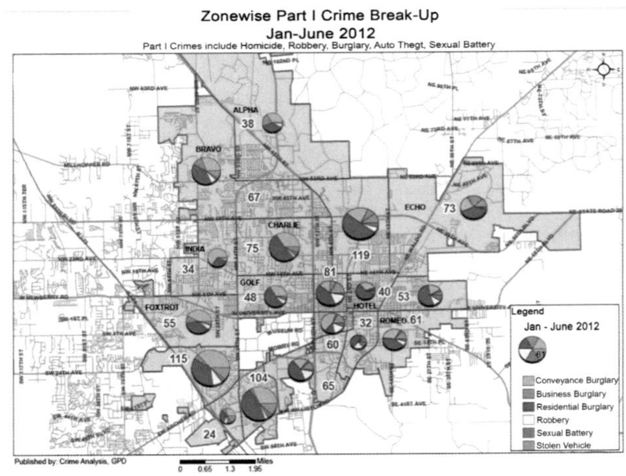

Figure 5.9. *Pie chart map example.*

Source: Rachel Boba Santos, Crime Analysis with Crime Mapping, ISBN: 9781506331034.

A pie chart map showing the Part I crime breakdown for each beat zone is shown in Figure 5.9. To represent the data for each zone, pies are positioned in the center of each zone. The slices show the percentage of each type of crime, and the pies' sizes are graduated to represent the overall amount of crime. The relative frequencies of values within a variable are shown in bar chart mapping, but the heights of the bars indicate the relative frequencies of incidents rather than percentages.

5.2.1.5. Interactive Crime Mapping

The phrase "interactive crime mapping" refers to streamlined geographic information systems that are accessible to inexperienced users via the Internet, as opposed to a specific kind of mapping. Many police agencies are moving toward enabling audiences to conduct analyses themselves through interactive crime mapping systems, rather than just posting analysis results. These systems are used by website users to map the results of database searches for information that piques their interest. This kind of format lessens the workload for department staff while also providing audienceter choice in the information they can access.

In order toTo offer their citizens an interactive crime mapping service, police departments have been forming business partnerships with internet companies more frequently in recent years. Police departments give these businesses, who have created interactive crime mapping software, their crime data r a fee so they can offer the service to the general publicpublic. Because of this partnership, police departments can avoid developing and maintaining the software themselves.

For this purpose, the majority of interactive crime mapping websites currently use single-symbol mapping; however, a few also use density mapping and area maps with graduated colors.

Some websites offer interactive features that enable users to query data just like in mapping systems, but the information they retrieve is presented in summary reports or case lists rather than maps. Numerous interactive crime mapping sites on both police and privaonducting an Internet search. But generally speaking, theseBut these apps aren't sophisticated or adaptable enough to be of any use to crime analysts. The users' familiarity with crime data and mapping is another problem with these websites. Because crime analysis and crime mappingmplicated fields of study, as this book makes clear, there'sthere is a chance that inexperienced users of Internet crime mapping systems will misuse or misunderstand the information they find and the maps they create.

5.2.2. Methods for Descriptive Crime Mapping

Thematic mapping, also known as choropleth mapping, is one kind of descriptive mapping that is frequently used to represent data summarized by statistical or administrative areas. It is especially helpful for getting a broad overview of the overall spatial distribution of crime (Eck, Chainey, Cameron, Leitner, and Wilson, 2005). This section explains the statistical methods—categorical, statistical, and manual—that crime analysts employ to create graduated-color and graduated-symbol maps. Geographic data can be displayed in a variety of ways, and it is crucial that analysts choose the ones that best suit their needs and the data they are analyzing.

5.2.2.1. By Category

Categorization of data allows for different types of symbols or symbols with varying colors or shades to be shown on a map. Since categorical variables have nominal rather than numeric values, crime asts typically employ this method for them. Race, gender, modemode of entry, point of entry, point of entry, weapon used, kind of location, kind of business, and land use are a few examples of categorical variables. Using this approach, the values found in each variable (e.g., distinct illustrations for each gender (male and female for the sex variable).

Shading by categorical value is mostly applied to polygon and point features, and it is only utilized with single-symbol maps. Since categorical mapping necessitates that each point be shaded in accordance with a single categorical value, it cannot be applied to graduated-size maps. A graduated-size map would, for instance, show a location with two robberies at it with a larger point than the points used for addresses with just one robbery. Because different kinds of weapons might have been used in the two robberies represented by that single point (e.g different types of firearms), one cannot shade tha bywith the weapon used during the robbery. e.g., one robberyrobber used a knife,other used a gun. The map in Figure 5.10 was made in order toto analyze a robbery. Because an interstate gives a thief a quick way out of the scene of a crime, the areas are shaded to show whether they cotate highways. The values that determine the different colorsassorted colors are "yes" (an interstate is present) and "no" (no interstate is present). The categorical variable mapped here is: Is there an interstate in the area? This map combined with a graduated-symbol map of robberies could be used by an analyst to assess whether areas with interstates have a higher rate of robberies. Rather than using shading to represent different busin uses different symbols. This map could be used by an analystAn analyst could use this map to help differentiate between locations based on how likely they are to be robbed.

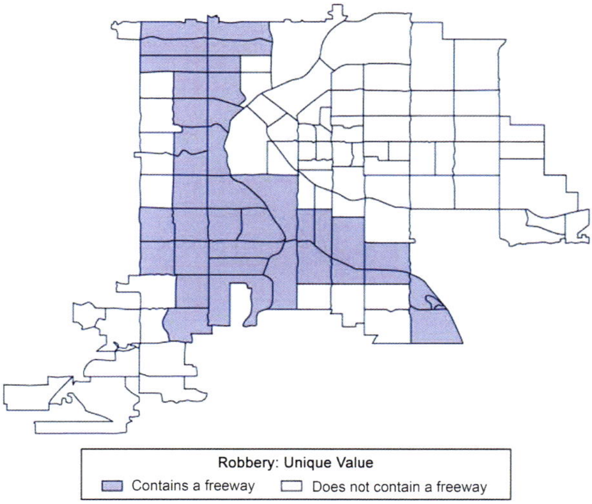

Figure 5.10. *Graduated-color map indicating presence of a freeway.*

Source: Rachel Boba Santos, Crime Analysis with Crime Mapping, ISBN: 9781506331034.

5.2.2.2. By Statistical Classification

A formula that establishes the break points for the size or shading of the data is a statistical classification used in mapping (details regarding break points are shown in a map's legend). A map's features can be identified from one another based on the categories that their values belong to. For example, the colors used to symbolize ranges may be broken down as follows:

- **White:** No crimes;
- **Light Gray:** 1 to 10 crimes;
- **Dark Gray:** 11 to 20 crimes;
- **Black:** 21 to 30 crimes.

An area feature, like a police beat, with 15 crimes would be shaded dark gray on a map created with these categories. A thematic map should not have more than six classes or shadings (Harries, 1999). In crime mapping, four statistical classifications are commonly employed: standard deviation, quantile, equal interval, and natural breaks. These divisions serve various functions for analysts.

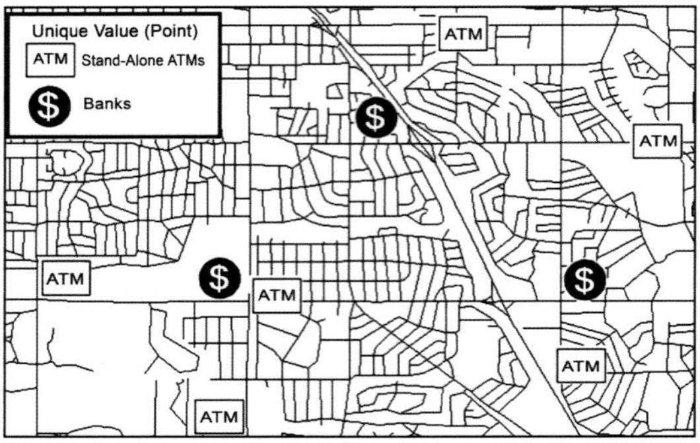

Figure 5.11. *Unique-symbol map indicating banks or stand-alone ATMs.*

Source: Rachel Boba Santos, Crime Analysis with Crime Mapping, ISBN: 9781506331034.

Using GIS software, an analyst using the natural breaks classification can locate the gaps in the data distribution that naturally serve as breakpoints for the classifications in the legend. This is one of the most commonly used classification types in crime analysis, and it is also the default type in many GIS programs. It works best for descriptive or exploratory analysis of a sample of data (e.g., a broad overview of an issue) and is unsuitable for long-term comparisons.

The point, line, and polygon maps in Figures 5.12, 5.13, and 5.14 show how the natural breaks are categorized. Observe that the categories' values in the map legends appear arbitrary, with unequal intervals. This is so because breakpoints in the distributions of the data being mapped have been used by the GIS to determine the ranges.

Three categories are used in Figure 5.12's graduated-size point map to show robberies at specific addresses. The data set naturally breaks at robberies at a single address between 1 and 4, 5 and 9, and 10 and 13. The data used to create this map is shown in Table 5.4, which shows a number of the addresses along with their respective counts of robberies.

The number of robberies along the street segments in a particular area (*listed in* Table 5.4) is shown in three categories on the graduated-size line map in Figure 5.13. The data exhibits natural breaks ranging from 1 to 7, 8 to 10, and 11 to 24 robberies per street segment. Figure 5.14's graduated-color polygon map displays the number of robberies by geographic area. The three map legends differ due to the different ways in which the data have been summed (e.g., by area, by street segment, and by address), which results in disparities in the data distributions' gaps.

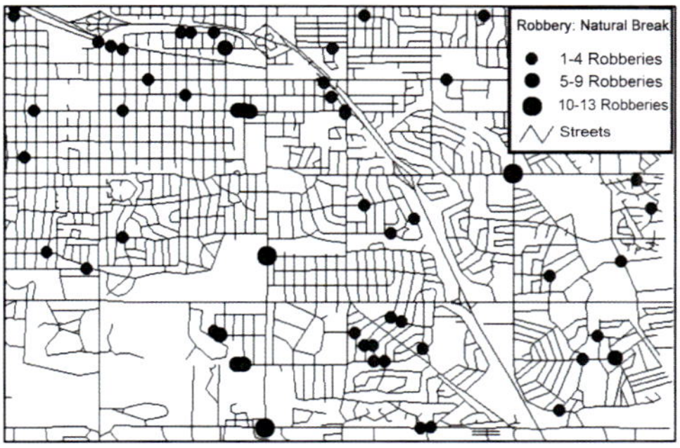

Figure 5.12. *Graduated-size point map: natural breaks classification.*

Source: Rachel Boba Santos, Crime Analysis with Crime Mapping, ISBN: 9781506331034.

Table 5.4. *Number of Robberies by Address*

Address	Number of Robberies
4980 E Main St	3
3920 S Clover Rd	10
930 S Bridge St	9
4500 N River Rd	4
3952 S Thompson St	0
230 S Bridge St	5
4560 N River Rd	1
465 S Bridge St	8
1520 S Bridge St	12

Source: Rachel Boba Santos, Crime Analysis with Crime Mapping, ISBN: 9781506331034.

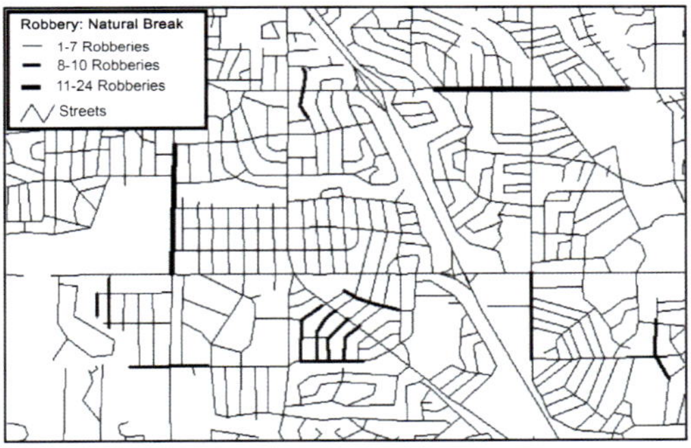

Figure 5.13. *Graduated-size line map: natural-breaks classification.*

Source: Rachel Boba Santos, Crime Analysis with Crime Mapping, ISBN: 9781506331034.

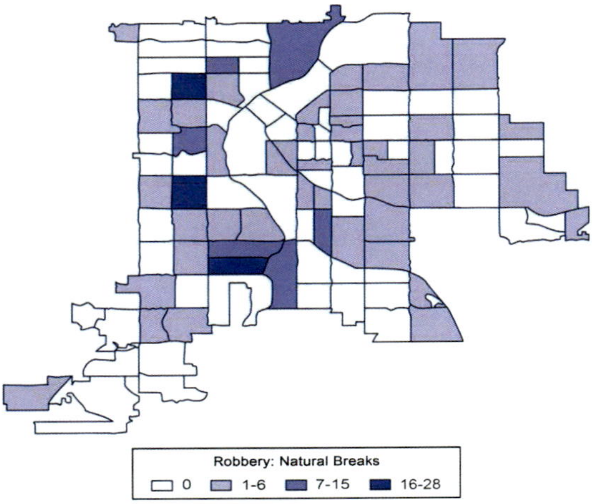

Figure 5.14. *Graduated-color polygon map: natural-breaks classification.*

Source: Rachel Boba Santos, Crime Analysis with Crime Mapping, ISBN: 9781506331034.

Although all of these classifications can be used to create graduated-size or graduated-color point and line maps, only polygon maps are used to illustrate statistical formulas in the following discussions of the remaining types of classifications. The following examples demonstrate how the analyst's choice of classifications can affect how the same data is displayed. They use the same data set as the example with the natural breaks.

Using a GIS, the analyst applies a statistical formula that splits the difference between the highest and lowest value into equal-sized ranges to arrive at an equal interval classification. The highest number of robberies per area in Figure 5.15 is 28, while the lowest is 0. Four categories were chosen, and the range for each is 7, which is 28 divided by 4 (e.g., 0–7, 8–14).

The results of the equal interval classification vary based on the data values (e.g., values between 0 and 80 would be split into four categories (0–20, 21–40, andh). The best data fo this kind of map are those with comparable incidentincidents that counts across all classes.

This classification is commonly used ps to help them understand the nature of the issues they are looking intothe nature of the issues into which they are looking. However, due to the skewed nature of most crime analysis data distributions, they typically do not provide police with such maps. e.g., take note of all the white spaces in Figure 5.15, and this classification usually produces unusable results for law enforcement.

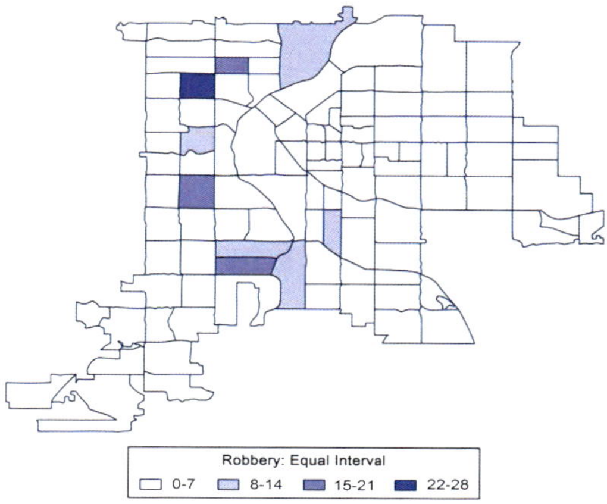

Figure 5.15. *Graduated-color polygon map: equal-interval classification.*

Source: Rachel Boba Santos, Crime Analysis with Crime Mapping, ISBN: 9781506331034.

By dividing the total number of records in the database by the total number of user-selected categories, an analyst creates a quantile map where each category has an equal number of records. Quantile classification prioritizes the number of records in the database over the values within the selected variable, as opposed to other classifications which are based on the values in the selected variable to be mapped.

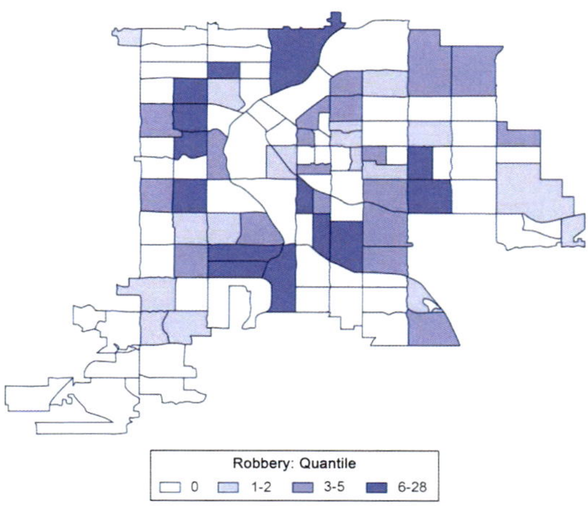

Figure 5.16. *Graduated-color polygon map: quantile classification.*

Source: Rachel Boba Santos, Crime Analysis with Crime Mapping, ISBN: 9781506331034.

The process that creates the quantile classification categories is demonstrated in the example that follows. 20 records with areas (polygons) and the quantity of robberies are included in Table 5.5. As a result, each range in a quantile map made from these data would contain five cases, since there are a total of twenty cases (20/4 = 5). The GIS program sorts the data by number of robberies (ascending) to identify the break points; the first five cases represent the first range, and so on. Table 5.6 displays the sorted data. Table 5.6 in gray indicates the break points for the four categories: 0 for robberies, 1 to 2 robberies, 3 to 5 robberies, and 6 to 28 robberies. The four categories' geographic units are shaded differently, with each color denoting 25% of the total number of records. A quantile map with four categories is shown in Figure 5.16. The values of the first, second, third, and fourth 25% of the cases provide the break points.

Table 5.5. *Number of Robberies by Area (Polygon)*

Area	Number of Robberies
1	6
2	0
3	0
4	2
5	0
6	0
7	5
8	15
9	2
10	3
11	4
12	3
13	22
14	23
15	5
16	1
17	2
18	0
19	1
20	28

Source: Rachel Boba Santos, Crime Analysis with Crime Mapping, ISBN: 9781506331034.

Quantile maps are most frequently used by crime analysts to compare data sets with highly disparate values. For instance, an analyst could compare the number of robberies and burglaries by area in a year using two quantile maps. The values of the categories would differ greatly in the legends of the maps because there are a lot fewer robberies than burglaries. No matter the actual frequencies, the analyst can use quantile maps to compare and identify areas within the highest 25% (using four ranges) for both types and to determine whether the areas with the highest rates of burglaries also had the highest rates of robberies. When an analyst employs the standard deviation classification, mean (i.e., average) and standard deviation of the chosen variable to ascertain the category break points, which are represented in the legend as standard deviations rather than whole numbers (e.g., standard deviation from the mean, +1, −1). By adding the total number of robberies within the polygons and dividing it by the total number of polygons, the GIS calculates the mean number of robberies within the polygons on the map shown in Figure 5.17. The break points for each category are then calculated by the GIS by computing the distribution's standard deviation and adding and subtracting it from the mean. Finding polygons, points, or lines that are outliers (+/− 3 standard deviations from the mean) and comparing the outliers from one database to another (much like a quantile) are the two main uses for this kind of map. In other words, the polygons with values significantly higher or lower than the mean for each data set are shaded a specific color. The analyst can compare dissimilar distributions across various maps because the standard deviation is a standardized measurement that offers the same measures relative to the distribution of a particular variable. Because the mean is frequently not a value that exists in the data distribution, it should be noted that in these maps, the mean value is typically not shaded in any particular area. For instance, a mean of 4.57 robberies does not exist in reality (i.e., four or five robberies are possible but not 4.57), hence none of the areas would be colored in this way.

Table 5.6. *Number of Robberies by Area, Sorted in Ascending Frequency to Determine Quantiles*

Area	Number of Robberies
2	0
5	0
6	0
18	0
3	0
16	1
19	1
17	2
4	2
9	2
10	3
12	3
11	4
15	5
7	5
1	6
8	15
13	22
14	23
20	28

Source: Rachel Boba Santos, Crime Analysis with Crime Mapping, ISBN: 9781506331034.

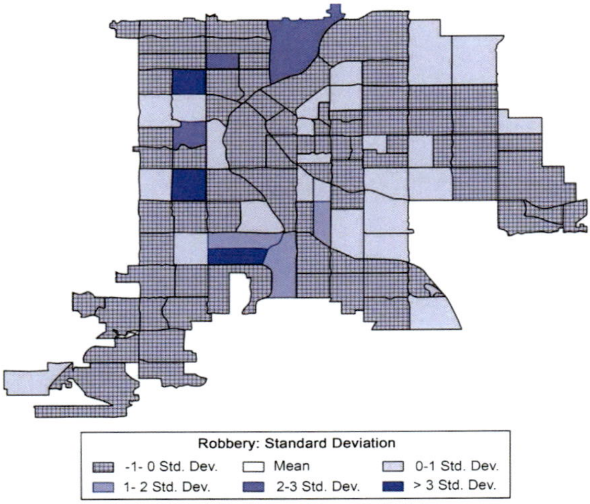

Figure 5.17. *Graduated-color polygon map: standard-deviation classification.*

Source: Rachel Boba Santos, Crime Analysis with Crime Mapping, ISBN: 9781506331034.

5.2.2.3. By Manual Method

The final kind of graduated map is called a "custom" map; in a map made by hand, the ranges shown in the legend are set by the map creator rather than by the values of any variables or statistical formulas.

When comparing multiple maps with the same kind of data over time, such as monthly robbery maps where the same colors represent the same ranges, crime analysts frequently use custom ranges.

Since the colors in the other classifications discussed so far represent different ranges each time the data changed in those classifications, it is not possible to compare the actual values of the variable mapped using any of those classifications.

Two maps with identical custom legends are shown in Figures 5.18 and 5.19, enabling the analyst to compare variations in robberies by area over two time periods (i.e., the same year (January and February). Observe that the fourth category label in these maps reads "or more" rather than having an upper value. When an analyst uses the same legend for multiple maps, they create these categories because the upper limit varies depending on the data set. Custom legends typically have break points that fall on 5, 10, 25, 50, 100, and so forth.

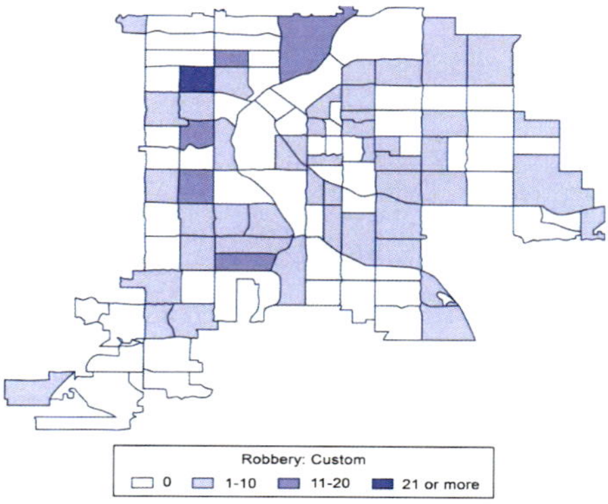

Figure 5.18. *Graduated-color polygon map: custom classification (January).*

Source: Rachel Boba Santos, Crime Analysis with Crime Mapping, ISBN: 9781506331034.

One of the most crucial steps in making a map is selecting the classification that will serve as the break points in the legend. Crime analysts don't just pick classifications at random; instead, they base their choiceexamined the data and the intended uses of the maps. They frequently take into accountconsider agency policies, regional laws, and the background of the issue under investigation when making these choices. For instance, if the city fines locations that have five or more alarms in a given time period, an analyst making a map to display the number of burglar alarms at particular locations in a city might choose "5 or more" as the highest range.

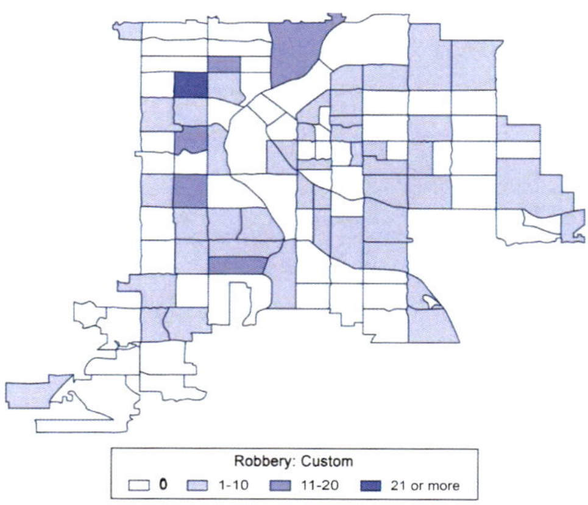

Figure 5.19. *Graduated-color polygon map: custom classification (February)*

Source: Rachel Boba Santos, Crime Analysis with Crime Mapping, ISBN: 9781506331034.

The various classifications have been demonstrated by the frequency of robberies in each of the maps that have been shown in this chapter thus far. Analysts can map a wide range of statistics besides frequency, though, including rates, means, and percentages. These maps might be more pertinent to the current problem than frequency.

Crime analysts should keep the following guidelines in mind when creating maps to describe data:

- In deciding which classification and how many categories to use, the analyst should first determine the purpose and audience of the map.
- Decisions regarding how a map should be made are part of the analysis process; the analyst should not rely on the default settings of a GIS program.
- With the exception of the custom or manual method classification, all of the classification methods are dependent on the data; that is, the ranges in the legend will differ from data set to data set, depending on the distributions and values within the data.
- When describing data using these classifications, the analyst should experiment with the classifications and the number of categories as well as with different statistics (e.g., rate vs. frequency). Often, comparisons among the different maps can provide insight into and promote understanding of a problem.
- The analyst should be aware that shading an entire area based on the aggregate number of events can give readers of the map the impression that the activity is occurring equally across the area, when in fact it may not be.
- When creating area maps, the analyst should not draw conclusions based on the area about individuals or particular locations within that area (i.e., ecological fallacy).

Table 5.7 provides a summary of mapping classification methods and some examples of their use.

Table 5.7. *Summary of Mapping Classification*

	Unique Value	Natural Breaks	Equal Interval	Quantile	Standard Deviation	Custom
Type of variable needed	Categorical	Numeric	Numeric	Numeric	Numeric	Any
Type of feature point (point, line, polygon)	All	All	All	All	All (typically polygon)	All
Ranges dictated by	Values of the variable	Data set	Data set	Data set	Data set	Crime analyist
How often used in strategic crime analysis	Often	Very often	Seldom	Seldom	Often	Very often
Practical example of use	Shading banks by whether they have drive-up ATMs	Mapping robberies for the past month using graduated symbols	Mapping the number of robberies per area to understand the skewed distribution	Comparing levels of bank robbery to levels of convenience store robbery	Determining areas with unusually high numbers of robberies	Comparing levels of robbery on a monthly basis

Source: Rachel Boba Santos, Crime Analysis with Crime Mapping, ISBN: 9781506331034.

5.2.3. Analytical Mapping: Density Mapping

Crime analysts utilize precise incident coordinates in analytical mapping to identifyrations of crime, and areas of disorder. Density mapping is the method most frequently usedmost frequently used method in crime analysis to investigate crime clusters and concentrations. Density mapping, in contrast to the mapping methods previously covered, does not restrict the analyst to looking at predefined areas (e.g., polygons), lines, or points; instead, the density findings display the ways in which the incidents concentrate and cluster over space. To create density maps, crime analysts employ both specialized software and standard GIS packages. There are several statistics and methods used in the process of creating density maps, but this section only provides a general overview and some examples.

The process of creating a simple density map includes the following components:

1. An arbitrary grid is placed over the study area. The analyst selects the size of the grid; however, in this type of map the size tends to be very small to approximate the immediate area of an incident location (i.e., the size used is typically between 50 and 100 feet).
2. A density "score" for each cell is derived as follows: The software searches a predetermined (by the map creator) radius around each

cell (the search radius), counts the number of incidents within that radius, and divides that count by the size of the search area.

3. The cells are shaded according to their resulting scores. Thus, a cell's score does not represent the number of incidents in that cell but the number of incidents "near" that cell divided by the area "around" that cell, approximating the concentration of activity. In other words, a cell may not contain any incidents at all but have a high score because it is surrounded by areas in which incidents have occurred. This is also how continuous shading is produced.
4. The legend for the map is created. Most GIS software programs default to an equal interval classification. The legend does not illustrate "real" counts of events; rather, it provides a ratio of events in an area by the size of the area (e.g., the number of incidents per square mile).

Visually distinct density maps can be produced from the same data by varying the cell size and search distance radius. The same data, for instance, is displayed in Figures 5.20 and 5.21 with 50-foot-sized cells and search radii of 0.5 miles and 2 miles, respectively. This approach can be used to analyze massive volumes of data and is not restricted by geographical boundaries. Analysts need to keep the following issues in mind when they use density mapping:

- Because density maps show crime locations as a continuous surface, they may give the impression that crimes have occurred in places where they actually have not occurred (Groff and La Vigne, 2002). In other words, the shading approximates areas that have high concentrations of crime, not the exact number and location of the crimes.
- Changes in cell sizes and search distances can result in very different maps. A general rule in crime analysis is to keep the grid cell size to about 50 to 100 feet (the approximate size of where a crime or call for service might occur) and adjust the search radius according to the scale of the study area.
- The legends can be confusing to those who are unfamiliar with density maps, and in practice, many crime analysts use legends with labels such as low density, medium density, and high density instead of ranges of numbers. However, such categories are not useful for cfferent databases (e.g., the same type of data for different time periods or different typesseveral types of data for the same time period). For example, if a map of 500 simple assaults is compared with a map of 50 aggravated assaults and the maps have categorical

legends, both maps may appear to show the same level of crimes because the colors and the values are the same. In contrast, if the legends show actual values, it will be clear that simple assault occurs at a much higher rate per square mile. Thus, for purposes of comparing similar data, "custom" legends should be used. It is also recommended that if low, medium, and high density labels are used that the values also be included in the legend, so users can compare legends across maps.

- Density maps have an inherent border bias because cells that are close to the edges of the study area may not have the potential for incidents to occur.

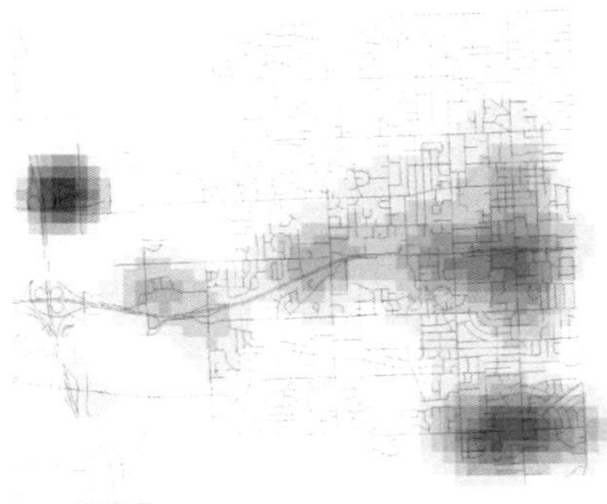

Figure 5.20. *Density map: search radius 0.5 miles.*

Source: Rachel Boba Santos, Crime Analysis with Crime Mapping, ISBN: 9781506331034.

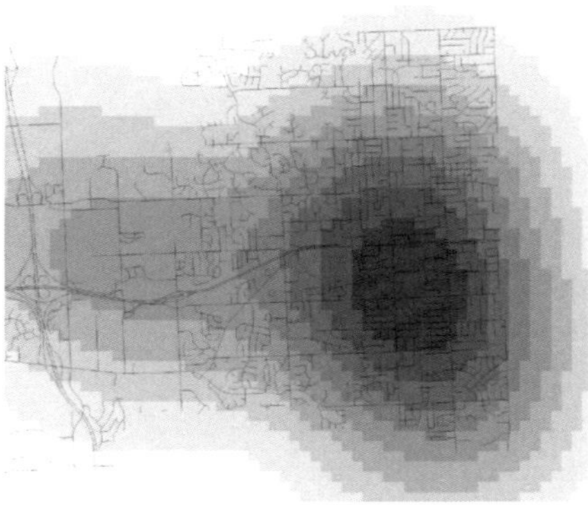

Figure 5.21. *Density map: search radius 2 miles.*

Source: Rachel Boba Santos, Crime Analysis with Crime Mapping, ISBN: 9781506331034.

REFERENCES

1. Bernasco, W. (2010). Modeling micro-level crime location choice: Application of the discrete choice framework to crime at places. *Journal of Quantitative Criminology, 26*, 113–138.
2. Bowers, K. J., & Johnson, S. D. (2003). Measuring the geographical displacement and diffusion of benefit effects of crime prevention activity. *Journal of Quantitative Criminology, 19*(3), 275–301.
3. Brantingham, P. J., Dyreson, D. A., & Brantingham, P. L. (1976). Crime seen through a cone of resolution. *American Behavioral Scientist, 20*, 261–273.
4. Brantingham, P. L., & Brantingham, P. J. (1981). Introduction: The dimensions of crime. In P. Brantingham & P. Brantingham (Eds.), *Environmental Criminology* (pp. 7–26). Beverly Hills, CA: Sage.
5. Chainey, S., & Ratcliffe, J. (2005). *GIS and Crime Mapping*. Hoboken, NJ: John Wiley & Sons.
6. Chainey, S., Tompson, L., & Uhlig, S. (2008). The utility of hotspot mapping for predicting spatial patterns of crime. *Security Journal, 21*(1, 2), 4–28.
7. Cornish, D., & Clarke, R. V. (2008). The rational choice perspective. In R. Wortley & L. Mazerolle (Eds.), *Environmental Criminology and Crime Analysis* (pp. 21–47). Cullompton, Devon: Willan Publishing.
8. Eck, J. E., Chainey, S. P., Cameron, J. G., Leitner, M., & Wilson, R. (2005). *Mapping Crime: Understanding Hot Spots*. Washington, DC: National Institute of Justice.
9. Fotheringham, A. S., Brunsdon, C., & Charlton, M. (2003). *Geographically Weighted Regression: The Analysis of Spatially Varying Relationships*. Chichester, UK: Wiley.
10. Groff, E. R., & La Vigne, N. G. (2002). Forecasting the future of predictive crime mapping. In N. Tilley (Ed.), *Analysis for Crime Prevention* (pp. 29–58). Monsey, NY: Criminal Justice Press.
11. Johnson, S. D. (2010). A brief history of the analysis of crime concentration. *European Journal of Applied Mathematics, 21*(4, 5), 349–370.
12. Johnson, S. D., Guerette, R. T., & Bowers, K. (2014). Crime displacement: What we know, what we don't know, and what it means for crime reduction. *Journal of Experimental Criminology, 10*(4), 549–571.
13. McDonnell, R., & Kemp, K. (1995). *International GIS Dictionary*. New York, NY: Wiley.

14. Oberwittler, D., & Wikström, P. O. (2009). Why small is better: Advancing the study of the role of behavioral contexts in crime causation. In D. Weisburd, W. I. M. Bernasco, & G. Bruinsma (Eds.), *Putting Crime in its Place: Units of Analysis in Spatial Crime Research* (pp. 35–59). New York, NY: Springer.
15. Openshaw, S. (1984). *The Modifiable Areal Unit Problem*. Norwich, UK: Geobooks.
16. Robinson, W. S. (1950). Ecological correlations and the behavior of individuals. *American Sociological Review, 15*, 351–357.
17. Schmid, C. (1960). Urban crime areas–Part I. *American Sociological Review, 25*, 527–543.
18. Tobler, W. R. (1970). A computer movie simulating urban growth in the Detroit region. *Economic Geography, 46*(sup1), 234–240.
19. Tompson, L. (2016). Explaining temporal patterns in street robbery (Ph.D. thesis). University College London.
20. Weisburd, D. (2015). The law of crime concentration and the criminology of place. *Criminology, 53*(2), 133–157.
21. Weisburd, D., & Green, L. (1995). Policing drug hot spots: The Jersey City drug market analysis experiment. *Justice Quarterly, 12*(4), 711–735.
22. Weisburd, D., Bernasco, W., & Bruinsma, G. (2008). *Putting Crime in its Place*. New York, NY: Springer.
23. Weisburd, D., Groff, E. R., & Yang, S. M. (2012). *The Criminology of Place: Street Segments and Our Understanding of the Crime Problem*. Oxford, UK: Oxford University Press.

Chapter 6

Crime Mapping and Analysis Using GIS

Contents

Introduction.. 240

6.1. Crime Mapping.. 241

6.2. GIS for Crime Mapping.. 242

6.3. Role of Geospatial Technology in Crime Mapping.............................. 246

6.4. Crime-Place Relationship and Role of Place in Assessing Crime........ 257

References... 273

INTRODUCTION

The traditional and age-old system of intelligence and criminal record maintenance has failed to live up to the requirements of the existing crime scenario. Manual processes neither provide accurate, reliable and comprehensive data round the clock nor does it help in trend prediction and decision support. It also results in lower productivity and ineffective utilization of manpower. The solution to this ever-increasing problem lies in the effective use of Information Technology.

Geographic Information System (GIS) uses geography and computer-generated maps as an interface for integrating and accessing massive amounts of location-based information. GIS allows police personnel to plan effectively for emergency response, determine mitigation priorities, analyse historical events, and predict future events. GIS can also be used to get critical information to emergency responders upon dispatch or while en route to an incident to assist in tactical planning and response. GIS helps identify potential suspects to increasrsinvestigators' suspect base when no leads are evident.

GIS plays an important role in crime mapping and analysis. Response capabilities often rely on a variety of data from multiple agencies and sources. The ability to access and process information quickly while displaying it in a spatial and visual medium allows agencies to allocate resources quickly and more effectively. In the 'mission-critical' nature of law enforcement, information about the location of a crime, incident, suspect, or victim is often crucial to determine the manner and size of the response. GIS software helps co-ordinate vast amounts of location-based data from multiple sources. It enables the user to layer the data and view the data most critical to tsueissue or mission. It is used world over by police departments, both large and small, to provide mapping solutions for crime analysis, criminal tracking, traffic safety, community policing, Intranet/Internet mapping, and numerous other tasks.

GIS helps crime officers determine potential crime sites by examining complex seemingly unrelated criteria and displaying them all in a graphical, layered, spatial interface or map. It also helps them map inmate populations, fixtures, and equipment to provide for the safety of inmates by separating gang members, identifying high-risk or potentially violent inmates, and identifying hazardous locations in an area. It reduces the potential for internal violence by providing better command and control. GIS functions, when combined with capabilities of location identification devices such as GPS facilitate tracking the movement of high-risk inmates or at-risk personnel throughout an area. It is more cost-effective for the crime analys withproduce the information than for patrol officers to do it themselves.

Virtually every operational activity in the police department includes spatial relationships. Traditionally, these activities have been supported by paper maps and pins. Police officers now have the ability to immediately generate maps directly relevant to the situation at hand. Police agencies collect vast amounts of data from many sources including called-for-services, arrests, first information reports and daily report. Data in this form, however, can be difficult to visualise. The same information displayed graphically provides a powmakingdecision-making tool for investigators, supervisors, and administrators. The visual format shows relationships and patterns that are buried in the data. GIS could also be used to explore the relationship between crime and the environment.

6.1. CRIME MAPPING

Crime analysts can visualize issues related to crime by using maps. Having a better knowledge of the places and reasons behind crimes can help combat them. Police can better protect citizens by mapping criminal activity. Patrols can be directed to areas where they are most needed by using simple maps that show the locations of crimes or concentrations of crimes. More intricate maps could be used by police department policy makers to spot patterns in criminal activity. Maps can also be very helpful in the investigation of criminal cases.

6.1.1. Display Spatial Patterns of Events

The easiest way to visualize the whole crime scene is with digital maps. The places where crimes, arrests, etc., occur. can be shown on maps regularly. Seeing local activities is made simple with this, as opposed to having to go through an events listing. Additionally, maps can be used to display multiple types of information simultaneously. Crime scenes can be represented by symbols based on the day of the week, the kind of crime, the suspect's modus operandi, or the frequency of the crime.

6.1.2. Integrate Community Characteristics

Features of the community (e.g., slums, marketplaces, universities, parks, areas with alcohol permits, red light districts, etc.,) can be frequently seen on maps when examining crime trends to determine the connection between these traits and the crime. To determine whether crime is concentrated near establishments that sell alcohol, the locations of violent assaults, robberies, and alcohol permits, for instance, can be shown. The simultaneous display of additional mapping data, such as public housing and bus routes, can be used to analyze correlations between crime and neighborhood features.

6.1.3. Producing Thematic Maps

At any given geographic level, maps can be created (e.g., zones, divisions, or police stations) to support the analysis of crime trends. It is possible to shade each response area to indicate how many crimes took place there over a given period of time. The more events that took place in the response area, the darker the shade. The shift in a region's crime rate can also be displayed using these theme maps. By shading each area based on whether there was an increase, decrease, or no change in the number of crime incidents, the percent change in the number of incidents can be shown.

6.2. GIS FOR CRIME MAPPING

Geographic Information Systems (GIS) are incredibly helpful tools with a wide range of applications in different fields, and crime mapping is one such use that is growing in popularity in this era of unmatched technological advancement. The way law enforcement agencies manage resource allocation, crime prevention, and investigations has completely changed as a result of the integration of geographical data and the pattern analysis capabilities of GIS technology.

A geographic information system is designed to gather, store, process, analyze, organize, and display spatial or geographic data. By fusing data, technology, and software, it processes geographic data and generates intelligent maps. The cornerstones of GIS are spatial data, attribute data, and a range of data analytic tools. In terms of crime mapping, attribute data pertains to the specifics of the crime, such as its type, date, and time, while spatial data is related to the locations of crime episodes. Police enforcement officers can make maps that show crime trends using GIS tools, and they can utilize that information to make more informed decisions.

6.2.1. Benefits of GIS in Crime Mapping

6.2.1.1. Improved Decision-Making

With the aid of visual representations of crime trends provided by GIS, law enforcement agencies can make data-driven decisions and identify patterns, allocate resources efficiently, and develop targeted interventions.

6.2.1.2. Resource Allocation

By analyzing patterns and criminal areas, GIS helps law enforcement agencies allocate resources as effectively as possible. This includes staff deployment that is strategically planned, heightened surveillance in high-risk areas, and the application of preventive measures meant to deter criminal activity.

6.2.1.3. Community Engagement

When crime statistics are made available to the public, it encourages transparency, increases awareness, and inspires people to actively contribute to enhancing neighborhood safety. As such, GIS maps are useful tools for enlisting local communities in efforts to prevent crime.

6.2.2. Techniques and Tools in GIS for Crime Mapping

6.2.2.1. Spatial Data Acquisition and Integration

6.2.2.1.1. Geocoding

Place names or addresses are converted into latitude and longitude coordinates on a map through the process of geocoding, which allows for the precise location of criminal incidents in crime mapping. Sophisticated geocoding methods use real-time data, spatial algorithms, and address databases to increase accuracy.

6.2.2.1.2. GPS Technology

The development of GPS technology has fundamentally altered the way spatial data is obtained, enabling law enforcement to obtain position data in real-time while on patrol or conducting investigations. By integrating GPS data into GIS platforms, crime mapping becomes more accurate and current, making it simpler to spot trends and crime hotspots.

6.2.2.1.3. Remote Sensing

Remote sensing technologies, such as satellite images and aerial photography, offer high-resolution spatial data that can be used to map crime. These resources offer a more comprehensive perspective that enables analysts to identify environmental elements, such as poorly lit areas or abandoned buildings, that may contribute to criminal activities.

6.2.2.2. Spatial Analysis Techniques

6.2.2.2.1. Kernel Density Estimation

By creating a smooth surface that highlights areas where criminal activity is concentrated, Kernel Density Estimation (KDE), a spatial analysis method, helps identify crime hotspots by estimating the density of criminal occurrences over a given region. With this information, law enforcement can allocate resources more effectively.

6.2.2.2.2. Spatial Autocorrelation

Spatial autocorrelation measures the degree of dispersion or clustering in the distribution of crime episodes. By identifying spatial patterns and linkages, researchers can gain a better understanding of how crime might spread throughout society.

6.2.2.2.3. Hot Spot Analysis

With the use of hotspot analysis, law enforcement can identify statistically significant clusters of high or low crime incidences and use this information to target specific locations for involvement and enforcement.

6.2.2.3. Data Visualization Tools

6.2.2.3.1. Geographic Information System (GIS) Software

GIS software, such as ArcGIS, QGIS, or MapInfo, provides an intuitive interface for the importation, analysis, and visualization of spatial data, and is the cornerstone of crime mapping. They offer a wide range of tools for creating themed maps, executing spatial queries, and sharing interactive maps with interested parties.

6.2.2.3.2. Web Mapping Applications

Web mapping applications like Leaflet and Google Maps API make it easier for the public to share crime maps, and law enforcement agencies can use these tools to create dynamic, approachable maps that increase openness and community involvement.

6.2.2.3.3. Dashboard Tools

With dashboard tools like Tableau or ArcGIS Dashboards, multiple data visualizations can be integrated to create a single, interactive interface. This allows for more informed decision-making when law enforcement dashboards presenting extensive crime statistics, trends, and hotspots are used.

6.2.3. Some Real-World Application

6.2.3.1. Los Angeles Police Department (LAPD)

By projecting crime data onto a computerized map, the Los Angeles Police Department (LAPD) uses geographic information systems (GIS) to map criminal activity and identify patterns and trends. This helps the department allocate resources more efficiently and improve situational awareness. This information improves community safety standards, guides patrol operations, and supports crime prevention programs.

6.2.3.2. New York City Police Department (NYPD)

The NYPD uses GIS technology to create thorough crime maps that aid in their investigations and community outreach. GIS allows law enforcement to visualize crime data over time, allowing them to identify evolving trends and adjust their strategies accordingly. Another way the government promotes transparency and community involvement is by making crime maps available to the general public.

6.2.4. Future Trends and Innovations

6.2.4.1. Spatial Analytics and Predictive Policing

Spatial analytics, a key component of GIS, will become even more significant in the context of crime mapping as advances in this field allow for the significant insights to be derived from geographical data, enabling law enforcement to identify patterns, trends, and hotspots. Predictive policing models, powered by machine learning algorithms, forecast potential future criminal activity based on historical crime data. As these models become more sophisticated, they may enhance proactive law enforcement strategies.

6.2.4.2. Artificial Intelligence in Crime Mapping

Artificial intelligence (AI) has revolutionized crime mapping by enabling large datasets to be analyzed by AI algorithms quickly and accurately. This allows AI algorithms to extract crucial information that may be challenging for human analysts to identify. GIS systems that integrate AI are now equipped with this capability. Object recognition, anomaly detection, and natural language processing are just a few uses of artificial intelligence that can improve crime mapping abilities.

6.2.4.3. Machine Learning for Crime Prediction

Mactechniques, particularly in the area ofaround predictive modeling, are transforming the field of crime mapping. By using hrime data, these algorithms are able tocan identify complex patterns and linkages that conventional analytical methods might overlook. As machine learning models develop, law enforcement agencies should expect more accurate forecasts and proactive steps to prevent crime.

6.2.4.4. Integration of Emerging Technologies

Law enforcement personnel may now view crime scenes in three dimensions thanks to the immersive experiences made possible by augmented reality (AR) and virtual reality (VR) technologies, which are broadening the scope of crime mapping through the integration of GIS with other technologies. This improved depiction facilitates more thoughtful decision-making and allows for a better understanding of the spatial context of crimes.

6.2.4.5. Privacy and Ethical Considerations

Concerns about responsible information use and individual privacy rights are raised by the massive collection and analysis of spatial data, and these concerns also follow as GIS technology advances. Achieving the ideal balance between mapping crimes with GIS technology and safeguarding privacy is a never-ending task that requires careful consideratiegal frameworks.

GIS has greatly alteredaltered the field of crime mapping by providing law enforcement agencies with powerful tools for evaluating and visualizing geographic data. The technical intricacies of GIS, such as data integration and spatial analytic techniques, facilitate more informed decision-making and the efficient use of resources. The use of GIS in crime mapping appears to have a bright future, despite ongoing challenges with data quality and privacy. As technology advances, the integration of GIS with crime prevention will become increasingly crucial in creating safer and more secure communities.

6.3. ROLE OF GEOSPATIAL TECHNOLOGY IN CRIME MAPPING

Crime is a human phenomenon that is defined as breaking any country's current legal framework and is subject to punishment under those laws. It is illegal in India under several sections of the Indian Penal Code (IPC). In underdeveloped and developing nations, like the third world, crime statistics are still manually arranged on paper copies. However, outside of a few major cities, crime maps in India are rarely available in digital or GIS format when it comes to crime locations, police station jurisdiction areas, administrative boundaries, etc. This restricts the potential for improved surveillance because of crime analysis techniques like hotspotting, zonation, navigational aids, criminal profiling, patterns of land use, topography, etc., cannot be examined and evaluated. GIS-based spatial analysis and crime mapping are widely acknowledged methods for studying and managing crime. This is the strongest IT equipment needed for law enforcement. In developed nations, law enforcement agencies have made extensive use of GIS to improve policing. In India, it is still in its infancy. Even though the police have begun to use GIS technology, it is only available in major cities. This is because developing a (spatial) system by looking at crime patterns and forecasting future criminal events and their likely locations is crucial because operational and tactical aspects are the main concerns.

GIS technology is still in its infancy in India. It is not regarded as a necessary tool in the police force because it is not sufficiently acknowledged in crime mapping and analysis, although the Ministry of Home Affairs' National Crime Records Bureau initiated GIS utilities despite a shortage of GIS specialists.

6.3.1. Why Geo-informatics in Crime Mapping?

The development of hardware, software, and information technology has made it easier to use for certain goals. GPS, GIS, and remote sensing data may be utilized for a number of criminal applications. All types of geographically referenced material can be efficiently captured, stored, manipulated, updated, and visualized with the help of GIS tools.

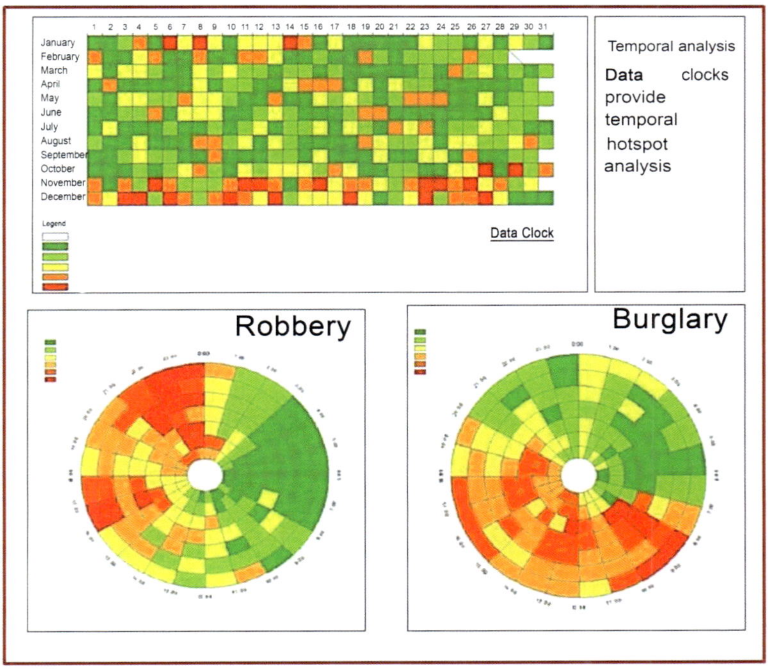

Figure 6.1. *Data clock of crime provideprovides temporal hotspot analysis.*

Source: https://vindhyabachao.org/embeds/crime-mapping-venhf-2017.pdf.

The crime mapping process can make use of both simple and complex data queries as well as data analysis techniques like hotspot generation and the comprehension of spatial and temporal trends and their pattern analysis. GPS data on crimes can be used to identify and update different types of crimes and their activities geographically. Delineating urban area buildings, roads, parks, shopping centers, police stations, and other features that are helpful for crime mapping, particularly in cities, can be successfully accomplished with the use of high resolution remote sensing data. Figure 6.1 provides a basic example of a data clock of crime that only saves the date and time and was utilized by Richard Weiss for temporal hotspot mapping. This study only shows that the majority of crimes occur in the months of November and December, while burglaries typically occur during the day and robberies primarily o night.

Based on the compared parameters, a better understanding of the place and crime and their relationship can be gained from the spatial relationship between crime location and other factors like demography, including education level, housing (pakkah, kachha, and jhuggis), and socioeconomic conditions, including employment status and laborer class people (Alves et al, 2013; Anderson and Anderson, 1984; Lawrence and Cohen, 1979; Cotte Poveda, 2012; Cusimano et al, 2010; Hojman, 2002; Hojman, 2004; Kelly, 2000; Levitt, 2001). The potential advantages and usefulness of crime prediction have drawn a lot of attention. (Gorr et al., 2003; Liao et al., 2010; Mohler et al., 2011; Wang et al., 2010; Alves et al., 2013; Gerber, 2014).

One of the most crucial factors in crime is location (Brantingham and Brantingham, 1991). Numerous details about the nature and characteristics of crime can be learned from the location of the crime and any other geographic information related to the criminal incident. This aids in improving the planning, evaluation, and analysis of criminal incidence prevention. Weisburd and McEwen (1997) looked at the spatial relationship between crime and education level. He discovered an inverse relationship between resident population education levels and violent crime hotspots. tion and identification have benefited greatly fromfrom mobile phone location identification in cellular networks, which is based on the streng waves received by the phone.

Despite the fact thatEven though GIS has been effectively applied in India for a number of purposes, including mapping urban areas (Ahmad and Goparaju, 2016), mapping forest changes (Ahmad and Goparaju 2017b), mapping agroforestry (Ahmad et al, 2017; Ahmad and Goparaju 2017a), etc. However, crime mapping continues to be ineffective in the field of crime.

In developed nations like Canada (Eikelboom et al., 2017), the USA (Jefferson, 2017; Bunting et al., 2017), and New Zealand (Curtis-Ham and Walton, 2017), crime mas are commonly employed. However, relatively littlelittle research has been done in this area, particularly in developing nations. The study conducted by Khalid et al. (2017) assessed and produced a hotspot mapping of crime in Faisalabad, Pakistan. The findings indicate that the frequency of crime events is influenced by the functional nature of various urban land uses, while street crimes are primarily ty's center. They ultimately came to the conclusionconcluded that there is actual potential for the hotspot analysis to influence police patrolling procedures. Wang et al. (2013) investigated crime mapping using actual data from a US city in the northeast. Esri ArcMap 10.1 comparison studies with the Hot Spot Analysis tool confirm that HOT can reliably map crime hotspots. District-level crime mapping in Rajasthan, India was completed by Malvika (2015). The study shows that, in lieu of more conventional crime recording techniques, the use of GIS and graphical tools, along with some significant statistics, is imperative for crime mapping. In the GIS domain, Karuppannan et al. (2004) investigated crime in Chennai, India. Because of its geographic referencing capabilities, the study demonstrated that GIS is a far more reliable and compatible tool for crime pattern analysis than the procedures used now.

Since there is very little GIS mapping, analysis, querying, or hotspot generation in India when evaluating crimes, this is seen as a potential research gap that, if appropriately interpolated in a timely manner, could be very beneficial for policy makers and law enforcement agencies alike.

The current study intends to apply state-by-state crime data for India from 2011 to 2015, generate a year-by-year crime map in the GIS domain, and comprehend the state-by-state temporal trend of crime. It is also represented as a map and recorded percent wise. Additionally, the crime trends for ten of India's largest cities were assessed.

The entire nation, including the four union territories of Delhi, Chandigarh, Pondicherry, and Daman and Diu, was included in the study area. The study area is roughly located between latitudes 8° 29' 40" N and 36° 54' 28" N and longitudes 68° 14' 45 " E and 97° 28' 30 " E. According to the World Crime Index, India ranks 10th in the world with 1.76 million crimes, or about 15% of altted in the United States (http://www . nationmaster .nationmaster. com/ country-info/stats/Crime/Total-crimes). India is home to more than 18% of the world's population, despite holding the equivalent of 2% of the world's land area.

According to the 2001 Indian census, 27.2% of people live in villages and the remaining 27.5% in towns. According to data from the 2011 Indian census, Delhi has the highest population density (9340) among all Indian cities, while Bihar has the highest population density (1102) among all states.

The vector file was obtained from the DIVA GIS website (http://www.divagis.com) for the nation and its various states. Data at diva-gis . org). Information on state-specific crimes (IPC crime registered) from 2011 to 2015 was obtained from the National Crime Rau of the Indian Ministry of Home Affairs.

In order toTo comprehend the temporal trend, we have also downloaded the crime data for India, broken down by year (murder, dacoity, robbery, burglary, theft, and riots), from 2001 to 2015. In order to comprehend the trend of different types of crimes in a city, we have also downloaded the crime data for the top 10 cities in India, which includes all metro areas, for the year 2015.

The analysis was completed using MS Excel, ARC, and GIS software. In the polygon vector attribute, six columns were created for the population of 2011 as well as the years 2015, 2014, 2013, 2012, and 2011. Each relevant column was filled with the population and crime rate broken down by state. Data from the India census is only available every ten years.

The most recent Indian census data from 2011 was used to determine the annual crime density in each state. Using the same 2011 population data that was available, we also evaluated crime density from 2011 to 2015 in our study.

Based on the data, we have also produced a crime map that displays the temporal density of crime as well as the percentage change in crime (both increase and decrease) by state when compared to the previous year's crime data. Since Telangana state was established in 2014, data was only accessible for those two years 2014 and 2015.

6.3.2. Temporal Trend of Various Crimes in India

Figures 6.2 and 6.3 provide data on crime in India by country. There was an increase in murder crimes in 2001, and while they showed a declining trend from 2001 to 2009, they showed an increasing trend from 2009 to 2012. Dacoity crime was higher in 2001 and 2002, but it also shows a declining temporal trend. In contrast, it has drastically decreased in 2015.

From 2001 to 2006, robberies were observed to be roughly under control. From 2006 onward, there was also a continuous upward trend, but from 2010 to 2014, there was a noticeable increase. The years 2001 and 2012 were the highest for riots, while 2014 and 2015 were the highest for burglaries. The year 2002 marked the lowest theft rate ever recorded, and it continued to rise steadily until 2015.

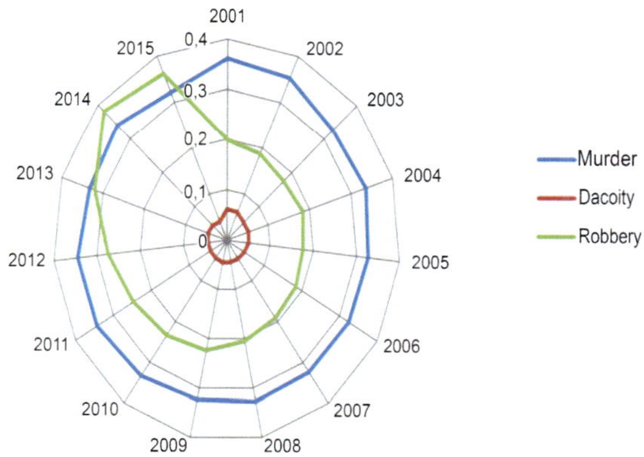

Figure 6.2. *Crime (murder, dacoity and robbery) in India in lakh from 2001–2015.*

Source: https://vindhyabachao.org/embeds/crime-mapping-venhf-2017.pdf.

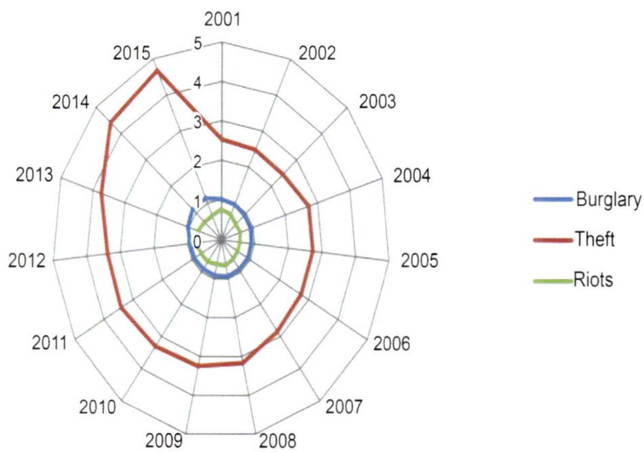

Figure 6.3. *Crime (burglary, theft, riots) in India in lakh from 2001–2015.*

Source: https://vindhyabachao.org/embeds/crime-mapping-venhf-2017.pdf.

6.3.3. State Wise Temporal Trend of Crime (IPC Crime Registered) in India

Figures 6.4a, 6.4c, 6.4e, 6.4g, and 6.4i, respectively, show the crime map generated for the years 2015, 2014, 2013, 2012, and 2011, while Figures 6.4b, 6.4d, 6.4f, and Figure 6.4h, respectively, show the percentage increase and decrease in crime for the years 2015, 2014, 2013, and 2012 compared to the year before.

State-by-state, the crime density values for 2015 range from 65.8 in Nagaland to 1140 points in Delhi, with Delhi having the highest value and the national average being 243.6. Kerala is the second-highest state, maintaining a score of 769.5, which is about three times higher than the national average. After analyzing the percentage change in crime for the year 2015, it was discovered that Daman and Diu had the biggest increase in crime, at 29.6%, when compared to the previous year. Kerala and Delhi came in second and third, with values of 24.3% and 23.9%, respectively. The year in question saw the greatest drop in crime, with Goa recording a value of 31.2%, and Sikkim recording 28.1%.

Similarly, state-by-state crime density values for 2014 range from 58.5 to 927.2, with Nagaland having the lowest and Delhi having the highest, while the national average was 235 points. Kerala continues to hold the second-highest value at 619. After analyzing the percentage change in crime for the year 2014, it was discovered that Delhi had the biggest increase in crime—94.3%—when compared to the previous year, while Mizoram came in second place with a value of 25.2%. Gujarat saw the largest decrease in crime that year, at 16.5%, and Chandigarh, at 21.0%.

State-by-state, the 2013 crime density values range from 61.5 to 527.9, with Nagaland having the lowest and Kerala having the highest, while the national average was 218.7. Delhi continues to hold the second-highest value at 477.6. After analyzing the percentage change in crime for the year 2013, it was discovered that Sikkim had the biggest increase in crime—61.2%—when compared to the previous year, while Delhi came in second with a value of 47.7%. Manipur saw the biggest drop in crime that year, at 15.0%, followed by Pondicherry at 12.3%.

State-by-state, the values for crime density in 2012 range from 55.1 to 475.9, with Nagaland having the lowest and Kerala having the highest, while the national average was 197.2.

Pondicherry, which maintains the value of 343.1, is the second highest. After analyzing the percentage change in crime for the year 2012, it was discovered that Assam had experienced a 16.4% increase in crime compared to the previous year, while Manipur had the second-highest value at 16.1%. The state with the biggest drop in crime that year was Himachal Pradesh, at 12.3%, followed by Sikkim, at 11.4%.

State-specific crime density values for 2011 range from 54.7 to 515.3, with Nagaland having the lowest and Kerala having the highest, while the national average was 192.1. Pondicherry maintains its position as the second-highest with 349.5.

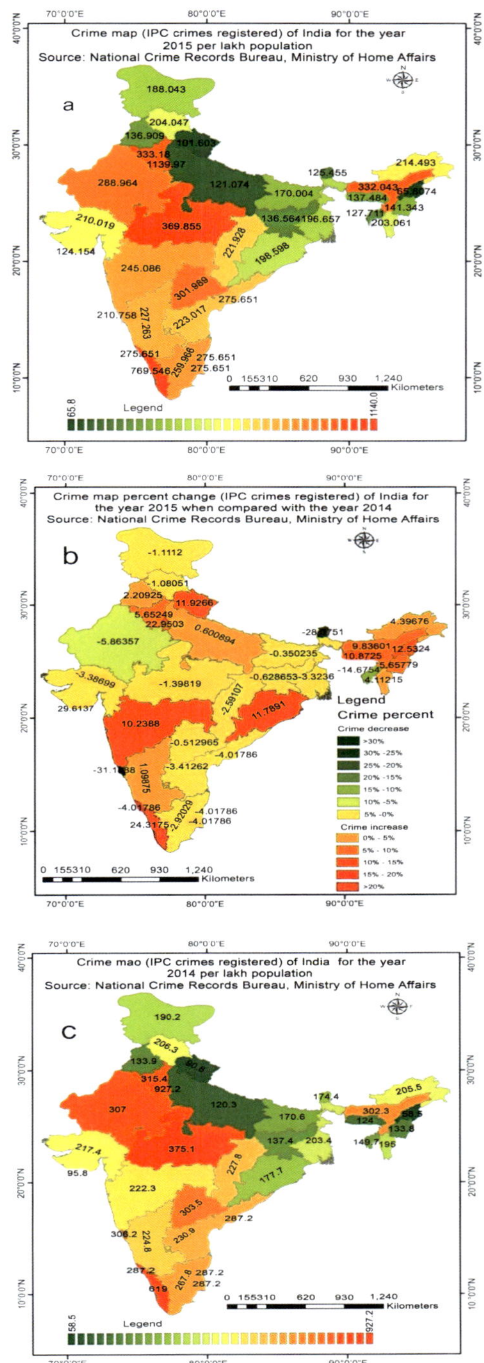
Crime map (IPC crimes registered) of India for the year
2015 per lakh population
Source: National Crime Records Bureau, Ministry of Home Affairs
a
Legend
65.8
1140.0
0 155310 620 930 1,240
Kilometers
Crime map percent change (IPC crimes registered) of India for
the year 2015 when compared with the year 2014
Source: National Crime Records Bureau, Ministry of Home Affairs
b
Legend
Crime percent
Crime decrease
>30%
30% -25%
25% -20%
20% -15%
15% -10%
10% -5%
5% -0%
Crime increase
0% - 5%
5% - 10%
10% - 15%
15% - 20%
>20%
0 155310 620 930 1,240
Kilometers
Crime mao (IPC crimes registered) of India for the year
2014 per lakh population
Source: National Crime Records Bureau, Ministry of Home Affairs
c
Legend
58.5
927.2
0 155310 620 930 1,240
Kilometers
70°0'0"E
80°0'0"E
90°0'0"E
10°0'0"N
20°0'0"N
30°0'0"N
40°0'0"N

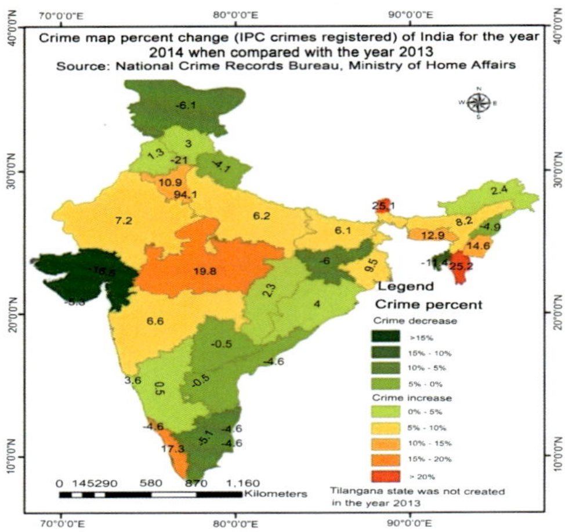
Crime map percent change (IPC crimes registered) of India for the year
2014 when compared with the year 2013
Source: National Crime Records Bureau, Ministry of Home Affairs
Legend
Crime percent
Crime decrease
>15%
15% - 10%
10% - 5%
5% - 0%
Crime increase
0% - 5%
5% - 10%
10% - 15%
15% - 20%
> 20%
0 145290 580 870 1,160
Kilometers
Tilangana state was not created
in the year 2013
70°0'0"E
80°0'0"E
90°0'0"E
40°0'0"N
30°0'0"N
20°0'0"N
10°0'0"N

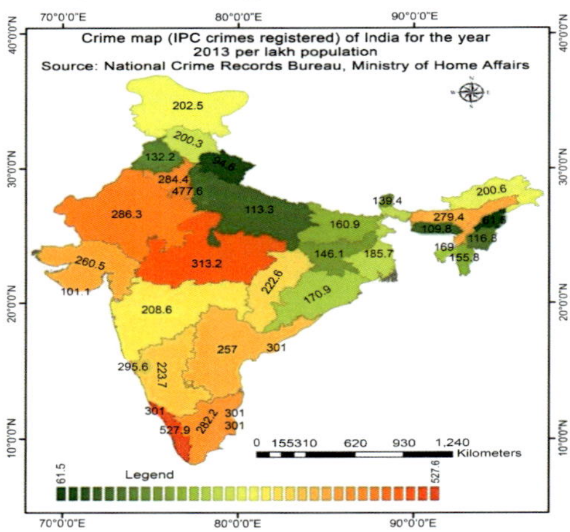
Crime map (IPC crimes registered) of India for the year
2013 per lakh population
Source: National Crime Records Bureau, Ministry of Home Affairs
0 155310 620 930 1,240
Kilometers
Legend
61.5
527.6
70°0'0"E
80°0'0"E
90°0'0"E
40°0'0"N
30°0'0"N
20°0'0"N
10°0'0"N

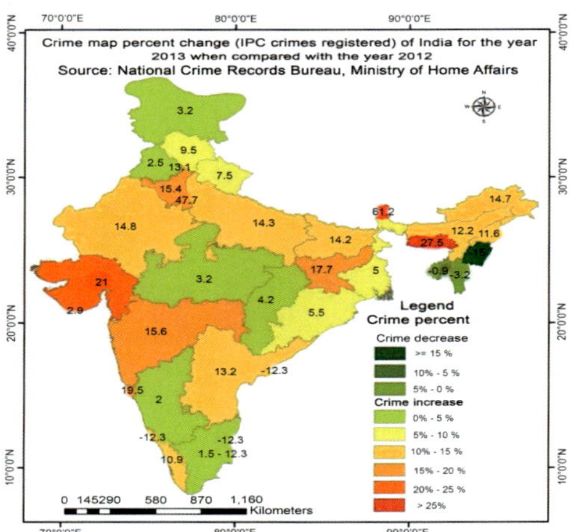
Crime map percent change (IPC crimes registered) of India for the year
2013 when compared with the year 2012
Source: National Crime Records Bureau, Ministry of Home Affairs
Legend
Crime percent
Crime decrease
>= 15 %
10% - 5 %
5% - 0 %
Crime increase
0% - 5 %
5% - 10 %
10% - 15 %
15% - 20 %
20% - 25 %
> 25%
0 145290 580 870 1,160
Kilometers
70°0'0"E
80°0'0"E
90°0'0"E
40°0'0"N
30°0'0"N
20°0'0"N
10°0'0"N

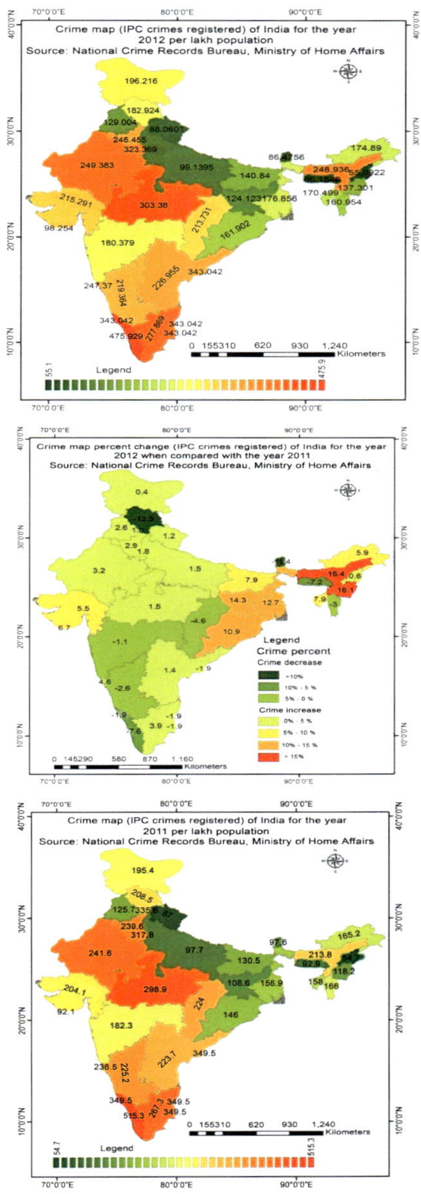

Figure 6.4. *Crime map of India (a: crime density 2015, b: crime map percent change 2015, c: crime density 2014, d: crime map percent change 2014, e: crime density 2013, f: crime map percent change 2013, g: crime density 2012, h: crime map percent change 2012, i: crime density 2011).*

Source: https://vindhyabachao.org/embeds/crime-mapping-venhf-2017.pdf.

6.3.4. City Crime Evaluation

Figure 6.5 presents the evaluation of ten cities, including the metro area, for the year 2015 based on higher crime data types. In terms of all crimes that are considered to be cognizable under the Indian Penal Code, the various city crime per lakh population ranges from 189.4 to 925.9. The city of Indore had the highest crime rate, while Chennai had the lowest.

The range of murder crimes per lakh population was found to be between 0.9 and 11.3 in Patna and between 0 and 11.3 in Mumbai. The rate of dacoity as a crime per lakh people ranged from 0 in Jaipur to 1.7 in Patna. Robbery rates, for example, were lowest in Kolkata (0.6) and highest in Delhi (31.1) per lakh population.

The IPC crime per lakh population for theft, rioting, burglary, and other crimes ranged from (1.1 to 57.17), (14.8 to 445.6), (0.5 to 35.4), and (147.7 to 576.2), respectively. When it comes to IPC crimes such as burglaries, Indore leads the way. Delhi ranked lowest for riots and highest for theft.

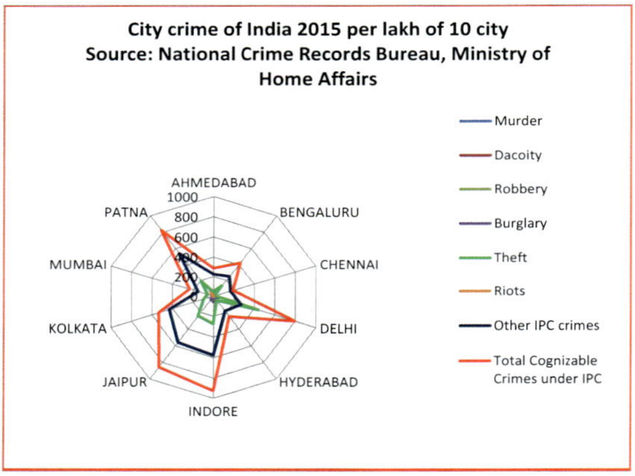

Figure 6.5. *City crime 2015 (Murder, dacoity, robbery, burglary, theft, riots and other IPC crime).*

Source: https://vindhyabachao.org/embeds/crime-mapp17.pdf.

GPS, GIS, and remote sensing are very helpfulextremely helpful add-on technologies for mapping, predicting, and identifying crimes. When combined with other thematic data sets, such as the locations of police stations, shopping centers, buildings, recreational centers with urban sprawl, girls' schools and colleges, mobile police van locations, installed cameras, etc., historical crime data and their locations can reveal a number of clues that can be very helpful for identifying and preventing crimes. In India, the implementation of the Unique Identification Number (UID) and its connection to mobile SIM cards will help further reduce crime. The information pertaining to different crime hotspots can be used to deploy police patrols, build new police stations, and install cameras.

The nature and rate of crime vary from state to state and city to city, with social, economic, mental health, geographic, and political factors being the main causes (http://lawnn . com/crime/). Overall, the state of Kerala has the highest rate of cognizable crimes, while Delhi, a union territory, tops the list.

The majority of crime incidents in Kerala are reported because the state has improved its policing and its citize aware of their rights. On the other hand, in order toto maintain a low crime rate, the police in the majority of other Indian states refuse to register crimes. There is a stark contrast between the rich and the poor in Delhi. A third of the city's population, mostly made up of migrants from other states seeking work, live in impoverished socioeconomic conditions with high rates of illiteracy in slums. They lack even the most basic amenities and ing conditions. Therefore, crime thrives as a result ofbecause of unemployment, poverty, and illiteracy. Additionally, because of the lengthy legal system, people have grown accustomed to committing crimes and believe they can get away with it easily.

According to an article published in the national newspaper Time of India (TOI, 2016), retired Supreme Court justice Markandey Katju attributes crime primarily to poverty. He further stated, "You cannot eradicate crime unless you establish a social and political order in which everyone has access to a decent life, which includes appropriate work, appropriate incomes, healthcare, education, and wholesome food for the kids. According to our research, crime in Nagaland is low and has been declining annually. Neingulo Krome, secretary general of the Naga People Movement for Human Rights, was quoted in the prestigious Indian "The Hindu" as saying, "Ours is a very peaceful society.. society." There are very few crimes committed in society, and anyone found to have criminal tendencies is typically shunned by the community, according to Singh (2016).

6.4. CRIME-PLACE RELATIONSHIP AND ROLE OF PLACE IN ASSESSING CRIME

According to Brantingham and Brantingham (1991), the crime's location is one of its most crucial elements. The location of a crime and any other geographic information related to a criminal incident can provide a wealth of information about the traits of potential offenders, aid in the development of preventative measures, aid in program evaluation, and aid in gaining a clearer understanding of potential environmental causes of criminal incidents. Analysts interested in identifying areas with a high crime rate need to know the locations of incidents.

It is evident to even the most uninformed person about criminal science that crime rates vary by place. There are some high-crime areas and some low-crime areas in almost every city. Researchers discovered this important fact almost 200 years ago. Rather than focusing on personal criminality, these researchers were more interested in areas with high rates of criminal activity, such as cities, counties, states, or towns. These researchers attempted to determine why crime rates varied amongst locations and whether these variations in crime were caused by the people who resided there or by the characteristics of those locations. In this regard, it is thought that criminal science long ago realized the significance of locations.

The "Compte general de l'administration de la justice criminelle en France" was the first crime report released by France and was based on data that was systematically gathered from geographical units (Beirne, 1993). Some French researchers became interested in this first crime report over time. These researchers examined how crime was distributed among geographical areas with various ecological and social features (Quetelet, 1842). Adolphe Quetelet, a renowned researcher, thoroughly examined the information from the "Comral de l'administration de la justice criminelle en France..France." He realized that, even though a region's periodically obtained crime data are typically regular, the crime data from various regions are not comparable or at the same level. Researchers were persuaded by this finding that factors other than personal characteristics account for the variations in crime rates across different regions.

One of the early theories, created by Park and Burgess in 1925, to explain the spatial arrangement of urban areas was the concentric zone theory. The University of Chicago's sociologists were interested in comprehending the consequences of the swift social transformations, specifically how they would affect morality and social order. A crime causation ecological analysis was first presented by Park and Burgess. Park and Burgess then looked at local features rather than criminals to find reasons for high crime rates. Their research enabled them to develop the concept of urban areas, which were defined as concentric zones extending from the city center to the suburbs. The concentric zone theory states that each distinct zone within a city has its own characteristics, organization, and population types.

Clifford R. Todd Shaw and Henry D. Todd McKay made another contribution to the study of crime and place that was closely related to the Park and Burgess studies (Shaw and McKay, 1942). Shaw and McKay, two criminologists interested in using the Parks and Burgess concentric zone theory to examine delinquency in Chicago, were influenced by Park and Burgess's research. These researchers computed the rates of delinquency for different geographic zones of Chicago and created crime maps using pins and the addresses of the criminals that they had collected. Shaw and McKay discovered that crime was concentrated in the city center and gradually decreased as one moved farther out from the center after creating maps akin to those of some other cities, such as Cincinnati and Boston.

Regarding the relationship between crime and place, hot spots and Crime Prevention through Environmental Design (CPTED) are also crucial areas of crime prevention. According to Crowe (2000:1), "appropriate design and efficient use of the built environment can lead to an improvement in the quality of liell as a decrease in the incidence of crime and fear of crime..crime." Hotspot studies represent yet another cutting-edge method for studying crime geography. Research conducted in 1989 by Sherman, Gartin, and Buerger revealed that a mere fraction of addresses were responsible for more than half of all requests. These locations are referred to as "crime hot spots..spots." The hot spot approach holds that certain areas harime than others, and that other areas are relatively crime-freecrime-free. Put differently, crime tends to cluster in some areas while disappearing in others. Some academics assert that law enforcement agencies can more effectively reduce crime if they concentrate their efforts on high-crime areas, citing hot spot research as support.

Furthermore, it becomes clear from analyzing a few key police tactics that these tactics are strongly place-based approaches to crime. Researchers acknowledge that crime is concentrated, so policing strategies are also moving toward place-based policing implementations like team policing, community policing, and problem-oriented policing. In these types of policing tactics, police officers ly tasked with overseeing a specific geographic region in order toto become acquainted with both the local community and the people they serve.

All in all, modern police agencies use GIS to create crime maps within their jurisdictions due to the significance of the place-crime relationship and technological advancements. Geographic Information System (GIS) and crime mapping are regarded as fundamental components of crime analysis, providing police executives with relevant and timely crime data.

6.4.1. History of Geographical Information Systems and Crime Mapping in Policing

GIS has been around for a while in manual form. The American Revolution's Battle of Yorktown in 1871 was depicted on a map created by French cartographer Louis Alexander Berthier that featured hinged overlays that displayed troop movements (Star and Estes, 1990). Despite theiions, these manual information systems were helpful at the time, buttime but using them was challenging due to a few issues. The information was not always current, and there were no established scales (Rogers and Craig, 1996).

In their study, Weisburd and McEwen (1997) provide a useful example of an early crime mapping implementation incident. Using French census data from 1825 to 1827, Guerry, an attorney, and Balbi, an ethnographer, produced maps of crime in relation to violence and property crime categories. Data from demographic studies and criminal statistics were combined. As clarified by Weisburd and McEwen.

They discovered that the northeastern region of France by comparing these maps. was better educated, that people in areas with high rates of property crime also tend to be better educated, and that higher educated people also tend to live in areas with higher rates of property crime (1997). According to Weisburd and McEwen, Guerry and Balbi discovered via their maps that there was an inverse relationship between resident population education levels and violent crime hotspots.

Mapping the distribution and demographics of crime had started by the middle of the 19th century. According to Garland (1997), "dangerous places" research and studies were quite popular in the 19th century. Regarding this matter, police agencies have long employed pin maps as a tool for pattern analysis of geographical information (Block, 1995). Traditionally, these maps feature pins placed on a map that displays criminal activity. Officers can learn a great deal about the distribution and density of crimes from these maps. An excellent general image of the locations and kinds of crimes may be obtained by the observer. However, creating pin maps requires a lot of work and time in its conventional forms. The previous crime patterns have vanished, even though they are renewed. Furthermore, pin maps may be too difficult to comprehend when multiple crime types—typically represented by pins of various colors—are combined. Put another way, computers were not used for mapping as much in the past as they are now. The maps served as the spatial databases in the past. People had to put in a lot of reading and research into maps before they could generate new information. Memory limitations also existed in the absence of computers. On the other hand, GIS can store as much data as the available computer hardware will allow. Among many other operations, GIS can multiply, divide, add, subtract, and combine data. The police can respond to extremely challenging inquiries with GIS. Additionally, the system integrates crime statistics with geographic data.

Even though the military was the first to use computerized mapping, police now use it extensively to map crimes. Not just in the US but also in certain other nations, police departments are finding extensive use for GIS and crime mapping. In addition, the US Department of Justice established the Crime

Mapping Research Center in the 1990s to support law enforcement and crime analysts. In the field of crime mapping, the Crime Mapping Research Center is now regarded as an authority.

6.4.2. GIS and Crime Mapping as Crime Analysis Method and Their Functions in Policing

Many contemporary movements and trends, including proactive policing, community policing, problem-oriented policing, and crime analysis, have an impact on policing these days. Law enforcement organizations generally accept these new policing techniques. Currently, crime analysis is one of the key components of these new policing movements. Given that GIS and crime macknowledged as widely used crime analysis techniques, it could be a good ideaan innovative idea to provide a brief overview of crime analysis before discussing the functions or advaf either tool. What precisely is crime analysis, then? It is believed thought that problem-oriented policing, a popular trend in policing that aims to identify patterns of crime, find solutions, and locate the resources required to address the issues, is where crime analysis originated. It is acknowledged in this regard that crime analysis is necessary to achieve the objectives of problem-oriented policing, which include identifying issues and their solutions as well as evaluating the outcomes. The mechanics of crime pattern recognition have been studied by some academics; this task is considered by some to be the core of crime analysis (Goldsmith, McGuire, Mollenkopf and Ross, 2000). Gill (2000) defines crime analysis as the process of identifying trends and connections in crime data and other relevant data sources in order to prioritize and focus police efforts. Using examples from earlier research, some academics provide a how-to manual for the fundamental processes of law enforcement crime analysis (Reuland, 1997).

To put it simply, crime analysis is policing that focuses on identifying and analyzing criminal issues in order toto solve criminal problems. Crime analysis in policing means that the police officer, or any individual or unit within a law enforcement agency, is in charge of processing data and supplying the agency with information. As a result, the organization can use the data to lessen, stop, and resolve issues related torder and crime. Crime analysis units use arrest and crime reports, police callscall for service, and other relevant data to accomplish this. Crime analysis units then collaborate with their local police departmentsefficient strategies and solutions to address the disorder and crime in light ofconsidering their findings. In order to capture criminals, prevent crime, lessen disorder, and assess organizational processes, crime analysis, according to Boba (2001), is "the qualitative and quantitative study of crime anorcement information in combination with socio-demographic and spatial factors..factors." Given this definition, there are four objectives for crime analysis. One of the main goals of crime analysis is to assist in the arrest of criminals. For instance, in a homicide case, an investigator might come across a particular tattoo on the potential criminal's body. The police analysis unit can assist investigators by looking up criminals with similar tattoos in a database. Helping field officers prevent crimes is another goal of crime analysis. The crime analysis unit can assist the police in addressing theft issues in residential areas by performing spatial analyses of theft, as well as analyses of the items taken from victims and the circumstances surrounding the theft. The third goal of a crime analysis unit is to lessen disorder, which is achieved by conducting research and disorder indicator analysis. The final goal is to support police agencies in making organizational decisions like forecasting staffing requirements, allocating resources, projecting the cost of crime prevention initiatives, and setting up police zones.

The Massachusetts Association of Crime Analysts suggests that crime analysis units should have the following abilities:

- **A Solid Understanding of Criminal Behavior:** Knowledge of the analyst's particular jurisdiction, knowledge of research methods, ability to collect, manage, collate, and query data, ability to understand and synthesize crime information, critical thinking skills, ability to calculate descriptive, inferential, and multivariate statistics, and to create meaningful charts and graphs based on those statistics, understanding of demographic analysis, strong computer skills, including databases, desktop publishing and word processing, spreadsheets, and statistical packages, ability to use a Geographic Information System and a thorough understanding of spatial analysis and spatial statistics, presentation skills, interpersonal communications skills.
- **With all of These Responsibilities:** A crime analyst functions for a law enforcement agency as a combination of an information systems specialist, criminologist, researcher, planner, and statistician.

Five categories of crime analysis exist (Boba, 2001). The tactical one provides data to support operational staff in identifying particular criminal activity and apprehending offenders for immediate criminal cases. Administrative crime analysis involves informing law enforcement administration, city council, city hall, and citizen groups about significant findings from crime analysis units. Strategic crime analysis is the accepted term for analysis used to identify long-term patterns of criminal activity. Intelligence analysis is the process of deterriminal activity in relation to specific people, places, and things. Last but not leastFinally, criminal investigative analysis looks for paan help solve ongoing serial criminal activity.

Crime analysis is becoming more and moreincreasingly popular among American police agencies due to its many valuable applications. The advancement and application of sophisticated computer technology, as well as the funding and dedication of this field of study, have all contributed to the growing popularity of crime analysis (Rich, 1996). To further enhance dissemination and make information about police services more useful, many law enforcement agencies are setting up specialized crime analysis divisions. The exclusive responsibility of these units is to gather data from all sources, analyze it, and look for patterns or connections that can be used for operational or managerial reasons. Conversely, some organizations are searching for high-tech ways to support them in effectively implementing different specialized crime analysis programs. These software-based technologically aided programs support police in carrying out efficient crime analysis. The International Association of Crime Analysts (IACA), for instance, has defined crime patterns for tactical analysis and is dedicated to a continuous process of professionalization through standards and knowledge development. Geographic information systems and crime mapping are software applications that are used by many disciplines and occupations, including law enforcement, and are crucial components of crime analysis. GIS has the special ability to layer various data sources—including police calls for service, arrest records, crime reports, the location of particular sites, and even citizen complaints—into digital map layers so that they can be analyzed. According to Olligschlaeger (1997), GIS is giving police departments a useful tool for analyzing vast amounts of data, which results in a thorough understanding of crime and its causes. "Spatial analysis, database management, and data visualization" are widely acknowledged as the three key functions of crime mapping and GIS. Thanks to the combined presence of the three components, crime mapping and GIS enable the connection of criminal behaviors and their numerous features with their geographic position. These elements can also accomplish overlay functions, which blend the location of criminal incidents with the demographics of the local communities. As of right now, no other implementation—aside from GIS and crime mapping—can successfully combine these two categories of analysis.

Posing more pertinent and vital questions to law enforcement officials about crimes and the jurisdictions in which they occur is another useful advantage of GIS and crime mapping. Therefore, in order to combat crime in their area, police officers tasked with patrolling may determine which particular areas require their attention and where they specifically need to patrol. Furthermore, mapping can give the general public specific information on criminal activity and crime (Saddler, 1999). Crime mapping and GIS provide the public with specific information about crime components, enabling the community to assist law enforcement and take part in neighborhood crime prevention efforts. It serves as a link between the police and the community in this way. By providing researchers with the ability to predict future patterns of crime mapping and GIS play a crucial role in equipping police departments to deal with future criminal issues within their jurisdictions.

Therefore, based on projected crime trends, crime mapping and GIS can be utilized to determine the best location for new facilities. Law enforcement agencies will use crime mapping and GIS as a useful tool to determine the best locations for new police checkpoints, headquarters, substations, and other facilities as their use of theaily.

The San Bernardino County, California, Sheriff's Department uses crime maps on a daily basisdaily as an example. This police unit shows the residences of some recorded sexual offenders through crime mapping. In this implementation, law enforcement locates the residences of child sex offenders on a map and uses that information to draw a buffer zone around each school, limiting the distance that the identified offenders can remain from potential victim areas. Similarly, a victim service provider can map and track the locations of victims who received protection by using GIS.

This can be accomplished by calculating the distance between the victims' residence and the potential attackers' residence, and then allocating the necessary patrols to the appropriate locations.

Ratcliffe (2002:214) gives concise information about the benefits of crime mapping-usage for police departments by referencing Wartell and McEwen (2001) as follows:

1. Providing crime maps on the Internet may provide a saving in police workload;
2. Increased community knowledge about crime may increase community co-operation;
3. Maps can assist in community policing and problem solving;
4. Maps can increase public awareness of neighborhood problems;
5. Maps can facilitate partnerships with researchers and other agencies;
6. Data provision by the police service can help prevent its figures from being misinterpreted;
7. Maps and data increase police department accountability.

Because of this, GIS and crime mapping support a wide range of spatial decision-making and problem-solving applications in crime patterns, and crime locations (Saddler, 1999). They also give police departments the chance to use more information more wisely (Nelson, 1999).

6.4.3. Specific Implementations: Compstat and Geographical Profiling

6.4.3.1. Compstat

GIS and crime mapping are being practically used by police department decision-making managers to help them make decisions about how best to allocate their manpower and other resources. Because the New York City Police Department regularly uses GIS and crime mapping, it has grown to be a crucial component of the COMSTAT implementation. William Bratton, the Police Commissioner of the New York City Police Department, launched CompStat in the beginning of 1990. The program has since gained acceptance as one of the most well-liked developments in law enforcement. Compstat was the recipient of the "Innovations in American Government" award in 1996.

"Goal oriented strategic management process that uses computer technology, operational strategy, and managerial accountability to structure the manner in which a police department provides crime-control services" is how Walsh (2001) defines Compstat. It has been called "possibly the single most important organizational/administrative innovation inpolicing during the latter half of the twentieth century" by George Kelling and William Sousa (2001:2). ."

COMPSTAT used GIS and crime mapping techniques during conference presentations, even though it is not a crime mapping method. Since the word "compstat" is an acronym for "computerstatistics," the use of computerized statistics is this program's most crucial feature. Police executives review these statistics in the New York Police Department's crime-strategy meetings in order to more effectively allocate resources. In these meetings, specific issues are presented and examined through the use of GIS and crime mapping. Police executives can perceive crime patterns in relation to area boundaries and neighborhood demographics with the help of crime maps and GIS. High level police managers become particularly aware of groups of criminal incidents and clusters during these periodic meetings.

After analyzing issues during the compstat process, poers concentrate resources on combating crime. For instance, a police commander may decide to reevaluatere-evaluate the police department's approach to local policing on game days if they observe an increase in crime close to the football stadium. Specifically, GIS and crime mapping help the New York Police Department identify crime hotspots through a compstat process. In other words, by displaying the locations of crime events, GIS aids in problem identification. Following that, resources may be more wi Compstat also reengineers the administration of law enforcement by making police chiefs directly liablepersonally liable for the amount of crime in their districts.

According to Willis, Mastrofski, and Weisburd (2004), they reviewed the entire literature and identified six key components of the compstat mission clarification: organizational flexibility, data-driven problem analysis, assessment of the department's effort to solve problems, internal accountability, and creative problem-solving strategies.

Many departments are gradually implementing compstat policing because Compstat combines all of the major recommendations made by current organizational development specialists. According to Silverman (1996), other police departments have increased their use of compstat as a result of widespread media coverage regarding New York's usage of compstat and its decline in crime. Willis, Mastrofski, and Weisburd (2004) report that since the inception of COMPSTAT in 1994, a third of large departments have implemented comparable programs, and another 26% plan to do so. According to Grubler's (1991) estimation, the fastest spreading technologies are required to reach a 90% expansion level.

Compstat was used in law enforcement prior to this implementation, ensuring the use of certain contemporary applications. To prevent crimes by analyzing GIS-based data, artificial neural networks and spatial decision systems can be developed. This was illustrated in a study conducted in İzmir, Turkey by Yavuz and Tecim (2012). Another example is the MANAGER model of the Arlington Police Department, which evaluates the effectiveness of police organization.

6.4.3.2. Geographical Profiling

While geographical profiling is an investigative technique, COMPSTAT is an operational management tool. In particular, geographic profiling focuses on the whereabouts of serial offenders in order to predict where they will eventually call home.

The background of geographical profiling is closely related to certain crime theories, including opportunity theory, rational choice the activity theory, claim Brantingham and Brantingham (1981). These three theories of crime generally explainexplain why many people lead routine lives. To be more precise, people leave their homes for work at a set time, travel to their daily activities after work, and then return home. The key idea behind this process is that individuals in every community identify certain locations—like their homes, workplaces, schools, bars, restaurants, and movie theaters— typically spend their time and feel safe and at ease because they are in familiar surroundings. Similar toLike this, every criminal has a daily schedule that they follow while committing crimes. In his paper, Ratcliffe (2004) succinctly compares the daily activities of criminals to those of regular people while taking criminal theories into accounHe also describes how geographic profiling makes use of this relationship to look into criminal activity: .:.".. Although offenders will engage in similar daily activities, they will also look for opportunities to offend in theas. Crime pattern theory can be thought of as the offender equivalent, indicating areas of likely criminalcriminal behavior, while Cohen and Felson's Routine Activity Theory can be interpreted as an indication of victim behavior (Robinson, 1999). When the victim and the offender get together, the offender makes a deliberate decision to seize (or not seize) any criminal opportunity that presents itself (Clarke and Felson, 1993).

By combining these concepts, profiling analyzes victim data and crime scene analysis to identify patterns of offending. The end productproduct is a map of crime scenes, where each point denotes a known location for the offender at any given time.."

Research on the distance between an offender's residence and the scene of the crime is a crucial component of geographical profiling. For many years, a key topic in criminology has been the study of the distance between a criminal's place of residence and the scene of the crime. The distance between the offender's residence and the scene of the offense is typically considered a depdies. The majority of crimes occur relatively close to the criminals' homes, according to research findingshomes. In other words, the farther a target is from the offender's residence, the less likely it is that the offender will select that target (Capone and Nichols, 1976).

Geographic profiling can be used to determine the likely locations of criminals in a given area based on information such as crime site clues and the fimes typically occur close to the criminals' residence. After that, it might draw a map of that likely spotspot to ascertain the criminal's most likely residence.

There are other applications for geographical profiling, even though it has primarily been used in cases of arson and serial homicide. It can be applied to target DNA testing of large populations, improve police information systems, prioritize suspects, increase patrol saturation, and, most recently, link with an external agency database (Rossmo, 2000).

6.4.4. Controversial Issues in Geographical Information Systems and Crime Mapping

Like any good technology or implementation, there are challenges and issues with the GIS and crime mapping. According to Weisburd and McEwen (1998), a number of academics and law enforcement officials have become irritated with the inconsistencies between the positive aspects of creating digital crime maps and the drawbacks of incorporating criminal justice data into them. These negative aspects or contentious issues and problems can be primarily listed as high implementation costs, resistance to police culture, challenges in pinpointing crime scenes precisely, concerns about accurate data, invasions of people's privacy, detrimental effects on social and economic life, consequences of "spatial labeling," and a few technical hiccups.

The use of GIS and crime mapping technologies can be challenging due to their high cost and some police cultures' resistance to change. Implementated technology are always costly. According to Rogers and Craig (1996), the primary determinant of whether or notwhether to use GIS or crime mapping is economic. This can be a significant obstacle to the advancement of this essential technology, particularly for sms that lack the funding to use GIS and crime mapping. Political and cultural factors are also taken into accountconsidered by certain police departments. These police cultures are resistant to technology and generally ignorant of technical issues, which makes them unwilling to use it. They made the decision to rely more on employee experience than on data derived from statistics (Block and Green, 1994).

Two other issues with using GIS and crime mapping are pinpointing the precise location of crimes and obtaining reliable information about them. It's critical to note the precise location of crimes. Some people might think that this would be a pretty simple case, with the police just needing to note the location of the crime. However, it is not that simple. For instance, should a knife attack in a bar be reported under the name or address of the bar? If an issue starts in one place and spreads to another, how should the incident's location be entered into the system? Moreover, accurately recording addresses is crucial because even a small typo can lead to issues with computer programs. For example, how can the location of an incident be entered into the system if it has two doors that may open to different streets or no door number? Ratcliffe (2001) enumerates 10-important points about the geocoding errors problems:

1. Out-of-date street directories that do not recognize new addresses or roads.
2. Abbreviations of street and road names (for example, 'gdns.' in place of 'gardens') that cannot be recognized by geocoding software.
3. Local name variations that do not match database entries.
4. Address duplication problems that are caused by dozens of streets with the same name across a city.
5. Non-existent addresses caused by typographical errors (for example, '3700 Chestnut Street' that should read '370 Chestnut Street').
6. Line simplification that does not reflect the true curves of a street and places geocoded points in the wrong place. Line simplification is the process of using sections of small, straight lines to represent

curved and winding roads. It is commonly done with GIS to reduce file sizes and to simplify the visualization of bending road s and shapes.

7. Noise in the address file that causes geo-coding software to skip records. Additional terms in addresses such as 'outside 12 Smith Street' or 'near 12 Smith Street' can be unreadable to many geo-coding programs.
8. The inability to geo-code non-address locations, such as 50m along a street, or in a rural location a few miles from a town.
9. General geo-coding imprecision that places a point some distance from the actual address.
10. Ambiguous or vague addresses that make it impossible to identify an actual address.

Furthermore, the success of any geographic profiling may depend on the accuracy of the records kept by those who are producing the data. However, the accuracy of the crime data entered into the system may not always be guaranteed. For instance, people sometimes report criminal incidents incorrectly or not at all. When compiling information for reports, police officers may occasionally fail to do their jobs accurately. Additionally, calls from the public regarding hot spot implementation are not limited to crimes; they can also involve minor matters like lost pets or escort services. Ainsworth (1995) claims that scientific studies have shown that calls from citizens to the police are not always connected to actual criminal issues but rather to other kinds of requests for assistance. If the requested services are not categorized as actual crime problems and other police services, it may be challenging to designate any location as a high-crime area in this situation.

The right to privacy is another contentious issue. Crime mapping and GIS may violate people's right to privacy and confidentiality. While a crime map is being created, specific details like the gender, age, place, time, ethnicity, and age of the perpetrators and victims should be input into the systems. In this instance, superimposing all of this data over particular crimes could unintentionally identify a victim or lead to the identification of potential suspects. According to Ratcliffe (2002), people can still access a specific address by placing on a map, even if it is not physically present. Furthermore, very few victims will disclose information about their mistreatment to law enforcement because they are aware that a minimal amount of online research could lead to their identification. How many rape victims, for instance, would want their address or identity to be accessible to the public online? Another contentious topic is the posting of crime maps online and its potential negative impact on areas with higher rates of crime than others. One of the most significant fallouts is that posting a map of a high-crime area online may have a direct impact on insurance costs in that area. Prices for both residential and commercial real estate may therefore decline. Additionally, a large number of competent public servants and employees might choose to relocate to an area with lower crime rates, which could have an impact on the caliber of services provided in that area. Imagine, for instance, that all the qualified educators in that situation went on to find employment elsewhere, which would have an impact on the standard of education that students in the area could receive. The concept of "Spatial Labeling," which Ratcliffe (2002) defines as "negative impressions and stigmas can be attached to an area, with a knock-on effect on the tolerance to crime of the residents and people passing through the region," is discussed in his study. Put another way, as Ratcliffe explains in Labeling Crime Theory, designating an area as having a high crime rate has a detrimental impact on that area. This crime theory holds that labels have an im how people behave, particularly when they are negative or stigmatizing labels like "deviant, criminal, or felon.. felon." These designations create a self-fulfilling prophecy for criminal activity. Consequently, an individual who bears a label is compelled to comply with the essential implications of that determination. In relation to this matter, Grabosky (1996) elucidates the adverse effect of designating a location as a "high-crime area": the act of designating a location as dangerouommunicates a signal. Individuals who are averse to risk and prioritize peace of mind are likely to steer clear ofavoid such a place, whereas those who generate and consume risk are drawn there. When warning signs of danger do not at first correspond with empirical reality, they can become self-fulfilling prophecies, changing the perception and reality of the location.

Another worry regarding crime mapping is potential technical problems that police agencies might run into when deciding to implement computerized mapping. Mazerolle, Bellucci, and Gajewski (1997) state that the first decision to be made is whether to set up a crime mapping system for analysts and police department planners or for street-level problem-solving officers. While any crime mapping system can have some positive effects on both groups, the group that uses it will determine how much of a benefit they receive from it. To put it another way, Mazerolle, Bellucci, and Gajewski claim that police department planners and street-level problem-solving officers will have different needs when it comes to systems, including data requirements and types of inquiries. Therefore, police departments that plan to implement a crime mapping system need to determine the system's goal. Mazerolle, Bellucci, and Gajewski also note that certain police agencies might not be able to incorporate PC mapping features into mainframe computing environments. This is yet another difficult technical problem that requires funding.

6.4.5. Policy Recommendations

The police departments have no control over crime maps that are available online. For this reason, before posting the crime map online, two crucial steps need to be taken. These include an explanation of the map's limitations that is posted data integrity that was used to create the map. Information provided to the public about crime is not the same asdifferent from information provided to criminal justice experts. Despite this, most criminal justice experts are conscious of the limitations associated with criminal justice research. Individuals lacking sufficient knowledge about criminal justice are ill-equipped to evaluate the crime distribution found online. At that point, creating crime maps for police departments is one of their most important duties. They have to ensure the highest standards of day and provide a satisfactory and honest explanation of any limitations on the data and mapping techniques.

In order toTo balance the public right to information with the privacy of the crime victim, mechanisms for ensuring privacy protection must be developed. This is because privacy is an important topic, just like a public right to information in a public information system. As an example of an implementation, the personal identification could simply be kept private for the duration of what's required and then be destroyed as soon as the process is finished. Numerous strategies could be created, like in the example below, to help those who create crime maps safeguard the addresses and identities of victims and, if necessary, offenders. Furthermore, data or information must only be used for mapping or analyzing crimes, and only authorized staff with the proper authorization may access it for investigative purposes. Because of this, GIS users—especially those who work with data layers—need to be aware of sensitive and private information and take appropriate safety measures to preserve people's rights and privacy.

Another thing to do is persuade the police of the value of GIS and crime mapping. They might need to be persuaded of the value of utilizing the crime mapping analysis tool and geographic information system. Presentations and educational programs can be arranged to break through the resistance of police cultures that are resistant to certain types of technology. There are ways to establish guidelines for police use of the system to avoid inaccuracies and incomplete data entry. Police can also be trained on the value of protecting people's privacy and the necessity of providing the crime mapping and analysis unit with accurate information.

The public nees to be made aware of the complexity of crime distribution in order to stop the negative effects of "spatial labeling.." According to Ratcliffe (2000), data from studies supports the idea that crime hotspots could shift over time. This implies that over time, any jurisdiction that is thought to have a high crime rate may prove to be the safest, and vice versa; a jurisdiction thought to have a low crime rate may prove to be the most dangerous. Crime map creators may be able to lessen public opinion bias against high-crime areas published online if they provide adequate information about how these areas are changing.

Is the internet always the best way for the entire community to share information about crimes? Another interesting application is the efficient use of television and other mass media to disseminate the results of crime analyses or to explain regional crime maps in cases where internet usage is restricted in the community. If not, only people with internet access will be able to make knowledgeable decisions about local crime.

Olligschlaeger (1997) asserts that researchers and practitioners are still getting to know geographic information systems and, as a result, all of its implementations. For this reason, it appears that more work is required to resolve some of the contentious issues.

Scholars should conduct thoroug research on these contentious GIS and crime mapping issues, particularly the detrimental effects of "spatial labeling.." As previously mentioned, designating an area as dangerous has significant ramifications for the local community. Despite this evident reality, not enough research has been done to determine what steps ca from an economic, sociological, or criminological standpoint to mitigate the detrimental effects of "spatial labeling..labeling." In summary, comprehensive scientific research is required to eliminate the effects of spatial labeling. Geographic Information Systems and crime mapping are widely used, but they are still in their infancy, and there are still some ethical and technical issues that need to be worked out. Police enforcement agencies in the US have a long history of utilizing cutting-edge, developed technologies to help with crime prevention and investigation. In many police departments, computers and information systems are used extensively for crime analysis. Two crucial elements of the criminal event are the crime's location and the perpetrators' use of the surrounding area. Because of this, the analysis and identification of crime patterns and trends depend heavily on the use of GIS and crime mapping. As previously mentioned, GIS and crime mapping assist a wide range of applications for spatial decision-making and problem-solving in relation to crime and crime locations. Agencies can use more data more wisely thanks to GIS.

It goes without saying that not all aspects of GIS and crime mapping are covered by the aforementioned advantages, issues, and policy implementations. For police departments that use or plan to use this technology, there might be a number of additional advantages, issues, and policy recommendations that must be followed. Of course, new research and analysis are needed to arrive at that new knowledge.

REFERENCES

1. Ahmad, F., & Goparaju, L. (2016). Analysis of urban sprawl dynamics using geospatial technology in Ranchi City, Jharkhand, India. *Journal of Environmental Geography, 9*(1, 2), 7–13.
2. Ahmad, F., & Goparaju, L. (2017a). Long term deforestation assessment in Jharkhand state, India: A grid based geospatial approach. *Biological Forum, 9*(1), 183–188.
3. Ahmad, F., & Goparaju, L. (2017b). Land evaluation in terms of agroforestry suitability, an approach to improve livelihood and reduce poverty: A FAO based methodology by geospatial solution: A case study of Palamu district, Jharkhand, India. *Ecological Questions, 25*, 67–84.
4. Ahmad, F., Goparaju, L., & Abdul Qayum, A. (2017). Agroforestry suitability analysis based upon nutrient availability mapping: A GIS based suitability mapping. *AIMS Agriculture and Food, 2*(2), 201–220.
5. Ainsworth, P. B. (1995). *Psychology and Policing in a Changing World*. Chichester: Wiley.
6. Alves, L. G., Ribeiro, H. V., Lenzi, E. K., & Mendes, R. S. (2013). Distance to the scaling law: A useful approach for unveiling relationships between crime and urban metrics. *PLoS One, 8*(8), 1–8.
7. Anderson, C. A., & Anderson, D. C. (1984). Ambient temperature and violent crime: Tests of the linear and curvilinear hypotheses. *Journal of Personality and Social Psychology, 46*(1), 91–97.
8. Beirne, P. (1993). *Inventing Criminology: Essays on the Rise of "Homo Criminalis"*. Albany, NY: State University of New York Press.
9. Block, C. R. (1995). STAC hot-spot areas: A statistical tool for law enforcement decisions. In C. R. Block, M. Dabdoub, & S. Fregly (Eds.), *Crime Analysis Through Computer Mapping* (pp. 15–32). Washington, DC: Police Executive Research Forum.
10. Block, C. R., & Green, L. A. (1994). *The Geoarchive Handbook: A Guide for Developing a Geographic Database as an Information Foundation for Community Policing*. Illinois Criminal Justice Information Authority.
11. Boba, R. (2001). *Introductory Guide to Crime Analysis and Mapping*. Report to the Office of Community Oriented Policing Services Cooperative Agreement.
12. Brantingham, P. J., & Brantingham, P. L. (1981). *Environmental Criminology*. Beverly Hills, CA: Sage.
13. Brantingham, P. J., & Brantingham, P. L. (1991). *Environmental Criminology* (Eds.). Prospect Heights, IL: Waveland Press.

14. Bunting, R. J., Chang, O. Y., Cowen, C., Hankins, R., Langston, S., Warner, A., & Roy, S. S. (2017). Spatial patterns of larceny and aggravated assault in Miami–Dade County, 2007–2015. *Professional Geographer*, 1–13.
15. Capone, D. L., & Nichols, W. W., Jr. (1976). Urban structure and criminal mobility. *American Behavioral Scientist, 20*, 199–213.
16. Clarke, R. V., & Felson, M. (1993). Introduction: Criminology, routine activity and rational choice. In R. V. Clarke & M. Felson (Eds.), *Routine Activity and Rational Choice* (Vol. 5, pp. 259–294). New Brunswick, NJ: Transaction Publisher.
17. Cotte Poveda, A. (2012). Violence and economic development in Colombian cities: A dynamic panel data analysis. *Journal of International Development, 24*(7), 809–827.
18. Crowe, T. D. (2000). *Crime Prevention Through Environmental Design: Applications of Architectural Design and Space Management Concepts* (2nd ed.). Oxford: Butterworth-Heinemann.
19. Curtis-Ham, S., & Walton, D. (2017). Mapping crime harm and priority locations in New Zealand: A comparison of spatial analysis methods. *Applied Geography*.
20. Cusimano, M., Marshall, S., Rinner, C., Jiang, D., & Chipman, M. (2010). Patterns of urban violent injury: A spatio-temporal analysis. *PLoS One, 5*(1), 1–9.
21. Eikelboom, A., Martini, E., Ruiz, L. L., et al. (2017). Public crime mapping in Canada: Interpreting RAIDS Online. *Cartographica: The International Journal for Geographic Information and Geovisualization, 52*(2), 108–115.
22. Encyclopaedia Britannica. (2016). *Compstat*. Retrieved from: http://global.britannica.com/topic/Compstat (accessed on 14 October 2024).
23. Garland, D. (1997). Of crimes and criminals: The development of criminology in Britain. In M. Maguire, R. Morgan, & R. Reiner (Eds.), *The Oxford Handbook of Criminology* (pp. 11–56). Oxford: Clarendon Press.
24. Gerber, M. S. (2014). Predicting crime using Twitter and kernel density estimation. *Decision Support Systems, 61*, 115–125.
25. Gill, P. (2000). *Rounding up the Usual Suspects? Developments in Contemporary Law Enforcement Intelligence*. Aldershot: Ashgate.
26. Goldsmith, V., McGuire, P., Mollenkopf, J., & Ross, T. (2000). *Analyzing Crime Patterns* (Eds.). Thousand Oaks, CA: Sage.

27. Gorr, W., Olligschlaeger, A., & Thompson, Y. (2003). Short-term forecasting of crime. *International Journal of Forecasting, 19*(4), 579–594.
28. Grabosky, P. (1996). Unintended consequences of crime prevention. In R. Homel & R. Clarke (Eds.), *Crime Prevention Studies* (Vol. 5, pp. 25–56). New York: Criminal Justice Press.
29. Grubler, A. (1991). Diffusion and long-term patterns and discontinuities. *Technological Forecasting and Social Change, 39*, 159–180.
30. Heikkila, E. J. (1998). GIS is dead; long live GIS! *Journal of the American Planning Association, 64*(3), 350.
31. Hojman, D. E. (2002). Explaining crime in Buenos Aires: The roles of inequality, unemployment, and structural change. *Bulletin of Latin American Research*, 121–128.
32. Hojman, D. E. (2004). Inequality, unemployment, and crime in Latin American cities. *Crime, Law, and Social Change, 41*(1), 33–51.
33. International Association of Crime Analysts. (2011). Crime pattern definitions for tactical analysis (White Paper 2011-01). Overland Park, KS: Author. Retrieved from: https://www.iadlest.org/Portals/0/Files/Documents/DDACTS/Webinars/Automation/Lessons/CRIME%20PATTERN%20DEFS_IACA.pdf?ver=SWBnC2STwP-bH4HfyRVOQA%3D%3D.
34. Jefferson, B. J. (2017). Predictable policing: Predictive crime mapping and geographies of policing and race. *Annals of the American Association of Geographers*, 1–16.
35. Karuppannan, J., Shanmugapriya, S., & Balamurugan, V. (2004). Crime mapping in India: A GIS implementation in Chennai city policing. *Geographic Information Sciences, 10*, 20–34.
36. Kelling, G. L., & Sousa, W. H. (2001). Do police matter? An analysis of the impact of New York City's police reforms. *Civic Report no. 22*. Center for Civic Innovation at the Manhattan Institute. nl
37. Kelly, M. (2000). Inequality and crime. *Review of Economics and Statistics, 82*(4), 530–539.
38. Khalid, S., Shoaib, F., Qian, T., et al. (2017). Network constrained spatio-temporal hotspot mapping of crimes in Faisalabad. *Applied Spatial Analysis*.
39. Lawrence, E., & Cohen, M. F. (1979). Social change and crime rate trends: A routine activity approach. *American Sociological Review, 44*(4), 588–608.

40. Levitt, S. D. (2001). Alternative strategies for identifying the link between unemployment and crime. *Journal of Quantitative Criminology, 17*(4), 377–390.

41. Liao, R., Wang, X., Li, L., & Qin, Z. (2010). A novel serial crime prediction model based on Bayesian learning theory. In *Proceedings of the 2010 IEEE International Conference on Machine Learning and Cybernetics* (Vol. 4, pp. 1757–1762).

42. Malvika, P. (2015). Crime mapping of Rajasthan (2013): A district-level analysis. *Asian Journal of Research in Social Sciences and Humanities, 5*(6), 139–152.

43. Mazerolle, L. G., Bellucci, C., & Gajewski, F. (1997). Crime mapping in police departments: The challenges of building a mapping system. In D. Weisburd & J. T. McEwen (Eds.), *Crime Mapping and Crime Prevention* (pp. 131–156). Monsey, NY: Criminal Justice Press.

44. Mohler, G. O., Short, M. B., Brantingham, P. J., Schoenberg, F. P., & Tita, G. E. (2011). Self-exciting point process modeling of crime. *Journal of the American Statistical Association, 106*(493), 100–108.

45. Nelson, L. (1999). GIS: The powerful weapon for law enforcement. *ESRI Arcuser Magazine*, Jan–March. Environmental Systems Research Institute, Inc.

46. Olligschlaeger, A. M. (1997). Artificial neural networks and crime mapping. In D. Weisburd & T. McEwen (Eds.), *Crime Mapping and Crime Prevention* (pp. 259–294). New York: Criminal Justice Press.

47. Özdemir, H. (2012). Compstat: Arlington (Teksas, ABD), polis müdürlüğü MANAGER yönetim modeli. In S. Özdemir & U. Argun (Eds.), *Suç önleme Sempozyumu Bildiriler Kitabı* (pp. 310–330). Bursa: Bursa Emniyet Müdürlüğü Yayınları.

48. Park, R., & Burgess, E. (1925). Urban ecology studies. *CSISS Classics*. Retrieved from: http://escholarship.org/uc/item/6f39q98d (accessed on 14 October 2024).

49. Quetelet, A. J. (1842). *Treatise on Man and the Development of his Faculties*. Edinburgh, SCOT: W. and R. Chambers.

50. Ratcliffe, J. H. (2000). Aoristic analysis: The spatial interpretation of unspecific temporal events. *International Journal of Geographical Information Science, 14*(7), 669–679.

51. Ratcliffe, J. H. (2001). On the accuracy of TIGER-type geocoded address data in relation to cadastral and census areal units. *International Journal of Geographical Information Science, 15*(5), 473–485.

52. Ratcliffe, J. H. (2002). Damned if you don't, damned if you do: Crime mapping and its applications. *Policing and Society, 12*(3), 211–225.
53. Ratcliffe, J. H. (2004). Crime mapping and the training needs of law enforcement. *European Journal on Criminal Policy and Research, 10*(1), 65–83.
54. Reno, J. (1999). Crime mapping and ESRI. In L. Nelson (Ed.), *Crime Mapping News* (Vol. 1, Issue 4, Fall 1999). Washington, DC: Police Foundation.
55. Reuland, M. (1997). Information management and crime analysis: Practitioners' recipes for success. Washington, DC: Police Executive Research Forum.
56. Rich, T. F. (1996). The Chicago Police Department's Information Collection for Automated Mapping (ICAM) Program. Washington, DC: U.S. Department of Justice, National Institute of Justice.
57. Robinson, M. B. (1999). Lifestyles, routine activities, and residential burglary victimization. *Journal of Crime and Justice, 22*(1), 27–56.
58. Rogers, R., & Craig, D. E. (1996). Geographic information systems: Computers in law enforcement. *Journal of Crime and Justice, 16*, 61–73.
59. Rossmo, D. K. (2000). *Geographic Profiling*. Boca Raton, FL: CRC Press.
60. Saddler, D. (1999). Why map crime? *Crime Mapping Research Center, National Institute of Justice, U.S. Department of Justice*, Washington, DC. Retrieved from: www.ojp.usdoj.gov/cmrc (accessed on 14 October 2024).
61. Shaw, C. R., & McKay, H. D. (1942). *Juvenile Delinquency and Urban Areas*. Chicago: University of Chicago Press.
62. Sherman, L. W., Gartin, P. R., & Buerger, M. E. (1989). Hot spots of predatory crime: Routine activities and the criminology of place. *Criminology, 27*, 27–55.
63. Star, J., & Estes, J. (1990). *Geographic Information Systems: An Introduction*. Englewood Cliffs, NJ: Prentice Hall.
64. The Massachusetts Association of Crime Analysts. (2012). What is crime analysis? Retrieved from: https://macrimeanalysts.org/.
65. Walsh, W. (2001). Compstat: An analysis of an emerging police paradigm. *Policing: An International Journal of Police Strategies and Management, 24*(3), 347–363.
66. Wang, D., Ding, W., Lo, H., et al. (2013). Crime hotspot mapping using crime-related factors: A spatial data mining approach. *Applied Intelligence, 39*, 772. https://doi.org/10.1007/s10489-012-0400-x.

67. Wang, P., Mathieu, R., Ke, J., & Cai, H. J. (2010). Predicting criminal recidivism with support vector machine. In *Proceedings of the 2010 IEEE International Conference on Management and Service Science* (pp. 1–9).
68. Wartell, J., & McEwen, J. T. (2001). Privacy in the information age: A guide for sharing crime maps and spatial data. *Institute for Law and Justice, NCJ 188739*. Washington, DC. Retrieved from: https://www.ncjrs.gov/pdffiles1/nij/188739.pdf (accessed on 14 October 2024).
69. Weisburd, D., & McEwen, T. (1997). Introduction: Crime mapping & crime prevention. In D. Weisburd & T. McEwen (Eds.), *Crime Mapping & Crime Prevention* (Vol. 8, pp. 1–21). Monsey, NY: Criminal Justice Press.
70. Weisburd, D., & McEwen, T. (1997). Introduction: Crime mapping and crime prevention. In D. Weisburd & T. McEwen (Eds.), *Crime Mapping and Crime Prevention* (Vol. 8, pp. 1–21). Monsey, NY: Criminal Justice Press.
71. Weisburd, D., & McEwen, T. (1998). *Crime Mapping and Crime Prevention Studies* (Vol. 8). Monsey, NY: Criminal Justice Press.
72. Willis, J. J., Mastrofski, S., & Weisburd, D. (2004). *Compstat in Practice: An In-Depth Analysis of Three Cities*. Washington, DC: The Police Foundation.
73. Yavuz, Ö., & Tecim, Y. (2012). CBS tabanlı suç önleme çalışmalarında yapay sinir ağları kullanılarak mekansal karar sistemi oluşturulması. In S. Özdemir & U. Argun (Eds.), *Suç Önleme Sempozyumu Bildiriler Kitabı* (pp. 295–310). Bursa: Bursa Emniyet Müdürlüğü Yayınları.

Chapter 7

Crime Analysis Purpose and Audience

Contents

Introduction 280
7.1. Crime Analysis Purpose 280
7.2. Crime Analysis Audiences 283
7.3. Crime Analysis Typology 285
7.4. Situational Awareness Examples 285
7.5. Crime Reduction Examples 291
References 301

INTRODUCTION

The purpose of crime analysis is to provide law enforcement agencies with actionable insights that enhance their ability to prevent, investigate, and respond to criminal activity. By systematically examining crime data, crime analysts help to identify patterns, trends, and emerging threats, enabling police departments to allocate resources more effectively, prioritize their efforts, and develop informed strategies for crime prevention and reduction. Toalgoal of crime analysis is to support the creation of safer communities by enabling law enforcement to act with precision and foresight.

Crime analysis serves multiple audiences, each with distinct needs and expectations. The primary audience is law enforcement professionals, including police officers, detectives, and command staff. For frontline officers and detectives, crime analysis provides critical information on where and when crimes are most likely to occur, which can guide patrol strategies and investigative focus. For command staff and decision-makers, crime analysis offers data-driven insights that inform strategic planning, resource allocation, and policy development. It helps in setting priorities, evaluating the effectiveness of policing initiatives, and making adjustments to improve outcomes.

Another important audience includes community leaders and the public. Crime analysis can be used to inform community policing efforts, helping to build trust and collaboration between law enforcement and the communities they serve. Public-facing crime reports and presentations based on crime analysis can educate residents about local crime trends, engage them in crime prevention efforts, and foster transparency and accountability within law enforcement agencies.

In addition, crime analysis can serve policymakers and researchers who rely on accurate data to shape criminal justice policies and study crime patterns. By providing a clear understanding of the nature and distribution of crime, analysts contribute to broader discussions on public safety and criminal justice reform.

The purpose of crime analysis is to enhance the effectiveness of law enforcement through data-driven insights, serving a diverse audience that includes police personnel, community members, policymakers, and researchers. Its impact is broad, influencing daily operations, long-term strategies, and the relationship between law enforcement and the communities they protect.

7.1. CRIME ANALYSIS PURPOSE

The temporal character and complexity of a problem can be used to classify it. In other words, more complex issues, like problem locations, take longer to develop than simpler issues, like isolated incidents, which usually show symptoms very quickly. These are divided into three categories in this book: (i) short-term problems, (ii) long-term problems, and (iii) immediate problems. The results of crime analysis are produced for various audiences and purposes within each problem category. This first section discusses the two different ways that results from crime analysis are used: to help with situational awareness and to direct strategies for reducing crime. The various audience types are covered in the section that follows.

7.1.1. Situational Awareness

Situational awareness in the context of law enforcement refers to the growth of an officer's perception of the workplace, rf rank. In order toTo achieve this goal, crime analysts generate "information" regarding crimes and other activities for police officers, giving them context regarding the times and locations of their daily work. Information is defined as knowledge that is shared regarding a specific fact or situation, and the results of a crime analysis information analysis only offer specifics about specific incidents (e.g., traffic accidents, arrests, crimes, and service requests) or total counts of occurrences over various time periods (e.g., for short-term issues, one week or month; for long-term issues, one or five years). A list or map of all parolees residing in a specific area, a count of crimes by geographic areas over a year, or a list of calls made to an address over a few days are a few examples of the information obtained from crime analysis. Crucially, the purpose of crime analysis information results is to simply report the facts; they do not offer interpretations, connections to other issues, or explanations for why the facts are happening. Therefore, information results are examined by personnel who must draw their own conclusions before taking any action; they do not direct or result in specific police responses. For instance, a robbery detective searching for suspects in a specific robbery they are investigating is given a list of current prisoner releases and the results of crime analysis information displayed in a map. The detective must review the data to pinpoint a specific parolee who may have carried out the robbery by considering the parolee's criminal history, place of residence, and physical characteristics, among other factors. The list includes all prisoner releases. As a result, the list of prisoner releases only provides the detective with information about each parolee, which they must then analyze and draw conclusions from in order to identify a possible lead.

7.1.2. Crime Reduction

The creation of crime analysis results with the aim of directing police in tharticular strategiesstrategies for crime reduction is the second purpose of the results, which is to support police in their effoce crime. In order toTo produce crime analysis results for this use, key elements of factual data are looked at (i.e., examined) by the crime analyst, and judgments regarding the connections between the facts are drawn. The outcomes of crime reduction analyses are used in the police context to identify and rank the information's component parts and y possible connectionsconnections can be made in order to guide police crime reduction tactics. These results are therefore "action oriented" in that police personnel are not required to examine them; rather, the results themselves direct police toward a variety of potential tactics that may be put into practice. For instance, an analyst has connected six recent residential burglaries since each case involved entry through the rear slider during the daytime within a two-block radius. These findings are used to send undercover crime suppression units to that area during the pattern, distribute crime prevention flyers to residents in the two-block area, and instruct officers to patrol and establish field contacts in the pattern area.

7.1.3. Contrasting the Purposes of Crime Analysis Results

The process by which situational awareness and crime reduction crime analysis results are developed is an important differentiator, even though it may appear that they are similar because they are based on the same data. In other words, situational awareness results usually involve a quick database search and the making of a list or a map. An analyst must determine the connections between the various facts in order to produce the results that will direct the reduction of crime. Crucially, for police agencies to effectively reduce crime, both forms of results must be used consistently. Information is necessary for officers, sergeants, managers, and commanders to comprehend the workplace and to prioritize and oversee particular crime reduction tactics based on analysis results. The following are several more examples of crime analysis results created for situational awareness and crime reduction to highlight their differences:

Situational Awareness Analysis Results

- List or map of all juveniles currently on probation in the jurisdiction;
- List of all calls for service at a particular address over several months;
- List of all burglaries occurring in a beat over 1 week;
- Counts of all crime by crime type for the past 6 months;
- Map of areas with the most Part I crime over 2 years.

Crime Reduction Analysis Results

- A list or map of the 10 most serious violent juvenile offenders on probation;

- A list of addresses with five or more false burglar alarm calls for service in the last 3 months;
- Six convenience store robberies thought to be committed by the same suspect;
- Ten apartment complexes that have the highest number of loud parties, fights, or public intoxication over 6 months;
- A map showing areas in which a specific type of crime has increased or decreased before and after a particular police strategy was implemented.

Crucially, crime analysts usually generate and disseminate results for these two purposes in somewhat different ways. While this is not a unique distinction, situational awareness information is usually generated automatically, and the outputs show comprehensive lists of the data's contents (e.g., all jail discharges, total counts of all UCR Part I offenses). This explains why information results are frequently generated by organizations without crime analysts or by employees who have not been assigned by analysts. However, analysis generated for the purpose of reducing crime is usually produced by analysts who, using a methodical process, eliminate irrelevant details and extraneous information, draw conclusions, and produce a product in a particular format with specific information. However, there are some analysis results for reducing crime that can be automated. In these situations, critical analytical choices are made prior to automation, resulting in an analytical product as the output (i.e., gives conclusions rather than just facts). The product guarantees that the outcomes have been ranked in order to direct police tactics.

7.2. CRIME ANALYSIS AUDIENCES

Differentiating the intended audience is crucial when determining the purpose of crime analysis results, as various audiences demand different kinds of analysis. This chapter focuses on crime analysis findings that are pertinent to internal police officers who apply and assess crime reduction strategies through tactical and strategic crime analysis. For situational awareness and crime reduction, various forms of analysis are needed by audiences within a police agency. The simplest method to group useful items is to consider the duration of the activity (i.e., the duration of the task) as well as the job duties of the individuals for whom the results are being produced (i.e., problem complexity) that they have to deal with.

The general relationship between responsibility and the temporal nature of an activity is shown in Figure 7.1. Even though there are areas where police agency employees' responsibilities overlap,-ranking employees typically handleoversee smaller-scale tasks on a shorter timescale, and higher-ranking employees (i.e., those with greater responsibility) handle activity over an extended period of time. To put it another way, first-line supervisors and line-level officers need the results of crime analyses to address short-term and immediate issues, like answering service requests and recent trends in crime, while managers and commanders (i.e., lieutenants and higher) need data on both short- and long-term activities.

Lists of sexual offenders, recently released inmates, and calls at specific addresses are a few examples of information results that help line-level officers with situational awareness. These results are likely to center on specific incidents. On the other hand, aggregate information—such as the total counts of crimes by category and patrol area—is likely to be the main focus of information results for police managers and commanders (e.g., district or beat). However, managers' and commanders' crime reduction results are likely to address more long-term activities, such as whether crimes are increasing or decreasing over time or an examination of parks, bars, or hotels where a disproportionate amount of activity is occurring, so that long-term solcan be initiated. Similarly, resultsthe results of crime reduction that facilitate responses from officers and sergeants are likely to address immediate activity and may include patterns of crime occurring in an area in the past few days or week.

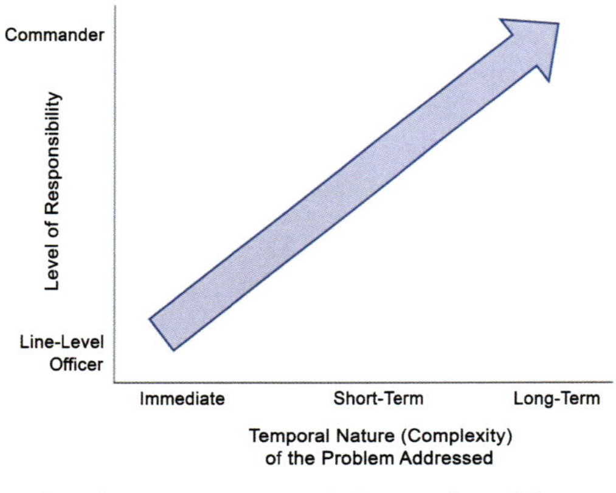

Figure 7.1. *Relationship between responsibility and problem complexity.*

Source: Adapted from Taylor and Boba (2011). Rachel Boba Santos, Crime Analysis with Crime Mapping, ISBN: 9781506331034.

Based on their roles within the company, three categories of internal police audiences are identified. Various sized agencies use different methods to allocate responsibilities to different ranks. Thus, the general terms and examples of what ranks are included in each are as follows:

1. Operational personnel refers to line-level officers (e.g., officers, corporals) and first-line supervisors (e.g., corporals, sergeants).
2. Management personnel refers to midlevel police managers, such as lieutenants and in some cases captains.
3. Command personnel refers to those who serve as the leadership of the police organization, such as the chief or sheriff, deputy chiefs, majors, and in some cases captains.

7.3. CRIME ANALYSIS TYPOLOGY

A crime analysis typology that helps us categorize crime analysis results and apply crime analysis in a real-world setting is created by dissecting possible crime analysis results by (i) problem category, (ii) crime analysis purpose, and (iii) internal police audience types. The typology is illustrated in Figure 7.2. The next two sections offer straightforward, yet accurate, examples for each of the typology's classifications. Keep in mind that there are numerous analyses that can be carried out to yield results in each typology classification, as well as numerous formats and styles that crime analysts may choose to employ. While instances may fall into more than one category (e.g., the same results might be helpful for various audiences). The goal is to provide the student a deeper understanding of the process of producing results for various problems, purposes, and audiences by showcasing at least one example in each category.

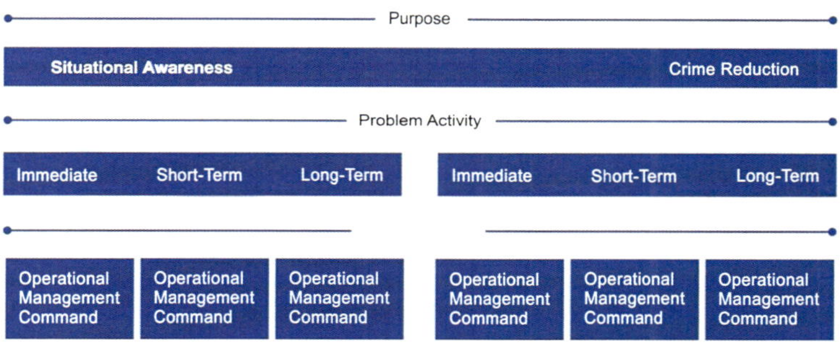

Figure 7.2. *Typology of crime analysis results.*

Source: Rachel Boba Santos, Crime Analysis with Crime Mapping, ISBN: 9781506331034.

7.4. SITUATIONAL AWARENESS EXAMPLES

For the operational, management, and command audiences within the internal police, this section provides situational awareness examples for immediate problems, short-term problems, and long-term problems. The crime analysis results displayed in each figure are described for each example, along with a discussion of possible applications.

7.4.1. Immediate

Isolated incidents that happen and are fixed in a matter of minutes, hours, or sometimes even days are referred to as "immediate" problems. Patrol officers and detectives who have received both basic and advanced investigative training respond to them using their investigative skills.

7.4.1.1. Operational

- **Description:** Table 7.1 is a list of calls for service produced on June 15, 2017, that occurred at one residential address in the previous 2 weeks (e.g., June 1, 2017, through June 14, 2017).
- **Potential Use:** Patrol officers might review this information before they respond to a new call for service at this address to make them aware of the previous contact with the police the residents have had (e.g., previous crime reports, arrests, etc.).

Table 7.1. *Calls for Service at 345 at S Apple ST*

Incident No.	Call Date	Day	Time	Call Type	Disposition
2017013294	6/1/2017	Wed	2102	Loud noise	No action taken
2017141524	6/5/2017	Sun	2012	Disturbance	Gone on arrival
2017142509	6/6/2017	Mon	1954	Domestic disturbance	Unable to locate
2017142640	6/6/2017	Mon	2325	Domestic disturbance	Arrest
2017142676	6/9/2017	Thu	1406	Barking dog	No action taken
2017142878	6/10/2017	Fri	2205	Criminal trespass	Report
2017143275	6/11/2017	Sat	0321	Domestic disturbance	Arrest
2017143496	6/13/2017	Mon	1604	Burglary	Report
2017144169	6/14/2017	Tue	1855	Parking violation	No action taken

Source: Rachel Boba Santos, Crime Analysis with Crime Mapping, ISBN: 9781506331034.

7.4.1.2. Management

- **Description:** Table 7.2 is a table that depicts an aggregate count of arrests that have occurred for each shift by district (e.g., days, evenings, midnights) in the previous 2 days.

- **Potential Use:** Patrol or criminal investigations managers might review this information to get a sense of shift productivity.

Table 7.2. *Arrests by District Per Shift*

Shift	District 1 Arrests	District 2 Arrests	District 3 Arrests	Total
Day shift	2	6	7	**15**
Evening shift	0	10	7	**17**
Midnight shift	6	14	2	**22**
Total	**8**	**30**	**16**	**54**

Source: Rachel Boba Santos, Crime Analysis with Crime Mapping, ISBN: 9781506331034.

7.4.1.3. Command

- **Description:** Table 7.3 is a list of all commercial robberies that occurred over the last 24 hours (from May 2, 2017, 9:00 a.m. to May 3, 2017, 9:00 a.m.), with the suspect description and a brief summary of each case.
- **Potential Use:** The chief and command staff might review this information to be aware of these serious gun crimes, as well as to be prepared for any questions about the cases that might come from the media or business associations.

Table 7.3. *Commercial Robberies, Previous 24 Hours*

Case #	Report Date	Time	Location	Business Name	Suspect Information	Short Description
20170132	5/2/2017	1800	470 Lake Rd	Cell Phones R Us	Black male, 22 years old, 200 pounds, 5'11"	Suspect entered business, pretended to be a customer, displayed a blue steel revolver, and demanded property.
20171425	5/2/2017	2200	2801 N Fithutt Ave	Harry's Food Store	Hispanic or Black male with shirt over his face, 20–30 years old, 180 pounds	Suspect entered business, displayed a handgun, and demanded property.
20171426	5/2/2017	2315	772 Farragut Ln	Subs and More	White male, 40 years old, 220 pounds, 6'	Suspect entered, exited, and returned. Suspect went to restroom, exited, attempted to get drink, waited in line, displayed black semiautomatic, and demanded property.
20171426	5/3/2017	0015	12516 E North Ave	Exgo Gas Station	White male, wearing a hoodie, 18 years old, 150 pounds, 5'6"	Suspect entered business, asked if clerk was alone, displayed handgun, and demanded property.
20171441	5/3/2017	0130	1959 N State St	Quick Mart	Asian male, beard, 18–25 years old, 160 pounds, 5'10"	Suspect entered business, made purchase, got second item, took to counter, produced handgun, and demanded property.

Source: Rachel Boba Santos, Crime Analysis with Crime Mapping, ISBN: 9781506331034.

7.4.2. Short-Term

Patterns and recurring incidents are short-term issues. A repeat incident is a collection of two or more similar incidents that have usually occurred to the same person or at thtion and are common. Interpersonal or noncriminalnon-criminal criminal incidents can lead to a crime report, but they don't always. Patterns are collections of two or more crimes that are reported to the police or uncovered by them. These groups are analyzed as a single unit because they have one or more important characteristics in common that set them apart from other types of crimes. These characteristics include the absence of a known victim-offender relationship and the generally short duration of the criminal activity (IACA, 2011b).

7.4.2.1. Operational

- **Description:** Figure 7.3 is a map depicting density and single symbols for car prowls (theft from vehicle) over 4 weeks and single symbols for offenders living nearby in 2015.
- **Potential Use:** Provides officers and sergeants information about where thefts from vehicles are occurring over 4 weeks in the southwest precinct as well as whether offenders live nearby. The density shading and the single symbols for the crimes represent the same crime data. The map is only descriptive as it does not provide conclusions that lead to specific crime reduction strategies; it only provides a general overview of where the thefts from vehicles are occurring. Additional analysis would be required to guide any specific crime reduction strategies.

7.4.2.2. Management

- **Description:** Table 7.4 is a chart depicting counts of types of calls for service in the most recent month compared to the previous month for one district.
- **Potential Use:** Managers can use this to compare number of calls by type in their district and to determine recent changes in calls for service for their own district. However, these results do not provide conclusions that lead to specific crime reduction strategies; they only provide an overview of general aggregated data.

7.4.2.3. Command

- **Description:** Table 7.4 depicts counts of selected Part I crime types for two districts for the most recent month compared to the previous month and the percentage change.

- **Potential Use:** Commanders can use this to determine changes from one month to the next and to compare districts. However, these results do not provide conclusions that lead to specific crime reduction strategies; they only provide an overview of general aggregated data.

Table 7.4. *Counts and Percentage of Change: Part I Crime Types*

	Eastern District				Southern District			
	Jan.	Feb.	Difference	Percentage of Change	Jan.	Feb.	Difference	Percentage of Change
Homicide	0	0	0	NC*	1	0	−1	−100%
Rape	3	5	2	67%	7	3	−4	−57%
Robbery	26	35	9	35%	56	50	−6	−11%
Aggravated assault	75	66	−9	−12%	125	174	49	39%
Burglary	154	190	36	23%	201	175	−26	−13%
Larceny	254	288	34	13%	341	325	−16	−5%
Auto theft	167	188	21	13%	154	122	−32	−21%
Arson	0	2	2	NC*	0	0	0	NC*
Total	**679**	**774**	**95**	**14%**	**885**	**849**	**−36**	**−4%**

Source: Rachel Boba Santos, Crime Analysis with Crime Mapping, ISBN: 9781506331034.

7.4.3. Long-Term

A series of related activities spanning several months, seasons, or years that are caused by systematic opportunities generated by routine behavior and surroundings is referred to as a long-term problem. Issues may include typical disorder behavior (e.g., loud parties or driving too fast in residential areas) in addition to significant criminal activity (e.g., rape on a date, or bank heist).

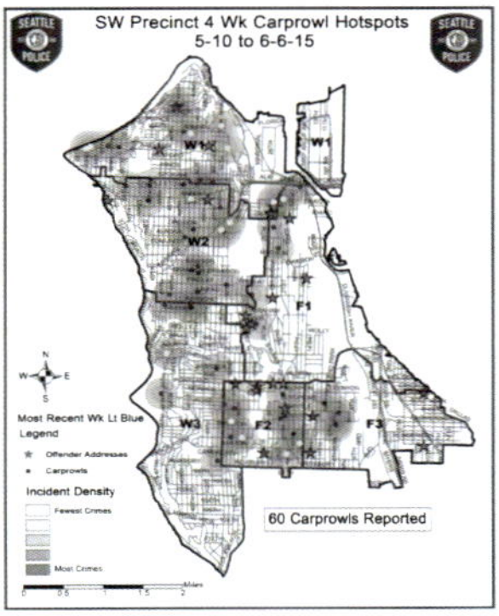

Figure 7.3. *Four weeks of car prowls in Seattle, Washington—2015: Southwest Precinct.*

Source: Seattle (Washington) Police Department, Detective Dan Benz. Rachel Boba Santos, Crime Analysis with Crime Mapping, ISBN: 9781506331034.

7.4.3.1. Operational

- **Description:** Figure 7.5 is a map depicting the city of Gainesville, Florida, with equal grids, graduated by color to indicate 2010 crime counts for the entire city for the last year.
- **Potential Use:** This alerts officers to the areas of the city that have the most crime over a long period of time. However, the map does not indicate the reason why these areas have the most crime or does it distinguish what types of Part I crimes are occurring where.

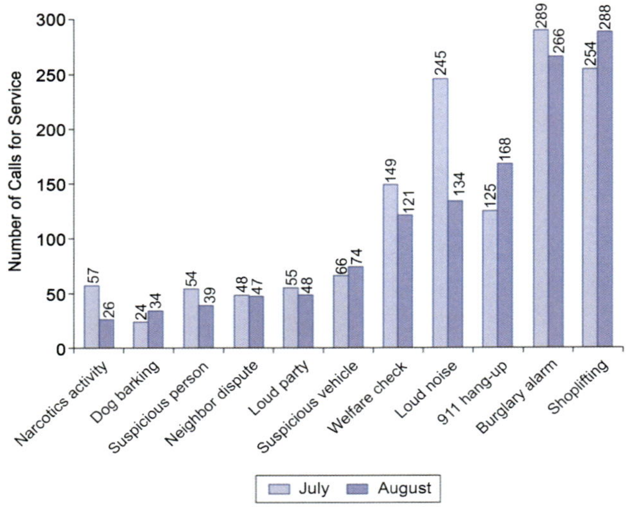

Figure 7.4. *Two months of calls-for-service comparison: District 4.*

Source: Rachel Boba Santos, Crime Analysis with Crime Mapping, ISBN: 9781506331034.

7.4.3.2. Management

- **Description:** Figure 7.6 is a line chart of the aggregate counts of residential burglary crime for each month for the last year for one region in the city.
- **Potential Use:** It provides managers information about increases or decreases in residential burglary in their region for 1 year.

7.4.3.3. Command

- **Description:** Figure 7.7 is a map that compares counties in California by their rates of unsolved homicides over 20 years.

- **Potential Use:** Command personnel, particularly those in county-level agencies, would review this map to compare their own levels of unsolved homicides to those of other counties in the state. Note that the map depicts the rate per unit of population, which helps to compare across counties of different populations.

7.5. CRIME REDUCTION EXAMPLES

Examples of crime reduction are shown here. The results of the crime analysis are described for each example, along with a discussion of possible applications. It should be noted that the remainder goes into great detail regarding the methods and analytical approaches used to get these results.

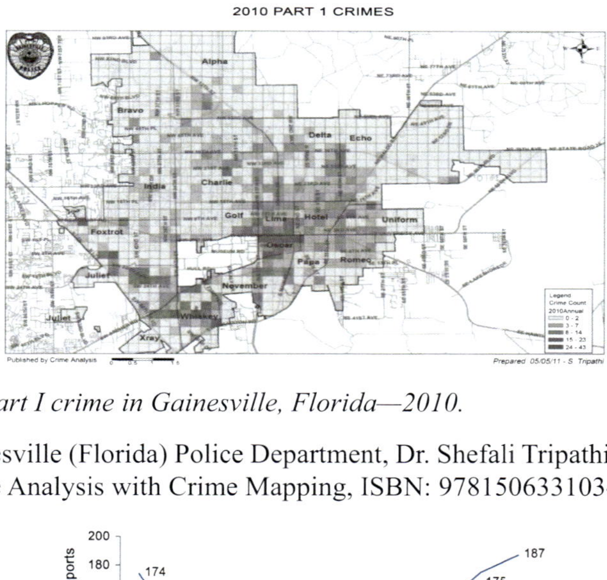

Figure 7.5. *Part I crime in Gainesville, Florida—2010.*

Source: Gainesville (Florida) Police Department, Dr. Shefali Tripathi. Rachel Boba Santos, Crime Analysis with Crime Mapping, ISBN: 9781506331034.

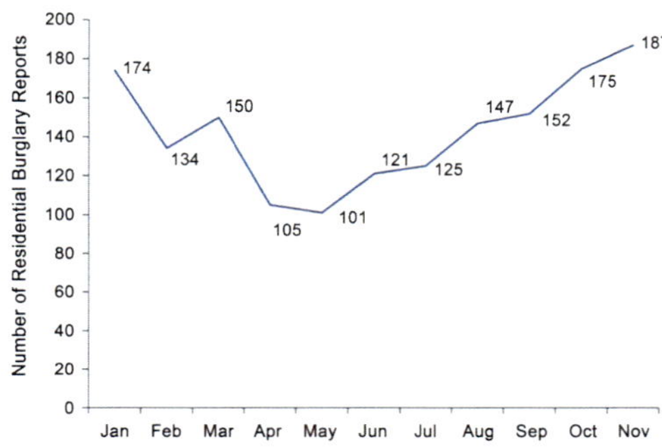

Figure 7.6. *Western region: residential burglary by month.*

Source: Rachel Boba Santos, Crime Analysis with Crime Mapping, ISBN: 9781506331034.

7.5.1. Immediate

7.5.1.1. Operational

- **Description:** Table 7.5 is a list of only four burglary offenders who have recently been released from jail and live in a three-block area where there have been reports of several residential burglaries that appear to be related.
- **Potential Use:** Officers and detectives might use this list to contact these burglars during their workday to determine if they might be responsible for the burglaries that have been occurring since they are known offenders who have been recently released and might be committing crime again. Research shows that offenders commit crime near where they live, so it makes sense for detectives to start their search for suspects with these individuals.

Table 7.5. *Release Burglary Offenders Living in Pattern Area*

Name	Date of Birth	Current Address	Race/Sex	Convictions
Jones, Mark	4/21/1986	156 E Main St	White/Male	Burglary, shoplifting, grand theft
Smith, John	7/17/1991	129 E Main St	Black/Male	Burglary, theft
Harold, Jason	8/1/1984	403 S Grand Ave	Hispanic/Male	Burglary, vandalism, robbery
Samuels, Denis	2/15/1988	470 S Grand Ave	White/Male	Burglary, auto theft, grand theft

Source. Rachel Boba Santos, Crime Analysis with Crime Mapping, ISBN: 9781506331034

7.5.1.2. Management

- **Description:** Table 7.6 is a short report that is either disseminated or read to patrol officers during their daily roll call. It contains brief descriptions of analytical results from the previous day and week as well as direction for responses based on analysis that officers will conduct during their uncommitted patrol time, which is the time officers have for proactive activity between dispatched calls for service and writing reports.
- **Potential Use:** This is a report that would be used by a variety of personnel. Managers help develop the report and use it to inform officers and sergeants about current short-term activity and long-term problems that are being addressed; it directs their proactive crime reduction responses. It can also be used by managers to hold their subordinates accountable (i.e., "Did you conduct the response outlined in the May 12th report, and if so, what did you do?").

Table 7.6. *Daily Roll Call Sheet*

District 1: Saturday, May 12, 2017		
Crime Patterns	**Analysis**	**Response**
Pattern #: 2017-089	Seven residential burglaries occurred in Beat 14 during the day over the last week; entry was made through the rear slider. Cash, jewelry, and small items were taken. No suspects.	Increase proactive patrols in Beat 14; conduct checks on suspicious subjects; continue to conduct thorough canvases on all burglary investigations and complete the security survey.
Pattern #: 2017-092B	Four street robberies have occurred in the Westwood area in the midmorning hours over the last several weeks. Two white males on foot approach victims from behind in a retail or apartment parking lot, threaten them with a weapon (or simulated weapon) and demand money and other possessions. Victims are primarily women.	Increase proactive patrols in Westwood area and in retail and apartment parking lots; make contact with business owners and apartment managers about pattern and crime prevention advice (see flyer developed by the Crime Prevention Unit for this pattern).
Problem Locations	**Analysis**	**Response**
Jay's Truck Stop: 1654 E Highway 176	Citizens have reported day laborers hanging around the truck stop causing disorder and traffic problems along Highway 176. Officers have also reported prostitution and drug activity.	Several weeks ago, Captain Smith (District 1) initiated contact with the truck stop's management to develop long-term solutions for this problem. However, because the activity has increased in recent weeks, officers are to patrol in the area, look for suspicious behavior, and give trespass citations (not warnings) to those individuals not on the property for business with the truck stop.

Source. Rachel Boba Santos, Crime Analysis with Crime Mapping, ISBN: 9781506331034.

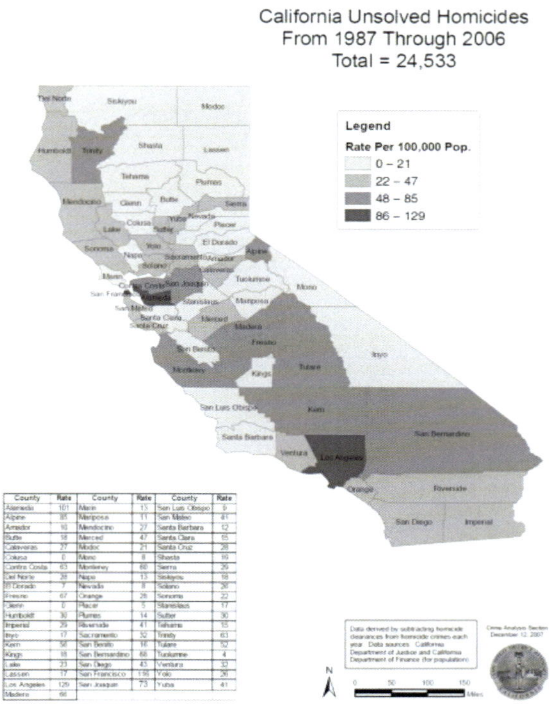

Figure 7.7. *California unsolved homicides, 1987–2006.*

Source: Rachel Boba Santos, Crime Analysis with Crime Mapping, ISBN: 9781506331034.

7.5.1.3. Command

- **Description:** Table 7.7 is an excerpt from a list of selected crimes that have occurred in a jurisdiction in the previous 1 to 3 days. This is an example of a report in which the analytical decision comes before the product is created and could also be automated. The types of crimes included in the report are those that were selected by the chief and command staff when the report was initially developed because they are a priority for the agency. Instead of waiting to hear about the crimes through a police report, this report provides information on a daily basis so that the agency leaders can take action or ensure responses are being implemented immediately. Some examples of crime types that are typically selected for such a report include homicides, attempted homicides, home invasion robberies, shootings, serious, violent gang-related incidents, hate crimes, damage to city property, crimes involving city officials, and stranger-on-stranger gun crime such as armed robbery, violent sex crimes, abductions, and serious aggravated battery. The types selected are often different in different police departments since they have contrasting amounts and types of crime as well as distinct priorities for crime reduction.
- **Potential Use:** The chief and command staff would discuss the list in each command briefing to ensure that crimes deemed a high priority are investigated thoroughly.

Table 7.7. *Command Briefing Report*

Case #	Offense	Location	Synopsis
201714248	Murder, attempted	1204 S Stonegate Dr	On 4/15/2017 at 2100, Suspect (Larry Thompson, B/M, 12/14/1991) and Victim (Thomas Gonzolez, H/M, 01/19/1990) got into an argument at the PubNGrub bar. A shot was fired by the suspect, and the victim suffered a bullet graze to his head. He was transported to St. Mary's Hospital and will survive. K-9 and Air Unit conducted a search for suspect, who was found in bushes on the next block and was arrested.
201714166	Aggravated assault	2519 W Wake Rd	On 4/14/2017 at 2000–2200, Suspect (Christopher Allen, W/M, 7/1/1986) fired shots in the air at Club Y. Suspect was apprehended immediately by security and off-duty officers. Said to be an initiation for a local skinhead group.
201714288	Burglary, other	2301 N Janey St	Sometime between 4/13/2017 at 1900 and 4/15/2017 at 0900, the Holy Trinity Church was vandalized, with approximately $50,000 in physical damage. Also, racist, antireligious graffiti was painted throughout the church.

Source: Rachel Boba Santos, Crime Analysis with Crime Mapping, ISBN: 9781506331034.

7.5.2. Short-Term

7.5.2.1. Operational

- **Description:** Table 7.8 is a report that identifies addresses with more than a certain level of disorder type of activity within one police precinct. This report is generated by selecting those addresses with three or more types of disorder calls for service (e.g., disturbance, loud noise, loitering, etc.,) that occur3 weeks. This example only shows three addresses, but there are likely moremore addresses that had at least three disorder calls. This is a report that can be automated because the analytical decisions are made before the report is created. That is, the agency has decided it wants to respond to addresses that have short–term disorder problems. Because the agency has to prioritize its response based on resources, in this example it has decided to only respond to addresses that have had three or more calls in 4 weeks. Another agency with more resources might lower the threshold to two calls, or one with even fewer resources might increase it to five calls for service so that fewer addresses are on the report.
- **Potential Use:** Operational personnel use these results to implement proactive problem-solving responses for these particular locations to prevent future calls for service and stop the problematic activity.

Table 7.8. *Top Addresses for Disorder: Precinct 33*

September 11, 2017–October 1, 2017					
124 E Main St (Righty's Bar)					
Date	**Time**	**Day**	**Call Type**	**Disposition**	**Case #**
9/30/2017	2200	Sat	Disturbance	Unable to locate	None
9/28/2017	1954	Thu	Loud noise	Citation issued	201709789
9/25/2017	2103	Mon	Loud noise	Warning issued	None
9/17/2017	2356	Sun	Disturbance	Peace restored	None
3519 SE Cedar Ave (Hotspot Gas and Go)					
Date	**Time**	**Day**	**Call Type**	**Disposition**	**Case #**
10/1/2017	0032	Sun	Loitering	Citation issued	2017121023
9/30/2017	2100	Sat	Disturbance	Trespass warning	None
9/15/2017	0120	Fri	Trespassing	Unable to locate	None
4428 N Grand Ave (Public Library)					
Date	**Time**	**Day**	**Call Type**	**Disposition**	**Case #**
9/30/2017	945	Sat	Loitering	Peace restored	None
9/29/2017	1034	Fri	Loitering	Warning issued	None
9/29/2017	1345	Fri	Disturbance	Arrest made	201709945
9/22/2017	1622	Fri	Disturbance	Peace restored	None
9/14/2017	1007	Thu	Loud noise	Peace restored	None

Source: Rachel Boba Santos, Crime Analysis with Crime Mapping, ISBN: 9781506331034.

7.5.2.2. Management

- **Description:** Table 7.9 is a brief summary of a crime pattern that includes information about the crimes an analyst has linked together by crime type (commercial burglary), the area of their occurrence (Beat 42), the method of the crimes (accessed through air conditioning ducts), and the time in which they occurred (overnight hours). These summaries are produced as crime patterns occur and are not a regularly produced report.
- **Potential Use:** This is another example in which multiple personnel would use the report. Management personnel use these results to direct operational personnel from the patrol division as well as other support divisions to collaboratively implement short-term crime reduction strategies. The responses would include directed and undercover patrol, providing crime prevention advice to residents in the pattern area, contacting the known offenders living in the pattern area, and so on. Note that the daily roll call report directs patrol resources on a variety of problems for a particular day, whereas this report directs a collaborative response of patrol, criminal investigations, crime prevention, and actions from the public information officer until the pattern is resolved.

7.5.2.3. Command

- **Description:** Figure 7.8 is a map depicting (with dots) the locations of all thefts from vehicles occurring over 3 months in District 2 as well as patterns of crimes (with large circles) that have been identified during the same time period. The labels for each pattern indicate the month in which the pattern was identified as well as its unique assigned number.
- **Potential Use:** This map, produced each month for the previous 3 months, assists command personnel in determining 1) whether proactive responses to these crime patterns are working, or 2) whether individual crime as well as crime patterns are continually occurring in the same area and might be escalating into larger long-term problems that may require additional response.

Table 7.9. *Crime Pattern Summary Information*

Hot Spot of Commercial Burglaries in Beat 42	
# of Incidents:	Five crimes, two attempts
Date range:	September 15, 2017–September 21, 2017
Time range:	All incidents occurred overnight (between 2000 and 0700) during the week
Target:	Commercial businesses in plazas with roof-accessed air conditioning ducts
Property taken:	Computers, printers, cash, and in two cases a safe
General location:	Northwest area of Beat 42
Method (MO):	In five cases, entry was made into the business through the roof via an air conditioning duct. In two cases, entry was made from a neighboring business (that was entered through the roof the same night). In all cases, only the most expensive equipment was taken, even if it was large and heavy. Burglar alarms were activated in only the two attempts; officers found evidence of attempted entry through the roof, but after a canvas of the area, no suspects were found.

Source: Rachel Boba Santos, Crime Analysis with Crime Mapping, ISBN: 9781506331034.

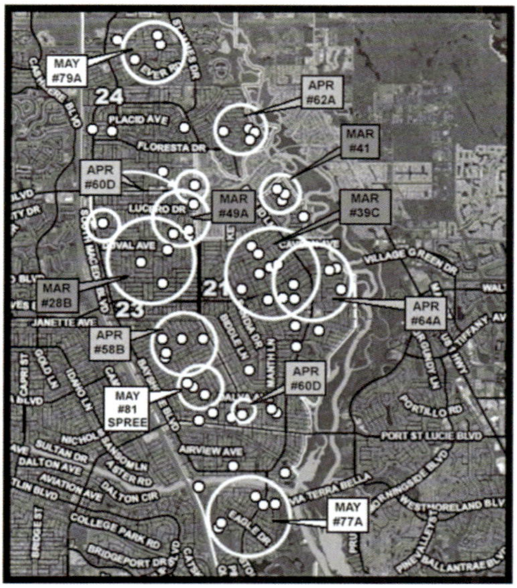

Figure 7.8. *Theft from vehicle incidents and patterns: April–May.*

Source: Port St. Lucie (Florida) Police Department, Michelle Chitolie. Rachel Boba Santos, Crime Analysis with Crime Mapping, ISBN: 9781506331034.

7.5.3. Long-Term

7.5.3.1. Operational

- **Description:** Table 7.10 is a list of the five offenders with the most violent criminal offenses that live in a particular area of the city. This report uses 6 months of arrest data to identify these offenders, so it is considered a long-term analysis report. Note that using 12 or even 24 months of data could result in different individuals on the report.
- **Potential Use:** Both patrol and criminal investigations personnel can use this information to implement responses to deter these offenders from future criminal activity.

7.5.3.2. Management

- **Description:** Figure 7.9 illustrates a comparison analysis created for an apartment community that was identified as a problem location. This example is a part of a more comprehensive analysis product that would be used to guide long-term crime reduction responses. The report shows a chart of the number of calls for service per year at ABC apartments, with a line depicting the city goal of calls for service, indicating that this complex consistently has high numbers of calls for service. It also shows that this community has almost 3 times as many calls for service per apartment unit than other communities in the city and provides a frequency of calls by building and the most common types of calls at the location. A number of call types are not counted in this report, including traffic collisions, lost or found property, vehicle impounds, any calls canceled prior to dispatch, or any officer-initiated CFS without associated case reports.

Table 7.10. *Top Violent Offenders Residing in District 5: January–June 2017*

Rank	Name	Date of Birth	Current Address	Race/Sex	Convictions	Corrections Status
1	Marshall, James	5/23/1956	1456 E Harvard Ave	White/Male	Armed robbery, auto theft, aggravated assault, domestic assault, stalking, DUI	On parole until 5/2019
2	Holden, John	4/12/1967	1219 S Harrison St	Black/Male	Sexual assault, armed robbery, assault of a police officer	On parole until 1/2018
3	Venarila, Manuel	8/24/1979	980 S Appenton Rd	Hispanic/Male	Domestic assault, sexual assault, DUI	On probation until 8/2021
4	Gregory, Josh	9/18/1983	1280 E Main St	Black/Male	Armed robbery, burglary, aggravated DUI, aggravated assault with a weapon	House arrest until 6/2019
5	Adams, Michael	1/12/1992	400 N Lexington St	White/Male	Sexual assault, stalking, domestic assault, armed robbery	Due to be released from prison 4/2018

Source: Rachel Boba Santos, Crime Analysis with Crime Mapping, ISBN: 9781506331034.

*Convicted of any type of violent crime, sexual or nonsexual, domestic or nondomestic.

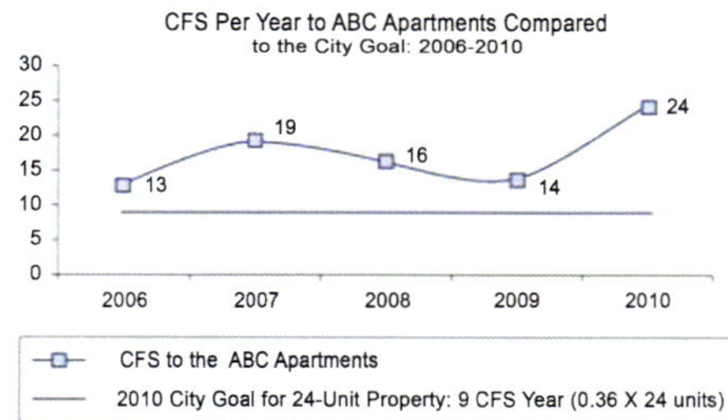

2010 Police CFS per unit, per year ratio for the ABC Apartments (24 CFS/24 units)

1.00

Median Police CFS per unit, per year ratio for city apartments with 8+ units

0.36

Compared to other city propeties, the ABC Apartments' 2010 CFS per unit per year ratio is

2.8 times higher

Total Number of CFS to Each Unit
From Most to Least

Address	Unit	2010 CFS
1234 ABC Street	Unit 5	9
1234 ABC Street	Unit 3	3
1234 ABC Street	Unit 22	3
1234 ABC Street	Unit 12	2
1234 ABC Street	Unit 7	1
1234 ABC Street	Unit 10	1
1234 ABC Street	Unit 11	1
1234 ABC Street	Unit 17	1
1234 ABC Street	No unit specified	3

Call Types to Your Complex From
Most Common to Least Common

CFS Type	2010 CFS
Domestic Violence	4
Psychological Evaluation	4
Vandalism	3
Disturbance - Family	2
Disturbance - Person	2
Check a Person's Well Being	1
Disturbance - Noise	1
Incident Evaluation	1
Other Incident	1
PR Contact	1
Staking	1
Suspicious Circumstances	1
Suspicious Person	1
Vehicle Theft	1

Figure 7.9. *Problem analysis results: ABC apartment.*
Source: Chula Vista (California) Police Department, Karin Schmerler. Rachel Boba Santos, Crime Analysis with Crime Mapping, ISBN: 9781506331034.

- **Potential Use:** Police managers use these results to understand what specific problem this apartment community is experiencing as well as how it compares to others in the city. Along with other information not shown here but covered in depth in Part III: Strategic Crime Analysis, the analysis helps to determine appropriate responses and prioritize which responses should be implemented first. It also establishes a baseline for comparison once the responses have been implemented to determine if the crime reduction strategies were effective. These and other measures would be collected again to show how the community compared to others in the city and how the specific problem addressed had been impacted.

7.5.3.3. Command

- **Description:** Figure 7.10 is an example of a chart that depicts monthly counts and the linear trend line of residential burglary before and after police response was implemented in November of 2017. For comparison, the chart includes the monthly counts and linear trend line for all other Part I property crime (commercial burglary, theft, and auto theft) for which specific proactive responses were not implemented. Including a comparison to other property crime occurring in the same jurisdiction assists in understanding whether property crime is going down generally or just for residential burglary, for which the agency has implemented specific crime reduction efforts. The chart provides linear trend lines for the crime occurring before and after the responses have been implemented, allowing the commanders to more easily see the differences.

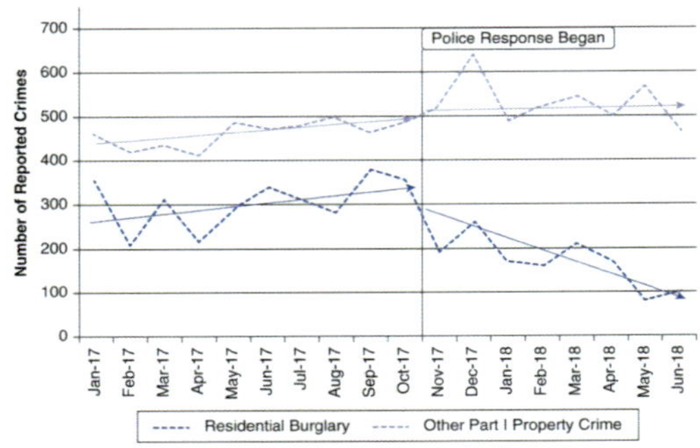

Figure 7.10. *Residential burglary response evaluation.*

Source: Rachel Boba Santos, Crime Analysis with Crime Mapping, ISBN: 9781506331034.

- **Potential Use:** Commanders would use these results to evaluate whether the agency's crime reduction efforts for residential burglary had been effective and whether the response could, if successful, be concluded or, if not, needed adjustment.

REFERENCES

1. Boba Santos, R. (2016). *Crime Analysis with Crime Mapping* (4th ed.). SAGE Publications.
2. Bruce, C. W., Hick, S., LaVigne, N., & Palmer, T. (2014). *Crime Analysis: A Guide for State, Local, and Tribal Law Enforcement Agencies* (2nd ed.). U.S. Department of Justice, Office of Community Oriented Policing Services.
3. Clarke, R. V., & Eck, J. E. (2005). *Crime Analysis for Problem Solvers in 60 Small Steps*. U.S. Department of Justice, Office of Community Oriented Policing Services.
4. Gottlieb, S., Arenberg, S., & Singh, R. (1994). *Crime Analysis: From First Report to Final Arrest*. Alpha Publishing.
5. International Association of Crime Analysts (IACA). (2021). Crime analysis and crime mapping information. Retrieved from: https://www.iaca.net/.
6. O'Shea, T. C., & Nicholls, K. (2003). *Crime Analysis in America: Findings and Recommendations*. U.S. Department of Justice, National Institute of Justice.
7. Ratcliffe, J. H. (2016). *Intelligence-Led Policing* (2nd ed.). Routledge.

Chapter **8**

Analyzing Repeat Victimization

Contents

Introduction 304

8.1. Patterns of Repeat Victimization 304

8.2. Understanding Your Local Repeat Victimization Pattern 318

8.3. Data Sources and Limitations of Revictimization 329

References 335

INTRODUCTION

Analyzing repeat victimization is a critical component of crime prevention and criminal justice, focusing on the phenomenon where certain individuals or locations experience multiple victimizations over time. Understanding this pattern is essential for developing targeted strategies to protect vulnerable populations and reduce overall crime rates.

Repeat victimization occurs when the same victim or location is targeted by offenders on more than one occasion. This can happen wittimea brief time frame or over a more extended period. The reasons for repeat victimization vary, but often include factors such as the attractiveness of the target, perceived vulnerability, and the offender's familiarity with the victim or location. In some cases, repeat victimization may result from a failure to adequately address the factors that led to the initial crime, leaving the victim or location exposed to further harm.

Analyzing repeat victimization involves examining crime data to identify patterns and trends. This analysis can reveal which individuals or locations are most at risk, allowing law enforcement and other stakeholders to implement targeted interventions. For instance, homes that have been burglarized are at a higher risk of being targeted again, particularly wierioda brief period after the initial incident. By recognizing this, police can increase patrols, provide crime prevention advice, or install security measures to deter future crimes.

The importance of analyzing repeat victimization lies in its potential to significantly reduce crime. Research has shown that a small proportion of victims accounortiona sizable proportion of crime, meaning that effectively addressing repeat victimization can lead to a substantial decrease in overall crime rates. Additionally, understanding the factors that contribute to repeat victimization can inform broader crime prevention strategies, making communities safer and more resilient.

Analyzing repeat victimization is crucial for identifying vulnerable targets, developing effective crime prevention strategies, and ultimately reducing crime. This analysis enables a more proactive and focused approach to law enforcement and community safety, helping to protect those most at risk.

8.1. PATTERNS OF REPEAT VICTIMIZATION

Repeat victimization (RV) as a concept and how it relates to other patterns in issues with public safety, like hotspots and repeat offenders. This explains information sources and how to assess the volume and nature of recurring victimization within your jurisdiction. This concludes by reviewing police practice and evaluative research responses to recurrent victimization. This is meant to be a tool to assist law enforcement in recognizing and comprehending patterns of recurring victimization related to various criminal and disorder issues. The manual focuses on methods for estimating the quantity of RV needed for particular public safety issues and how analysis of RV in general can be applied to create more potent solutions. This book is not meant to be a how-to for particular issues like car theft, domestic abuse, or break-ins. For a more thorough understanding of these issues, you are urged to consult other guides.

Police and community members have been working hard to prevent crime for decades. Some of the strategies used to do this include marking property, starting Neighborhood Watches, conducting surveys, hardening targets, improving lighting, and installing electronic security systems.

Even though there are many successful crime prevention initiatives, the people, homes, and organizations least likely to experience victimization tend to implement them. Strategies for preventing crime work best when they target those who are most likely to become victims.

Linking crime prevention strategies with likely victims is a challenge because of the difficulty in predicting the most likely victims of crime. Taking steps to prevent that offense from occurring would be easier, if only police knew:

- What stores will be robbed?
- Whose homes will be burglarized?
- Which college students will be sexually assaulted?

It is often painfully evident that certain people, homes, or businesses are more likely to become victims of crime than others. Such vulnerability could be caused by alcohol abuse, neglecting to secure property, being physically alone, participating in risky activities, or living near groups of people who are likely to commit crimes. Even though the majority of people and places are not victims of crime, those who experience victimization on a regular basis are at the highest risk of experiencing it again. The most reliable indicator of victimization in the past is prior victimization. More than any other aspect of crime, it is a more accurate indicator of victimization in the future. Repeat victimization is not only predictable, but it is also possible to calculate the period of time during which victimization is likely to occur again because subsequent offenses are always characterized by their rapidity. After an initial offense, a week passes before most repeat victims occur again, and in some cases, within 24 hours. The highest chance of being victimized again occurs right after the first offense in all crime types, and this window of increased risk gradually closes over the ensuing weeks and months. Given the likelihood of recurrent victimization and the brief window of time following the initial victimization, police have a very specific window of opportunity to act swiftly to stop further offenses. The effectiveness of police can be significantly increased by employing strategies to decrease victimization. Reducing recurrent victimization can lead to decreased crime, better crime prevention resource efficiency, and the capture of criminals. Additionally, it can save resources for both patrol and investigation.

8.1.1. Defining Repeat Victimization

Repetition as a victim is, in essence, a form of criminal pattern. Numerous well-known crime patterns exist, such as crime series, hotspots, and repeat offenders. Certain offenses involve more than one crime pattern, even though recurrent victimization is one distinct pattern. According to most definitions, repeat victimization, also known as revictimization, is when a victim or target experiences the same kind of crime incident more than once within a set amount of time, like a year. The term "repeated victimization" describes the total number of offenses—both initial and subsequent—that a victim or target has to deal with. If someone breaks into someone's home twice in a year or ten times, those incidences are regarded as repeats. The percentage of victims (individuals or addresses) who experience repeated victimiza given time periodtime for a particular type of crime, like robbery or burglary, is typically used to report the amount of repeat victimization. The percentage of offenses that result in repeat victims is another way to measure repeat victimization; this number is typically referred to as repeat offenses. Although both numbers are significant, they should not be interpreted equally, so caution should be used when interpreting them. When data 3are available, we report the proportions of repeat offenders as well as repeat victims in this guide.

For example, the first row in Table 8.1 would be stated as:

- 46% of all sexual assaults were experienced by persons suffering two or more victimizations during the data period.

Similarly, the second row in Table 8.2 would read:

- 11% of assault victims suffered 25% of all assaults over the 25-year period.

And the first row in Table 8.3 would read:

- 40% of all burglaries were experienced by the 19% of victims who were victimized twice or more duringing, victimizationVictimization refers to human experiences, such as those of victims of domestic abuse. However, since a victim can be a person, a residential property, a company at a particular address, or even a chain of businesses with several locations, repeat victimization is better understood as repeat targets. Even cars have the potential to reoccur. We go over how to identify repeat victims in police data using the victim's name, address, and other identifiers later in this guide.

8.1.2. The Extent of Repeat Victimization

The prevalence of repeated victimization is high and contributes significantly to overall cri Although almost allall crime problems involve revictimization, the precise amount of crime linked to this phenomenon varies over time, between locations, and between crime problem are a reflection ofreflect the localized nature of crime as well as significant variations in the kinds and quantities of data used to calculate victimization rates. The prevalence of repeat victimization is evident in three main sources of information: crime reports, interviews with offenders, and surveys of victims. The prevalence of revictimization is the same in all of these sources, despite their respective shortcomings.

Table 8.1. *Estimates of Repeat Victimization International Victimization Survey*

Offenses	Repeat Offenses
Sexual assault	46%
Assault	41%
Robbery	27%
Vandalism to vehicle	25%
Theft from vehicle	21%
Vehicle theft	20%
Burglary	17%

Source: https://popcenter.asu.edu/sites/default/files/analyzing_repeat_victimization.pdf.

Comparative data from global victimization surveys reveals that violent crimes like robberies and assaults are more likely to result in repeat victimization than property crimes (*see* Table 8.1). According to Table 8.2, victims of assault frequently experience a high rate of victimization again, and domestic violence is one of the crimes that is most likely to recur.

Table 8.2. *Estimates of Repeat Victimization for Assault*

Offense	Repeat Offenses	Repeat Victims	Data Source and Time Period
Assault	25%	11.4%	Emergency room reports, 25 years, Netherlands[2]
Sexual assault	85%	67%	Victim surveys, adult experience, Los Angeles, California[3]
Domestic violence	n/a	44%	Victimization survey, one year, Great Britain[4]
Assaults of youth	90%	59%	National Youth Survey, one year, United States[5]

Source: https://popcenter.asu.edu/sites/default/files/analyzing_repeat_victimization.pdf.

According to data from the British Crime Survey, property crime also frequently results in repeat victims (*see* Table 8.3).

Table 8.3. *Estimates of Repeat Victimization for Property Crime: British Crime Survey*

Offense	Repeat Offenses	Repeat Victims
Residential burglary[6]	40%	19%
Vehicle crime (thefts of/from)[7]	46%	24%
Vandalism[8]	n/a	30%

Source: https://popcenter.asu.edu/sites/default/files/analyzing_repeat_victimization.pdf.

Police records also reveal strong evidence of revictimization for issues ranging from bank robberies to domestic violence and burglaries, even though many studies of repeat victimization are based on victim surveys (*see* Table 8.4). Crime reports, like victimization surveys, reveal the highest rate of recurrent victimization related to domestic abuse.

Table 8.4. *Estimates of Repeat Victimization: Crime Reports*

Offense	Repeat Offenses	Repeat Victims	Location
Domestic violence	62%	28%	Merseyside, England[9]
	42%	31%	West Yorkshire, England[10]
Commercial robbery	65%	32%	Indianapolis, Indiana[11]
Gas station robbery	62%	37%	Australia[12]
Bank robbery	58%	36%	England[13]
Residential burglary	32%	15%	Nottinghamshire, England[14]
	13%	7%	Merseyside, England[15]
	32%	16%	Beenleigh, Australia[16]
	25%	9%	Enschede, Netherlands[17]
Commercial burglary	66%	36%	Austin, Texas[18]
	33%	14%	Merseyside, England[19]
Residential and commercial burglary	39%	18%	Charlotte, North Carolina[20]

Source: https://popcenter.asu.edu/sites/default/files/analyzing_repeat_victimization.pdf.

Some repeat offenses are linked to chronic victims, who are victimized more frequently and experienr more offenses in a givenin each period of time, even though many repeat victims only experience two victimizations during a reporting period. According to the British Crime Survey, 7% of victims of vehicle and burglary crimes experience three or more victimizations in a year (*see* Table 8.5), whereas 23% of victims of domestic violence experience this concentration of recurrent victimization.

These chronic victims report a disproportionate number of offenses, which makes up a larger portion of overall victimization. For instance, 21% of all burglaries involve victims who make up 7% of the total (*see* Table 8.6).

Table 8.5. *Concentration of Repeats Among Victims*

	Type of Victimization		
	Burglary	**Vehicle Crime (Theft of/from)**	**Domestic Violence**
One offense	81%	76%	56%
Two offenses	13%	17%	21%
Three or more	7%	7%	23%

Source: https://popcenter.asu.edu/sites/default/files/analyzing_repeat_victimization.pdf.

Table 8.6. *Contribution of Repeat Victims to Burglaries*

Offense	**Victims**	**Proportion of Offenses**
One burglary	81%	60%
Two burglaries	13%	19%
Three or more burglaries	7%	21%

Source: https://popcenter.asu.edu/sites/default/files/analyzing_repeat_victimization.pdf.

Due to data limitations, virtually all estimates of repeat victimization, despite strong evidence of it, are conservative. Since victimization surveys record offenses that go unreported to the police, they reveal the highest rates of recurrent victimization. However, panel surveys rely on a victim's recollection of several incidents, while longitudinal surveys lose respondents over time because victims frequently move. Repeat victimization is supported by offender interviews, however these studies have been few and the reliability of the offenders is dubious.

Police estimates of repeat victimization are decreased by unreported crime, and some evidence even points to a decreased likelihood of repeat victims calling the police. When estimating repeats, police may also take into account the victimization of the same person in multiple contexts, such as crimes reported from hospitals or police stations. Additionally, recording procedures for a series of crimes, the use of brief time frames (such as a single year), and a small number of offenses may conceal repeats that the police are able to identify.

8.1.3. When Repeat Victimization Occurs

Recurring offenses happen fast; many happen within a week of the first offense, and some happen even within 24 hours. This is a crucial and consistent characteristic of victimization that happens again. An early RV study revealed that the first week following an initial burglary was when there was the greatest chance of another burglary. Once the initial period of heightened risk has passed, the likelihood of a repeat offense rapidly diminishes, bringing the victim's risk of victimization back to that of unaffected individuals or properties. Figure 8.1 illustrates this common pattern, which indicates that 60% of repeat burglaries happened within a month of the first offense and 10% happened in the second month. There is very little chance of a repeat offense after the second month. RV continuously exhibits a predictable pattern called a time course, which consists of a brief but high-risk phase followed by a sharp decline and a leveling off of risk. The amount of time there is a higher chance of becoming a victim varies depending on the level of crime in the area. Determining the period of increased risk is essential because it is during this time that preventive measures must be implemented in order to stop subsequent offenses. When it comes to offenses that have a brief but high-risk time course, prompt preventive action is necessary. A two-day or one-week delay could mean missing the chance to stop a recurrence.

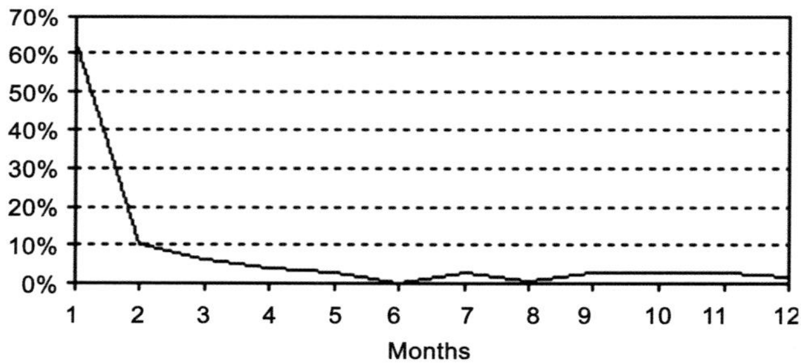

Figure 8.1. *Time course between repeat commercial burglaries Montgomery County, MD.*

Source: https://popcenter.asu.edu/sites/default/files/analyzing_repeat_victtion.pdf.

According tosome research, there could be a bounce—a tiny increase in the percentage of revictimization that happens after the risk seems to be gradually decreasing—interspersed with the predictable time course of repeat victimization (*see* Figure 8.2). The replacement of property with insurance money may be the cause of the time course boult appears likely that some repeat offenders may use a "cool down" period, believing victims should remain vigilant for several months following an offense but then becoming less vigilant.

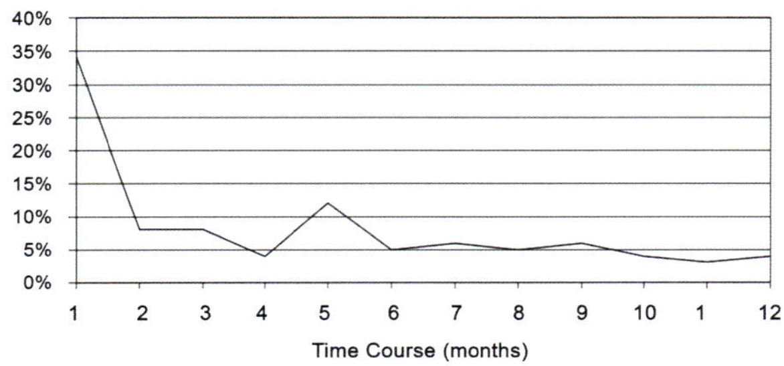

Figure 8.2. *Time course between repeat commercial burglaries: Indianapolis, IN.*

Source: https://popcenter.asu.edu/sites/default/files/analyzing_repeat_victimization.pdf.

There is evidence that the amount of time that elapses between a first and a second offense depends on the kind tic violence appears to havehas a brief time course (*see* Table 8.7), with 15% of repeat offenses taking place in a single day. Depending on the temporal distribution of the data, the time course of RV can be computed by hours, days, weeks, months, or even years between offenses. Apart from the variation based on the type of crime, it is probable that the time course could also differ based on the study location. For instance, research conducted in Florida revealed that 25% of recurrent burglaries happened within a week, whereas research conducted in Merseyside revealed that 11% of repeats happened in a comparable amount of time. Although the time period for reporting repeat victimization varies, the statement of such findings is straightforward. For example, the first row in Table 8.7 would be stated as:

- Of repeat incidents of domestic violence, 15% occurred within 24 hours of the initial incident while 35% of repeat incidents occurred within five weeks.

Table 8.7. *Time Course of Repeat Victimization by Offense Type: Crime Reports*

Offense	Proportion of Repeats by Time Period	Where/Study
Domestic violence	15% within 24 hours 35% within five weeks	Merseyside, England[25]
Bank robbery	33% within three months	England[26]
Residential burglary	25% within a week 51% within a month	Tallahassee, Florida[27]
	11% within one week 33% within one month	Merseyside, England[28]
Non-residential burglary	17% within one week 43% within one month	Merseyside, England[29]
Property crime at schools	70% within a month	Merseyside, England[30]

Source: https://popcenter.asu.edu/sites/default/files/analyzing_repeat_victimization.pdf.

8.1.4. Why Repeat Victimization Occurs

The boost explanation, which is related to the role of repeat offenders, and the flag explanation, which is related to the vulnerability or attractiveness of specific victims, are the two main causes of victimization that occur again.

According to the flag explanation, some targets are disproportionately vulnerable to crime or exceptionally attractive to criminals, and these traits typically don't change over time. In these situations, various perpetrators victimize the victim on multiple occasions.

- Some locations, such as corner properties, may have higher victimization because offenders can easily determine if no one is home. Similarly, apartments with sliding glass doors are particularly vulnerable to break-ins.
- Some businesses, such as convenience stores, are easily accessible and open long hours, which increases exposure to crime.
- Some jobs, such as taxi driving or delivering pizzas, routinely put employees at higher risk than do other jobs. People who routinely spend time in risky places, such as bars, are at greater risk of victimization.
- Hot products, such as vehicles desirable for joyriding, are at higher risk of being stolen.

According to the boost explanation, victimization that occurs again shows that the first offense was successful. From their experience, certain offenders learn vital information about a target and utilize that knowledge to commit new crimes. This information could include methods for getting past security, easy access to a property, or moments when a target is unattended. For instance, thieves who target specific car brands might be aware of how to get around the locking or electronic security systems. This boost pattern is even evident in fraudulent victimization, since some cases of recurring victimization may be explained by insurance fraud.

- During initial offenses, offenders may spot but be unable to carry away all the desirable property. These offenders may return for property left behind; or the offenders may tell others about the property, leading different offenders to revictimize the same property. Since many victims will eventually replace stolen property, such as electronics, original offenders may also return after a period of time to steal the replacement property—presumably brand new.
- Some victims may be unable to protect themselves from further victimization. An unrepaired window or door may increase

vulnerability and make repeat victimization even easier than an initial offense. For example, once victimized, a domestic violence victim faces a high likelihood of revictimization if no protective measures are taken to prevent subsequent offenses.

- Interviews with offenders suggest that much repeat victimization may be related to boost explanations— experienced offenders can reliably calculate both the risks and rewards of offending. Half to two-thirds of offenders report burglarizing or robbing a specific property twice or more. Among domestic violence offenders, as many as two-thirds of incidents are committed by repeat offenders.

Reasons for a boost and a flag may overlap and differ depending on the type of offense.

For instance, bank robberies are more likely to happen again if the first one resulted in a sizable profit; banks were less likely to be robbed again when the financial losses were minimal. Studies on recurrent victimization—for banks and other targets—indicate that while most targets are never victimized at all, most offenses are highly concentrated on a small number of victims.

8.1.5. How Repeat Victimization Relates to Other Crime Patterns

Research has revealed several types of repeat victimization:

- True repeat victims are the exact same targets that were initially victimized, such as the same house and the same occupants who were burglarized three times within a year.
- Near victims are victims or targets that are physically close to the original victim and may be similar in important ways. Apartments close to a burglarized unit will tend to contain similar goods, have similar physical vulnerabilities, and a common layout.
- Virtual rectims that are virtually identicalidentical to the original victim in important ways.of convenience stores or fast foodfast-food restaurants may have identical store layouts and management practices, such as having a single clerk on duty or informal cash handling procedures. The new occupants of a dwelling that had been previously burglarized are another type of virtual repeat.
- Chronic victims are repeat victims who suffer from different types of victimization over time—such as burglary, domestic violence, and robbery. This phenomenon is also known as multiple victimization.

For some crimes, repeat victimization is related to other common crime patterns:

- Hot spots are geographic areas in which crime is clustered. Hot spots may be hot because of the frequency of the same type of crime, such as burglaries, or hot spots may include different types of crimes. For many crimes, repeat victimization contributes to hot spots.
- Hot products are goods that are frequently stolen, and their desirability may underlie repeat victimization. Stores that sell CDs, beer, or gasoline may suffer repeat victimization. Some products, including vehicles, become hotuse of the product's vulnerability—vulnerability, for example, vehicles wcks that are easy to defeat.
- RepeatRepeating offenders are individuals who commit multiple crimes. Some offenders specialize in a single crime type, while others commit complementary offenses—such as breaking into a house and stealing a vehicle to transport the goods, or stealing a license plate to be used in the commission of another crime, such as a commercial robbery.
- Crime series aof one crime type that appear to beare the work of the same offender. The offenses may be clustered in space or time, or reflect a distinctive modus operandi, such as a serial rapist who targets college students. Common series involve property crime at similar targets, such as robberies of convenience stores.
- Risky facilities are locations such as colleges or shopping areas that routinely attract or generate a disproportionate amount of crime. For example, lots where students routinely park may generate more larcenies from vehicles because the vehicles of students may routinely contain desirable electronic equipment.

Thescrime patterns are not exclusive ofto one another and may even overlap. However, the identification of recurring victimization frequently offers crucial hints regarding the causes of recurrence and enables law enforcement to concentrate on preventative measures.

8.1.6. Where Repeat Victimization Occurs

Repeat victimization is most prevalent in high-crime areas for many crime-related issues. Crimes like sexual assault and domestic abuse typically don't have geographic concentrations, but other places that are frequently targeted for victimization—like banks, convenience stores, and low-cost lodging—might. People and places in high-crime areas are more likely to become victims of many crimes for the first time, and they might not have the resources to immediately improve security measures and preventfense. Hot spots are relatively smallsmall geographic areas where offenses are clustered. In high crime areas, crime is concentrated among repeat victims to such an extent that recurrent offenses can create hot spots. Because of this, incident maps may be dominated by symbols scaled to represent the number of offenses at particular addresses; hence, exprts came up with the term "hot dots.."

Maps of incidents are frequently used to locate hotspots and can be used to find victims who have been victimized again. On maps that are scaled to reflect the number of incidents, icons or symbols should be used; otherwise, overlapping points might not be visible, hiding RV. Additionally, the amount of recurring victimization that can be identified on maps may be distorted by data decisions. Short time periods—a week, month, or even quarter—may conceal recurrent victimization; imprecise address information—a single address for occurrences at a sizable apartment building, for example—may conceal specific RV locations (Figure 8.3).

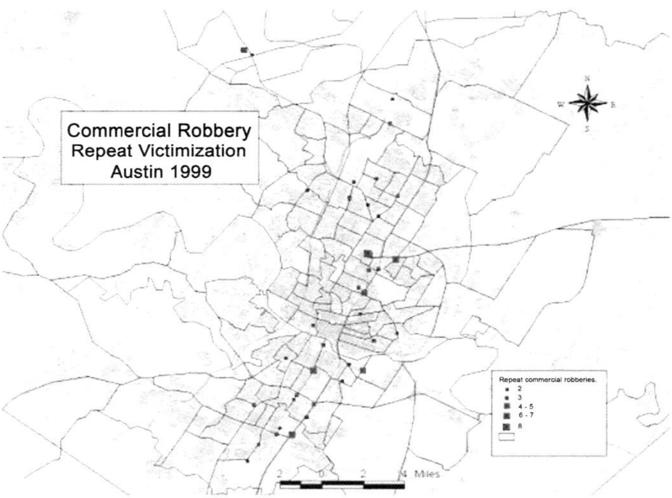

Figure 8.3. *Repeat commercial robberies.*

Source: https://popcenter.asu.edu/sites/default/files/analyzing_repeat_victimization.pdf.

Because most incident maps show the frequency and geographic distribution of offenses rather than taking into consideration the concentration of crimes, they may conceal RV in densely populated areas. In areas with high population density, like those with multi-family homes, most maps fail to distinguish between individual apartment units and apartment buildings, which can make up large apartment complexes.

This is also true for repeat victimization: crime is not always correlated with geography. For instance, it is improbable that victims of domestic abuse are concentrated in one area.

Even recurrent instances of domestic abuse might not happen at the same location; instead, the victim may experience one offense at home and another at work.

Geographically, certain crimes like burglaries are clustered; repeat burglaries are even more logically clustered. Therefore, the percentage of repeat burglaries that take place in smaller geographic areas may be hidden by citywide burglary data. This implies that in order to study RV, various geographic levels of analysis must be used. Offenses like bank robberies and domestic violence, in contrast to burglaries, may require the use of data from the entire jurisdiction.

8.1.7. Overlooking Repeat Victimization

Even though repeat victimization is a well-established phenomenon, most people and properties within a jurisdiction are not victims of crime, especially within a period of one or two years, so it is easy to overlook the significance of repeat victimization in crime pattern analysis.

Consider a study in which 10,828 burglaries were reported to police in 1990:

- 97% of the city's estimated 300,000 addresses were not burglarized;
- 3% of the jurisdiction's addresses (8,116) were burglarized.

At first, repeat victimization appears minimal:

- 82% of the victims (6,616 addresses) suffered only one burglary during the year;
- 18% of victims (1,500 addresses) suffered two or more burglaries.

Analysis sheds further light on revictimization:

- 61% of all burglaries (6,616) occurred at addresses with only one offense;
- 39% of all burglaries (4,212) occurred at addresses with two or more offenses.

Even though it might still seem insignificant, Figure 8.4 graphically illustrates that revictimization accounts for a disproportionately high percentage of all burglaries: 18% of victims accounted for 39% of burglaries. 2,712 fewer burglaries—a 25% decrease in burglaries—would have occurred in the jurisdiction if subsequent offenses had been avoided.

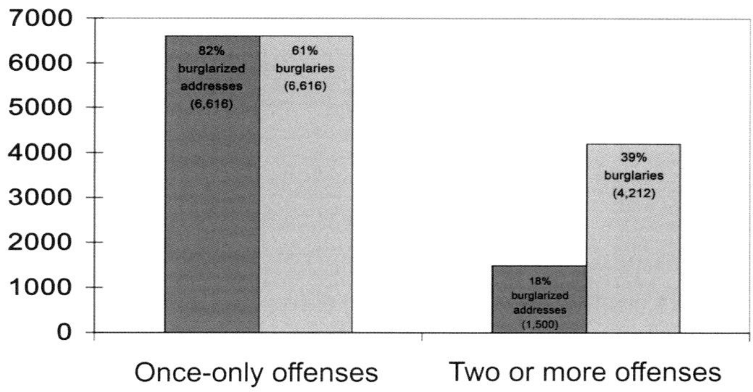

Figure 8.4. *Distribution of burglaries by address and frequency.*

Source: https://popcenter.asu.edu/sites/default/files/analyzing_repeat_victimization.pdf.

- Serve as a catalyst for developing more effective responses for problems that generate much of the workload for police.
- Reveal limitations of existing data and police practices, and advance improvements in data quality and victim services.
- Provide insight into patterns underlying recurring crime problems.
- Prioritize the development and delivery of crime prevention and victim services.

Although recognizing repeat victimization is an important step, working out precisely what to do about revictimization will require additional effort on the part of police.

8.1.8. Special Concerns about Repeat Victimization

The crime pattern can be used as a tool to develop responses to reduce revictimization once an agency analyzes repeat victimization and establishes the frequency and time course of repeats by offense type. Focusing on victims raises a number of special concerns that police should consider:

- **Blaming the Victim:** Victims may be vulnerable because they are unable, or have failed to secure their property, or have placed themselves in high-risk settings. The behaviors of individuals—such as using poor judgment while under the influence of drugs or alcohol—may contribute to victimization. In most cases, police should provide information to the victim about the increased risk of victimization but must be careful about implying blame.

- **Increasing Fearfulness:** For offenses such as burglary that are unlikely to be solved, the primary role of police is often to comfort victims. Warning victims about the likelihood of being revictimized may make victims more fearful.
- **Violating Privacy of Victims:** Although victimization increases the risk of revictimization to the original victim, it also increases the risks to persons and properties that are either nearby or virtually identical to the initial victim. While police may be concerned about violating the privacy of an initial victim by warning others, this information may prevent other vulnerable persons or places from being victimized.
- **Displacing Crime:** It is often believed that thwarting one offense will result in a motivated offender simply picking another target. Unless there are virtual victims, the likelihood of displacement is low. For example, preventing repeat domestic violence is unlikely to result in the displacement of violence to another victim. If there are virtual victims available—such as similar nearby houses to be burglarized or similar unsecured parking lots for vehicle theft—police should consider these as candidates for similar crime prevention strategies. Rather than causing displacement, crime prevention efforts focused on victims are just as likely to produce bonus effects. For example, reducing opportunities for vehicle theft may also reduce theft from vehicles.
- **Unintended Consequences:** Focusing on repeat victimization to reduce offending may have unintended consequences. In a study in New York City, researchers found that follow-up visits and educational services to victims of domestic violence resulted in increased calls for police service, and mandatory arrest for some domestic violence offenders increases revictimization.

8.2. UNDERSTANDING YOUR LOCAL REPEAT VICTIMIZATION PATTERN

Only a broad overview of repeated victimization is provided in this guide's content. You must integrate the fundamental ideas of repeat victimization with a more detailed comprehension of your local issue, as locations and types of crime problems differ in their prevalence of repeat victimization. You can create a response plan that is more successful by thoroughly analyzing the local issue.

Calculating the frequency and distribution of recurrent victimization is essential to creating a successful response.

8.2.1. Selecting the Problem

Examining a cluster of problems may be desirable, depending on the crime problem under consideration and its assumed relationship to other related problems. For instance, convenience stores that experience robberies may also experience burglaries, shoplifting, or larceny on a regular basis. Reasoning from experience shoun of problems to be studied.

Despite the fact thatEven though the nature of the data being used may require starting with a broad problem, every attempt should be made to narrow the problem down to one that has more similarities than differences in order to avoid an excessively broad problem. Vandalism, for instance, encompasses both graffiti and property destruction, but each needs to be looked at separately.

For the problem being examined, determine the appropriate "unit of analysis" by deciding if the relevant "victim" is an individual or household, an address, a business, or a group of victims such as convenience stores or an individual chain store.

8.2.2. Selecting Data

Existing police data, such as crime reports, are most often used to document repeat victimization. In selecting data, attention should be given to:

- **Determining the Appropriate Time Frame:** For most crime problems, it is best to use at least three calendar years of data. You can then define repeat victims as persons or places victimized more than once during the three years. If you use only a single year of data, an address burglarized in December will not be identified as a repeat if the next burglary at the address occurred in January. Shorter time periods of data will generally underestimate the amount of repeat victimization.
- **Determining Data Sufficiency:** As a general rule, it can be easier to detect repeat victimization for offenses that are common than for offenses that are rare. While the magnitude of problems varies from one jurisdiction to another, it may be useful to have 100 offenses or more per year to detect repeat. While one may find repeats even among 10 bank robberies per year in a small town, analyzing a larger number of robberies will produce more reliable findings. When there are few offenses of one type, you can increase the amount of data by incorporating multiple years, up to ten years or more, or by broadening the geographic scope of analysis, such as incorporating offenses that occur in neighboring jurisdictions.

- **Choosing a Denominator:** To best calculate repeat victimization, it is useful to know the population or number of possible victims of a similar type. For example, if you want to determine the number of repeat robberies of convenience stores, it is helpful to know the number of convenience stores. For demographic information, such as households, such data can be found in the U.S. Census; for other denominators, sources such as business licenses or tax records can be used to determine the population.
- **Identifying Key Variables:** Data should routinely include victim name, address (including street number, building name or number, apartment or suite number, and direction), and date and time of the offense. If the victim is a business, the business name and the type of business should be examined. Variables examined should also include the outcome such as the type or value of property taken or damaged, whether the offense was attempted or completed, the amount of force used in the offense, the level of harm, and so forth. Additional variables may be useful, and you can identify these by reading the literature on the specific type of problem being considered.
- **Determining Data Limitations:** Police data routinely have limitations, including underreporting, delayed reporting, data errors, and imprecise address information. When selecting data, you should identify the limitations of the data you will use, think through the implications of these limitations, and determine whether the data can be improved with a reasonable amount of effort. Detecting the limitations of different data and techniques for improving data quality are discussed in appendices A and B.

8.2.3. Analysis Tasks

It is usually not necessary to use complex statistical procedures for basic analysis of victimization that occurs repeatedly. A spreadsheet containing various descriptive variables is usually used to hold the data. These variables are then used to sort the data, grouping related victims together based on a specific variable.

8.2.3.1. Mapping Locations

Point maps are useful for the initial detection of many types of revictimization. These maps show the locations of calls for service, offenses, and arrests for crimes like assaults, robberies, and burglaries as .s or points. It is helpful to have points whose sizes correspond to the quantity of incidents that happen at specific addresses. Point maps are less helpful in crowded areas of high-rise apartments or office buildings. In rural areas or places with few addresses, like parks, farms, and large parking lots, point maps are also less helpful unless these locations have global positioning system (GPS) coordinates est *Sorting Offense Data by Address*

In essence, mappingMapping is the process of projecting a table or chart onto a spatial layer. Sorting data by address allows us to achieve the same goal: by organizing the street names and numbers, we produce a table like Figure 8.5. The victim's name is not included in this table, but the data would allow you to count the number of offenses that have occurred at each location after sorting.

Police Beat	Census Tract	Census Block	Street Number	Street Direction	Street Name	Street Type
12	12500	4005	645		H	ST
12	12500	4005	645		H	ST
31	13412	1004	4420		BONITA	RD
14	12303	2013	295		E	ST
13	13000	1000	352		H	ST
13	12700	2000	444		3RD	AV
31	13409	1000	386	E	H	ST
31	13409	1000	358	E	H	ST
31	13413	2003	1020		TIERRA DEL REY	
31	13409	1000	354	E	H	ST
31	13409	5009	599		TELEGRAOH CANYON	RD
31	13409	5009	591		TELEGRAPH CANYON	RD
31	13409	5009	591		TELEGRAPH CANYON	RD
14	12302	1006	279		F	ST
14	12302	1006	279		F	ST
14	12302	1006	279		F	ST
14	12302	1006	279		F	ST

Figure 8.5. Distribution of burglaries by address and frequency.

Source: https://popcenter.asu.edu/sites/default/files/analyzing_repeat_victimization.pdf.

8.2.3.3. Sorting Offense Data by Victim Name

The victim's name can be used as the primary sorting characteristic for police data. Addresses and other unique information can be used to verify and fix any apparent errors in the database. This method can be used to analyze offense data as well as calls-for-service data.

8.2.3.4. Counting Victims and Offenses

Most electronic databases, including Microsoft® Excel and SPSS®, have a procedure for counting the number of unique addresses or names once the data have been sorted and matched. Making a table with the number of victims and offenses is the best way to display repeat data (*see* Figure 8.6). To report the percentage of households or offenses in each row, additional columns may be used.

Number of burglaries	Number of victims burglarized (address or households)	Total burglaries
0	F (Total population or households – E)	0
1	A	A
2	B	2 x B
3	C	3 x C
4 or more	D	F – (A + 2B + 3C)
Total	E (A +B + C + D)	F

Figure 8.6. *Sample table for recording number of victimizations: residential burglary.*

Source: https://popcenter.asu.edu/sites/default/files/analyzing_repeat_victimization.pdf.

Once the numbers in this table are input, percentages (*as shown in* Table 8.6) offer a convenient means of observing the ratios of offenses encountered by recurrent victims and figuring out what percentage of all victims have been victimized again.

8.2.3.5. Cleaning Data

Many errors are found when data is sorted and matched. These might seem insignificant (for instance, when a road type is listed as a street in one record and an avenue in another), but they can lower the number of matches and underestimate the frequency of victimization. Usually, the errors can be fixed by sorting and confirming the correct version using a different variable. For instance, the addresses 599 and 591 Telegraph Canyon are shown in Figure 8.5. If the victim's name is looked up, it might be discovered that the 599 address was entered incorrectly and should have been changed to 591.

8.2.3.6. Calculating Time Course

The term "time course" refers to the interval of time between an initial offense and a subsequent offense (or between the second and third, or third and fourth). By deducting the date of the second offense from the date of the first offense, the majority of software can quickly calculate the time course in days. When the data set is larger than 12 months, the process is only marginally more difficult because the year must be converted in order for the software to understand

January. 1, 2001, which is 365 days after January 1. 1, 2000. The average number of days between repeat events, the range between the shortest and longest time between events, and percentiles such as the percentage of repeat events occurring within a week, 30 days, 6 months, or 12 months are all examples of time courses that are commonly reported using descriptive statistics. The temporal distribution of the data should be examined for natural or significant breaks before deciding on a reporting period for percentiles.

8.2.3.7. Calculating Rate

The degree of victimization and recurrent victimization are related to exposure in many crime situations. For instance, if a city has 118 convenience stores, and 75 of them are Handy Andy® locations, then Handy Andy robberies are probably more common than those at other stores. Longer operating hours, more residents, more foot or vehicle traffic, and so forth can all increase exposure.

8.2.4. Planning Further Analysis

Further analysis is likely to be required, but the analysis of repeat victimization, its concentration, and its time course may clearly point to specific responses that will eliminate or reduce a problem. In the absence of additional investigation, the majority of police will try to capture one or more offenders at the scene of repeated victimization through surveillance or undercover operations. This response might be approcases where there is a connection between the repeatrepeat offending and victimization, but it might take a lot of resources and won't always improve the general state of the properties or the behaviors of those who are more likely to become victims.

8.2.4.1. Collecting Additional Information

The preliminary examination of recurrent victimization could reveal clear vulnerabilities associated with these individuals. These vulnerabilities may be related to attributes for which information will need to be gathered, such as store hours, victim age (young or old), environmental factors, management techniques, employed crime prevention devices, victim conduct, and so on. Every analysis ought to be focused on variables that the police or other relevant parties could influence. Investigators and patrol officers frequently have knowledge of the elements that lead to high rates of recurrent victimization.

8.2.4.2. Examining Victim-Suspect Relationships

In certain cases, the nature of the police response and the extent of revictimization can be inferred from the relationship between the victim and the suspect. These connections could account for a large number of recurrences of victims being targeted for personal or property abuse.

8.2.4.3. Determining the Role of Boosts

Repeat offenders may not always be immediately apparent, but they frequently play a part in certain crimes, such as domestic abuse. It is important to analyze the role that repeat offenders play in victimization patterns. If a single habitual offender—a worker, a relative, or someone else—is the cause of a large amount of victimization, this information will direct efforts to identify the best course of action, such as heightened short-term surveillance or panic or other temporary alarms. Recurrent victimization that persists after an offender is caught raises suspicions rather than clarifies them.

8.2.4.4. Comparing Victims and Non-Victims

The distinctions between victims and non-victims, or between one-time victims and those who are victimized repeatedly, even chronically, are frequently brought to light when repeat victimization is the focus. Convenience store robberies may be common, but some stores never experience them. The distribution of crime in low-cost motels is likely due to management practices more so than geographic location. Comparisons can show the typical number of offenses for specific victim groups, locations, or business groups.

A literature review on the subject and conversations with patrol officers and investigators can help identify the variables that need to be looked at. The way of entry, the kind of property taken, the security measures in place, the closeness to places where crime is likely to occur, like bars or schools, and other factors can all be significant in property offenses. Factors like the victim-suspect relationship and drug or alcohol use may be crucial in cases of personal victimization, such as sexual assault or domestic violence. Variables like management styles, security features, customer demographics, or the kind of goods being sold may provide light on the differences between victims and non-victims in cases of commercial offenses.

Public records, like tax and business licenses, can be used to gather information about certain victim types, like budget hotels, bars, schools, banks, and convenience stores. Important details regarding variations in victimization may be obtained by utilizing cross-tabulations or by establishing correlations between significant variables. However, depending on the nature of the issue, you might wish to look for more help in more intricate statistical models. Giving this information could be useful when putting responses into action that call for adjustments to victim behaviors or management techniques.

8.2.5. Responding to Repeat Victimization

Since the risk of repeat victimization is highest in the short term, responses with the greatest potential for being effective have the following characteristics:

Responses emphasize quick action—within 24 hours if possible—to prevent a subsequent offense.

- Highest priority is accorded repeat victims with the most victimization, and these victims receive an increased level or amount of the response. This type of graded response deploys the easiest or least expensive measures to first-time victims and increases the intensity of the response if subsequent victimizations occur.
- Responses to repeat victimization may be temporary since the increased risk of revictimization is most acute in the short-term.

8.2.6. Types of Responses to Repeat Victimization

There are three primary ways of responding to RV:

- Protecting victims by blocking future opportunities against these specific persons or places;
- Shifting responsibility for repeat victimization;
- Increasing actual or perceived risks of apprehension for offenders, primarily repeat offenders.

These types of responses may be combined, depending on the type of problem.

8.2.6.1. Protecting Victims

1. **Quickly Blocking Visual Signs of Victimization:** Obvious signs of property damage should be removed immediately to block visual signs of vulnerability. Needy victims may need assistance in quickly securing properties.
2. **Improving Physical Security:** While it is not practical to provide security surveys to all potential victims, properties that have been victimized once or more should be assessed for vulnerability, and protective actions should be taken rapidly.
3. **Target Hardening:** Improved security, such as hardware, can be installed; lighting can be improved; security lighting installed; visibility improved such as by unobstructing views of cash registers; and so forth.
4. **Rapidly Blocking Access to Targets:** Installing bandit or anti-robbery screens at victimized properties; placing targeted products

behind counters, in locked cases, or out of reach; and moving or removing targets such as telephone booths, signs, vending machines, or vehicles.

5. **Removing or Protecting Targets:** Some targets cannot be physically moved but victimization can be reduced by installing driveway barriers where vehicles cannot be garaged; and obstructing access to alleys, walls, signs, or culverts using fences, gates, vegetation, baffles, or sprinklers.
6. **Regulating or Controlling Access:** Access to locations that are repeatedly victimized, such as parks, bathrooms, libraries, and schools can be controlled in different ways including fees, passes, identification cards, or parking permits.

8.2.6.2. Shifting Responsibility for Repeat Victimization

1. **Educating Victims or Eliminating Excuses for Risky Behaviors:** Victim behaviors, such as failing to secure property or walking alone, may contribute to victimization. Once victimized, victims can be educated about their risk of being victimized again. Services such as escorts for women walking alone on college campuses, access to shelters or protective custody for domestic violence victims, and crime prevention devices such as dead bolt locks can eliminate excuses for risky behavior.
2. **Changing Management Practices:** Management practices, such as increasing the number of employees or adopting security features, may reduce repeat victimization. For example, access controls can be installed in parking lots, retail stores can require receipts for returned merchandise, apartment complexes can screen visitors, gasoline stations can adopt pre-pay policies, stores can limit and secure cash on hand, bars can monitor drinking, the number of customers can be limited, access to hot products can be controlled, or the number of employees can be increased during "hot times."

Some businesses may choose to accept repeated victimization as a cost of doing business, given the potential costs and inconveniences associated with making changes to their management practices. In these situations, law enforcement ought to think about taking action to promote the use of preventative measures. Some property owners may be persuaded to take protective measures by information and unofficial requests. Some repeat victims may be convinced to adopt crime prevention strategies through the use of publicity, user fees, or even civil actions, since predictable repeat victimization reduces the amount of police service available to unwilling victims.

8.2.6.3. Increasing Risks to Offenders

1. **Temporarily Increasing Surveillance:** For a variety of offenses, including vandalism, burglary, and domestic abuse, police patrols, security guards, and staff members can temporarily increase informal and formal surveillance for targeted locations and individuals.
   - Temporary surveillance can be increased through "cocoon watch," a type of Neighborhood Watch in which nearby residents are informed of an offense and asked to be particularly vigilant.
   - Electronic surveillance, including CCTV and portable burglar alarms, can also be temporarily used in many settings.
   - Domestic violence victims may be provided with panic alarms to quickly contact police about repeat offenses.
2. **Reducing Rewards:** Reducing the rewards for committing crimes and concentrating on areas, people, or property that have been victimized can help discourage repeat offenders.
   - Tracking devices, such as units temporarily placed in vehicles, can be used to detect offenders.
   - Marking or etching property with identification makes it difficult to sell property, and ink packs in cash packs limit use.
   - Cash control procedures in retail stores limit the amount to be stolen, and return policies can reduce shoplifting.
3. **Monitoring Repeat Victimization:** Assigning precise accountability for recognizing and keeping an eye on recurrent victimization is crucial. Depending on the nature of the offense and the frequency of revictimization, different people may be in charge of keeping an eye on repeat victims. The identification and monitoring of repeat victimization may involve call dispatchers, crime analysts, crime prevention staff, specialists like victims service personnel, responding officers, and investigators; however, the locus of responsibility should be made clear as the allocation of responsibility may differ depending on the specifics of each crime problem.

It is important to proceed cautiously when concentrating on raising the likelihood that offenders will be apprehended, even though some successful responses to recurring victimizations may concentrate on doing so.

It takes a lot of resources and is not always successful to capture elusive criminals, especially when it comes to property crimes. An ender may be apprehended in certain circumstances as a result ofbecause of tactical or short-term police actions like baiting, stings, or surveillance to prevent theof specific people or locations. Police should take into accountconsider whether the initial characteristics of the vulnerable victim or location are likely to remain unchanged and thus attract other offenders, even though these offenders may be accountable for multiple offenses.

Longer-term initiatives to stop revictimizatiothe traits of certain types of repeat victims are probably goinggoing to be the most successful and efficient crime reduction tactics. For instance, implementing pre-pay procedures at petrol stations where there are frequent fuel drive-offs will be more advantageous in the long run than apprehending one or more offenders.

8.2.7. Measuring Your Effectiveness

Measurement tells you how successful your efforts have been and offers suggestions for changing your approach if necessary to get the desired outcome.

Measurements of your issue should be taken both before and after you implement solutions to ascertain how serious the issue is and whether they have been successful.

In cases where issues are geographical in nature, steps ought to be taken for a target group as well as the surrounding region to identify any spatial displacement and, if feasible, a comparable area to serve as a benchmark. In many situations, action should be taken to address the issue at hand as well as any issues that may cause offenses to shift, like from residential to commercial burglaries.

The following are potentially useful measures of the effectiveness of responses focused on repeat victimization:

- Reduction in the number or frequency of reported incidents;
- Reduction in the proportion of repeat offenses;
- Reduction in the number or frequency of calls for service;
- Reduction in repeat calls for service;
- Reduction in the proportion of repeat victims;
- Reduction in completed offenses;
- Education of value of property taken or harm associated with offenses; and
- Increase in arrests associated with offensesuffered by repeat victims.

8.3. DATA SOURCES AND LIMITATIONS OFOF REVICTIMIZATION

The quantity of revictimization that can be identified depends on the kind and caliber of the data used to estimate RV. This could therefore obscure important aspects of revictimization and restrict our ability to assess the effects of lessening revictimization.

8.3.1. Police Data

The most common method of identifying repeat victimization is through recorded crime data; however, common issues like the following frequently obscure the true level of repeat victimization.

- **Underreporting:** Much victimization is unreported but reporting varies from one offense to another. Virtually all bank robberies, vehicle crashes, and most vehicle thefts and commercial robberies are reported. On the other hand, most domestic violence, much theft, and much vandalism are unreported. Underreporting will limit the ability to detect repeat victimization.
- **Incomplete or Inaccurate Crime Reports:** Offense reports completed by responding officers are rarely used for analysis, and often contain incomplete or inaccurate information about offenses, including poor address or victim informatg information. Analysis of repeat victimization will likely provideprovide an opportunity to involve line personnel in improving the quality of their initial reports; this may contribute to reductions in their workload and provide opportunities to participate in the most effective crime prevention strategies.
- **Time Period Covered by the Data:** A single year of offense data is customarily used for crime analysis but provides a weak basis for detecting repeat victimization. Undercounting occurs when offenses straddle calendar years, with an initial offense occurring late in one calendar year and a recurrence early in the next year. The problem is more common when the time course between offenses is longer. While this data may be all that is available to police, truncating data by calendar year substantially masks repeat offenses.
- **Data Accuracy:** Police data are fraught with errors that reduce the amount of repeat victimization that can be detected. Some errors reflect data entry problems or errors on reports such as misspelled victim or street names, or erroneous street numbers. Basic inconsistencies in data, such as the use of a street suffix or direction

(such as north or south), may reduce data quality. Accuracy of data is also affected by victim reporting—victims may delay reporting, may fail to recall key elements such as all types of property taken, may fail to report suspect information, or may provide false information to police such as claiming that properties were secured.

- **Data Precision:** Even in offense reports, police data often fail to record all the elements of a unique address. Street number, apartment building or building name, floor, and apartment or suite number are often necessary for accurately detecting revictimization at addresses. For large properties, such as parks, parking lots, or sporting venues; or in locations without an address, such as pedestrian or bicycle paths, along creeks or in canyons, or within alleys; very precise address information will be unavailable. Some properties, such as schools or businesses, may have multiple addresses, including different streets. Police data may fail to distinguish between types of residential properties, such as apartments or single-family dwellings, or a type of commercial enterprise.
- **Imprecise Victim Names:** Detecting revictimization of individuals involves matching recorded victim names. But victims may alter their name, move after being victimized, be victimized in different locations, and households may contain individuals with different names who report separate incidents. When a commercial location is victimized, recording victim names should be standardized to consistently distinguish a corporate name from a store name or acronym.
- **Hierarchical Crime Classification and Recording Inconsistencies:** Hierarchical classification of offenses may mask revictimization for some offense types. For example, the occurrence of a burglary at the address where domestic violence has occurred may result in undercounting burglary or domestic violence revictimization. Some offenses are not consistently classified—an attempted break-in of a motor vehicle may be reported as vandalism.
- **Victim Groups:** "Virtual" repeat victims may comprise groups, for example, specific restaurant chains, a specific chain of convenience stores or gasoline stations, college students, or surface parking lots.
- **Boundary Issues:** Repeat victimization may occur across territorial boundaries, particularly for victim groups. For example, a specific chain of fast food restaurants may be robbed but offenses occur in different jurisdictions or police districts, and therefore are not easily detected. In areas where offender mobility is high, RV may be masked.

8.3.2. Victim Surveys

Victim surveys provide better information than police data because they address a common issue with police data, which is underreporting. Random surveys usually don't make sense financially because the victimization rate for any given offense is typically very low. Police, however, can use two basic methods to survey for repeat victimization:

- **Victim Follow-Up Surveys:** After being victimized once, victims are surveyed to find out if they have been victimized again and whether or not they have called the police. Offense reports, also known as call histories, are used to create a sampling frame. Depending on the time course for the offense type under consideration, the duration could be 30 days, 3, 6, or 12 months.
- **Modified Offense Reports:** A simple way for police to incorporate revictimization surveys into routine police work is to modify offense reports and/or the initial investigation of responding officers to include a few basic questions about victimization such as:
  - Have you previously been victimized?
  - Were you a victim of the same or a different type of offense?
  - Were you victimized at this address or another address?
  - How many times were you victimized?
  - When did the victimization occur?
  - Did you report the victimization to the police?

Inquiries regarding past victimization should be utilized to identify victims who are at high risk and to help develop the best possible responses. Inquiries from victims ought to be pertinent to the particular issue under consideration.

Police may wish to conduct more extensive surveys in specific situations. One can survey a whole group of people, like all managers of convenience stores, all managers of low-cost motels, all women on small college campuses, all principals of public schools, and all homebuilders. Certain surveys, like those on crime prevention that evaluate lighting and building layouts, may be observational in nature.

In general, methodological issues must be considered in victim surveys:

- **Continuous Data:** Unlike police data, which are collected continuously over time, data obtained from victim surveys are usually discrete, and data collection occurs at a single point in time. Ideally, surveys of victims should follow victims over time to detect if and when further victimizations occur.

- **Attrition:** Victim surveys will be subject to attrition as some victims move or refuse to be surveyed. Attrition may be more likely for individuals who have been revictimized, thus distorting the amount of revictimization detected. Conversely, some studies suggest that victims who are pleased with the police response to an offense are more likely to call the police again.
- **Accuracy:** Victims may be unable to recall incidents accurately—particularly dates of incidents—or may be reluctant to discuss victimization, particularly incidents such as domestic violence or sexual assault. Surveys relating to such problems must be sensitive to the presence of an offender or others who may inhibit honesty. Victims may not consider some types of victimization crime or may not consider themselves victims.

8.3.3. Other Data Sources and Methods of Repeat Victimization

Even though there are other sources of information about revictimization already in existence, data about repeat victimization might still need to be gathered. Observations of the environment can yield important data. To increase the quantity and quality of information about offenses, properties that are susceptible to graffiti, such as transit corridors, pedestrian tunnels, or walls in urban areas that are prone to vandalism, should be monitored. These observations could be made every day, every week, or at vulnerable times like the weeks after school breaks. Interviews with convicted or seasoned offendould advance knowledge about recurrent victimization. These interviews won'twill not yield an empirical estimate of the frequency of recurrent victimization, but the insights from offenders may offer insight into target selection and a chance to stop recurrent victimization. Additional data sources that have been employed to identify recurrent victimization include inventory systems, hospital admissions and treatment in emergency rooms, as well as admissions to domestic violence shelters.

8.3.4. Improving Data Integrity

Different problems have different data limitations in terms of their magnitude and significance. For certain issues, da quality are rarely a problem—for example, bank robbery data are very accuratefully accurate and trustworthy in identifying revictimization. Inadequate data obscures the victimization of victims in other issues, like home invasions and domestic abuse. While data quality can often be improved, a decision to undertake such effort should consider the following factors:

- Extent of data limitations for problem being examined;
- Presumed value of improving data quality, including short-term and long-term benefits;
- Availability of alternate data or methods to improve data quality;
- Resources necessary to improve data quality.

Depending on the issue under investigation, more trustworthy data might be required. For example, highly credible data might be required to inform, motivate, persuade, or threaten private property owners to take expensive preventive measures if the data indicate that they ought to.

To lay the groundwork for a response, including winning support from those who might contribute to a decrease in victimization, it is crucial to meticulously record the degree of recurring victimization. The integrity of data can be readily enhanced, depending on the kind of problem being studied:

- **Collecting Additional Data:** Offense reports can easily be modified so that victims are asked a short series of questions about prior victimization.
- **Creating Data Layers:** In most jurisdictions, common types of locations—bars and nightclubs, budget motels, schools, banks, movie theatres, convenience stores, gasoline stations—will routinely generate similar types of crimes. For example, assaults will occur at the bars, vandalism at schools, robberies at banks, beer runs at convenience stores and so on. Police should integrate location identifiers into their records management systems so offenses among these location groups can be routinely monitored.
- **Combining Data Sources:** For some problems, victim interviews will provide better information about the impact of responses to problems such as domestic violence than police records. Crime reports may underestimate or overestimate the impact of responses—increased reporting does not demonstrate increased victimization and reduced reporting does not demonstrate reduced victimization. Conducting follow-up surveys with victims who previously reported an offense to the police provides more reliable measures of revictimization. Other data sources—such as calls for service, offense reports, arrests, property recovered, and warrants—can also be combined to create more comprehensive databases, for example, facilitating searches by both name, address and unique identifiers when available.
- **Increasing Data Precision:** Incident reporting forms and police records can be revised to improve specific location information.

Whenever possible, police should avoid recording offense locations as intersections or hundred block addresses. Each unit of an address should be routinely recorded—including building name or number, floor, office suite, or apartment number. For properties that have multiple addresses (such as an apartment complex that has addresses on more than one street), records management systems should be modified to link addresses. An alternative is to use mapping to reveal near-repeat offenses that are recorded on different streets. For offenses that occur in large public or private spaces such as parks or parking lots, police can use global positioning system (GPS) equipment to record precise coordinates for offenses.

- **Improving Data Quality:** Simple procedures, such as mapping offenses, can identify "match rates," or the proportion of offenses that can be linked to valid addresses. Consistent recording of offense types is very important. The distinctions between some offenses may seem trivial but have implications affecting revictimization. For example, if appliances are stolen from a house under construction, this might be classified as larceny or theft from a construction site, residential burglary, or commercial burglary. Offense classifications and recording practices should be monitored to ensure consistent classification and recording methods.
- **Data Sharing:** To detect revictimization across boundaries and jurisdictions, police agencies should routinely share data about victims. This is practical for counties or neighboring jurisdictions that participate in regional information networks. Individual victims may (unsuccessfully) relocate to avoid revictimization and revictimization of commercial properties. Virtual victims may be especially common across boundaries.

REFERENCES

1. Ashton, J., Brown, I., Senior, B., & Pease, K. (1998). Repeat victimisation: Offender accounts. *International Journal of Risk Security and Crime Prevention, 3*(4), 269–279.
2. Bennett, T. (1995). Identifying, explaining, and targeting burglary 'hot spots'. *European Journal of Criminal Policy and Research, 3*(3), 113–123.
3. Bennett, T., & Durie, L. (1999). *Preventing Residential Burglary in Cambridge: From Crime Audits to Targeted Strategies*. Police Research Series, Paper 108. London: Home Office.
4. Bowers, K., Hirschfield, A., & Johnson, S. (1998). Victimization revisited: A case study of non-residential repeat burglary in Merseyside. *British Journal of Criminology, 38*(3), 429–452.
5. Budd, T. (1999). Burglary of domestic dwellings: Findings from the British Crime Survey. *Bulletin 4/99*. London: Home Office.
6. Burquest, R., Farrell, G., & Pease, K. (1992). Lessons from schools. *Policing, 8*(2), 48–155.
7. Clarke, R., Perkins, E., & Smith, D. Jr. (2001). Explaining repeat residential burglaries: An analysis of property stolen. In G. Farrell & K. Pease (Eds.), *Repeat Victimization. Crime Prevention Studies, Vol. 12* (pp. 119–132). Monsey, NY: Criminal Justice Press.
8. Davis, R., & Maxwell, C. (2003). Preventing repeat incidents of family violence: A reanalysis of data from three field tests. *Final Report*. Washington, D.C.: National Institute of Justice.
9. Farrell, G., & Bouloukos, A. (2001). International overview: A cross-national comparison of rates of repeat victimization. In G. Farrell & K. Pease (Eds.), *Repeat Victimization. Crime Prevention Studies, Vol. 12* (pp. 17–30). Monsey, NY: Criminal Justice Press.
10. Felson, R., Messner, S., & Hoskin, A. (1999). The victim-offender relationship and calling the police in assaults. *Criminology, 37*(4), 931–947.
11. Hanmer, J., Griffiths, S., & Jerwood, D. (1999). *Arresting Evidence: Domestic Violence and Repeat Victimisation*. Police Research Series, Paper 104. London: Home Office.
12. Hotaling, G., & Buzawa, E. (2003). Forgoing criminal justice assistance: The non-reporting of new incidents of abuse in a court sample of domestic violence victims. *Final Report to the National Institute of Justice*. Washington, D.C.: National Institute of Justice.

13. Johnson, S., Bowers, K., & Hirschfield, A. (1997). New insights into the spatial and temporal distribution of repeat victimization. *British Journal of Criminology, 37*(2), 224–241.

14. Kingma, J. (1999). Repeat victimization of victims of violence: A retrospective study from a hospital emergency department for the period 1971–1995. *Journal of Interpersonal Violence, 14*(1), 79–90.

15. Kinsholt, G. (2001). Vehicle-related thefts: Practice message from the British Crime Survey. *Briefing Note*. London: Home Office.

16. Kleemans, E. (2001). Repeat burglary victimization: Results of empirical research in the Netherlands. In G. Farrell & K. Pease (Eds.), *Repeat Victimization. Crime Prevention Studies, Vol. 12* (pp. 233–246). Monsey, NY: Criminal Justice Press.

17. Lauritsen, J., & Quinet, K. (1995). Repeat victimization among adolescents and young adults. *Journal of Quantitative Criminology, 11*(2), 143-166.

18. LeBeau, J., & Vincent, K. (1998). Mapping it out: Repeat-address burglar alarms and burglaries. In D. Weisburd & T. McEwen (Eds.), *Crime Mapping and Crime Prevention. Crime Prevention Studies, Vol. 8* (pp. 289–310). Monsey, NY: Criminal Justice Press.

19. Lloyd, S., Farrell, G., & Pease, K. (1994). *Preventing Repeated Domestic Violence: A Demonstration Project on Merseyside.* Home Office Crime Prevention Unit Paper 49. London: Home Office.

20. Lynch, J., Berbaum, M., & Planty, M. (1998). *Investigating Repeated Victimization with the NCVS.* Final Report NCJ# 193415. Washington, D.C.: National Institute of Justice.

21. Matthews, R., Pease, C., & Pease, K. (2001). Repeated bank robbery: Theme and variations. In G. Farrell & K. Pease (Eds.), *Repeat Victimization. Crime Prevention Studies, Vol. 12* (pp. 153–166). Monsey, NY: Criminal Justice Press.

22. Mukherjee, S., & Carcach, C. (1998). *Repeat Victimisation in Australia.* Research and Public Policy Series, No. 15. Canberra: Australian Institute of Criminology.

23. Pease, K., & Laycock, G. (1996). *Revictimization: Reducing the Heat on Hot Victims.* Washington, D.C.: National Institute of Justice.

24. Polvi, N., Looman, T., Humphries, C., & Pease, K. (1991). The time course of repeat burglary victimization. *British Journal of Criminology, 31*(4), 411–414.

25. Ratcliffe, J., & McCullagh, M. (1998). Identifying repeat victimization with GIS. *British Journal of Criminology, 38*(4), 651–662.

26. Robinson, M. (1998). Burglary revictimization: The time period of heightened risk. *British Journal of Criminology, 38*(1), 78–87.
27. Schmerler, K., Wartell, J., & Weisel, D. (2004). Applied research in crime analysis and problem solving. In C. W. Bruce, J. Cooper, & S. Hick (Eds.), *Exploring Crime Analysis: Readings on Essential Skills* (pp. 109–120). Oakland Park, KS: IACA Press.
28. Sorenson, S., Siegel, J., Golding, J., & Stein, J. (1991). Repeated sexual victimization. *Violence and Victims, 6*(4), 299–308.
29. Taylor, N. (2004). Petrol service stations as victims of crime: Their risks and vulnerabilities. *Crime Prevention and Community Safety: An International Journal, 6*(1), 31–41.
30. Townsley, M., Homel, R., & Chaseling, J. (2000). Repeat burglary victimisation: Spatial and temporal patterns. *Australian and New Zealand Journal of Criminology, 33*(1), 37–63.
31. Trickett, A., Osborn, D., Seymour, J., & Pease, K. (1992). What is different about high crime areas? *British Journal of Criminology, 32*(1), 81–90.
32. Van Dijk, J. (2001). Attitudes of victims and repeat victims toward the police: Results of the International Crime Victims Survey. In G. Farrell & K. Pease (Eds.), *Repeat Victimization. Crime Prevention Studies, Vol. 12* (pp. 143–152). Monsey, NY: Criminal Justice Press.
33. Weisel, D. L. (2001). Repeat victimization for commercial burglary and robbery: How much and where? Presentation at the U.S. Department of Justice, National Institute of Justice, Crime Mapping Research Conference, Dallas, TX (December).

Chapter **9**

Pattern Identification Process

Contents

Introduction 340
9.1. Crime Pattern Identification Process 340
9.2. Persons Crime and Property Crime 352
9.3. Potential Responses to Patterns by Police 355
9.4. Identifying Meaningful Patterns 360
9.5. Property Crime Pattern Key Characteristics and Examples 367
9.6. Describing and Disseminating Known Patterns 377
References 388

INTRODUCTION

Identifying meaningful and useful patterns in crime is a crucial aspect of modern criminology and public safety, providing insights that can help prevent crime, allocate resources effectively, and develop targeted interventions. As crime continues to evolve with changes in technology, society, and the economy, the ability to detect patterns in criminal behavior, locations, and demographics has become increasingly important for law enforcement agencies, policymakers, and researchers.

One of the primary methods for identifying crime patterns is through crime mapping and spatial analysis. By examining the geographic distribution of crimes, analysts can identify hotspots—areas with a high concentration of criminal activity. These patterns often reveal underlying social, economic, and environmental factors that contribute to crime, such as poverty, unemployment, and lack of social services. Understanding these correlations allows for the development of focused strategies to address the root causes of crime in specific areas.

Temporal patterns, such as the times of day or days of the week when crimes are most likely to occur, also provide valuable insights. For example, certain types of crimes, like burglaries or assaults, may peak during specific times, helping law enforcement to optimize patrol schedules and deploy resources more effectively.

Moreover, with the advent of big data and advanced analytics, the ability to identify patterns in crime has reached new heights. Machine learning algorithms and predictive analytics can process vast amounts of data to uncover hidden trends and predict future crime occurrences with greater accuracy. This predictive approach allows for proactive crime prevention, rather than reactive responses, enabling law enforcement to anticipate and mitigate potential threats before they materialize.

Overall, the identification of meaningful and useful patterns in crime is integral to developing smarter, more efficient strategies for crime prevention and public safety, ultimately contributing to safer communities.

9.1. CRIME PATTERN IDENTIFICATION PROCESS

Law enforcement and criminologists employ the crime pattern identification process as a methodical way to examine crime data, identify patterns, and create plans for stopping and opposing illegal activity. With the development of technology and data analytics, this process has grown more complex, enabling quicker and more precise insights into criminal activity.

Data collection is the initial stage in the identification of criminal patterns. This entails compiling comprehensive data on crimes that have been reported, including the nature of the crime, the place, the time, and the attributes of the perpetrators and victims. Police reports, emergency calls, surveillance systems, and even social media are common sources of this information. Since the quality of the data greatly influences the quality of the analysis, accurate and thorough data collection is essential.

Following collection, the data is sorted and examined using a variety of techniques. Geographic information systems (GIS) are frequently used in crime mapping, a technique that involves visualizing crime data on maps. This aids in locating spatial patterns, such as high-crime-activity areas known as "crme hotspots.." Another important technique is temporal analysis, which looks at crime timing to find patterns according to the day of the week, season, or time ofay. The data isare then subjected to sophisticated analytical techniques, such as machine learning algorithms and statistical techniques. These instruments can reveal more profound trends and relationships that might not be immediately apparent, like links between various crime kinds or the influence of socioeconomic variables on crime rates. A more recent development, predictive analytics forecasts probable future crime occurrences using historical data, enabling proactive law enfoimately, decisionsDecisions are made with the knowledge gathered from the analysis. This could entail boosting police presence in particular regions, modifying patrol plans, or launching neighborhood-based programs designed to deal with the underlying causes of crime. Thus, the process of identifying crime patterns is an essential tool in contemporary policing, improving the capacity to safeguard communities through data-driven tactics.

9.1.1. Pattern Identification Methodology

The primary objective of tactical crime analysis is pattern identification, which includes, among other things, making connections between crimes based on person, vehicle, and modus operandi (MO) attributes. The majority of the work done for tactical crime analysis is pattern identification. This section explains the different kinds of tactical crime analysis patterns that are found, the methods used to find patterns (e.g., induction and deduction), as well as the methodical techniques for identifying and finalizing patterns initially.

9.1.2. Types of Patterns

A crime pattern is a collection of two or more crimes that are reported to the police or uncovered by them. These crimes are analyzed as a single unit because: (i) they are notable and distinct crimes that share one or more key characteristics;

(ii) there is no known relationship between the victim and the offender; and (iii) the criminal activity is usually short-, 2011b). In order toTo organize pattern recognition and establish a common vocabulary for discussing patterns among police departments and their communities, the International Association of Crime Analysts (2011b) divided crime patterns into seven primary categories. The following are definitions of the seven types according to the IACA (2011b):

- Series is a group of similar crimes thought to be committed by the same individual or group of individuals acting in concert. Examples: Four commercial arsons citywide in which a black male between the ages of 45 and 50 wearing yellow sweatpants, a black hooded sweatshirt, and a yellow "Yankees" cap was observed leaving the commercial structures immediately after the fire alarm was triggered; five home invasion–style robberies involving two to three white males in their 20s wearing stockings over their faces, displaying a silver, double-barreled shotgun, and driving a red 2000 to 2010 Honda Civic.
- Spree is a specific type of series characterized by high frequency of criminal activity within a remarkably short time frame, to the extent that the activity appears almost continuous. Examples: A rash of thefts from autos at a parking garage over the course of 1 hour; multiple apartments in a high-rise building burglarized during daytime hours on a single day.
- Hot prey refers to a group of crimes, committed by one or more individuals, involving victims who share similar physical characteristics and/or engage in similar behavior. Examples: five home invasion robberies of new immigrant Asian families occurring throughout the city over 6 weeks; seven fraudulent check scams targeting elderly victims over 1 week; 10 robberies, committed by different offenders, of intoxicated persons walking home alone from the bars on the weekend over 2 months.
- Hot spot refers to a group of similar crimes committed by one or more individuals at locations within close proximity to one another (IACA, 2011b); it is also called a micro-time hot spot (Santos and Santos, 2015d). It is important to more clearly differentiate micro-time hot spots from long-term or macro-time hot spots (i.e., problem areas) since the micro-time hot spot is the most common type of pattern identified by crime analysts. Thus, a micro-time hot spot is the emergence of several closely related crimes within a few minutes' travel distance from one another (i.e., micro-place) that occurs within a relatively short period of time (i.e., micro-time)—a crime "flare-up" (Santos and Santos, 2015c). Examples: four daytime burglaries

over the past 2 weeks at a suburban residential subdivision, with no notable similarities in method of entry or known suspects; 10 commercial burglaries over the course of 3 weeks at businesses located within a 0.5-mile radius during overnight hours.

- Hot setting refers to a group of similar crimes committed by one or more individuals that are primarily related by type of place where the crimes occurred. Examples: seven late-night robberies of 24-hour convenience stores throughout the city by different offenders over 2 weeks; five burglaries of duplex homes adjacent to the same abandoned railway bed over a single weekend; 10 thefts from commercial vans/trucks parked at night in residential neighborhoods over 3 weeks.
- Hot place refers to a group of similar crimes committed by one or more individuals at the same location. Examples: a local movie theatre that has experienced 10 thefts from auto, three incidents of graffiti on the building, and two strong-arm robberies in the parking lot over the course of 1 month; an apartment community that has experienced two stranger-on-stranger sexual assaults, one drug-related shooting, and five residential burglaries within 3 weeks.
- Hot product refers to a group of crimes committed by one or more individuals in which a unique type of property is targeted for theft. Clarke (1999) coined this term, defining hot products as "those consumer items that are most attractive to thieves." Examples: four thefts of handguns taken out of vehicles at residential and commercial places in 2 weeks; 15 burglaries of vacant homes and construction sites in which only copper wiring and piping was taken over 6 weeks; 10 thefts of laptops and smartphones occurring across one college campus during the first month of school.

It is noteworthy that these pattern types are not exclusive of one another (i.e., a pattern can have multiple types). However, the most specific type should be selected when choosing which to apply to a pattern of crimes. For instance, it is both a series and a hot setting if a pattern of the same suspect robbing convenience stores is found. Because the title "series" gives more specific information about the pattern—the same suspect is more specific than the same type of place—the analyst would label it as such.

9.1.3. Deduction and Induction

One of two general situations arises when a crime analyst attempts to find a pattern: either the analyst has a large number of cases from which to find a pattern, or the analyst has one crime that can be linked to other crimes. These investigative techniques are known as deduction and induction, respectively, in the social sciences.

When employing the deductive method, a researcher begins with broad concepts regarding the phenomenon of interest and proceeds to particular facts that corroborate these conceptual frameworks. By employing this technique, pattern analysis analysts look at all crimes simultaneously and look for patterns. Based on shared characteristics, Figure 9.1 shows how an analyst would infer a pattern from a large number of incidents. The analyst starts by looking through every burglary before concentrating on commercial burglaries, followed by those that happen in Beat 46 and at doctor's offices. Lastly, the analyst concentrates on business burglaries in Beat 46 that take place at doctors' offices during the night and on the weekends when the establishments are closed. Critical thinking and commonalities among the incidents are the basis for each level of the analyst's decision-making. For instance, the analysts would search for crimes in Beat 46 at a different type of location if there was only one commercial burglary in Beat 46, which occurred at doctors' offices.

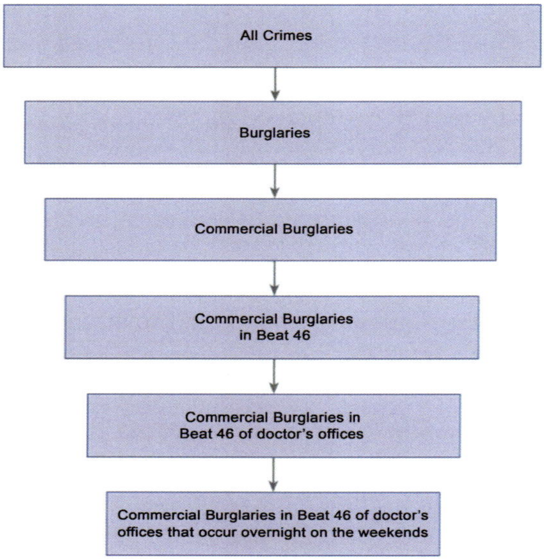

Figure 9.1. *Pattern identification: deduction.*

Source. Rachel Boba Ss, Crime Analysis Withwith Crime Mapping, ISBN: 9781506331034.

On the other hand, the inductive approach entails connecting particular facts or concepts to broader ideas. When conducting pattern analysis, an analyst employing induction first concentrates on a single crime before searching for patterns in a collection of other crimes. An analyst would apply the inductive method to identify a robbery pattern, as shown in Figure 9.2. In the first instance, a white man poses as a woman and robs a bank. The analyst searches for additional robberies that have traits similar to the first one, starting with this one.

There are multiple ways in which crime analysts can locate the case for which they start the inductive method of pattern identification. One method is to look for anomalies in the crime database, which entails finding unique or uncommon traits that are comparatively uncommon for that particular crime type and/or jurisdiction (e.g., a man posing as a woman robbing a business; grand theft of priceless paintings; and commercial burglaries where the perpetrator makes an opening in the wall of a nysts may also be notifiedare notified about cases by detectives who are looking into crimend connecting the dots.s, or by other law enforcement officers who receive reports or notice unusual criminal activity.

9.1.4. Initial Pattern Identification

Analysts need to be adept at critical thinking and able to find similarities between the ferime incidents in order toto identify patterns in crime (Paulsen et al., 2009). This process necessitates analytical abilities and knowledge of crime, but it is neither mathematical nor precisely defined. As a general guide for pattern analysis, a two-step procedure for finding a pattern is provided in this chapter. In order to confirm that the pattern discovered is valid, the analyst must first connect all of the cases that could form a pattern (initial pattern identification). This process is followed by a closer examination of thoown as pattern finalizationfinalization, and covered later in this chapter. To identify patterns initially, crime analysts employ three methods: (i) ad hoc linking, (ii) weights and thresholds, and (iii) query method. Analysts can examine cases inductively or deductively by using any of these techniques.

Ad hoc linking, the most informal method of pattern identification, is when people link cases together by memory while they are going about their daily business. Despite the lack of systematicity in this approach, analysts frequently use it to find numerous patterns. The query method and the weights and thresholds method are the two other more formal techniques that analysts typically use to follow up on ad hoc linking. Using a combination of deductive and inductive reasoning, the analyst searches a database and creates links between cases that share similar features in the query method.

The second way to find preliminary patterns is mathematically, where the analyst gives weights to different aspects of crimes and then aggregates the weights for each crime using a statistical or other kind of program. After the weights are established, the analyst has two options: using the inductive method, they can match the characteristics of one case to the entire database, or using the deductive method, they can search for any cases that share a certain threshold of similarity with one another. Different weights for different types of crimes (e.g., bank robbery, street robbery, commercial burglary, and residential burglary) and traits (e.g., point of entry, description of the suspect, and time).

Since crime analysts employ the query method the most out of the three, it is covered in greater detail here. Querying is an iterative process used in initial pattern identification, wherein the analyst manipulates, searches, and sorts crime characteristics in a database matrix to create links between crimes that share similar characteristics. In order to find patterns, the analyst first employs induction or deduction.

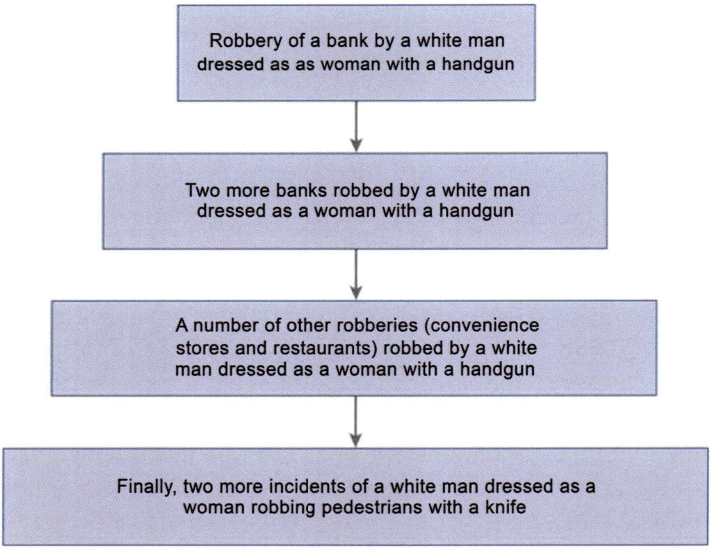

Figure 9.2. *Pattern identification: induction.*

Source: Rachel Boba Santos, Crime Analysis With Crime Mapping, ISBN: 9781506331034.

The analyst usually sorts the crime report cases in order to view the results more conveniently and examine them visually. As the analyst can see, there are several instances where the side door, another window, and the master bedroom window were used as entry points. Even more intriguingly, the table demonstrates that the closets were thoroughly searched during the crimes where the perpetrator broke through the window of the master bedroom. These cases could represent the start of a first trend. Cases where the criminal forced the sliding door open to enter the house could form another pattern. In order to determine whether there are any additional early parallels, the analyst would examine the times and dates of these incidents as well as the police report narratives.

In order to enable analysts to compare multiple cases and columns quickly and scan fields for relevant information, pattern analysis requires the use of electronic data matrices through software like Microsoft Excel or Access, IMB's SPSS, or specialized crime analysis software. An analyst could arrange the matrix, for example, so that the variables most relevant to robberies—such as location type, weapon, suspect's actions against the victim, and suspect description—are easily analyzed together in order to identify a series of robberies. An analyst may arrange the matrix so that the data on the point of entry, the method of entry, the property taken, and the location are near to one another in order to spot a pattern of residential burglaries. If a matrix's variables are positioned fixedly (e.g., as they were initially kept in the database or as a paper matrix), the analyst is probably going to have trouble seeing the pertinent variables by various crime categories.

The analysis query method is straightforward but effective. It takes into account the analyst's requirement to visually inspect data in order to spot patterns. The analyst can "see" patterns in the data by adjusting the matrix and using data queries to group, sort, and improve the outcomes.

9.1.5. Pattern Finalization

The process of narrowing down the initial list of crimes and identifying those that are closely connected and share important traits is known as "pattern finalization.." For instance, all crimes committed at businesses in a specific area during the previous month could be included in the initial identification of a commercial burglary pattern. While concluding this pattern, the analyst may exclude a few afternoon crimes that happened during the week because the remaining crimes happened at night or on the weekends. Three steps make up the inductive methodology for finalizing a pattern: identifying the principal case, identifying other important cases within the pattern, and identifying any further related cases.

9.1.6. Identifying the Principal Case

The first step for the analyst is to choose a crime from the initial list that most accurately illustrates the pattern and has the greatest amount of detail. The other crucial cases in the pattern are then identified by the analyst using this principal case as a guide. The analyst bases his or her method for identifying the principal case on the salient features of that specific category of crime (e.g., suspicious behavior in the case of robberies, and the kind and proximity of residential burglary locations. When two crimes have almost all of the same essential elements, an analyst may occasionally distinguish between two principal cases. One or two main cases can be handled using the procedures that follow. The primary case in this process would be the one that started the initial pattern identification if the analyst had employed the inductive method.

9.1.7. Identifying Other Key Cases in the Pattern

The analyst must determine which characteristics areative of the pattern in order toto find the cases that are closely related to the principal case. Typically, these characteristics are the same ones that were used to determine the principal case (e.g., suspicious behavior in the case of robberies, and the kind and proximity of residential burglary locations. Subsequently, the analyst applies an inductive method to compare the salient features of each crime in the original list with the main case. Since it is rarely known if crimes are genuinely related, the analyst's final decisions about which crimes should be included in the pattern are based on critical thinking.

9.1.8. Identifying Additional Related Cases

By now, the analyst has decided which crimes from the original pattern should be included in the final pattern and which ones should be left out. The analyst can make sure that no more crimes have gone unnoticed by running a second query against the original database using the essential elements of the final pattern. Furthermore, the analyst must investigate additional databases that might hold crimes associated with the pattern, moving from databases of recent crimes (e.g., those in the last four months) to databases that are older or archived. Once more, the analyst queries the archived data using the salient features of the principal case. The secret to a successful pattern analysis is thoroughness. Analysts search individual databases maintained by numerous law enforcement agencies, which might ncted to tactical data, in order toto find possible connections to prevailing patterns.

Since criminals do not confine themselves to the boundaries of police jurisdiction, analysts also ask nearby police departments for assistance in concluding patterns. Before publishing the pattern bulletin, analysts would speak with other analysts to see if they had any similar crimes, especially in cases of larger-scale crimes like commercial robberies and burglaries. Consequently, an analyst must consult all internal and external sources that may contain pertinent data before concluding and disseminating information about a pattern.

9.1.9. Identifying Investigative Leads

Finding investigative leads for both unique crimes and trends is the second objective of tactical crime analysis. Given that many crimes lack identified suspects (e.g., the identities and residences of the perpetrators), tactical crime analysts will collaborate with investigators to support the inquiry by pointing out possible suspects for specific crimes as well as trends. The analyst's first step in locating an investigative lead for a pattern is to locate the most pertinent and trustworthy suspect description or other information that can be used to connect an individual, much like in locating the principal case (e.g., dates, times, and locations of a burglary can be connected to the details of a suspicious person's field information. As with pattern identification, suspect identification requires thoroughness and critical thinking; analysts must be sure to take into account all plausible suspects. For instance, it would be illogical to omit either Black or White people from a list of possible leads if witnesses have described a suspect as a pale Black man or a tan White man with an unidentifiable accent. In fact, considering this general description, it would be prudent for the analyst to also include Native Americans, Arabic speakers, and Hispanics, as these groups may also contain individuals who match the witnesses' description. In certain cases, analysts can deduce details about a suspect from the available data, including strength (e.g., a door smashed during the crime), the usage of implements (e.g., scratches on a window), as well as entry to a place (e.g., The crime took place within a 15-minute time frame. many hours).

After identifying a key suspect description, the analyst compares the description's attributes with information from multiple databases containing information on offenders and suspects. The following databases would be searched with an emphasis on an offender's current residence and its proximity to the crimes in the pattern, as theory and research suggest that offenders commit crimes close to where they live.

- **Arrest Database:** This database is contained in the agency's RMS and includes information on individuals that have been arrested by the analyst's agency. A search of the arrest database by residential address, type of crime, MO, and suspect description can produce the names of individuals who have been arrested for committing the type of crime of the pattern and/or who live in the pattern area.
- **Probation and Parole Database:** This database is housed in the department of corrections and contains records of individuals who have been or are on parole or probation. A search of this database can produce names of individuals who were convicted of a particular type of crime and were recently released from prison or are currently on probation or parole.

- **NCIC Database:** This database contains records of all individuals throughout the United States who have been arrested and/or convicted of crimes. This database is often too broad if a crime analyst does not know the name or address of an offender, but it can be used in conjunction with other databases to provide information on an individual.
- **Registered Sex of Ender Database:** This database contains information on individuals who have been arrested and convicted of sex crimes and have registered with the state as required by law. While the individuals will be in the other databases mentioned in this section, it provides a mechanism to search only sex offenders living in the jurisdiction, no matter where they committed their crimes (i.e., sex offenders are required to register based on where they live; they also must re-register when they move). Analysts can search the sex offender database by residential address, description, and type of crimes committed to identify potential suspects for related sex crimes (e.g., sex offenders convicted for abusing children living in the area of a current pattern of child abduction).
- **Field Information Database:** As discussed earlier in this chapter, this database contains information about individuals who have exhibited suspicious behavior and individuals who have unique features and have been contacted by police officers. Analysts may identify potential leads by searching this database for information that matches a current pattern by proximity to the pattern, time of day of week (e.g., suspicious vehicle in an area), unique features (e.g., a person with particular scars, marks, or tattoos), or other unique information (e.g., a person found behind a commercial place with a hammer or other tools that can be used for burglary).
- **Vehicle Databases:** These are databases in which vehicles are represented as cases. They can be either a departmental database that lists vehicles that have been in crashes, stolen, recovered, found, or used in a crime within the analyst's jurisdiction or a database maintained by the state's motor vehicle division that has records of all registered vehicles. Both types of databases allow searches by various characteristics (e.g., VIN, plate number, and make/model) of vehicles, and analysts search them to identify the owners of vehicles used in the commission of crimes and identify potential suspects. Officers and citizens are more likely to identify vehicles than people, and vehicle ownership can be easily determined with tag information. They can also be identified or the possible vehicles narrowed down

with less specific information through more complex searches. In more recent years, some agencies have implemented license plate reader technology equipment that captures license plates of vehicles that drive by (Koper, Lum, Willis, Woods, and Hibdon, 2015). The vehicle plate information is captured as well as the date, time, and location of when the plate was read. Analysts can search the database to identify cars that were in the vicinity of individual crimes or of patterns.

Apart from these databases, analysts also review data from other sources, such as people contacted by state troopers, private security firms, federal agencies, local sheriff offices, and other organizations that gather information on criminals. These data are frequently shared by analysts via both official forums and networks and more casual means (e.g., e-mails).

9.1.10. Clearing Cases

Helping police clear cases is one of tactical crime analysis's other objectives. This is the procedure that connects open cases to a recently resolved case in an effort to close them and strengthen case against a specific suspect. It'sIt is crucial to remember that while crime analysts support this process, detectives and prosecutors are legally tasked with deciding whether or not cases can be connected. For instance, a suspect in two residential burglaries in a specific area is apprehended by a detective. An analyst who has been looking through data for the last six months discovers that four more burglaries have occurred in that area. With this knowledge, the investigator could question the suspect (e.g., "Did you commit these as well?"), or fingerprints or DNA evidence could link the suspect to the other cases. If the crimes are connected, one arrest clears six burglaries instead of two, the police department closes four more burglary cases, and the prosecutor can charge the person with additional crimes.

The process of clearing cases is inductive. Since one crime (the solved case) is identified and compared with others to see if any meaningful relationships exist, it adheres to the pattern finalization method. Closing entire patterns is another part of clearing cases. Analysts reexamine previously released data on recognized patterns for arrested individuals' connections to recent arrests during this process. An AK-47 was allegedly used by a suspect in a recent spate of robberies, according to a published crime pattern. Four months later, there were still robberies, but patrol officers arrested a man who had an AK-47 in his car during a traffic stop. In an effort to connect the suspect to these crimes and clear his name, a crime analyst would compare this person's description to the suspect description in the robbery pattern and forward this information to the officers for further gun comparisons or so they can use the pattern information in the suspect's interview. The methods of pattern recognition, lead generation, and case resolution are systematic and require particular techniques and methods; however, the analyst's critical thinking, informed by their skills, experience, and the task at hand, shapes each analysis situation in a unique way. These procedures are less technical and more intellectual.

9.2. PERSONS CRIME AND PROPERTY CRIME

The distinction between patterns of property crime and patterns of person crime serves as a guide for pattern identification in tactical crime analysis. That is to say, since the traits that connect crimes involving people to one another are fundamentally distinct from those connecting crimes involving property, people and property crimes are typically investigated independently. Crimes against persons are those in which the victim is the intended victim of the offender. Indecent exposure, public sexual indecency, stranger sexual assault, and robbery are the crimes that are frequently investigated for a person's crime pattern analysis. Some analysts may look at the crimes of other people through pattern analysis (e.g., violent assaults, and shootings between strangers), but since these are the most frequent, the topic of this discussion will be restricted to robberies, stranger sexual assault, indecent exposure, and public indecency.

Since the victims of most crimes are also the witnesses, analysts can learn a great deal about the suspect's actions, description, and any vehicles involved in the crime. Because so much information about each crime is used to link incidents by offender, series or sprees of crimes are the types of patterns that are typically found for individuals. Analysts find patterns involving hot settings, hot prey, or hot spots less frequently. While there are no common suspects in these kinds of patterns, they do have similar traits like proximity, victim type, and location. The following are examples of some specific persons crime patterns:

- **Series, Indecent Exposure:** A suspect on a mountain bike approaches female pedestrians and exposes himself. Four incidents have occurred over a 1-month period, and the suspect's description, bicycle description, and actions are very similar in all four incidents.
- **Spree, Carjacking:** Three carjackings have occurred within the city in a period of 3 hours. Two suspects use a car to cut the victim off in traffic and force the victim to stop; then one suspect approaches the victim's car and orders the victim out of the car at gunpoint. That suspect drives away in the victim's car, and the other drives away in the suspect car.
- **Hot Place, Mall Parking Lot:** Several incidents of robbery of pedestrians and indecent exposure have occurred in a mall parking

lot near the movie theaters over a 1-month period. The crimes appear to have been committed by different people, based on various suspect descriptions by witnesses.

- **Hot Prey, Female Pedestrians:** Several types of vehicles have been observed driving through a residential area during evening hours. On several occasions, the driver of each vehicle is alone and exposed himself to a female pedestrian. Because the incidents have all occurred at night, officers have not been able to obtain detailed suspect and vehicle descriptions, but the targeted victims have all been women walking on the street.
- **Hot Setting, Convenience Stores:** Several incidents of strongarm robbery have occurred in the past week at a particular chain of convenience stores throughout the city, yet different MOs and suspect descriptions indicate that multiple suspects are responsible for the crimes.

9.2.1. Property Crimes

Crimes against property refer to those in which the perpetrator targets tangible assets. Theft from vehicles, auto theft, residential burglary, and commercial burglary are the crimes that are frequently investigated for property crime pattern analysis. Theft from buildings, criminal trespass, grand theft, and criminal damage incidents are also investigated in relation to these other crimes or if they show overt property theft and vandalism (e.g., vandalism of mailboxes, theft of building supplies). Since witnesses are frequently absent when property crimes are committed, crime analysts typically have little to no suspect data at their disposal to utilize for pattern recognition. Analysts typically use information on the different categories of crimes (e.g., home versus. business burglary), the kinds of environments (e.g., apartment complexes, single-family homes, and workplace buildings), as well as the incidents' proximity. To a somewhat lesser extent, temporal characteristics and modus operandi (MO) are also employed. Hot spots, hot settings, hot products, and sprees are the patterns that are most frequently found in the analysis of property crimes. Here are some examples:

- **Micro-Time Hot Spot, Residential Burglaries:** Three residential burglaries have occurred in a specific neighborhood within a 0.15-mile radius of one another. In all of the burglaries, suspects gained entry to the homes by breaking or prying open a rear window. Various types of property have been taken, from small electronics to jewelry and cash. Suspect information is not available, as there have been no witnesses to any of the incidents.

- **Hot Place, Apartment Community:** Ten incidents of theft from vehicle have occurred at the same 100-unit apartment community over 14 days. All incidents have occurred overnight, with several nights having multiple cars hit. Property taken varies from cash and electronics to parts of the vehicles (e.g., emblems, car covers). In some cases, no force was used, and in all cases, no suspect information is available.
- **Hot Setting, New Home Construction Sites:** Seven burglaries have occurred in the past 6 days at new home construction sites at a new 500-home development. Suspects break into or enter unlocked houses in their final stages of construction to steal appliances or on-site construction equipment. The incidents have all taken place at night, and no suspect information has been obtained. Different tire marks have been found at the scenes, indicating the use of several different types of vehicles.
- **Hot Product, Pool Equipment:** 15 thefts from residential backyard pools have occurred over a 4-week period during the day and night. Portable pool equipment is the only property taken in each incident.
- **Spree, Vandalism of Vehicles:** 13 vehicles along the same street were damaged over 1 night. It seems as though the same suspect(s) committed the crimes because the cars were next to one another and damaged in the same way— taillights broken; mirrors damaged— with what seems to be a baseball bat.

Crime analysts sometimes look at both property and person crimes together, even though they should be examined for different reasons. Some examples of such patterns include the following:

- **Series, Burglary and Robbery:** Two "cat" burglaries (when the suspect enters the house at night while the residents are home) and two robberies of residents walking down the street have occurred in the same neighborhood. Suspect information is available and similar for all of these incidents.
- **Spree, Burglary and Carjacking:** A young man burglarizes a business suite late at night and leaves the scene by carjacking a vehicle. The man then crashes the vehicle into a different retail store's front window, enters the store, and steals additional property. All of these incidents take place within a 1-hour period.
- **Hot Place, Water Park:** Over the past 2 weeks, a water park had 10 thefts from vehicle and four robberies of customers in its parking lot, as well as five public sexual indecency incidents inside the park

itself. There are a range of suspect descriptions, and there have been no crimes at the park in the 2 months previous while it has been open.

- **Hot Product, Video Games and Consoles:** During the past 2 months, nine houses across the city have been burglarized, and video game consoles and games have been the only property taken. In addition, two robberies have occurred in which video games have been taken from individuals in a gaming store's parking lot, and there was one commercial burglary from a large box store in which 50 gaming consoles were taken.

9.3. POTENTIAL RESPONSES TO PATTERNS BY POLICE

To find significant and practical patterns, crime analysts must comprehend how police apply the findings of pattern analysis for responses aimed at reducing crime. The problem-solving process's scanning and analysis phases are represented by patterns, or SARA (scanning, analysis, response, assessment). As a result, the response is customized in accordance with the precise pattern information that the analysis results provide. For instance, if a neighborhood's daytime residential burglaries are a pattern, stopping those crimes during the day would be a successful way to break that pattern. It is not considered a failure of the response if there are more burglaries that happen at night, in a different neighborhood, or to businesses in that area because the response to the pattern would not address burglaries with these characteristics (e.g., at night, to establishments, or somewhere else). Similar to recurring events, the goal is to pinpoint specific activities and react suitably to these short-term, smaller-scale issues in order to prevent them from growing into longer-term, more significant issues.

Police responses to patterns are generally simple and center on both crime prevention and the arrest and deterrence of offenders (Boba and Santos, 2011; Bruce, 2008b). To be more precise, the following details the methods that police usually employ to identify patterns. Notably, the times and locations of the crimes within the pattern—which could occur on any day of the week or at any hour of the day—are observed by the directed patrol, field contacts, surveillance, and sting operations. In contrast, normal business hours are when the pattern investigation and case clearing, direct communication with potential victims, and public dissemination of pattern information take place (i.e., weekdays starting at 8 a.m. up until 5 p.m.) and/or regular wake-up times on any given day.

- **Directed Patrol:** This strategy focuses on police patrol in the areas and at the times in which a pattern is occurring. Police patrol in cars, on bikes, or on foot. The objective of the directed patrol is for the police to arrest offenders committing a crime or to deter offenders by increasing guardianship and the offenders' perceived risk of being caught.
- **Field Contacts:** While conducting directed patrol, police officers make contact with individuals in the pattern area and, in some cases, at the time when the pattern is occurring (i.e., daylight hours for residential burglary). They contact individuals who appear to be suspicious and/or who might have information about the crime pattern. This strategy can deter potential offenders from committing crime by talking to them specifically, as well as provide potential investigative leads or intelligence that can help solve the individual crimes or the entire pattern. (For more information on both directed patrol and field contacts, see the Center for Problem-Oriented Policing [POP Center] response guide The Benefits and Consequences of Police Crackdowns (Scott, 2004)).
- **Surveillance:** This response involves the police to watch and wait in a particular area at a particular time for a crime to happen in order to make an arrest. This is different than directed patrol in which officers drive around the entire area because surveillance is often static and focused on one street block or location. When officers conduct surveillance, this response is used only in the most specific patterns (e.g., robberies of one movie theater's employees when they leave work at the end of the night). This is because personnel costs are very high (e.g., officer overtime). However, with modern technology, static or movable surveillance cameras can be used to observe and record the activity around a particular location or street block. (For more information, see the POP Center response guide Sting Operations (Newman, 2007) and Video Surveillance of Public Places (Ratcliffe, 2006).
- **"Sting" or "Bait" Operations:** This response requires a situation in which people or property that have been targeted in a particular pattern are put out as "bait" for offenders. Police then directly observe the bait or have electronic monitoring that allows them to arrest the offender or record (on video) offenders committing the crimes when the bait is taken. Some examples include a "bait car" for theft from vehicle or vehicle theft, or an undercover police officer for a robbery (For more information, see the POP Center response guide Sting Operations (Newman, 2007).

- **Investigating the Pattern and Clearing Cases:** Because a pattern becomes a unit of response for the police department, in addition to being assigned individual crimes, detectives can be assigned a pattern to investigate. The detective would then investigate all the crimes in the pattern together, looking at how, for example, fingerprints and evidence might cross over cases, which allows them to piece together information about the suspect, victims, and related information from the group of related cases (instead of one case at a time). Notably, not all crime reports taken by patrol officers in the field are actually assigned to detectives to investigate. This might be because of lack of evidence or just because the police department prioritizes based on its resources. Thus, in any given pattern, there might be cases that are not otherwise being investigated, so doing this gives the detectives the opportunity to clear more cases. That is, if an arrest is made related to one or more crimes in that pattern, the pattern can be used to clear the other related cases.
- **Contacting Potential Victims Directly:** Crime prevention education works best when it is targeted at specific victims, times, and areas. This response can include either volunteers or police officers contacting specific groups of citizens, residents, or businesses that are most relevant to a particular pattern. The contact can be made in person, over the phone (e.g., reverse 911), through a letter via postal mail, through flyers left at homes or businesses, or through the Internet, e-mail, or social media. The information would include details of the pattern, crime prevention advice, and contact information for the police. Crime prevention advice would include suggestions with immediate results (e.g., lock doors and windows) and those with more long term results (e.g., installing video surveillance equipment or alarms). (For more information about crime prevention publicity campaigns, see the POP Center response guide Crime Prevention Publicity Campaigns (Barthe, 2006).
- **Providing Pattern Information to the Public:** By disseminating patterns to the general public, police encourage the public to provide additional information ("tips") on known crimes as well as to report crimes that have not yet been reported. Also, when offenders see that the police know about their activities, they might be deterred from continuing their offending. Information about patterns also would provide specific crime prevention advice and would encourage individuals to protect themselves. Media such as newspaers, radio, television, and the Internet are used to provide this information. (For

more information about crime prevention publicity campaigns, see the POP Center response guide Crivention Publicity Campaigns (Barthe, 2006)).

Here'sHere is a quick rundown of how police can use these responses for individual person crimes and property crimes.

9.3.1. Persons Crime

As was previously mentioned, people's crime patterns are usually series or sprees, which indicates to the analyst that they believe the same individual or group of individuals has committed all of the crimes. The pattern will include specific MO information and descriptions of the suspect, so police responses are concentrated on improving the investigation and making it easier to apprehend the offender(s). A person's criminal history can raise the possibility that they will be arrested because when several crimes are connected, all the details come together to paint a fuller picture of the suspect and his actions. For instance, the rape victim might give a general description of the suspect along with particular details regarding the suspect's behavior. The victim might have given a more thorough description of the suspect in a different rape incident that has been connected by the suspect's actions. The investigators have more comprehensive information by combining the details from the two crimes, which may raise the possibility of an arrest.

Police use directed patrols and surveillance to address individuals' crime patterns. To help with this process, crime analysts can use information about crime patterns to try and predict when and where the offender might strike again. When an offence is successful, offenders frequently repeat the same actions, and they may select comparable circumstances to carry out their crimes depending on their own daily routines and areas of activity. The only method to determine whether a criminal is ris actions is to connect crimes that are similar tolike one another. For example, patrol officers can concentrate their uncommitted patrol time in these areas, stopping suspicious people, and detectives can conduct surveillance on locations where it seems likely that people might be robbed if the offender has been robbing people at bank ATMs around malls on weekends during the evening.

In response to an individual's crime patterns, police also provide crime prevention education to potential victims and managers of particular locations. For instance, when a spate of convenience store robberies occurs, police may give managers of convenience stores pamphlets containing situational crime prevention advice. At a time when there is a spate of stranger rapes at bars in which the suspect is giving his victims a "date rape" drug, they may also educate bar owners, managers, and customers about crime prevention.

Lastly, police usually inform the public about an individual's criminal history. Information about a person's criminal history is typically shared with the public via the media (e.g., newspapers, radio, TV, the Internet, and social media). Usually, series about stranger rape, robberies, and similar crimes are publicized. While single-victim cases are frequently covered by the media, crimes involving multiple people are far more serious and attract greater attention because the suspect is acting in the same way. Once this information is made available to the public, a variety of things may occur. It is possible to report crimes that have already been committed but have not been reported to the authorities. Witnesses to crimes that are already part of a pattern may come forward with more information when they realize the crimes are part of a larger series, which is another effect of media exposure. Last but not least, giving the public access to pattern information enables them to defend themselves. Because the shooters were targeting people in public spaces, the media's coverage of the Washington, DC, sniper case in 2002—in which ten people appeared to be shot at random in public spaces—encouraged residents of the DC area to stay indoors and only venture outside when absolutely necessary.

9.3.2. Property Crime

Police responses to property crime patterns concentrate more on victim education and deterrence than on apprehending suspects because the probability of arresting suspects for property crime is significantly lower than for person crime. The most crucial way that police address patterns of property crime is by warning prospective victims to take precautions. People are far more likely to use crime prevention techniques if they perceive an immediate threat, as was previously mentioned. Police target particular individuals in pattern areas based on patterns in property crimes. Techniques like reverse 911 (i.e., police can notify potential victims in a number of ways, including by going door-to-door, leaving an automated phone message for a group of residents in a specific area, and writing letters to residents or businesses to advise them of the pattern and suggest pertinent crime prevention measures. Other strategies include, but are not limited to, meeting with particular neighborhood or business groups and publishing patterns online or on social media. The intention is to provide details about the trend in crime as well as particular measures that individuals can take to safeguard their property (e.g., lock their car doors), alter actions that lead to criminal activity (e.g., take valuables out of their cars), or raise consciousness (e.g., watch out for shady characters in their neighborhoods).

Since property crimes are frequently connected by proximity, i.e., hot spots), police use targeted patrol to discourage criminal activity and, infrequently, apprehend criminals as they are. Hotspot policing is effective in lowering crime, particularly when it comes to transient problems like patterns. In order to raise police visibility and increase offenders' perception of the risk of being caught, directed patrol can be carried out in police cars, on bikes, or on foot. Furthermore, police have the ability to establish field contacts with suspicious individuals and vehicles while conducting this kind of patrol. By enhancing police contact, this can serve as a deterrent to crime and possibly lead to leads for future investigations into specific crimes and patterns.

In certain cases, property crime patterns can aid in the arrest of suspects, but after a suspect is taken into custody for a single crime, they usually aid in the resolution of subsequent cases. For instance, a crime analyst can create a pattern of vehicle burglaries that occur in the same location at the same time as a suspect who has been arrested by a detective for breaking into cars in a specific area. After receiving that information, the detective could use it to question the suspect or go over the proof to determine whether he had committed any of these crimes.

Lastly, police use tactics like bait operations and surveillance to target and apprehend offenders in the act when it comes to highly specific and focused patterns of property crime, though these patterns are less frequent. A few instances are a pattern of auto theft where a particular kind of car (like a Honda Civic) is customized for racing, a pattern of theft from a vehicle where a particular kind of property (like smartphones, high-end stereo speakers, or pricey wheels) is taken from a vehicle, or a pattern of commercial burglary where the perpetrators drive a car through the glass window of a specific electronics store. Police frequently employ bait cars that contain the desired property to identify these patterns, or they may employ individual surveillance (e.g., undercover investigators) or mobile or stationary video surveillance equipment to keep an eye on areas that resemble those in the pattern in the hopes of apprehending the criminal in the act.

9.4. IDENTIFYING MEANINGFUL PATTERNS

Tactical crime patterns are typically composed of several incidents of a single kind of crime. But occasionally—as was previously mentioned—similar kinds of crimes combine to form a single pattern. For instance, failed break-ins can be categorized as criminal damage and investigated in addition to successful ones. Additionally, rape, indecent exposure, and public sexual indecency can form a pattern if the offender is becoming more violent or exhibits different behaviors depending on the situation. It's crucial to remember that police officers categorize similar crimes differently according to particular legal standards. Nevertheless, crimes with different legal codes can nonetheless share similarities in their nature and constitute a similar crime pattern. In order to spot patterns, a crime analyst must consider the type of activity as well as its classification. Due to the fact that modus operandi (MO) traits can be extremely particular (e.g., a thief who makes the victim take off their clothes), they can clearly connect incidents that happened months or even years apart. It is not possible to fully establish a pattern by MO, though. Put another way, it is impossible to confirm that a specific suspect has committed every crime with a similar MO unless they are apprehended and make a confession. Patterns are typically connected in additional ways as well (e.g., suspicious description, kind of location). It is improbable that an offender would purposefully or accidently imitate another offender's vehicle or physical attributes, but it is simple to imitate general MO traits; for instance, a suspect might enter a bank and use a gun and a note to demand money from a clerk.

The possibility that an offender's MO may change as a result of situational circumstances is another element that can complicate the analysis of MO characteristics. For instance, within the same crime pattern, an offender may use more or less violence based on the victim's response. In certain situations, a burglar might decide against using his typical method of breaking in—kick the door—because it is much easier to enter through the open side window. Furthermore, traits that are predicated on witness accounts are frequently problematic. The accuracy of witness accounts can be impacted by elements like lighting, the length of time the victim and perpetrator were together, and fear. It's critical to keep in mind that establishing a pattern of crimes for police response does not establish sufficient evidence to prosecute an offender in court. As a result, the patterns are essentially the analyst's "best guess" that must be used to guide police toward specific actions. The pattern is far less significant than probable cause and the rules of evidence in the event that a suspect is taken into custody.

9.4.1. Persons Crime Pattern Key Characteristics and Examples

Crime analysts must consider possible police responses when they see any pattern and ensure that the patterns are targeted, pertinent, and useful for putting the right responses into action.

Arresting the suspect or suspects is the primary goal of a person's response to a crime pattern. In order to establish series and spree patterns, the investigation of an individual's crimes would thus concentrate on connecting crimes through dubious actions and descriptions. The following sections provide examples and a discussion of the salient features of the two types of person crimes that are most frequently investigated, robbery and sex crimes, to aid in the pattern finalization process.

9.4.1.1. Robbery Patterns

The actions of the suspect(s) during the crime and the kind of victim or location are important features of robbery patterns. Even though a robber may use various techniques to commit his crimes, it is harder to connect those acts as a pattern. It makes sense to use the type of place to differentiate robbery patterns because research indicates that criminals who commit street robberies differ from those who commit commercial robberies (Wright and Decker, 1997). Suspect descriptions are crucial for analyzing a person's patterns, but as was previously mentioned, since witnesses are not always trustworthy, the significance of the descriptions is viewed as secondary to the behavior of the suspect.

For instance, if the suspect's actions during one robbery are similar to those during another, e.g., brandishing a gun, and hitting the victims after robbing them) but the suspect in one crime is described as an Arabic man with curly hair, and the suspect in the other as a Hispanic man. The analyst may combine both descriptions into the pattern even though the victims' descriptions may not be exact, but the suspects' actions are strikingly similar.

While the businesses themselves are usually dispersed throughout a community (e.g., neighborhood), robberies at commercial locations are less likely to be identified through proximity of the incidents. g. proximity matters in street robbery patterns where criminals may target victims in familiar areas (e.g., two Best Buy stores are unlikely to be situated next to one another). e.g., theory of crime patterns. Therefore, even within a single category of crime, the essential traits may vary slightly. Finally, because the thief can travel and escape after committing the crime, proximity becomes less significant when a vehicle is used in the robbery. Because of this, certain robbery patterns cross jurisdictional lines, and gathering information from a nearby agency is usually a necessary step in the finalization of a robbery pattern.

9.4.1.1.1. Example: Hot Prey, Street Robberies, Seattle, Washington

Six strong-arm robberies made up this robbery pattern (i.e., victims physically threatened) and one instance of an armed robbery (i.e., teenagers (young people under 18) who were walking through the city on their way to or from high school over a 14-day period were threatened with a handgun by the victim. Suspects in the crimes were described differently in each case (e.g., white males and black males), indicating that the pattern is not sequential. Because the victims were all male or female students who were walking alone to or from school, it is known as a "hot prey" pattern. When the victim's phone was produced, the suspect in each case demanded to use it, threatened, physically attacked, and took the phone away from the victims. A gun-wielding suspect confronted the victim in one of the crimes and demanded the victim's cell phone. The suspect in every crime usually made their escape on foot. In separate incidents, money and a backpack were taken.

Detectives' response, depending on the pattern's nature, may involve looking into related crimes collectively (e.g., the robberies with weapons vs. the strong-arm robberies) in order to determine possible culprits. In order to educate parents about crime prevention and to gather more information from the public to help identify and detain the offenders, the pattern could be made public. Police could get in direct contact with school administrators to inform them of the threat and provide parents and students with self-defense strategies. Finally, to discourage offenders, police could patrol in a targeted manner before and after school hours in areas that are accessible by foot from high schools.

9.4.1.1.2. Example: Series, Commercial Robberies, Salisbury, Maryland

Given the similarity of the suspect descriptions across all the crimes, this pattern of commercial robberies seems to be a series. e.g., a white man of about six feet tall. Since it features robberies at a single kind of location, it is also a hot setting and hot product (i.e., retail pharmacies) that focus on a particular product (i.e., oxycontin). In the early afternoon hours of November through February in the city of Salisbury, there are three distinct locally owned (i.e., nonfranchised) pharmacies were targeted by a white man with a mask and gloves who asked the pharmacy clerk for "oxy" while brandishing a handgun.

The suspect used his own bag to transport the pilfered goods. The suspect stole more than 20 pill bottles, each containing five to thirty milligrams of medication—worth thousands of dollars—from each store. In every robbery, cash was also taken, but no video evidence was gathered. In one instance, fingerprints were removed.

Detectives' responses, depending on the pattern, might involve looking into all three crimes at once (e.g., investigating video evidence, speaking with victims and witnesses again while keeping in mind the other crimes), collaborating with detectives from nearby agencies that investigated comparable robberies, making direct contact with neighborhood pharmacies, and disclosing the pattern to the media so that the public can offer more information to apprehend the perpetrators. Since the crimes are not close to one another in terms of time or location, directed patrol is probably not the best course of action in this pattern. Additionally, it is difficult to predict that they will focus patrol on particular days, times, or pharmacy locations.

9.4.1.1.3. Example: Series and Hot Prey, Cell Phone Robberies, Fairfax County, Virginia

Six robberies over the course of two months make up this pattern of robberies. All of the victims were people who used Facebook or Craigslist to try to buy or sell an iPhone. This is a series based on the MO's similarity, and it's also a hot prey pattern based on the victims' similarities and the manner in which they are victimized. Social media was used by the victims and suspects in each crime to establish contact. When they finally met in person, the suspect intimidated the victim and forcibly took the money or iPhone. In two cases, the suspect threatened the victim with a gun, but nothing happened. Additionally, the suspect drove an older model, brown or green, four-door car in two of the cases. The incidents happened at different times of day and night in public parking lots all over the county.

Detectives' responses, depending on the pattern, might involve looking into every crime collectively (e.g., reviewing the evidence, speaking with the victims again, and keeping an eye on social media correspondence while considering all connected crimes). More importantly, the police could use the pattern to alert the public about the dangers of buying and selling cell phones to strangers online and offer tips on how to prevent crimes when engaging in such transactions. Certain police departments advise, for instance, that people complete these transactions at the police department. In order to give the police additional information that they could use to identify the offender or offenders and put an end to the crimes, the media release could also ask for information from bystanders who may have been victims but did not report the crimes to the authorities. Setting up a sting operation to find and apprehend this offender would be a suitable response, but directed patrol would not be the right course of action for this pattern since the locations of the crimes depend on the conversation between the victim and the offender and could be anywhere.

9.4.1.1.4. Example: Series and Hot Spot, Home Invasion Robberies, Salisbury, Maryland

Two occurrences in which two black males wearing ski masks forced entry into two-story single-family homes at around 10:00 p.m. comprise this robbery pattern. When the occupants were at their houses. Once inside the houses, the criminals demanded money from the victims while threatening them with handguns. The crimes happened within a 5-day period and a radius of 0.13 miles. This is a series because the suspects seem to be the same in every crime, but it could also be a hot spot because the crimes are all in the same neighborhood and close to one another. A little over $400 in cash was taken in the first robbery.

The victim in the second robbery informed the suspects that his money was behind one of the speakers in his car. After entering the car, the thieves took the speaker but left no cash behind. Because the perpetrators threatened the victims before stealing anything, these crimes are classified as robberies rather than burglaries, which is why they are called "home invasions." Even though the residents were present when the crimes occurred, they would still be classified as burglaries if the perpetrators had entered the house and taken the belongings without posing a threat to them.

Detectives' responses, given the pattern, might involve looking into these two crimes jointly (e.g., analyzing the data, speaking with victims again while keeping in mind the two connected crimes). Due to the close proximity and shared residential neighborhood of these crimes, the police were able to carry out targeted patrols, apprehend suspicious individuals who fit the suspect descriptions, and make contact with local residents who might have been potential victims. Another way to gather information would be to issue a media release (i.e., intelligence) from people who may have witnessed something or who may have been the victims of comparable crimes but chose not to report them in order to compile additional information that will help identify the perpetrators and put an end to the series. The circles that contain numbers (i.e., 1 and 2) stand for the crimes; the light gray boxes are the home addresses of known gun offenders that detectives may get in touch with as part of their response; the dark gray boxes are the locations of field interview cards for suspicious people in the area around the time of the pattern.

9.4.1.2. Sexual Crime–Related Patterns

Because sex crimes are less common than robberies and property crimes, they are not as frequently identified as other crime patterns in tactical crime analysis. There are very few stranger rape patterns because most rapes are perpetrated by acquaintances. Although they happen more frequently than stranger rapes, incidents of public sexual indecency and indecent exposure are still quite uncommon. Because sex crimes are uncommon and the offenders' methods are distinct, identifying patterns for all of them may be easier than for other types of crimes.

Important features of sexual crime patterns include the suspect(s)'s actions during the crime (i.e., series), as well as the kind of victim (i.e., warm prey). Suspect descriptions, like those in robbery patterns, are significant but not as reliable as the suspect's actions. Especially in these situations, the victims are taken aback and dismayed by the actions and might find it difficult to recognize the culprit (e.g., a rapist approaching them from behind or a flasher emerging from behind a tree). Cases within a sexual crime pattern, however, might be closer to one another than with robberies. Someone who is approaching strangers on the street might be doing so in a place like a park where there are lots of people walking around with little supervision. To find his victims, a rapist targeting college students would need to travel to an academic community. Since many of these crimes go unreported, it is especially crucial to educate the public and particular groups of potential victims about the patterns of sex crimes. Victims may be more inclined to report a crime if they are aware that the offender is committing multiple offenses and that other people have also been victimized. These unreported incidents may add details to a pattern that will help with the investigation and capture of the perpetrator.

9.4.1.2.1. Example: Series, Indecent Exposure, Gainesville, Florida

This pattern included four distinct occurrences over a period of several weeks in which a male Hispanic was observed engaging in sexual acts while driving a silver, compact, four-door car. In the first incident, two female students at Gainesville High School witnessed a Hispanic man in his mid-to late-40s engaging in sexual behavior in a silver car close to a Citgo station during the afternoon. The identical two female students noticed a silver car that looked similar at the Citgo station's gas pump two weeks later in the morning before classes. The male driver was pumping gas while engaging in a sexual act. He was dressed in long, dark shorts. The suspect stared at the victims while he masturbated, but he got into his car and left when one of the victims tried to take a picture of him for evidence. In the aftermath of class at Gainesville High School, a third incident involved a female student witnessing a man driving a silver car. The subject was masturbating and not wearing pants when she passed the car. After these crimes, a fourth incident was reported, although it happened a month earlier. That afternoon, a young woman saw a Hispanic man sitting in what appeared to be a gold four-door car, masturbating while wearing khaki shorts. The victim pointed out that the vehicle's color description might not be accurate because it was raining that day.

Detectives may look into these crimes as a pattern based on the pattern's nature, paying close attention to any available video evidence from the businesses and school. In an effort to catch the criminal, they may also carry out surveillance at particular locations. That is, the police may conduct surveillance at those times and locations if it looks that the offender has a pattern of appearing at specific businesses near the high school and in the school parking lot at similar times. Additionally, since the offender probably prefers to be where young women are walking around, patrol officers could conduct directed patrol around the high school before and after school and keep an eye out for the vehicle and suspect as described. In order to warn students about the pattern, the police could get in touch with the school administration. They could also request that any additional sightings of the man be reported right away, since it's likely that he does this far more frequently than is being reported. Finally, the police may decide against publicizing this pattern in the media because doing so could cause the suspect to temporarily alter or cease his behavior in an effort to avoid being apprehended.

9.4.1.2.2. Example: Series, Stranger Rape

In the 1990s, when I worked as a crime analyst, we noticed a pattern: a white male suspect would approach Asian students on college campuses and ask them for directions to a certain place while speaking to them in either Chinese or Japanese. He would ask them to get in his car if they responded but could not speak English. He threatened to rape them if they obeyed. The suspect first made contact with the women in a small neighborhood near the university where international students lived, but the crimes took place across a number of locations. But the suspect's particular actions were what connected the crimes.

We received additional reports of women who were not Asian but had dark hair and eyes being approached but not raped after officers responded to the pattern by releasing information to the public through the media. These women gave more details about the suspect's car and physical characteristics even though they had not been harmed. Once detectives had pieced together details regarding the suspect's vehicle (e.g., fragments of the license plate and a description) from the different victims and observers.

9.5. PROPERTY CRIME PATTERN KEY CHARACTERISTICS AND EXAMPLES

Crime analysts primarily focus on connecting these crimes through the type of crime, type of place, and proximity in location and time. This is because the primary goal of police responses to property crime patterns is to help victims protect their property and deter offenders. Hot spots, hot settings, hot products, and sprees are the common patterns that are discovered. As previously mentioned, the means of committing a property crime frequently rely on the openings provided by the property's managers or guardians (e.g., unsecured doors, visible valuables, windows in a house with broken locks). Only very specific factors are used to link crimes, such as entry method, point of entry, and type of property taken; these factors typically point to a crime series or sprees (same suspect). As an analyst, I once discovered a crime series in which homes were broken into by drilling a hole in the garage door, releasing the door lock cable with a hanger, and then entering the house through the unlocked internal garage door. A spree could be defined as a three-hour period during which a number of cars in the same parking lot are broken into. The motives may vary from car to car, but it is improbable that several criminals would carry out these offenses in one location and in such a short amount of time, indicating that the pattern is more of a series than a spree, even in the absence of any suspicious activity.

9.5.1. Theft from Vehicle Patterns

Theft from vehicles is the crime type that tactical crime analysis looks at the most often and is the subject of the most patterns in police departments. Due to the fact that many of these thefts take place in the absence of witnesses and when car doors are left unlocked, there is frequently little to no suspect information and minimal MO information.

As a result, the main traits of theft from vehicle patterns are mostly determined by the kind of location where the cars are kept (e.g., companies against. dwellings), the proximity of the thefts, and the moment they happened. The crime analyst often lacks suspect information and must identify patterns primarily by proximity, even though a single offender may be carrying out these crimes throughout the entire city (hot spots).

Significantly, since protecting victims and discouraging criminals from committing crimes in a specific area is the main objective rather than making arrests, micro-time hot spot patterns are useful for police responses. Particular patterns could be recognized by MO (e.g., breaking a window with a window puncher or spark plug) and the kind of property taken (e.g., hot item (such as GPS devices or cell phones) or kind of location (e.g., hot environment (gyms, day care centers). In the end, proximity plays a significant role in determining the majority of these patterns.

9.5.1.1. Example: Micro-Time Hot Spot, Thefts From Vehicles, Port St. Lucie, Florida

Six unlocked cars in a residential neighborhood that were parked in the driveway or on the street were the target of unidentified suspects. Within a 0.41-mile radius, the incidents happened over the course of eight days during the late evening or early morning. Loose change and other items left in the cars were among the stolen property, but nothing of great value.

Given the pattern's nature and the fact that the crimes are taking place in a residential neighborhood, detectives may decide to look into the crimes jointly and get in touch with residents who have a history of theft from vehicles. Officers may respond by conducting directed patrol within the pattern area, establishing contacts with residents in the area through social media, door-to-door visits, flyers, or reverse 911, alerting them to the pattern and offering targeted advice on preventcrime.

9.5.1.2. Example: Spree and Hot Setting, Thefts Fromfrom Vehicles at Retail Parking Lots, Port St. Lucie, Florida

Sunday afternoon, from 4:00 p.m. and 10:00 at night. within a few miles of one another, three cars were broken into in public parking lots (heated settings) at a restaurant, movie theater, and retail store. Two of the incidents involved the "popping" of the driver's door lock. e.g., extracted using a drill or another instrument from the door). There was no indication of force applied to the vehicle in the other incident. One car had a cell phone stolen, another had a purse containing credit cards and a wallet, and the third had nothing. Within a few hours of the first theft and within 50 miles of the times and locations of the crimes, the credit cards were used at two restaurants and a gas station.

Given the pattern, detective responses might involve looking into these crimes jointly because, given the times, places, and MO (popping the door lock), it is likely that the same person or people commi addition, crime prevention officers might get in touch withcontact particular establishments in the pattern area to advise staff members and clients about crime prevention and to warn them to be on the lookout for suspicious individuals in parking lots. Since crimes occur so quickly and it's unclear if offenders will return, directed patrol and in-person surveillance by police would not be practical in this situation. Installing video surveillance, however, might help identify criminals after the fact so that they can be apprded and prosecuted.

9.5.1.3. Example: Hot Setting, Thefts Fromfrom Vehicles, Gainesville, Florida

Unknown suspects targeted seven unlocked cars at apartment complexes (hot setting) over the course of four weeks. These incidents mostly happened in the early afternoon and evening, with one taking place at 10:00 a.m. Several things that were left in the car were among the stolen property. One incident involved the theft of a gun that was used in a shooting. Nothing was taken in another incident.

Detectives could look into these crimes as a single pattern based on the pattern's nature and get in touch with residents of these apartment buildings or those close by who have a history of stealing vehicles. In addition, police may carry out targeted patrols, establish field contacts with neighbors and management in these apartment complexes, and advise residents to lock their cars and remove valuables. Finally, because offenders appear to be returning to commit additional crimes, police may also conduct a bait vehicle operation at any of the two communities there victimized twice.

9.5.1.4. Example: Hot Place, Thefts Fromfrom Vehicles at the YMCA, Gainesville, Florida

In the YMCA parking lot, there were ten car thefts from February to June that happened on three separate days. Six cars were broken into on February 24 between 5:45 p.m. and 7:30 p.m. while positioned in the lot's front row. On March 6, someone broke into two cars between 5:00 p.m. and 8:00 p.m. in the evening. and between 9:50 a.m.oon on June 10 two vehicles were victims. and 11:00 a.m. All ofAll the vehicles had been unlocked, and the items taken from them varied. It should be noted that the locked cars in the parking lots escaped damage. Gives pattern and the repeated activity at this particular locationlocation over a period of months, police could collaborate with YMCA managers to encourage staff members and members to lock their cars, remove valuables, install security cameras, and restrict parking lot access. It would also be possible to inform staff members and guests of this fact and urge them to report anything suspicious as soon as possible, since the perpetrators hit multiple cars at once.

9.5.2. Vehicle Theft Patterns

Vehicle theft is comparable to theft from a vehicle, but since the entire vehicle is missing, there is even less data to look through for patterns. When a vehicle is recovered, information about how and why it was stolen can be inferred from its condition (e.g., no items taken and the car is empty of gas could point to joyriing), but cars are usually found days or weeks after the original crime, if at all, making it difficult to pinpoint specific crime trends right away. The main factors for car theft are therefore just proximity (hot spot), time, type of place (hot setting), and type of vehicle (hot product) because there isn't much data to connect these crimes.

9.5.2.1. Example: Hot Product, Moped Thefts, Roanoke, Virginia

Four more recent model (2009–2015) mopeds were taken over the course of 19 days, during the day, from in front of a house. eft there in plain sight. All of the mopeds had their handle barshandlebars and front wheels locked, but none of them were fastened to a building. This implied that the perpetrator was not allowed to drive or push the moped off the property. Prior to the theft, a white male juvenile, approximately 15 to 18 years old, was observed in one of the incidents. The pattern area is home to two known offenders who fit the suspect's description. One has a history of stealing motorbikes, while the other has a history of vandalism and car theft (e.g., theft of a car. Officers' responses are probably going to involve spreading the pattern throughout this neighborhood and putting it in the media to notify city moped owners, according to the information this pattern provides. Officers may undertake directed patrols in the neighborhood during the day, and detectives would get in touch with any known offenders who may reside there.

9.5.2.2. Example: Hot Product, Auto Theft of Pickup Trucks, Arlington, Texas

In Sector Z, there were 23 motor vehicle thefts and 13 attempts to steal fzed pickup trucks between August 1 and September 13. These theftsthieves all took place during the night. There were only seven cars found, and five of those were found by a jurisdiction that whermore, rather than being taken from the street, practically allall of the vehicles were taken from the victims' driveways. Prying open the door or e lock was the most popular way to gain access. Then, in order toto take the car, the suspects broke the ignition or damaged the steering column. There was only one car with a broken window, and in that instance, the suspects also harmed the door locks.

Given the information this pattern provides, officers' responses are probably going to involve publicizing the pattern in the media because it would be challenging to identify particular potential victims (i.e., those who possess these kinds of cars and leave them parked in their driveways). One of the locations where a number of the most recent incidents took place might be the site of a bait operation. The police's ability to use this latter course of action, though, would depend on their ability to obtain a car that fit the targets' descriptions.

9.5.3. Residential Burglary Patterns

Both residential and commercial settings are targets of burglaries, and while a single perpetrator may target both over a few weeks, it is challenging to connect these crimes due to a lack of suspect information. Because of this, as well as the fact that residential and commercial locations present distinct burglary opportunities, residential and commercial burglary crimes are typically investigated independently.

The type of residence and proximity are important factors in determining patterns of residential burglary. Once more, the intention behind addressing patterns of property crime is to inform potential victims and discourage criminal activity. Single-family, multifamily, mobile home communities, and similar residential types are frequently identified by patterns because of the differences in burglary opportunities among them. The significance of proximity (hot spots) stems from the fact that homes near one another frequently have similar features, making crime prevention strategies consistent between them. Additionally, a targeted area is where police officers can patrol most effectively when directed. While crimes that happen on different days and times would not necessarily be eliminated from a pattern when they occurred at the same type of residence in the same area, commonalities in the time of day and day of the week can be important for residential burglary patterns when they are very specific. Finally, MO matters when it comes to patterns of residential burglary, especially when it's highly specific. A crime analyst could still connect the two homes even though the suspects entered one through a sliding glass door and the other through an open window in the same neighborhood.

9.5.3.1. Example: Micro-Time Hot Spot, Residential Burglaries, Port St. Lucie, Florida

Unknown suspects broke into three houses in a 0.35-mile radius over the course of four days during the day and early evening. Cash, a video game console, and electronics for cleaning the house were among the stolen goods. Since the screen door was left open in one incident and no signs of force were discovered in the other, there was no use of force in either of the two incidents. Although nothing was taken during the third attempt at burglary, the front door lock was broken by being kicked in.

Officers' responses will probably involve directed patrol and field contacts in the pattern area, depending on the pattern's nature. 35-mile radius) in addition to having direct conversations with locals (possible victims) in the pattern area to offer guidance on preventing crimes. To inform them of the pattern, the police could also get in touch with the local neighborhood association. As possible leads, detectives may collaborate to look into the crimes and get in touch with well-known residential burglars who reside in the pattern area.

9.5.3.2. Example: Hot Setting, Burglaries of Sheds at Apartment Complexes, Frederick, Maryland

In four different apartment buildings, there were multiple shed burglaries in each building. Since the sheds are not used as homes, technically speaking, these are burglaries at residential locations of "other buildings" rather than residential ones. Over the course of four weeks, during the night, there were burglaries. The suspects typically removed the hinge locks or chopped the padlocks off the sheds. Numerous tools, sizable laundry and kitchen appliances, snow and lawn equipment, compressors, and ladders were among the stolen goods. A male black suspect, estimated to be 50 years old, is reported to be driving a gray van.

Detectives could look into these crimes jointly based on the pattern, concentrating on the suspect's description, any potential video footage, and fingerprint evidence, in addition to reaching out to known criminals who may be residing in or near the apartment buildings. Patrol officers may respond by getting in touch directly with apartment managers, who can then get in touch with residents, issue warnings, and assist in enhancing the security of the sheds on their properties. During the night, police may also carry out targeted patrols, identify and speak with any suspicious individuals in or near apartment complexes, and keep an eye out for the suspect.

9.5.4. Commercial Burglary Patterns

Similar to residential burglary patterns, proximity and type of business are key indicators of commercial burglary patterns. There will be trends in the form of burglaries of various business types in close proximity to one another—hot spots. Nonetheless, business type is frequently a connecting factor in commercial burglaries (e.g., electronics stores, and/or by a particular MO (e.g., traversing a wider region within a city or even across jurisdictional boundaries (for example, by breaking through the wall of the next company in a plaza or entering through an air conditioning vent on the roof). Unless the MO is extremely specific and indicates a series, residential burglaries are rarely identified across jurisdictional boundaries or neighborhoods. To find more burglaries at nearby businesses, crime analysts may look through burglar alarm service requests. The call could reveal additional locations that criminals may have attempted to target but were unsuccessful, and it would provide additional information to help develop responses and strengthen the pattern investigation, even though there may be little to no information available beyond the date, time, and location of the alarm. In pattern areas, this can also be applied to residential burglar alarms.

9.5.4.1. Example: Series and Hot Setting, Radio Shack Burglaries, Fairfax County, Virginia

Over a dozen burglaries at Radio Shack locations in Fairfax County and throughout the state of Maryland occurred between January and June, all with similar methods of entry. According to the MO and surveillance images, the same suspect is thought to have committed these crimes (i.e., series). This pattern is also considered a "hot setting" because all of the incidents took place at Radio Shack stores. Observe that it is not a hot spot because numerous locations (i.e., a hot spot is just one place). The suspect, a tall, thin black man, smashes the front door with a rock or brick while sporting a light-colored hoodie. The surveillance footage reveals that as soon as the suspect enters, he or she heads straight for the stock area in back and makes aim for the "cage" that houses expensive goods. The suspect takes easily accessible items and carries a bag, screwdriver, crow bar, and other tools to help open the cage.

The crimes in the pattern would be examined collectively to identify and capture the suspect, depending on the pattern's nature. Given that he would be familiar with the design of Radio Shack stores and their policies, it is probable that the suspect is a current or former employee of the company. e.g., where and how they keep things secure). In order to stop these crimes from happening in the long run, the police would also collaborate with Radio Shack store managers and especially corporate executives to alter employee policies, security procedures, and store layouts. Since the crimes are widespread in terms of dates and geographic area, directed patrol at Radio Shack stores would not be a realistic response. It would essentially be the responsibility of the Radio Shack stores and business leaders to take precautions and safeguard their own assets.

9.5.4.2. Example: Hot Spot and Hot Product, Commercial Burglaries, Fairfax County, Virginia

Cell phones and electronic tablets were taken in six commercial burglaries that occurred along Richmond Highway in a period of five months. A grocery store, a check-cashing store, and a "dollar" store were among the enterprises. Three hits were made on one location, two on another, and one on the third. In every case, the suspect(s) smash the front glass door with a rock they find nearby. Surveillance footage appears to show that the suspect(s) are one or two black males who enter the store and take only cell phones and electronic tablets. The break-ins happened exclusively during the week, between 1:00 a.m., and three in the morning. The pattern is popular since the locations are near to one another within the same business district. Nevertheless, since the same kind of property was taken in each crime, this activity also serves as a hot product. Furthermore, if the analyst determines from the surveillance footage that the same offender or offenders committed all the crimes, then this pattern may also be regarded as a series.

Detectives could look into these crimes together because of the pattern. However, since this is a commercial area and an "activity space" for a variety of people who may or may not live nearby, they would not necessarily contact known offenders who reside in the area. Working with the specific stores that were harmed to strengthen their security is another way to respond, particularly since two of the locations were harmed twice. In order to inform them of the activity and give them information on crime prevention and security, police may also get in touch with other companies that sell cell phones and tablets along the commercial district highway. Finally, since the offenders have been returning to these and similar stores over the course of several months, and since they have been successful in doing so, they are probably going to keep going until they are apprehended, patrol officers may undertake directed patrol around these and similar stores after midnight on weekdays.

9.5.5. Hot Product Patterns

Certain property crime patterns are typified by a common kind of property that is taken in a variety of crimes and/or locations rather than by a single crime type, one suspect, or the location in which they occur. According to Clarke (1999), a hot product is a kind of property that is frequently targeted, or more accurately, "those consumer items that are most attractive to thieves.." An item usually meets one of the following requirements to be considered a hot product: it must be "concealable, removable, available, valuable, enjoyable, and disposable.." Examples consist of valuable metal (e.g., handguns, laptop computers, tablets, smartphones, and catalytic converters (which produce gold, copper, and platinum). Patterns in tactical crime analysis center on recently taken items, but these are usually items that araken over a longer period of time, like electronics and jewelry. ..

The qualities of the product that is taken are the most important factors in determining a hot product pattern. Items can be used in similar kinds of crimes (e.g., theft) or in a., burglary, robbery, and theft). Crucially, the crime analyst lookscrime analysts look for very specific characteristics in order to identify hot product patterns. For instance, even though cash is the "hottest" product, because it is taken from cars, robberies, and burglaries so frequently, a crime analyst would not be able to spot a hot product pattern involving cash theft. But if money is linked to a popular product trend in each of the crimes (e.g., heist, break-in, and car theft) the money consisted of thousands of dollars stored in $100 bills within a zip bag intended for bank deposits. In spite of the fact that the perpetrators might not have been the same, this would make the pattern and the stolen property distinct.

9.5.5.1. Example: Hot Product and Hot Setting, Burglaries of Tractor Trailer Tires and Wheels, Greensboro, North Carolina

Eight break-ins at truck and trailer dealershipce between February and May, a three-month period, during which timewhich 10 to 50 tractor trailer wheels and/or tires were taken. Suspects took off the tires and wheels from trailers that already had them, or they broke the fence or the locks on the gates leading to the storage yard in the majority of the incidents. In other words, the wheels and tires were mounted on the trailers rather than being stacked. The suspects occasionally carried "blocks" to support the trailers while the tires were being removed. Five of the crimes happened over the weekend, and the rest happened during the night when the businesses were closed. Because of the particular skills, knowledge, and tools required to remove the tires from the crime scene and transport them, this pattern is probably also a series.

Given the pattern, it is likely that the suspects are removing the property from the crime scenes using large trucks or flatbed trailers. As a result, patrol officers could conduct directed patrol and stop large vehicles that are traveling in the vicinity of the victimized area and other similar locations on the weekends and overnight.

Investigators could look into these crimes as a pattern in order to compile any evidence they find. They might look for people or at businesses that sell trailer tires and wheels in other jurisdictions, either new or used, but they wouldn't get in touch with local offenders. Additionally, police may get in touch with any dealerships that resemble them (i.e., possible victims) to share details about the pattern, ask for details about potential suspects, and gather intelligence regarding the nature of the trailer tire and wheel industry.

9.5.5.2. Example: Hot Product, Packages Left on Residential Doorsteps, Fullerton, California

In the city, there were four package thefts in October and November. In each instance, the package was stolen before the homeowner could get it back from the mail delivery truck, which had left it in plain sight of the street and close to the front door. The crimes happened between when the package was dropped off, which was usually in the late morning or early oon, and when the victim got home and/or realized the package wasn'twas not there, which was occasionally a day or two later. None of the crimes have any suspicious information, and the items taken ranged from clothing to tiny electronics.

There are only a few answers because of the patte. For instance, given the wide dispersion of the crimes' time periodtime and location, it is unlikely that the same individual committed them all. Given that these crimes occur just before Christmas, a media release reminding people to request "signature only" deliveries or have their packages delivered to more secure locations would probably be the best course of action. The delivery companies may be notified by the police of the pattern, and their staff may be instructed to leave packages in more secure locations.

9.6. DESCRIBING AND DISSEMINATING KNOWN PATTERNS

An important part of the larger crime analysis process is summarizing and distributing patterns in crime, which help to inform the public, legislators, and law enforcement about new trends and direct crime prevention tactics. It is ensured that the insights obtained from the analysis of crime data are converted into practical steps that can improve public safety through the effective communication of these patterns. It is necessary to clearly and concisely sd articulate the major conclusions from crime data analysis in order toto describe crime patterns. This includes describing the common crime types, the most affected geographic areas (crime hotspots), the times of year or seasons when particular crimes are more likely to happen, and any significant changes in crime trends over time. Furthermore, analysts could delineate the demographic attributes of both perpetrators and victims, in addition to noting any discernible associations among distinct categories of criminal activity. Precise descriptions of crime patterns that combine qualitative and quantitative data to paint a complete picture are required. Maps, graphs, and charts are examples of visual aids that are frequently used to simplify complex data. Heat maps, for example, can be used to visually depict crime hotspots, and trend lines can be used to display the rise or fall in a particular type of crime over a given time period. Sharing these outlined patterns with pertinent parties, such as law enforcement organizations, civic leaders, legislators, and the general public, is known as dissemination. Making sure people in positions to act on the information are informed is the aim. Internal briefings, reports, and strategic meetings may be used by law enforcement to discuss the patterns in relation to operational planning and resource allocation. Public distribution is also essential because it provides communities with information about regional trends in crime. Public safety announcements, press releases, and community gatherings can all be used to accomplish this. In the modern era, a lot of police departments also disseminate information about crime patterns online and through social media, increasing public accessibility. Transparency has the potential to improve public cooperation in efforts to prevent crime, build trust between the community and law enforcement, and raise general awareness of safety-related issues. ..

9.6.1. Describing Known Patterns

Information about a crime pattern typically concentrates on the methods used to commit the crimes (i.e., modus operandi [MO]), the people who carried them out (i.e., suspect description), at the time they happened (i.e., time series analysis), as well as the locations of them (i.e., spatial analysis). Rather than repeating the specifics of each crime report, the objective of summarizing these aspects of a pattern is to compile all the data from the crimes into a single unit of analysis. This section is crucial because it discusses the description of a pattern and offers more guidance on recognizing and completing patterns as a result.

9.6.2. Modus Operandi Summary

Crime analysts find patterns that represent educated guesses about the relationships between incidents based on a range of characteristics. As such, analysts should exercise caution when communicating the findings and not present the information with undue conf is warranted. Every crime's method of operation will only be nearly identicalsmall number of patterns. It is more common for them to all be somewhat uniqueunique. When describing a pattern's method of operation, one should concentrate on the traits that set the crimes in the pattern apart from other concurrent crimes and that are common to all of them. For example, the following were the MOs for five crimes linked together for a street robbery series:

- Two black males approached the victim on the sidewalk in a residential area. They had their T-shirts pulled over their heads, flashed a handgun, demanded money, and took $46 from the victim.
- Two black males wore black ski masks, threatened the victim with a handgun, demanding money while on a residential sidewalk. The suspects took $50 in cash and fired one gunshot after the robbery but did not hit anything.
- One suspect wore a white Halloween mask; the other suspect wore nothing on his head. After threatening the victim with a handgun, the suspect(s) fired two or three gunshots toward the victim but did not take any money.
- Two black males approached victim outside of the victim's home, showed the victim a handgun, and demanded money. Suspect(s) took $10 and fired five gunshots into the air. No one was hurt.
- Three black males approached victim right outside victim's home, put gun to victim's head, and removed $30 from his wallet.

Although the number of offenders varies and each MO is slightly different, based on the data presented here and additional data not displayed (e.g., the places where the robberies took place, detailed descriptions of the perpetrators), the crimes have been connected. Accordingly, the following would be an MO summary for the pattern:

Using an unidentified handgun, one to three unidentified black males approach victims as they are strolling down a residential street or outside their residence and demand money. The suspects once put the gun to the victim's head. The suspects in three of the robberies wore ski masks, Halloween masks, or T-shirts over their faces. After the robbery, the suspects in three of the incidents fired one to five rounds, either in the air or toward the victims, but no one was hit. In one incident, the suspects took no money, and in the other four, they took between $10 and $50.

The MO summary does not aim to repeat what transpired in each case separately; rather, it combines and synthesizes the information from the incidents. Even though there was only one crime, it is still crucial to summarize the facts and highlight anything unusual, like the suspects putting a gun to the victim's head. Even though the crimes themselves may have only taken a few minutes, this example is fairly complex because it involved a human victim and there was a lot of interaction between the suspects and victims. Summaries of property crimes are typically much simpler, particularly in cases where there is no forced entry into a building or vehicle.

9.6.3. Suspect and Vehicle Descriptions

When describing a pattern, descriptions of the suspect and the vehicle are handled similarly. Most patterns consist of several distinct suspect descriptions varying in specificity from the various cases that comprise the pattern. The intention is to give as much detail as possible about the general descriptions of the suspects while leaving out any of the case descriptions. The physical description is given more weight than the person's actual physical state (e.g., weight and height compared to. clothes). For example, the following is a list of suspect descriptions from a stranger rape pattern:

- White male, average height, medium build;
- White male, 5'10" to 6' tall, 180 to 200 pounds, brown hair;
- White male, 6'1" tall, 210 pounds, brown curly hair, tattoo of snake on right arm.

A white male with brown curly hair, standing 5'10" to 6'1" tall, weighing 180–210 pounds, and sporting a snake tattoo on his right arm would be the description for the entire pattern. Regarding height and weight, the general description incorporates all three accounts; however, it is more detailed regarding the tattoo and hair because those details were only mentioned by one witness and do not contradict the accounts given by the other witnesses. The analyst must make sure to note discrepancies in descriptions when there is contradicting information present but the incidents are still deemed related. Misrepresentation frequently occurs when characterizing the physical state of the individual or vehicle (e.g., a dirty car or an inebriated individual), so just because the witness accounts differ doesn't imply they are unrelated. The method for handling vehicle descriptions is the same: details about the vehicle are condensed to the greatest extent possible while keeping all possible scenarios included, and the official description (e.g., tag, make, model, and color) are prioritized over the state of the car (e.g., a dent on the fender).

9.6.4. Time Series Analysis

The temporal aspect of the crime, which is captured by the time of day, day(s) of the week, and the order in which the incidents occurred, is a crucial feature of crime incidents for both describing and identifying patterns. Time series analysis, also referred to as temporal analysis, is the technique used to investigate these features (Paulsen, Bair, and Helms, 2009). Because crime analysts typically analyze fewer than 25 cases, central tendency statistics like mean and standard deviation are inappropriate. Instead, the temporal aspect of patterns is described using counts and percentages.

9.6.5. Exact Time

Examining events like robberies and sexual assault that have a precise time of occurrence is known as exact time series analysis. Using military time, which allows for the application of mathematical operations like addition and subtraction, and rounding time variables to the closest hour are standard procedures in the field of crime analysis. Although rounding slightly reduces accuracy, it is an acceptable trade-off for results that are intelligible and easy to understand. For instance, a crime that happened at 9:35 a.m. would be rounded to 09:00–09:59, with the crime occurring at 10:15 p.m. be rounded to the nearest 22:00 or 22:59. The goal of this analysis is to arrange the data so that a summary of the entire pattern is shown, even though it might be intriguing to know the precise moment of each crime. A different method of presenting the time series analysis of this pattern is to calculate the percentage of each robbery that has occurred overall. Stated differently, the number of incidents within an hour is no longer the measure of its worth. Rather, it is the total number of incidents divided by the number of incidents that occurred during that hour. Since there are 15 cases in total in this example, each incident is worth 6:7% (i.e., 1/15).

9.6.5.1. Exact Day of Week

Applying the same technique to calculate the frequency of crimes, the percentage of total crimes by day, and the number of crimes by day of the week. Bar charts are commonly used by crime analysts to display data regarding the days of the week.

9.6.5.2. Exact Time of Day and Day of Week

The two methods discussed in the earlier sections each provide information about the day of the week and the time of day. Analysts must, however, be aware of the day and time combinations that are most typical for the pattern's incidents.

9.6.5.3. Exact Date: Intervals Between Events

Lastly, examining the number of days that elapse between crimes in a pattern can help an analyst understand the nature of the pattern. For instance, if the take from each robbery is small, a person committing robberies to fund a drug habit may commit crimes more frequently over time. When performing this kind of analysis, analysts must be cautious not to make any assumptions about patterns or offenders, though, as numerous variables can affect how long it takes between incidents (e.g., weather, employment, illness, and opportunity).

The x-axis displays the pattern's date range; the y-axis shows the number of days between each incident and the next; and the lines show the times at which the crimes occurred within that range. According to Helms (2004), this graph is known as a tempogram; it indicates that crime is either increasing in frequency or is accelerating. When mapping patterns, analysts can also incorporate information about the time intervals between events—a technique that will be covered later in this chapter in the section on spatial analysis. This kind of study can make it clear whether a pattern has a specific tempo, or if it is steadily increasing, decreasing, or at an equilibrium. The time between events gets shorter in a pattern with an increasing tempo as it goes along. The time between events gets longer as a pattern with a decreasing tempo moves forward. The tempo is stable when the time between cases stays relatively constant. A crime analyst can assist in predicting future incidents in a pattern by looking at the gaps between cases in the pattern.

9.6.6. Weighted Time Span Analysis

Since only time span information is available for certain types of crimes (usually property crimes), exact time of day and day of week time series methods are inappropriate (i.e., the offense happened between 7:00 a.m. and five o'clock. a.m.). Time span information can still assist an analyst in connecting cases and better comprehending a recognized crime pattern, even though it is not as precise as exact time information. A crime-related time span's length and its beginning and ending points are two crucial factors to consider. For instance, a period of time starting at 4:00 p.m. culminating at 1same as one that starts at 4:00 a.m. and concluding at noon. Despite the fact thatEven though they both last eight hours. Furthermore, a one-hour time span is fare reliable for estimating the time of a crime than a five-hour time span. In timethe time series analysis, it is crucial that analysts look at both sides of time spans.

Every time span in the weighted time span analysis method is given a value of 1, and every hour in the time span represents a percentage of the time span. For instance, if there are five hours in a day, then each hour represents one-fifth of the total time and has a value of (i.e., 20%of five hours is one hour. Comparably, in an 8-hour period, each hour is one-eighth of a time, and it is given a value of (12.5%) cases that indicate, for every crime, the length of the time span, the assigned value (weight) of 1 hour of the time span, the first possible time the crime occurred, that time rounded, and the last possible time the crime occurred, that time rounded. e.g., in Case 1, where the duration is six hours, the value of each hour is 1/6, or 17.

The analyst places these values in the appropriate hours of the day and examines them collectively after giving each hour a value within the time frame of each case. The crucial columns are located on the right: Percentage of Total is the "total" for that hour of the day divided by the total of all the hours of the day (e.g., Total is the sum of the values by hour of the day). e.g., the "total" for the hours of 1000 to 1059 is 1.12, or 9.4% of the total for all of the hours in the day.

9.6.7. Spatial Analysis of Patterns

The geographic component of crime patterns is another important feature. Spatial analysis is a tool that crime analysts use to recognize and comprehend patterns in crime. Although there is currently advanced work being done in tactical spatial analysis by academics and practitioners, the discussion that follows is limited to fundamental methods.

The most prevalent pattern that crime analysts find is the micro-time hot spot. They are usually found by looking through data spanning one to two weeks. The emergence of multiple closely related crimes within a few minutes' travel time from one another is indicative of a micro-time hot spot (i.e., microplace) that takes place in a comparatively brief amount of time (i.e., micro-time)—a "flare-up" in criminal activity (Santos and Santos, 2015c). Micro-time hot spots, on the other hand, are not stable over time; instead, they emerge in a specific location and may not reappear there for months, years, or ever. Clusters of recurring incidents that happen in stable, long-term problem areas as well as in other areas that are not used to high crime rates or that continue to experience crime problems are known as micro-time hot spots. They are crucial to recognize and separate from problem areaf this. A crime analyst must comprehend how a microtime hot spot develops in order toto recognize and characterize one. A set of standards for defining a micro-time hot spot should be created as part of the crime analyst's pattern analysis process. This will help to ensure that patterns related to micro-time hot spots are consistently found and allow law enforcement to take appropriate action. Based on the size of the jurisdiction, the zoning, and the kind of crime under investigation, each crime analyst would choose the criteria (e.g., patterns of residential burglary are typically closer together than those of commercial burglary.

This shows how a property crime micro-time hot spot has developed based on the following criteria, which were created for residential crime in a suburban jurisdiction with average levels of property crime: (i) two or more incidents of residential theft from vehicles or burglaries; (ii) occurring one to 14 days after another; and (iii) occurring within a 0.25-mile radius.

A map in the left panel depicts a micro-time hot spot at the time of initial identification, where two crimes were committed within a 4-day period, within a radius of 0.10 miles. e.g., February 1–5. Additional Crimes 3 and 4 are depicted on the map in the middle panel. These crimes take place two and three days later, respectively, and are included in the micro-time hot spot because they are situated within a 0.25-mile radius of the mean center of the two initial crimes. The micro-time hot spot is depicted in the right panel map as it continues to flare up because Crime 6 occurs just 7 days after Crime 4 and falls within a 0.25-mile radius. Since Crime 5 is outside of the maximum permitted 0.25 mile radius, it is not included in the micro-time hot spot.

Since Crime 7 happened 25 days after Crime 6, the micro-time hot spot is thought to have cooled off after that. e.g., over 14 days) subsequent to Crime 6. So, in this example, the micro-time hot spot started with two crimes that occurred over the course of four days within a 0.10-mile radius. Before "cooling off," it continued to "flare up," with three more crimes occurring within a 0.25-mile radius. It continued for another 12 days. Crucially, it is plausible that a new micro-time hot spot may emerge around Crimes 5 and 7, respectively, in terms of space and time, but they would each need to satisfy the requirements for a new micro-time hot spot (i.e., two crimes in a span of 14 days and 0.50 miles. Stated differently, a crime that is already within a micro-time hot spot cannot be added to another one, and although two micro-time hot spots may be adjacent, they do not overlap in terms of time or space.

When analyzing property crimes like residential burglaries, auto thefts from vehicles, and auto thefts, or person crimes like street robberies, the geographic proximity of the incidents is a crucial factor. When doing pattern identification, analysts must take into account more than just the locations of incidents. To complete the pattern, the crime analyst would not only adhere to predetermined criteria but also consider attributes like the type of place, time, day, and MO.

9.6.8. Pattern Bulletins

Crime analysts use a format called a pattern bulletin to provide officers, detectives, and (in some cases) citizens with tactical information related to crime patterns.

Such a bulletin typically includes the following elements:

- **Publish Date:** This is the date the bulletin was initially published (disseminated to the police department) by the crime analyst.
- **Bulletin Number:** This is the sequential number of the bulletin. Normally, crime analysts use the year and a range of numbers (e.g., 2017–001, 2017–002). Also, when a bulletin is updated with new information, such as additional crimes or an arrest, the date is changed with an updated date, and a letter is added to the bulletin number (2017–001A). Multiple updates use letters in order (e.g., A, B, C, D, etc.). This is done so that the subsequent versions of the same pattern bulletin can be easily referenced. An additional consideration is that crime pattern bulletins should be numbered separately from other tactical bulletins, such as arrest bulletins and BOLOs (i.e., be on the lookout).
- **Amended Date:** Oftentimes, in an effort to get information to sworn personnel quickly, the crime analyst publishes a pattern before all the information is available (i.e., officers are still finalizing a crime report), and there may be mistakes or missing information in the first version of the bulletin. Thus, when more or corrected information about the original pattern comes about, a crime analyst will "fix" (i.e., amend) it, publish the bulletin again, and add an amended date so that individuals know the difference between the original and amended bulletin. The amended date does not replace the original publish date and both should be included; however, when a bulletin has been amended multiple times, only the most recent updated date is included.
- **Updated Date:** A bulletin is updated when there is additional activity linked to the pattern after the bulletin has been published. Where amending the bulletin is correcting, changing, or adding information of the original bulletin, updating a bulletin is adding new information about activity that occurred after the original publication (i.e., additional crimes 2 days after initial publication; FI cards taken in the pattern area after publication; an arrest). When an update to a bulletin is published, as noted earlier, the bulletin number is changed to include a letter (e.g., A, B, C) at the end, so the

updated date corresponds with this change. When multiple updates to a bulletin are created, the bulletin letter reflects how many times there has been an update, and the updated date reflects how long the pattern has been active (i.e., crimes are continuing) for response. (Note: Amending a bulletin has nothing to do with how long it has been active). For example, bulletin 2017-045, with a publish date of March 1, 2017, has been updated several times and is now 2017-045C, with a date of April 3, 2017. These two components indicate that the pattern has been updated three times and has been active for 34 days. The update date does not replace the original publish date on the bulletin (i.e., both should be listed); however, when a bulletin has been updated multiple times, only the most recent updated date is included.

- **Title:** The title contains the type of pattern (e.g., series, hot spot), the type of crime (e.g., robbery, burglary), and the location of the pattern (e.g., address, neighborhood, police beat, entire city). The title also may include other information, depending on the type of pattern (e.g., type of place for a hot setting, type of property for hot product).
- **Number of Incidents:** This is the total number of incidents in the pattern. The bulletin also may describe other incidents that are discussed as possibly related (e.g., five burglaries and two burglar alarm calls).
- **Date Range:** The date of the first and last crimes in the pattern.
- **Days and Times:** A summary of the days of week and times of day when the overall pattern is occurring.
- **Summary of MO:** A short, straightforward narrative in bullet form describing the suspects' actions in the incidents in the pattern.
- **Property Taken (if Relevant):** A summary of the types of property or unique property taken.
- **Suspect Information:** The most specific description(s) of the suspect(s) possible that covers all crimes.
- **Vehicle Information:** The most specific description of the vehicle possible that covers all crimes.
- **Weapons (if Relevant):** The most specific description of the weapons used that covers all possible descriptions.
- **Known of Enders (if Relevant):** Because we know individuals commit crimes near where they live (particularly burglaries, thefts, and robberies in residential areas), crime analysts include offenders

who have been arrested or convicted of the pattern crime type and who report their residences in the pattern. Each person's information is included on the bulletin (e.g., picture, name, date of birth, and crimes committed). Note that offenders should be individuals who are most likely to have committed the crime and thus should be prioritized and the number kept low (e.g., between three and five offenders on a bulletin).

- **Field Interviews and Other Information:** Information about field interviews, suspicious persons, or vehicles in the area that might be related to the pattern or information from other crimes that might be related but not enough to be considered a crime within the pattern.
- **List of Cases:** A list of the incidents in the pattern with detailed information about each case. This would include a map reference number, case number, date/time span of crime's occurrence (not of the report), time/time span of crime's occurrence, and address of the crime. Other information in the list would depend on the type of crime and pattern and would include other characteristics, such as location name, suspect's actions, individual suspect descriptions, victim type, point of entry, method of entry, property taken, and whether fingerprints and evidence were collected. Importantly, the cases are listed by chronology; most analysts place the most recent crimes at the bottom of the list.
- **Map of the Incidents in the Pattern:** Single-symbol map with numbers next to the symbols corresponding to the list of cases so that the numbers indicate the sequence of the crimes; higher numbers are more recent crimes. The addresses of known-offender residences, field interview locations, or other relevant locations (e.g., all Radio Shacks in a pattern in which 3 of 12 stores were victimized) would also be mapped using different symbols than the crimes. The map should also include a circle drawn so its edges touch the outermost crimes in the pattern with a notation about the length of the circle's radius. Instead of providing a scale on the map, the circle and its radius tell the officers the relative distance of all crimes in the pattern and the area in which to implement the responses, if appropriate.

The formats and contents of pattern bulletins differ by police agency and frequently by analyst across the United States. In the past 22 years, we have looked through and assessed hundreds of bulletins, offered suggestions, trained crime analysts to create pattern bulletins, and collaborated with police departments to put effective patterns responses into practice. Additionally, police departments create other kinds of tactical crime analysis bulletins, like arrest bulletins (i.e., details regarding a criminal's arrests for one or more crimes in a pattern), BOLOs (i.e., "be on the lookout" for a specific suspect, car, or other item.), as well as police safety alerts. Tactical crime analysis bulletins have traditionally been given to police officers in internal mailboxes or during briefings on paper. However, a lot of police departments have started sending out bulletins via email or uploading them to intranet websites in recent years. These approaches are better since they're less costly (e.g., paper and the price of printing and copying), and officers get better-quality products (e.g., color maps in comparison to. copies in black and white).

Crime pattern responses can be recorded in the system in agencies where officers use laptops in their cars to access a police department intranet site. For instance, in Port St. The Lucie (Florida) Police Department posts pattern bulletins to the agency management system (i.e., the department's website) as soon as the crime analysts identify a pattern. i.e., SmartForce®) for examination by supervisors and other sworn officers stationed nearby. A discussion board template (i.e., Officers can share information about their responses, as well as their knowledge of the patern area, known offenders, or conducted field interviews, by using the feature "thread.." With this kind of setup, the crime analyst can quickly update the bulletin or make changes to it and post it to the thread so that all of the officers can see it right away while they are responding. Software utilized by the Greensboro (North Carolina) Police Department is another illustration (i.e., CrimeView). Police managers can designate a region and give officers a "mission" or response using the software. Officers can then input the responses they have put into practice by clicking on the mission.

Last but not least, the bulletins designed for police agencies are "watered down" or sanitized when they are distributed to the public with information about patterns. Notifications meant for the general public won't contain any information that could violate privacy or endanger an ongoing investigation. For instance, if a pattern of burglaries includes places that are privately owned (e.g., single-family homes), the bulletin for the public would only contain details about the MO, times, dates, and general locations; the precise addresses of the burglarized homes would not be disclosed because it is not required for local homeowners to take precautions. For example, if cars are being broken into repeatedly in a specific nightclub's parking lot, that location would be specified because it would be important for citizens to have that information in order to protect their belongings there. Exact address information would be provided for publicly frequented locations included in the pattern.

REFERENCES

1. Basu, S., Banerjee, A., & Mooney, R. (2002). Semi-supervised clustering by seeding. In *Proceedings of the International Conference on Machine Learning* (pp. 19–26).
2. Berk, R., Sherman, L., Barnes, G., Kurtz, E., & Ahlman, L. (2009). Forecasting murder within a population of probationers and parolees: A high stakes application of statistical learning. *Journal of the Royal Statistical Society: Series A (Statistics in Society), 172*(1), 191–211.
3. Boba, R. (2005). *Crime Analysis and Crime Mapping*. SAGE.
4. Boriah, S., Chandola, V., & Kumar, V. (2008). Similarity measures for categorical data: A comparative evaluation. In *Proceedings of the Eighth SIAM International Conference on Data Mining* (pp. 243–254).
5. Brown, D. E., & Hagen, S. (2003). Data association methods with applications to law enforcement. *Decision Support Systems, 34*(4), 369–378.
6. Buczak, A. L., & Gifford, C. M. (2010). Fuzzy association rule mining for community crime pattern discovery. In *ACM SIGKDD Workshop on Intelligence and Security Informatics*.
7. Chen, H., Chung, W., Xu, J., Wang, G., Qin, Y., & Chau, M. (2004). Crime data mining: A general framework and some examples. *Computer, 37*(4), 50–56.
8. Dahbur, K., & Muscarello, T. (2003). Classification system for serial criminal patterns. *Artificial Intelligence and Law, 11*(4), 251–269.
9. Eck, J., Chainey, S., Cameron, J., & Wilson, R. (2005). *Mapping Crime: Understanding Hotspots*. National Institute of Justice, NIJ Special Report.
10. Ghahramani, Z., & Heller, K. (2005). Bayesian sets. In *Proceedings of Neural Information Processing Systems*.
11. Gwinn, S. L., Bruce, C., Cooper, J. P., & Hick, S. (2008). *Exploring Crime Analysis: Readings on Essential Skills* (2nd ed.). BookSurge, LLC.
12. Hauck, R. V., Atabakhsb, H., Ongvasith, P., Gupta, H., & Chen, H. (2002). Using COPLINK to analyze criminal-justice data. *Computer, 35*(3), 30–37.
13. Letham, B., Rudin, C., & Heller, K. (2013). Growing a list. *Data Mining and Knowledge Discovery*. (To appear).
14. Lin, S., & Brown, D. E. (2003). An outlier-based data association method for linking criminal incidents. In *Proceedings of the Third SIAM International Conference on Data Mining*.

15. Mohler, G. O., Short, M. B., Brantingham, P. J., Schoenberg, F. P., & Tita, G. E. (2011). Self-exciting point process modeling of crime. *Journal of the American Statistical Association, 106*(493), 100–108.
16. Nath, S. V. (2006). Crime pattern detection using data mining. In *Proceedings of Web Intelligence and Intelligent Agent Technology Workshops* (pp. 41–44).
17. Ng, V., Chan, S., Lau, D., & Ying, C. M. (2007). Incremental mining for temporal association rules for crime pattern discoveries. In *Proceedings of the 18th Australasian Database Conference, Vol. 63* (pp. 123–132).
18. Pearsall, B. (2010). Predictive policing: The future of law enforcement? *National Institute of Justice Journal, 266*, 16–19.
19. Ratcliffe, J. H., & Rengert, G. F. (2008). Near-repeat patterns in Philadelphia shootings. *Security Journal, 21*(1), 58–76.
20. Short, M. B., D'Orsogna, M. R., Pasour, V. B., Tita, G. E., Brantingham, P. J., Bertozzi, A. L., & Chayes, L. B. (2008). A statistical model of criminal behavior. *Mathematical Models and Methods in Applied Sciences, 18*, 1249–1267.
21. Short, M. B., D'Orsogna, M., Brantingham, P., & Tita, G. (2009). Measuring and modeling repeat and near-repeat burglary effects. *Journal of Quantitative Criminology, 25*(3), 325–339.
22. Wagstaff, K., Cardie, C., Rogers, S., & Schrödl, S. (2001). Constrained k-means clustering with background knowledge. In *Proceedings of the International Conference on Machine Learning* (pp. 577–584).
23. Wang, G., Chen, H., & Atabakhsh, H. (2004). Automatically detecting deceptive criminal identities. *Communications of the ACM, 47*(3), 70–76.

Chapter **10**

Administrative Crime Analysis

Contents

Introduction 392

10.1. Overview of Administrative Crime Analysis 392

10.2. Crime Reduction Accountability 394

10.3. Crime Reduction Goal Development 396

10.4. Crime Analysis for Weekly Action-Oriented Accountability Meetings 399

10.5. Crime Analysis for Monthly Evaluation-Orientedetings 402

References 417

INTRODUCTION

Administrative Crime Analysis is a critical function within law enforcement agencies, focusing on the evaluation of data to support internal operations, strategic planning, and policy development. Unlike tactical or strategic crime analysis, which primarily addresses immediate crime trends and long-term patterns, administrative crime analysis is concerned with the internal workings of a police department, ensuring that it operates efficiently and effectively.

The primary objective of administrative crime analysis is to provide data-driven insights that inform decision-making at the managerial and executive levels. This includes analyzing crime statistics, call-for-service records, personnel deployment, and resource allocation to identify areas of improvement within the agency. By doing so, administrative crime analysts help ensure that law enforcement resources are used optimally, maximizing the agency's ability to prevent and respond to crime.

This form of analysis also plays a significant role in evaluating the effectiveness of various law enforcement programs and policies. For instance, by assessing the impact of community policing initiatives or the deployment of new technologies, analysts can offer recommendations for adjustments or expansions that align with the agency's goals. This evidence-based approach ensures that policies are not only effective but also aligned with current trends and community needs. Administrative crime analysis also supports transparency and accountability within the agency. Reports generated by analysts are often used to communicate with stakeholders, including government officials, community leaders, and the public, about the agency's performance and use of resources. This transparency is crucial for maintaining public trust and securing funding for future initiatives. Furthermore, administrative crime analysis facilitates inter-agency collaboration by sharing insights and best practices across different jurisdictions. This coordination helps create a more unified approach to public safety and crime prevention. Administrative crime analysis is essential for the efficient management of law enforcement agencies, providing the insights needed for strategic decision-making, policy evaluation, and resource optimization. Through careful analysis, it ensures that agencies are well-prepared to meet the challenges of modern policing.

10.1. OVERVIEW OF ADMINISTRATIVE CRIME ANALYSIS

0Compared to the tactical and strategic forms of crime analysis that we have already covered; administrative crime analysis is distinct. Administrative crime analysis is, by definition, the presentation of compelling results from crime research and analysis grounded in legal, political, and practical considerations for audiences that include members of the city government or council, the police administration, and the general public.

Administrative crime analysis, then, differs significantly from the other types of crime analysis previously discussed in that it pertains to findings presentations as opposed to statistical analysis or research. Determining crime trends or solving crimes are not the goals of administrative crime analysis. Rather, the choice of what information to present and how to present it is more important. Frequently, the information that is offered is only the "tip of the iceberg" in terms of all the research and analysis that has already been completed (Santos, 2013). For instance, an executive summary of a report may be provided instead of the entire report in administrative crime analysis.

10.1.1. Why Is It Called Administrative Crime Analysis?

The reason administrative crime analysis got its name is that it focuses on the administrative requirements of the community, the government, and the police department (International Association of Crime Analysts, 2014). It can refer to a broad range of methods and outputs that are produced on demand as well as on a regular basis in the context of crime analysis. These methods and goods include printouts of data, charts, maps, and statistics. In addition, they consist of cost-benefit evaluations of police programs, reports to community groups, media requests, officer activity reports, statistics supplied for grant applications, and workload calculations by area and shift. According to the International Association of Crime Analysts (2014), a fourth category of crime analysis, known as operations crime analysis or police operations crime analysis, may include some of the later reports.

10.1.2. Areas of Administrative Crime Analysis

Yes, in a nutshell, is the response to this query. Planning, community relations, funding, and many other aspects of a police agency's operations are supported by administrative crime analysis, which is a legitimate and valuable subset of crime analysis (International Association of Crime Analysts, 2014). It is a fact of life for crime analysts that they frequently engage in non-analytical activities. Processes and techniques of administrative crime analysis include:

1. Districting and redistricting analysis;
2. Patrol staffing analysis;
3. Cost-benefit analysis;
4. Resource deployment for special events (International Association of Crime Analysts, 2014).

10.1.3. Reports Do Administrative Crime Analysts Present

The type of report is primarily determined by the intended audience, even though the administrative crime analyst will prepare reports and products in accordance with the demands and requirements of the police administration.

One could argue that informing audiences is administrative crime analysis's main goal. Because these audiences may differ depending on the circumstances, so too will the kind and volume of information. Administrative crime analysts may be preparing a presentation for the following audiences: media, citizens, neighborhood associations, police executives, and members of the city council, or any combination of these. Information should be prepared and presented in a way that is appropriate for the target audience. Nonetheless, the data must always be straightforward, understandable, and brief and must never reveal sensitive information (Boba, 2001).

Reports and presentations can be varied because there is a wide range of administrative and statistical reports, research, and other projects that are not concentrated on the short- or long-term reduction or eliminon of a pattern or trend. ..

Administrative crime analysis is frequently carried out to inform and support officials in the city government and law enforcement about the scope of crime and the impact that disorder and crime have on the community. The city council and the police administration will occasionally ask for long-term comparisons of the different types of crimes that occur in the city on a quarterly, semiannual, or annual basis.

10.2. CRIME REDUCTION ACCOUNTABILITY

The process by which police officers are held accountable for putting strategies to lessen crime and disturbance in the community into practice is known as accountability. The fundamental idea of accountability for crime reduction is that, in addition to responding to service requests and conducting criminal investigations, individuals, groups, and departments within a police department must assume accountability for carrying out crime reduction initiatives. The New York Police Department's (NYPD) Compstat program launched the trend in 1994 for police departments to have a formalized structure of accountability for aiding in crime reduction. What began as a pilot program in one department has spread throughout many police departments across the globe as standard procedure; most, however, have modified it to suit their own requirements rather than adopting the NYPD's model. Over the past ten years, the concept of stratified policing (Santos and Santos, 2015b) has broadened and clarified the Compstat framework, allowing for the stratification of accountability based on the various problem categories and ranks within the police organization. As a result, this chapter's discussion of accountability will be divided into sections that focus on crime analysis products for various objectives.

A police organization's crime reduction accountability procedures are focused on setting reasonable expectations, recording the activities that reduce crime, methodically assessing the activities' advancement, and assessing the effectiveness of the efforts at every stage. The implementation and maintenance of consistent and effective crime reduction efforts across the entire organization is guaranteed by an accountability process. Crime analysis plays a vital role in the accountability framework. Crime analysts develop standard products that are used to pinpoint issues and allocate resources, monitor managers' success in lowering crime, and assess the overall effectiveness of the organization in lowering crime and disturbance.

Regularly scheduled meetings comprise the formal structure police departments establish to support their accountability process, whether they are using stratified policing or Compstat. Every kind of meeting has a set agenda, a set list of attendees, and standardized crime analysis results. Meetings for Compstat may take place once a week, once every two weeks, or once a month. Three different meeting types are outlined in the structure of stratified policing: daily, weekly, and monthly meetings. These meetings are all ccted in tandem with one another.

It'sIt is significant that accountability takes place during these meetings, as well as the evaluation of crime reduction initiatives. When it comes to creating the materials and presentations that are used to track and evaluate efforts to reduce crime analysts are essential. While the previous chapters covered specific products used by police to guide their efforts in crime prevention and reduction, this chapter covers specific products designed to make sure people are correctly implementing strategies and to evaluate the effectiveness of their efforts.

Every kind of accountability meeting has a different goal, talks about different kinds of crime reduction initiatives, and has a different mix of personnel in terms of rank and type. The purpose of the daily and weekly meetings is to make sure that police officers are responding, so they are action-oriented. i.e., the "action") promptly, cooperatively, and suitably. Because they are used to evaluate both the advancement and efficacy of long-term crime reduction initiatives as well as the overall success of short-term crime reduction initiatives, monthly meetings are evaluation-oriented. The following is a brief description of each type of meeting:

- Dailyaccountabilitymeetingsfacilitateaction-orientedaccountability for strategies implemented for immediate and short-term activity.

The primary type of daily meeting is the "shift briefing" in which supervisors give patrol officers their crime reduction "mission" for that day based on crime analysis.

- Weekly accountability meetings facilitate action-oriented accountability within and/or among divisions (e.g., patrol, investigations, crime prevention, and media relations) so that police employees can come together to develop, coordinate, and assess strategies implemented for short-term activity. The main focus of weekly meetings is on patterns, as they require a coordinated response. These meetings are used for district commanders to "report out" what they are doing and for their bosses to ensure they are implementing the right number and type of responses, as well as decide whether the responses are working.
- Monthly accountability meetings facilitate evaluation oriented accountability within patrol districts and investigations, as well as across the entire police department. Patrol and criminal investigations commanders are held accountable for their specific geographic area or division by the police chief. The meetings are used to discuss whether all short-term crime reduction activities are effective rather than if responses to individual patterns are effective. That is, the discussion is focused on the combined responses to all patterns to determine if crime is going down and/or are there fewer patterns emerging. The meetings are also used to discuss whether long-term problems are emerging from unresolved short-term problems (e.g., residential burglary patterns are occurring in a neighborhood month after month) and to monitor the progress of ongoing long-term crime reduction strategies (e.g., determining whether implementing crime prevention through environmental design (CPTED) in an apartment community has reduced crime and disorder incidents). In addition, every 12 months the monthly meeting is used for evaluation-oriented accountability for all types of activity at the broadest level. That is, long-term trends of crime and disorder based on the crime reduction goals are examined to determine if all the efforts are making a difference, whether adjustments need to be made, and/or if new crime reduction goals need to be defined.

10.3. CRIME REDUCTION GOAL DEVELOPMENT

Prior to implementing accountability, the police department needs to establish clear objectives and a shared purpose for its efforts to reduce crime so that people are aware of what is expected of them. Formalized crime reduction goals are used to guide staff and provide specific measures to assess the agency's success in reducing crime and disorder, as opposed to a police chief simply declaring, "We will reduce crime.." These objectives differ from the goals and objectives that are typically developed in police organizations for a three-to five-year strategic plan that addresses the organization's overall growth, the number of officers that will be required, the need for new divisions or units, and the requirements for equipment.

Every crime reduction goal has a specified outcome, success indicators, baseline and target measurements, strategies, and performance measurements to ensure that they are applicable and actionable in the police department's daily operations. Crucially, distinct outcomes, strategies, and outputs are used to evaluate the process (i.e., whether tactics were applied appropriately) and effect (i.e., whether the tactics reduced criminal activity).

Crime analysts will play a crucial role in helping the department's leaders decide which crimes and disorder types to choose as goals, what the indicators and targets should be, and what degree of reduction the agency should try to achieve. However, they should not be in charge of creating crime reduction goals on their own. The following are descriptions of each component and the role of the crime analyst:

- **Crime Reduction Goal:** This is the desired outcome and is generally stated. It denotes a specific type of activity (e.g., violent crime, burglary, disorder) as well as the geographic area (e.g., countywide, citywide, district, beat). Most likely, very large and/or diverse jurisdictions will develop goals for geographic regions separately. The crime analyst would provide trend analysis for several years of different types and subtypes of crime and disorder for the entire jurisdiction and by geographic area to support initial goal development.
- **Success Indicator (i.e., Outcome):** This component specifies the type of activity that is used to measure the impact of the crime reduction strategies. The purpose of this component is to denote the specific measurement relevant to the crime reduction goal. The crime analysts would make suggestions for these measures as the "data expert" of the police department, knowing that using general measurements such as Uniform Crime Report (UCR) Part I Crime categories can mask changes in the specific crimes that are being addressed. For example, instead of using all UCR Part I violent crime (homicide, rape, robbery, and aggravated assault) to measure a goal to reduce violent crime, the success indicator measures specific types of violent crime that the agency has identified as concerns,

such as non-domestic aggravated assault and street robbery. Similarly, instead of using data for all burglaries to measure a goal pertaining to property crime and burglary, the success indicator can measure residential or commercial burglary separately, or even more specifically, it can measure residential burglary at single-family homes versus multi-family homes (i.e., apartments).

The level of intended success is also specified by the success indicator. This is typically shown as the portion of the activity type that has decreased (e.g., a reduction of 10%). The percentage of value is determined by taking into account past patterns in the activity, the quantity of police resources at hand, and an assessment made qualitatively by the leaders of the police department based on their expertise and understanding of what constitutes a reasonable target for reducing crime. What would be a reasonable goal for the upcoming year by the crime analyst's trend analysis. Last but not leastFinally, there are instances where geographic areas are mentioned in the success indicator rather than the goal statement as a whole. The geographic area within a success indicator indicates that while the jurisdiction as a whole may be the ultimate goal, a specific area will receive priority for responses. Alternatively, it may imply that responses will be given priority within a specific beat, even though the objective may be for a single precinct within a large jurisdiction. Crime analysis, which determines which area has the highest concentration of a particular crime or is most likely to see an increase in crime, would also be used to inform this.

- **Baseline:** This is the initial measurement of the success indicator. The actual value is listed, as well as the time period under consideration and the method of computation. The measurement can reflect frequency or counts of a year of data, or it can reflect a rate or an average over several years. This would depend on the data that is available and the nature of the activity. The crime analyst leads the development of the baseline measure and identifies these numbers through the trend analysis conducted for the previous components.
- **Target:** This is the desired level of success (i.e., reduction of crime) and is computed based on the percentage indicated in the success indicator and the baseline measurement. It is typically computed for 1 year, which is the evaluation period of the crime reduction goal. The crime analyst very easily computes the target once the previous components are designated.
- **Strategies:** The strategies listed here for each crime reduction goal address crime reduction efforts that the police department will implement simultaneously at each level of the organization. That is, a crime reduction goal is selected because it is important to the

police department and the jurisdiction; thus, the crime or disorder is addressed at immediate, short-term, and long-term levels. Because there are different strategies that are effective at different levels, this component designates what specific responses will be systematically implemented at each level. The crime analysts have a small role in choosing the strategies, but they may assist by providing insight about evidence-based policing research—for example.

- **Performance Indicators (i.e., Outputs):** These elements specify the activity to be measured and are developed based on the strategies outlined in the previous component. Examples include patrol officer activity, such as hours of directed patrol, as well as the number of arrests and cleared cases, which are measures of strategies used to address crime patterns. They also include rate of success in addressing specific types of problems, such as percentage of patterns and problem locations that were resolved successfully, and an analysis of the operational costs of implementing particular responses, such as overtime pay for officers and equipment purchases. The crime analyst would work with the leadership to decide the best measures for each strategy and data availability. That is, some things may not be currently tracked, and new data may need to be collected.

An example of a crime reduction goal and its elements is provided in Table 10.1. Given the broad nature of crime reduction goals and their potential for multiple category breakdown within the success indicator, an agency ought to aim for no more than three to five goals annually.

Using the methods and resources covered in this book thus far, the crime analyst conducts tactical and strategic crime analysis to lead and assist the department after crime reduction goals are developed and strategies are put into action. The remainder of the chapter discusses additional crime analysis products that were made especially for accountability in weekly and monthly meetings; although they serve different purposes, they are based on the same approaches that were just covered.

10.4. CRIME ANALYSIS FOR WEEKLY ACTION-ORIENTED ACCOUNTABILITY MEETINGS

Time spent developing products for weekly meetings that display weekly or monthly crime or disorder counts should not be spent by crime analysts. Weekly statistics are not required since they do not influence immediate actions, as accountability in weekly meetings is focused on taking action. As a result, the majority of the crime analysis findings that are discussed during weekly meetings were initially created as a component of tactical crime analysis (i.e., recurrent incident reports and crime pattern bulletins)—yet another justification for not needing weekly statistics.

The weekly repeat incident reports, for instance, are used to pinpoint response locations. Since the weekly product always includes the last 28 days of service calls, it is also used to assess the effectiveness of responses. Therefore, if a location received a response one week, the effectiveness of the response would be assessed using the product for the following week (i.e., no more calls at that address for the next two weeks). Because the data from the original product can be used for both accountability and response, a separate accountability product is not required for recurring incidents.

Table 10.1. *Example of Crime Reduction Goal Components*

Parameter	Goal: Violent Crime
Goal	Reduce violent crime throughout the jurisdiction
Success indicator (outcomes)	Reduce non-domestic aggravated assault and street robbery by 10% (focus on District 1 and District 2)
Baseline	Non-domestic aggravated assaults: 550 Street robbery: 450 Baseline time period: Jan–Dec 2016
Target	Non-domestic aggravated assault: [550 * .90 =] 495 Street robbery: [450 * .90 =] 445 Target date: Jan–Dec 2017
Strategies	Identify and respond to patterns (short-term) Identify and respond to problem areas (long-term) Identify and address repeat offenders
Performance indicator (outputs)	Number of patterns responded to and number resolved Number of problem areas responded to and crime reduced Number of repeat burglary offenders responded to Number of directed patrol hours in patterns and problem areas Number of arrests and clearances Number of known offenders contacted Cost analysis of responses deployed

Source: https://in.sagepub.com/sites/default/files/upm-assets/78468_book_item_78468.pdf.

Furthermore, because crime analysts update crime pattern bulletins in real time as new crimes occur, police leaders can determine from the bulletins themselves whether the responses are working (e.g., if there were no more crimes in the pattern for two weeks, it would be deemed successful. Therefore, to ascertain whether responses to a specific pattern are effective, no new statistics are required. For pattern accountability, the crime analyst would, nevertheless, produce a weekly product with data on the specified performance metrics for the pattern responses that will be covered. The crime analyst, individual patrol managers, and/or software that tracks crime reduction responses would all collect this data. The responses to the four active patterns that will be discussed in the weekly meeting are displayed in Table 10.2.

Table 10.2 shows us that pattern 35E has been in effect for 45 days and has been updated five times with 11 new crimes. Additionally, it is evident that substantial resources (e.g., 200 hours of directed patrol) were used to address the pattern. The action-oriented accountability would probably be to keep up the response because crime is still happening. In contrast, there haven't been any new crimes in Pattern 36 in the last 14 days. Police leaders would likely decide to stop responding and record it as a success after two or three weeks without any new crimes, as this is typically the recommended response time to patterns. Finally, in the last 20 days, Pattern 38B has seen two updates and five new crimes. With the fewest responses out of the four patterns, the patrol bureau commander would probably question the district captain in charge of the pattern as to why more resources haven't been allocated given the persistence of crime. Although there may be a valid explanation for the disparity, the police leaders can make sure that resources are being used sensibly and appropriately, identify successful efforts, and act quickly if necessary by making this table and comparing the response levels of the active patterns.

For recurring incidents, a similar kind of product might be made; however, since the solutions to those issues are typically more diverse, a more inventive approach to gauging the degree of response would have to be devised depending on the kind of recurring incidents dealt with. For instance, hours of contact with the family, the kinds and quantity of social service referrals made, arrests, restraining orders, and so forth could all be included in data related to response to domestic violence repeat incidents. In conclusion, there are very few products that would be made especially for a weekly accountability meeting and would focus on response, rather than on weekly crime or calls-for-service counts and statistics, because crime analysts are conducting action-oriented products every day. Finally, it is neither realistic nor effective to have weekly talks about crime analysis for accountability because long-term issues call for long-term solutions.

Table 10.2. *Response Statistics by Pattern*

Bulletin #	Days Active	Additional Crimes	Directed Patrol Hours	FI Cards Taken	Known Offenders Contacted	Reverse 911	Potential Victim Contacts	Arrests	Clearances
2017-35E	45	11	200	15	4	1	25	0	0
2017-36	14	0	65	3	3	1	12	2	5
2017-37A	17	3	84	10	5	1	0	0	0
2017-38B	20	5	21	0	1	0	0	0	0

Source: https://in.sagepub.com/sites/default/files/upm-assets/78468_book_item_78468.pdf.

10.5. CRIME ANALYSIS FOR MONTHLY EVALUATION-ORIENTEDETINGS

Accountability meetings are evaluation-focused on a monthly basismonthly, so crime analysts look at long-term trends month by month to track how well responses to recurring incidents, crime patterns, and persistent issues are working. A monthly review serves the objective of confirming that efforts to reduce crime are being implemented consistently and seem to be effective across the board. Monthly meetings are used to track the overall numbers of certain call types for service and crimes handled in the short term. Strategic analysis products that have already been produced and support the problem-solving process (as outlined in Part VI) would be discussed in monthly meetings, much like pattern bulletins that have already been created are discussed at weekly meetings. Monthly meetings are used to monitor long-term issues until it is determined that a thorough assessment of the solutions to that specific issue is necessary, and short-term issues until the crime reduction goals are evaluated.

Crime analysis for monthly accountability concentrates on trends rather than numerical differences or changes in percentage from month to month, year to date, or year to year because crime counts can vary greatly from month to month. The monthly crime analysis products that are produced by the crime analyst should be standard, pertinent, uncomplicated, and free of needless complexity or statistical detail. As a result, this section offers samples of a variety of products along with an explanation of their creation process and intended use in the monthly accountability process. Every product has the potential to analyze various types of disorders and crimes.

10.5.1. Crime and Disorder Monthly Trend Charts

Monthly, a chart depicting crime and disorder trends is constructed, featuring bars for the most recent six months contrasted with the equivalent six-month span from the preceding year. The chart includes a trend line for each time frame and showcases the percentage shift from the initial six-month period to the subsequent one. This tool is designed to assess the progress of crime decrease initiatives for a specific activity across the previous six months, compared to the same period the year prior, while also taking into account seasonal fluctuations, such as an uptick in crime during the summer months. A police chief might employ this tool to pinpoint any potential shortcomings in the implemented strategies and determine if additional dialogue and/or action are necessary in the upcoming month. In my experience collaborating with various police departments, discovered that six months is the optimal timeframe for tracking monthly trends. Longer durations prove more suitable for evaluating the effectiveness of crime reduction efforts in their entirety. For every monthly meeting, the same chart would be made, but the months would be updated to reflect the most recent six months (i.e., rolling time interval). Furthermore, distinct regions and various crime and disorder activities identified in the crime reduction goals may have the same chart made for them. For every monthly meeting, a crime analyst might create several iterations of this same product.

A bar chart displaying the counts and trend lines for a particular type of crime is presented in Figure 10.1. As we can see, although monthly fluctuations in crime rates are common, the overall trends indicate that the 2016 6-month trend was both more frequent (i.e., between 150 and 200) and remained flat over the course of the six months, whereas the 2017 trend is lower (i.e., falling between roughly 130 and 85) and is declining. From June to November 2017, there are 39% fewer crimes overall, according to the percentage change.

An accountable police leader would view this as a successful outcome. Nevertheless, examining the individual bars, he or she may draw attention to the fact that November 2017 is higher following a decline in every month from July to October 2017. Leaders haauthority to hold people accountable for ensuring that this increase doesn'tdoes not happen again in the upcoming months.

For each problem level and the crime reduction objectives, a monthly trend chart is alsong various kinds of service requests and criminal activity on a monthly basismonthly. See the following examples:

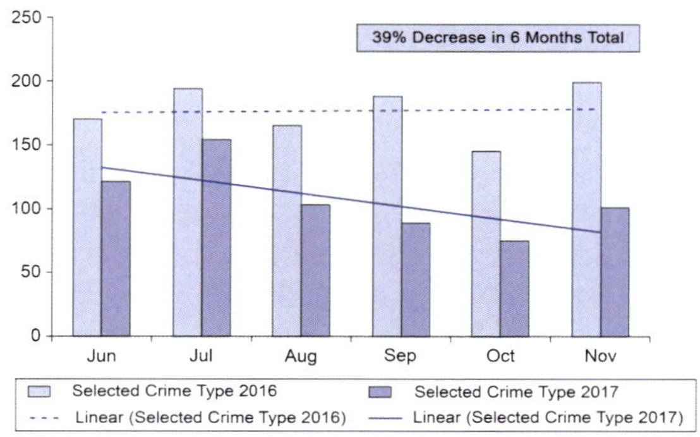

Figure 10.1. *Monthly trend chart.*

Source: https://in.sagepub.com/sites/default/files/upm-assets/78468_book_item_78468.pdf.

- **Repeat Incidents:** Charts for domestic violence calls for service in the entire jurisdiction and by geographic area (e.g., district) could be created to monitor the effect of the responses to domestic violence repeat incidents by district and across the jurisdiction.

- **Patterns:** Charts for street robbery in the entire jurisdiction and/ or by geographic area could be created to monitor the effect of the response to street robbery crime patterns and incidents, as well as compare progress across geographic areas.
- **Problems:** A chart for apartment complex burglaries could be created to monitor the effect of responses to a specifically selected problem of burglaries in apartment complexes.
- **Crime Reduction Goals:** Using the crime reduction goal example from the beginning of the chapter, charts would be made for non-domestic, aggravated assault, and street robbery separately to monitor the goal's success indicators. These products could also be broken down into geographic areas to determine if one area was doing better or worse than the others.

The following product is a bar and line chart combination that is generated monthly for the last six months and shows a month-by-month breakdown of selected crime or disorder activity for the current six months, the previous 12 months, and an average monthly for the previous five years.

This product's goal is to forecast the amount of activity that can be expected over the next six months by taking into account the previous six months, the previous 12 months, and the previous few years. If there were unusually high or low values over the previous 12 months, it may be useful to include an average.

Along with the counts of crimes from June to May of the previous year and the average for each month over the preceding five years, Figure 10.2 presents the same data as Figure 10.1.

According to the chart, there have been fewer crimes this year than there have been over the previous five years. However, the department may anticipate a rise in crime (i.e., violent crimes) based on data for the upcoming six months. e.g., even though the total figures are lower than in pres, observe how the 2016 and 5-year averages begin to rise in December. Similar toLike the preceding chart, the goal is to produce a product that is easy to interpret in order to track trends. A sophisticated predictive analysis is not required because it is not designed to systematically predict future crimes.

10.5.2. Problem Comparison Chart

The tactics outlined for a goal of reducing crime frequently refer to long-term solutions for trouble spots, neighborhoods, and criminals. Police leaders will discuss analysis and progress reports for pre-created problems during the monthly meeting. Therefore, the goal of a problem comparison chart is to enable them to compare multiple locations, areas, and offenders simultaneously to obtain a more comprehensive picture. Police chiefs can use the product to compare issues by setting the targeted crime counts side by side and to monitor the counts individually.

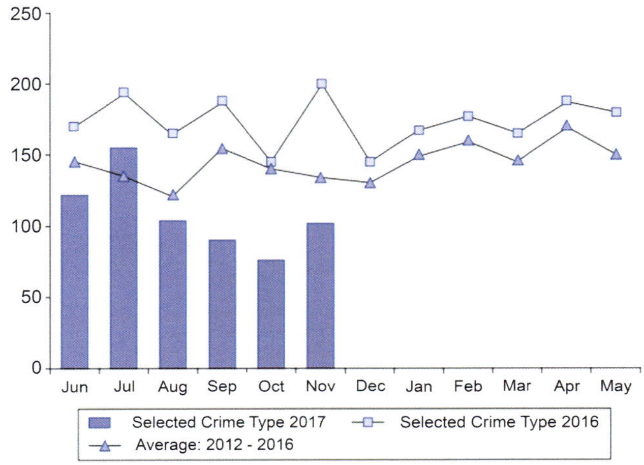

Figure 10.2. *Average trend analysis for 6 months, 1 year, and 5 years.*

Source: https://in.sagepub.com/sites/default/files/upm-assets/78468_book_item_78468.pdf.

This product is a bar chart that compares data from the same six months last year to the most recent six months, showing various locations, areas, offenders, and their counts. Like with the earlier products, a fresh chart would be made every month using the last six months (i.e., rolling time interval). Since this product shows problems rather than sequential months, a trend line is not used; instead, the difference between the 6-month totals is represented as a percentage of change.

Ten trouble spots that were determined by an 80/20 analysis and chosen for long-term crime reduction are shown in Figure 10.3. It demonstrates that while crime has decreased in eight problem areas, it has increased in Problem Areas (PA) 2 and 5, with a 20% overall decrease in crime over a six-month period for all problem areas. These findings suggest that while most of the problem areas' current crime reduction strategies appear to be effective, PA 2 and PA 5 still require improvement.

This product is used to keep an eye on various kinds of problems, criminal activity, and service calls. Rates may also be used to create it rather than crime counts. Some examples follow:

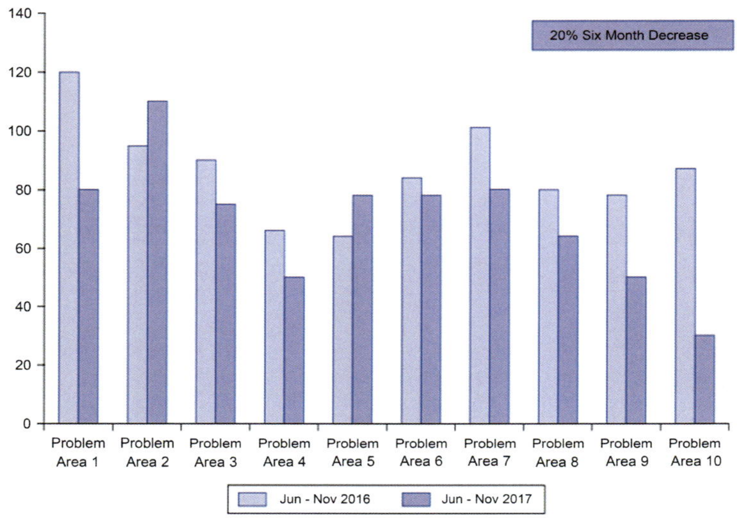

Figure 10.3. *Problem areas: 6-month comparison.*

Source: https://in.sagepub.com/sites/default/files/upm-assets/78468_book_item_78468.pdf.

- **Problem Locations:** Charts might be created for assaults at selected bars, loud parties at apartment communities, and disorder activity at budget motels.
- **Problem Areas:** Charts might be created for problem areas of robbery, aggravated assault, and disorder calls for service. Remember that problem areas may be defined at different scales, so a chart could be created by street block, by a cluster of blocks, or by various-sized areas. The most important aspect of creating this product for problem areas is to have areas with predefined and static boundaries so the crime and disorder activity can be counted accurately and consistently over time.
- **Problem Offenders:** This chart might include the number of arrests and/or police contacts for problem offenders. Note that this product would primarily be used and reviewed monthly for offenders that were being contacted and not for all offenders on a particular problem offender list.
- **Rates:** Charts might be created using crime per population of the problem area, loud parties per apartment unit, and assaults per occupancy of the bar.

10.5.3. Crime Pattern Trend Map

Maps can be used in addition to charts to track both short- and long-term activity and the police department's objectives for reducing crime. The purpose of the crime pattern trend map is to ascertain whether the patterns are becoming long-term problem areas by clustering over several months. It is a single-symbol map that shows all crimes of that kind that have occurred during a specific time frame. Ellipses indicate crimes that are included in pattern bulletins on the map. The fact that the crimes inside particular patterns are marked sets this apart from a simple single-symbol or density map. This product cannot be made by a crime analyst who does not perform pattern analysis. The monthly map's time period is rolling and includes six months' worth of pattern and crime incident data, just like it did for all the previous products. Keep in mind that crime patterns that cluster in space, like street robberies, residential burglaries, and residential vehicle theft, are best represented by these maps. For the sake of clarity, additional details such as the pattern number, the bulletin publication date, and whether an arrest was made are not displayed here but could potentially be included on the map for each pattern.

Eleven patterns were identified during this time period, five of which appear to have recurred in the same location (Figure 10.4). Police leaders would use their own discretion to determine whether to treat this cluster of patterns as a long-term problem area given the indications that the current short-term solutions are ineffective, or whether to keep an eye on it over the coming months.

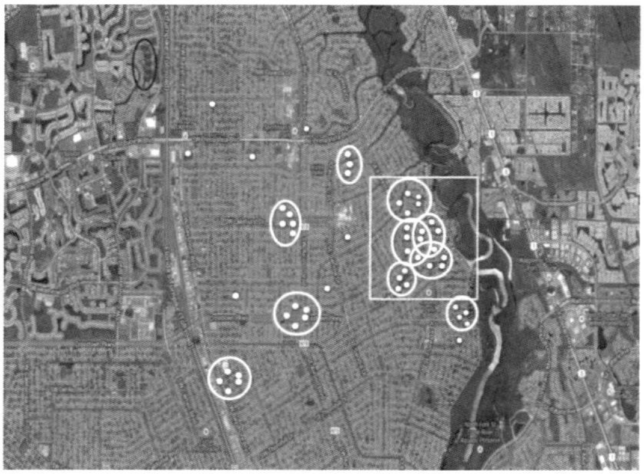

Figure 10.4. *Selected crime incidents and patterns: June–November 2017.*

Source: https://in.sagepub.com/sites/default/files/upm-assets/78468_book_item_78468.pdf.

10.6. Crime Analysis for Assessment of Crime Reduction Goals

Since the goals for reducing crime are set for 12-month periods, a crime analyst will develop new products every 12-month period to evaluate the performance indicators (i.e., outputs) and how they affect the success metrics (i.e., results) of the objectives for reducing crime. Data on crime and disorder from the police department, operational data on costs for implementing responses like personnel time and equipment, documentation of crime reduction strategies, and comparison data from nearby jurisdictions, the state, and federal sources are some of the sources of the data used for assessment.

10.6.1. Performance Indicator (Output) Products

To determine whether crime reduction tactics have been successfully and economically implemented, a wide range of products could be developed. They would stand for both the content analysis of the initiatives aimed at reducing crime (e.g., arrests, patrol reactions, clearances) as well as an evaluation of the tactics' financial implications.

One example of a performance indicator product designed for annual accountability is Figure 10.5. Data for one crime reduction goal's performance indicators are included, and it also addresses how issues, patterns, and recurring incidents are handled. Since weekly and monthly discussions are held to discuss crime reduction activities in greater detail, at this level of accountability, the activities are combined to represent totals for the entire year that is being examined. For every objective related to reducing crime, a different product would be made. Depending on the objective, a different product for every patrol division or geographic area (e.g., patrol in comparison. investigations) could potentially be made.

From top to bottom, Figure 10.5 shows outputs for the 12-month period:

- The number of individual patterns of crime responded to;
- The average number of hours of directed patrol expended by pattern;
- The number of arrests made, based on pattern response;
- The number of cases cleared, based on pattern response;
- The number of individual problem areas responded to;
- The average amount of directed patrol in each problem area per week;
- The total number of arrests made in the problem areas;
- The number of problem offenders that were contacted.

Although the values shown in Figure 10.5 may not make much sense in this particular textbook, the leadership of the police agency would actually understand what these numbers mean given their resources and expectations for the years' worth of crime reduction initiatives. The crime analyst would produce a product that contrasts the values for the current and prior year if the police department maintained the same goal of reducing crime the following year.

Since the responses are implemented in addition to the regular police duties of responding to service requests and conducting criminal investigations, it is also crucial to analyze the costs associated with the crime reduction initiatives. A cost analysis would look at the amount of overtime and scheduled staff hours as well as other expenses needed for each level of crime reduction initiatives (e.g., the use of bait vehicles, and the acquisition of extra equipment). These cost analyses can be carried out for all short-term strategies combined, or for a single crime reduction goal at a time (e.g., pattern responses) during the target time frame. In deciding which facts and figures to use and how to present the information, the crime analyst's contribution to the cost analysis is substantial. The crime analyst would collaborate with sworn administrative data, and budget personnel to perform the cost analysis rather than working alone.

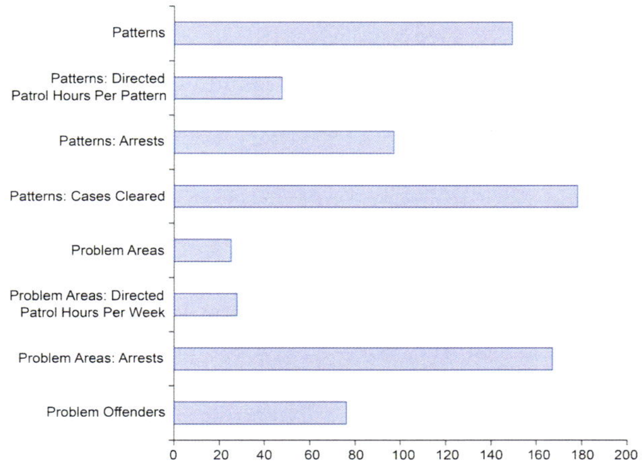

Figure 10.5. *Performance indicators (output): January–December 2017.*

Source: https://in.sagepub.com/sites/default/files/upm-assets/78468_book_item_78468.pdf.

10.6.2. Success Indicator (Outcome) Products

The initial step in evaluating each crime reduction goal is calculating the actual percentage change between the baseline and current counts to see if the police department has achieved the reduction percentage it designated as the success indicator. Further investigation is necessary to better understand the context of thes, regardless of whether the agency achieves its goal of reducing crime. In other words, a policethe police department's own efforts at reducing crime do not necessarily account for a 10% drop in violent crime. It's possible that because it was an exceptionally cold and wet year, fewer people were breaking the law outside, which is why other police departments in the area are reporting similar drops in violent crime. In a similar crimes not explicitly targeted may have decreased according to the agency. Therefore, in order toto have confidence in the overall results, the products presented in this section are meant to help the crime analyst tell the "story" behind the statistics by drawing comparisons with other crime types, prior years, and other jurisdictions.

10.6.2.1. Crime and Disorder Long-Term Trend Charts

The first crime and disorder long-term trend product is a line chart that shows the percentage change between each year and the previous, the linear trend line for the full three years of data, and the monthly frequency of crimes. This chart's objective is to assess each police department strategy's effect on a specific crime reduction goal over a two-year period. To provide context, a three-year dataset is used to determine the month-by-month relationship between the most recent year and the preceding two years. For this product, the usual duration is three to five years, but three years is the minimum that should be used.

For each category of crime or other activity designated as a goal for reducing crime, a separate version of the same chart would be made (i.e., distinct charts for street robbery and non-domestic aggravated assault). To compare various geographic areas over an extended period of time, particularly those mentioned in the success indicator component, separate charts could be made for each area. Figure 10.6 illustrates the decline in crime that persisted in 2017 after the police department started responding to residential burglaries. There was a 27% decrease in the percentage of change from 2016 to 2017 compared to an 8% decrease from 2015 to 2016. Both a visual examination of the chart and the results of the percentage differences seem to suggest that the impact and the police department's response were timed.

The following product is a chart that makes use of the same data from Figure 10.6 regarding residential burglaries, but it overlays the years on a 12-month calendar so that the seasonal variations can be evaluated. A single chart should only include three years at a time because after that, the lines get jumbled and confusing. The crime analyst may also utilize averages, like those in Figure 10.2, if they wish to take into account periods longer than three years.

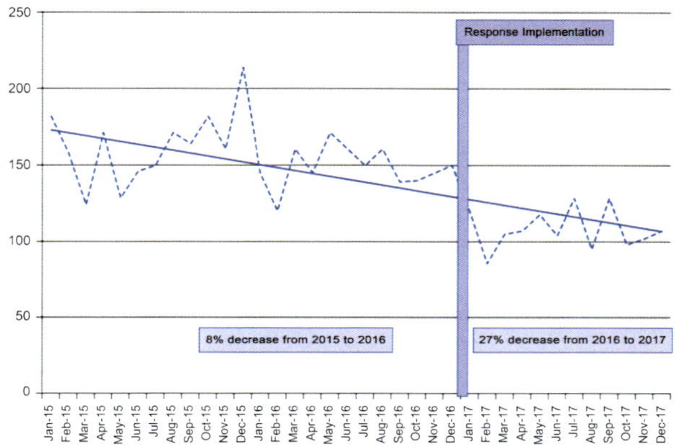

Figure 10.6. *Long-term residential burglary trend chart for 3 years.*

Source: https://in.sagepub.com/sites/default/files/upm-assets/78468_book_item_78468.pdf.

Although the current year has the lowest counts, Figure 10.7 demonstrates that the seasonal patterns seem to be similar to those of prior years. Every year, there is a decline in activity from January to February, followed by an increase through May and a decline in June. This graph demonstrates that seasonal patterns remained unaffected even though crime decreased in 2017 as a result of crime reduction measures. Even though crime is down overall in 2018, police chiefs may still want to think about modifying and enhancing their response during those months, since summertime crime is always on the rise.

10.6.2.2. Crime Trend Comparison Charts

To help ascertain whether declines are coming from the police department's own efforts to reduce crime and not from other sources (e.g., It is crucial to compare the baseline and target data for the crime reduction goal with other data, such as data from comparable crime types that were not chosen as crime reduction goals and data from other jurisdictions., spatial displacement, population growth, economy, or natural disasters). Depending on the objective and the data the analyst has access to, these trend charts usually show two to three years' worth of data. Finding the best comparison and acquiring the information required to produce the product are the duties of the crime analyst. Think about a police department that responded to residential burglaries as part of its crime reduction goal and saw a 20% reduction in crime. Comparatively, during the same time period, the department only witnessed a 5% decrease in residential vehicle thefts, while a nearby jurisdiction witnessed a 7% increase in residential burglaries.

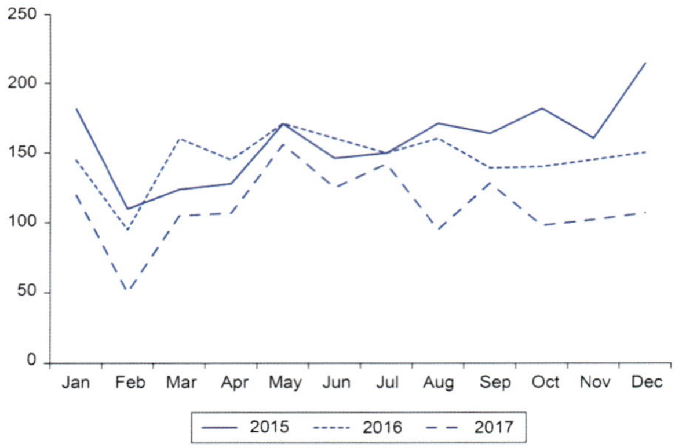

Figure 10.7. *Seasonal residential burglary trend chart for 3 years.*

Source: https://in.sagepub.com/sites/default/files/upm-assets/78468_book_item_78468.pdf.

Based on these findings, law enforcement officials may determine that the police department's actions were the reason behind the notable decline in residential burglaries. It appears that something different enabled the 20% decrease in residential burglary because other property crime in residential areas that was not addressed as a crime reduction goal saw a much smaller reduction and a neighboring jurisdiction saw an increase. Although the results do not conclusively link the reduction to the police department, the additional analysis strengthens the reporting of the 20% reduction relative to reporting it in isolation.

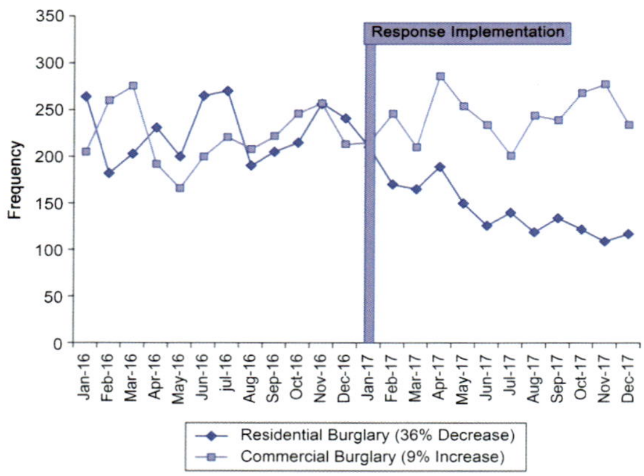

Figure 10.8. *Crime type comparison chart.*

Source: https://in.sagepub.com/sites/default/files/upm-assets/78468_book_item_78468.pdf.

The monthly counts of residential and commercial burglaries for the current year compared to the previous year are shown in Figure 10.8. The police department only responded to service requests and looked into criminal incidents; it did not address commercial burglaries. The aim of crime reduction was to lower the number of residential burglaries. e.g., fundamental law enforcement services). The percentage increase and decrease for each type in the legend are displayed in the chart. Visual examination of the chart reveals that, since the responses started, the monthly counts for residential burglaries appear to have decreased. According to the legend, overall, residential burglary decreased by 36% between 2016 and 2017, while commercial burglary increased by 9% during that same period. A similar chart that contrasts data from one jurisdiction with the jurisdiction of the crime analyst can be found in Figure 10.9. It is unlikely that crime analysts will find a jurisdiction nearly identical in size and population to their own, so a rate is used instead of monthly counts to compare jurisdictions with different populations. The monthly rates of residential burglary for the two jurisdictions are displayed in Figure 10.9. The comparison jurisdiction's rate of crime per 100,000 people and the crime analyst's rate per 100,000 people show similar trends in 2016. However, in 2017, after residential burglary crime reduction strategies were put into place, the crime rate decreased by 23% while it increased by 15% in the other jurisdiction. To bolster the case even further, more charts with different jurisdictions could be made. It is crucial that the crime analyst chooses additional jurisdictions with comparable zoning, even though their populations may differ (e.g., home versus. commercial) as well as additional traits (e.g., suburban/rural vs. urban area, college town, or getaway spot).

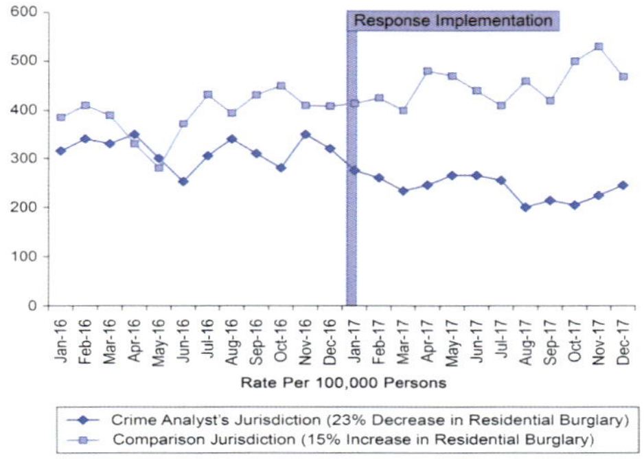

Figure 10.9. *Jurisdiction comparison chart.*

Source: https://in.sagepub.com/sites/default/files/upm-assets/78468_book_item_78468.pdf.

Notably, population isn't always the most useful measure when comparing particular kinds of crime (e.g., business burglary). Population is frequently the most realistic and useful comparison measure because it is unfortunately difficult to obtain comparison measures from other jurisdictions. Additionally, obtaining specific crime (e.g., residential break-ins at apartment buildings) and information on service requests (e.g., disorder calls only) from other jurisdictions, therefore it might occasionally be necessary to create these products by year using more generic categories (e.g., all calls made by citizens, or all break-ins). Finally, when a jurisdiction's population shifts during the course of the year, an analyst should exercise caution (e.g., a university town where summer enrollment is terminated) or is growing or shrinking over a number of years (e.g., a rise brought about by new industries or a fall brought on by the closure of a sizable factory). These factors necessitate extreme caution when performing the analysis and drawing conclusions based on broader data.

10.6.2.3. Yearly Comparison Maps

For the purpose of accountability, police leaders can also benefit from using yearly comparison maps to see long-term changes in activity. The analyst makes unique maps for every year so that variations can be observed from one to the next. Crime analysis products are frequently presented using presentation software during an annual accountability meeting. This makes it easier to see changes over time and allows maps to be animated than when they are static. Although analysts may produce maps on a quarterly or monthly basis, producing 12 or 24 maps for animation—rather than just two—takes a lot of work, so it should only be undertaken when the outcomes are significant.

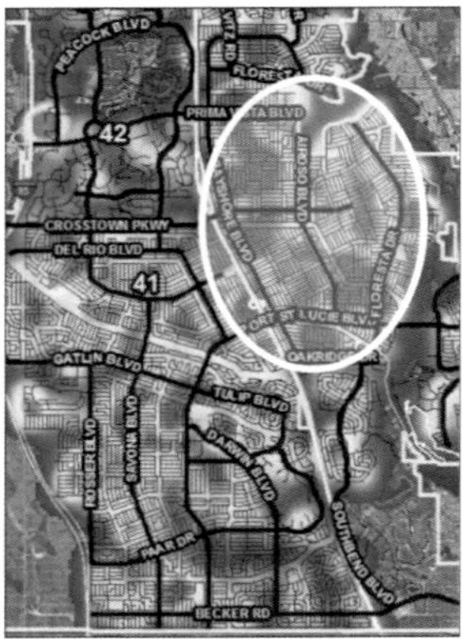

Figure 10.10. *Density map of crime reduction goal: 2016.*

Source: https://in.sagepub.com/sites/default/files/upm-assets/78468_book_item_78468.pdf.

Density maps of a chosen crime for the years 2016 and 2017 are shown in Figures 10.10 and 10.11, respectively. A graduated area map could also be used to produce the same goods. The legends are not displayed here, but the analyst should create "custom" legends for cross-temporal comparisons so that the years can be compared and each color category corresponds to the same values on each map. The maps were originally made in color, where the differences are more noticeable, even though they are displayed here in black and white. When we combine the two maps, we can observe how the problem areas in the large circled area changed in terms of crime density between 2016 and 2017. This indicates that these areas have improved. To illustrate how things have changed over time, more annual maps will be made.

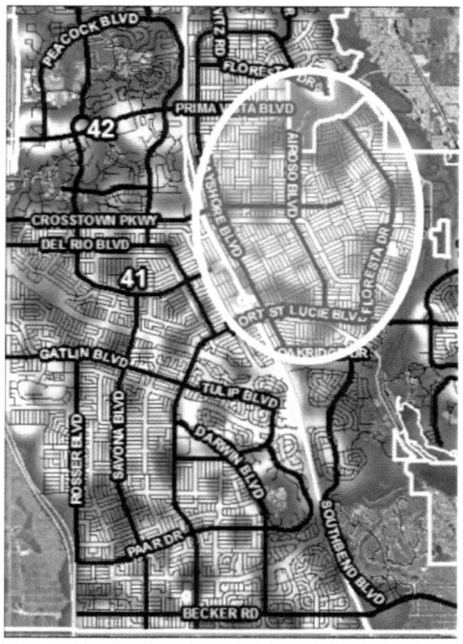

Figure 10.11. *Density map of crime reduction goal: 2017.*

Source: https://in.sagepub.com/sites/default/files/upm-assets/78468_book_item_78468.pdf.

10.6.3. Administrative Crime Analysis: Low-Priority Analysis

Some experts in the field believe that administrative crime analysis has gotten a bad rap over the years (Bruce, 2008). Bruce (2008) suggests that the category in question is low priority. However, this kind of crime analysis might actually keep a lot of analysts in jobs. It is extremely valuable for the police department to have someone who can respond to almost any question, provide information on demand, and organize data in an aesthetically pleasing manner, as Christopher Bruce (2008) notes. Additionally, both the product and the analyst become valuable assets when their work has the potential to significantly impact public safety or reduce crime rates.

10.6.4. How Administrative Crime Analysts Gather Data

Because of the nature of many of the products that administrative crime analysts produce, qualitative information is frequently useful even though a large portion of the data they use to prepare reports and presentations may come from the data found in police files.

There might only be a few standard police reports relevant to this assignment, for instance, if the analyst was asked to put together a presentation on the relationships between the police and the community over the previous three years. The analyst could locate and utilize reports about violent protests directed at the police or official complaints to the department regarding police brutality as sources of information. However, the analyst might have to employ qualitative techniques, like focus groups, interviews, reading through old newspaper articles, and reading locals' blogs or public email forums, in order to compile a more thorough report.

Interviews with patrol officers or potential employees of the community policing unit may be conducted by the analyst. You may learn a lot by probing them about the current situation of police-community relations and how it has evolved over the last three years. In a similar vein, organizing focus groups with police officers or community leaders may yield insightful findings and suggestions. Newspapers, however, typically have a pulse on the community, so looking through editorials and stories from the previous three years may provide the analyst with a broad understanding of how the public views the police.

Media outlets such as newspapers, news broadcasts, blogs, and Internet forums are likely to provide a deeper understanding of the issues that local residents care about. After obtaining this data, the analyst can then compare it with the police administration's messaging, mission statements, and stated goals to present a clear picture of the current and past three years' true states of police—community relations as well as what remains to be done to improve them.

REFERENCES

1. Boba, R. (2001). *Introductory Guide to Crime Analysis and Mapping.* Washington, DC: Community Oriented Policing Office, U.S. Department of Justice. Retrieved from: https://cops.usdoj.gov/ric/Publications/cops-w0273-pub.pdf (accessed on 14 October 2024).
2. Bruce, C. W. (2008). Crime analysis publications. In S. L. Gwinn, C. Bruce, J. P. Cooper, & S. R. Hick (Eds.), *Exploring Crime Analysis: Readings on Essential Skills* (pp. 342–363). Overland Park, KS: International Association of Crime Analysts.
3. International Association of Crime Analysts. (2014). *Definition and Types of Crime Analysis: Standards, Methods (Technology Methods)*. White Paper 2014-02. Overland Park, KS: International Association of Crime Analysts.
4. Santos, R. B. (2013). *Crime Analysis with Crime Mapping*. Thousand Oaks, CA: Sage.
5. Stevenson, M. R. (2013). *Crime Analysis: The History and Development of a Discipline* (Undergraduate honors thesis, Western Oregon University). Digital commons@WOU. Retrieved from: https://typeset.io/pdf/crime-analysis-the-history-and-development-of-a-discipline-34eghzx97g.pdf.

INDEX

A

Academic research 85
Accountability system 78, 83
Administrative crime analysis 20, 169, 173, 174, 177, 178, 262, 392, 393, 394, 415
Advanced analytical tools 162
Agency management system (AMS) 183
Aggregate analysis 13
Analysis Tasks 320
Analytical induction 141, 142
Analytical Mapping 233
Analyzing crime 112
Analyzing Documents 125
Anti-social behavior 116
Armed robberies 73
Arrest records 2, 162, 182, 187, 194, 263
Assessment models 124

B

Bibliographical database 114
Body language 145
Bookshop databases 114
British Crime Survey (BCS) 121
Business management system 183
Business registries 181

C

Canadian Society of Evidence-Based Policing (Can-SEBP) 82
Case law 112, 154, 155, 156
Categorical data 3, 388
Centre for Longitudinal Studies (CLS) 118
Child care 119
Chronological fashion 134
Civil law 155
Closed-circuit television systems (CCTVs) 184
Code violations 5, 200
Commercial law 155
Commission on Accreditation for Law Enforcement Agencies (CALEA) 10
Communication skills 102
Community collaboration 74

Community groups 62, 175, 393
Community issues 90
Community organizations 183
Community policing 2, 11, 15, 54, 61, 62, 69, 84, 162, 175, 240, 259, 261, 264, 280, 392, 416
Complex analysis 18
Complex statistical analysis 8
Compstat model 45, 66
Computer-aided dispatch (CAD) 181, 203, 214
Computer-aided dispatch systems 14
Computer science 18
Computer skills 176, 262
Computer software 58
Computer system 163, 164, 183, 190
Computer technology 4, 11, 14, 263, 265
Conceptual model 25
Confidentiality policies 145
Confirm information 90
Content analysis 3, 125, 126, 408
Conventional model 61
Conventional police 60, 90
Conventional police model 60
Coordinate Systems 214
Correlational analysis 142
Crime Analysis 1, 2, 4, 7, 8, 10, 14, 16, 18, 21, 24, 27, 31, 42, 43, 44, 45, 46, 47, 49, 50, 52, 55, 56, 58, 59, 69, 70, 79, 87, 90, 104, 107, 108, 161, 162, 163, 168, 171, 172, 173, 174, 176, 179, 180, 182, 185, 187, 188, 191, 192, 196, 197, 205, 209, 210, 211, 213, 216, 218, 219, 220, 223, 224, 225, 226, 227, 228, 229, 230, 231, 233, 235, 236, 261, 273, 279, 280, 282, 283, 284, 285, 286, 287, 289, 290, 291, 292, 293, 294, 295, 297, 298, 299, 300, 301, 337, 344, 346, 388, 391, 392, 393, 399, 402, 408, 415, 417
Crime Analysis Unit 10, 21, 42
Crime dynamics 56
Crime hotspots 56, 87, 133, 162, 243, 248, 249, 257, 260, 265, 271, 341, 377
Crime Incidents 185, 187
Crime Intelligence Analysis 169
Crime landscape 162
Crime Mapping 4, 6, 12, 15, 27, 31, 43, 44, 47, 48, 51, 52, 53, 58, 59, 70, 79, 104, 105, 107, 163, 176, 177, 180, 187, 188, 191, 192, 196, 197, 205, 207, 209, 210, 211, 213, 216, 218, 219, 220, 221, 223, 224, 225, 226, 227, 228, 229, 230, 231, 233, 235, 236, 239, 241, 242, 243, 245, 246, 247, 259, 261, 267, 276, 277, 278, 284, 285, 286, 287, 289, 290, 291, 292, 293, 294, 295, 297, 298, 299, 300, 301, 336, 337, 344, 346, 388, 417
Crime Pattern Theory 30
Crime phenomenon 39
Crime prevention 2, 3, 4, 5, 11, 25, 28, 36, 38, 39, 40, 41, 42, 43, 44, 45, 46, 48, 52, 53, 63, 68, 69, 78, 87, 97, 108, 120, 133, 162, 195, 208, 217, 236, 242, 245, 246, 259, 262, 263, 272, 275, 278, 280, 282, 296, 304, 305, 306, 317, 318, 323, 326, 327, 329, 331, 340, 355, 357, 358, 359, 363, 369, 372, 375, 377, 392, 395, 396
Crime Prevention Through Environmental Design (CPTED) 5

Crime rates 13, 32, 57, 65, 68, 71, 87, 123, 125, 208, 258, 270, 304, 341, 382, 403, 415
Crime reduction 5, 9, 23, 24, 40, 48, 50, 57, 58, 59, 60, 61, 64, 65, 68, 69, 70, 77, 78, 104, 107, 123, 132, 173, 174, 178, 183, 236, 281, 282, 283, 284, 288, 289, 291, 292, 294, 296, 298, 299, 300, 328, 394, 395, 396, 397, 398, 399, 400, 402, 403, 404, 405, 408, 409, 410, 411, 412, 413, 414, 415
Crime statistics 9, 57, 61, 69, 89, 96, 120, 122, 123, 198, 199, 217, 243, 244, 246, 260, 392
Crime surveys 147
Criminal apprehension 3, 4, 5
Criminal behavior 2, 7, 24, 26, 29, 340, 389
Criminal investigative analysis 172, 176, 262
Criminal justice 2, 15, 18, 19, 21, 24, 25, 52, 99, 119, 122, 123, 124, 136, 138, 139, 140, 143, 144, 145, 147, 157, 173, 184, 185, 267, 271, 280, 304, 335
Criminal Justice Information Services (CJIS) 184
Criminal justice system 2, 119, 122, 124, 136, 138, 139, 143, 144
Criminal statistics 12, 120, 124, 260
Criminological law 32
Criminological research 116, 123, 124, 125, 135, 136, 145
Criminological theories 24, 25, 29
Critical analysis 115
Critical essays 113
Cultural barriers 90, 91, 95

D

Data Analysis 134
Database management system (DBMS) 203
Databases 179, 185, 192, 350
Data collection 3, 17, 51, 116, 117, 124, 134, 135, 138, 139, 149, 162, 163, 164, 165, 166, 167, 173, 175, 179, 194, 195, 331, 341
Data Collection 131, 148, 194, 197
Data Considerations 197
Data documentation 117
Data entry 18, 19, 24, 163, 182, 196, 203, 271, 329
Data examination 162
Data Integrity 201, 332
Data Matrix 179, 180
Data Modification Subcycle 166
Data originates 163
Demographic information 150, 208, 320
Descriptive Crime Mapping 217, 222
Digital data 116, 117, 164
Direct observation 194
Disorder data 62, 67
Disorder Policing 65
Document analysis 125
Dog barking 189
Domestic violence 73, 122, 202, 307, 308, 309, 311, 313, 316, 318, 324, 326, 329, 330, 332, 333, 335, 401, 403
Drug addiction 172
Drug Market Analysis Program 14

E

Economic and Social Data Service (ESDS) 117
Economic downturn 57

Effective Communication 102
Effective crime analysts 96
Electronic crime 14, 164
Electronic data 4, 119, 122, 203, 347
Electronic database 164, 185, 199
Electronic media 167
Electronic records management systems 14
Emergency number 188
Environmental criminology 25, 32, 36, 41, 63, 109
Environmental elements 25, 243
Environmental law 155
Environmental policies 155
Environmental protection 154
Environmental regulation 154
Environmental surveys 194
Ethnographic research 128
Evidence-based analysis 95
Evidence-based practice (EBP) 96
Evidence collection 57

F

Family members 65
Field information 182, 198, 349
File maintenance 18
Forcing police agencies 95
Foreign court 155

G

Geographical data 165, 242, 245
Geographical Information Systems 259, 267
Geographic boundaries 60, 174
Geographic data 7, 165, 180, 181, 185, 203, 208, 213, 215, 242, 246, 260
Geographic display 181
Geographic zoning 173
Geography 14, 18, 21, 114, 177, 240, 259, 316
Globalized society 155
Government departments 114, 119, 122
Government organization 119
Government policy 119, 123
Group interviewing 143
Group Interviews 142
Group members 129, 130

H

Health care 119
Historical records 113
Hot Spots Policing 64
Human resource 86
Human rights 154, 155

I

Immediate Problems 72
Information-Sharing Platforms 183
Integrated Automated Fingerprint Identification System (IAFIS) 184
Intelligence analysis 15, 68, 106, 169, 171, 176, 177, 178
Intelligence-led policing (ILP) 67
Intentional resistance 91
International agencies 177
International Association of Crime Analysts (IACA) 11, 47, 168, 263, 301
International business operations 155
International Court of Justice 155
International law 155
Internet 6, 62, 167, 170, 202, 203, 204, 217, 221, 240, 264, 357, 359, 416
Interpersonal skills 102, 143

J

Jail management system (JMS) 184

Job Descriptions 17
Judicial precedent 154

L

Labor market 119
Large-scale mainframe mapping systems 14
Law enforcement 2, 3, 4, 5, 6, 7, 10, 14, 15, 16, 17, 19, 25, 29, 47, 49, 50, 51, 52, 56, 60, 67, 69, 71, 79, 80, 81, 84, 86, 87, 88, 91, 93, 94, 96, 98, 100, 101, 104, 108, 109, 112, 137, 162, 168, 171, 185, 197, 198, 199, 201, 203, 208, 226, 240, 242, 243, 244, 245, 246, 249, 259, 261, 262, 263, 264, 265, 266, 267, 269, 273, 276, 277, 280, 281, 304, 305, 314, 326, 340, 345, 348, 377, 383, 388, 389, 392, 394, 412, 413
Legal academics 155
Legal innovation 155
Legal system 112, 136, 153, 157, 257
Legal systems , 155
Library catalogues 114
Local governments 155
Long-Term Problems 72, 74

M

Magnetic resonance imaging (MRI) 57, 58
Manage performance 123
Matrices 179
Media organizations 178
Media relations 78, 396
Medical analogy 62
Medical diagnosis 59
Mental illness 139
Microsoft Access 179, 203
Modern policing 2, 80, 88, 95, 392
MRI data analysis 58
MRI scanner 69

N

National Child Development Study (NCDS) 118
National Crime Information Center (NCIC) 184, 185
National Incident Based Reporting System (NIBRS) 199
National Incident-Based Reporting System (NIBRS) 184
Natural scientists 126
News media 125, 167
Newspaper readership 119
Numerous academics 91
Numerous factors 128

O

Observational methods 126, 135
Office for National Statistics (ONS) 119
Operations analysis 174, 177
Organizational Chart 21

P

Partner organizations 183
Passport Office 119
Patrol strategies 2, 280
Pattern analysis 8, 74, 242, 248, 249, 260, 316, 344, 345, 347, 348, 352, 353, 355, 383, 407
Pattern Finalization 347
Personal communication 11
Police agency 2, 18, 19, 62, 72, 73, 77, 108, 173, 177, 179, 198, 283, 386, 393, 409
Police culture 17, 89, 95, 96, 103, 268

Police Data 329
Police decision-making 80, 81, 82
Police departments 6, 11, 18, 71, 83, 87, 88, 90, 180, 202, 221
Police hierarchy 88, 92, 93, 101, 102
Police leaders 97, 101, 400, 401, 414
Police leadership 101
Police management 11, 15, 67, 167
Police officers 25, 164, 241
Police procedures 17, 84, 103, 167, 201
Police record management system 59
Policy analysis 125
Political discourse 112
Political science 18, 19, 21
Population surveys 148
Poverty 13, 118, 119, 157, 257, 273, 340
Predictive analytics 56, 87, 340, 341
Predictive policing 42, 47, 68, 205, 245, 389
Predictive Policing 68, 245
Predict potential crime occurrences 162
Preliminary hypothesis 141
Primary Data 181, 194, 197
Private Property 38
Private sectors 114
Problem Analysis Triangle 26
Problematic behavior 75, 76
Problem-oriented policing (POP) 63
Problem-solving methodology 67, 68
Problem-solving techniques 14, 61, 64, 66
Problem-specific 84
Psychology 18, 114
Public and private sector agencies 114
Public safety 2, 15, 56, 61, 87, 109, 162, 181, 208, 280, 304, 305, 340, 377, 392, 415

Q

Qualitative Data 116
Quality control 165, 167, 182
Quantitative Data 117
Quantitative information 3

R

Radiologist 57, 58
Raising awareness 38
Random patrols 61, 81, 84, 87, 88, 100
Raster Data 212
Rational choice theory 28, 29
Rational Choice Theory 28
Recorded Crime Statistics (RCS) 120
Record management system 165
Records Management System 182
Regional legislatures 155
Relational database management 183
Relational databases 179
Repeat Victimization 33, 46, 54, 303, 304, 306, 307, 308, 310, 311, 312, 313, 314, 316, 317, 318, 325, 326, 327, 332, 335, 336, 337
Research consumers 136
Research methodology 17, 19, 96, 115, 116, 126, 135, 142
Resource allocation 79, 162, 242, 280, 377, 392
Risk Society 124
RMS (records management system) 180
Routine Activities Theory 31

S

Scientific data 112, 124
Secondary analysis 116, 117, 118
Secondary Data 180
Securities regulation 154

Selling drugs 76
Short-Term Problems 72, 73
Situational Awareness 281, 282, 285
Social disorder 61, 133
Social disorders 66
Social disorganization 13, 24
Social environments 135
Social factors
Social habits 172
Social network analysis 162
Social observation 126
Social phenomena 126
Social science 3, 32, 100, 138, 142, 150
Sociodemographic 3, 4, 181
Sociology 18, 19, 21, 24, 114
Software applications 68, 164, 203, 263
Software package 146
Software programs 179, 182, 203, 215, 234
Spatial analysis 4, 7, 12, 13, 14, 15, 20, 21, 64, 162, 178, 208, 214, 243, 246, 262, 274, 340, 377, 381, 382
Spatial Analysis 243, 275, 382
SQL Server 179
Staff members 22, 99, 148, 163, 327, 369, 370
Standard model 60, 61, 87, 96
Statistics Commission 122, 123
Street network 181
Superficial analyses 95
Surveillance cameras 356
Surveillance systems 162, 341
Systematic information 2
Systematic meta-analysis 63

T

Tabular Data 180
Tactical analysis 18, 47, 74, 89, 172, 263, 275
Tactical crime analysis 12, 20, 35, 169, 171, 172, 173, 176, 177, 178, 341, 349, 351, 352, 365, 368, 375, 386, 400
Telecommunications 181
Temporal analysis 4, 162, 208, 274, 341, 380
Three-dimensional visualization 6
Time Series Analysis 380
Traditional model 84, 88
Traffic crashes 72, 73, 185, 190, 191
Traffic Crashes 191
Troublesome youth 73

U

Uniform Crime Reporting (UCR) 184, 198

V

Vector Data 209
Vehicle identification number 193
Verbal interaction 147
Victim Surveys 331
Voice recorder 145
Volume crime analysis 95, 105

W

Web-based hardware 183
Websites 178
Weighted Time Span Analysis 381

FSC
www.fsc.org
MIX
Papier | Fördert gute Waldnutzung
FSC® C083411

Kolibri 360 GmbH
Ferdinand-Jühlke-Straße 7
99095 Erfurt, Deutschland
produktsicherheit@kolibri360.de